A TALE OF
MANY RAILWAYS

An Autobiography and History
of
Alan Keef Ltd

Alf Fisher.

From the owner of a junior de Winton to the
owner of a senior de Winton.

Alan Keef

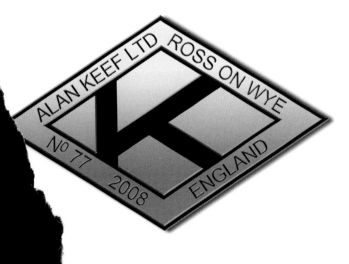

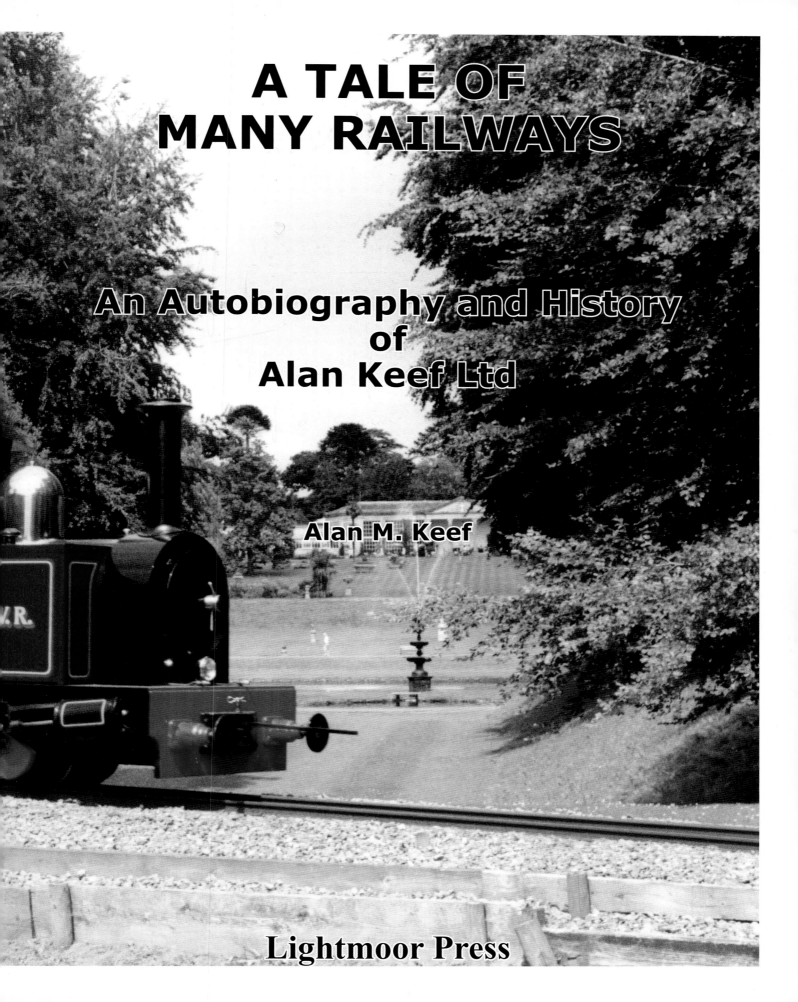

A TALE OF
MANY RAILWAYS

An Autobiography and History
of
Alan Keef Ltd

Alan M. Keef

Lightmoor Press

Behind every good man stands a better woman (Anon)

To Susan, who has encouraged and put up with me for all these years.

© Alan M. Keef and Lightmoor Press 2008.
Designed by Nigel Nicholson. Cover design by Neil Parkhouse.

British Library Cataloguing-in-Publication Data. A catalogue
record for this book is available from the British Library.
ISBN 9781899889303

LIGHTMOOR PRESS
Unit 144B, Lydney Trading Estate, Harbour Road, Lydney, Gloucestershire GL15 5EJ
www.lightmoor.co.uk
Lightmoor Press is an imprint of Black Dwarf Lightmoor Publications Ltd.

Printed by Craft Print, Singapore.

Front Cover: *Mark Timothy* pauses with a winter train at Coltishall Station on the Bure Valley Railway, Norfolk.

The glorious scenery of Loch Finn forms the backdrop for this rebuilt Simplex T series locomotive working push/pull with an ex-County Donegal Railways railcar on the Fintown Railway, Ireland.

Back Cover: At Star Lane Brickworks, Southend on Sea, this 40SD is the last locomotive to carry a Simplex works number, although Alan Keef Ltd built it at the time of the take-over. *Dennis Wilby.*

Brand new K.40 locomotive *Mary* emerges into the daylight of the pit bottom on the Mansfield Waste Water Scheme for Kier Construction.

Alan Keef admires his 38th locomotive creation, *Tryntje*, on commissioning trials at de Efteling theme park, Holland. *Tony Steenmeyer.*

Previous page: The new order at Bicton Park Gardens, Devon. Locomotive AK61 of 2000, subsequently named *Sir Walter Raleigh*, crosses the end of the avenue with a rake of new carriages.

Contents

AK26 of 1988 and AK28 of 1989 were basically identical Simplex 3½-ton locomotives fitted with Deutz engines for Butterley Building Products for their brickworks near Southend. Here No. 28 brings in three skips of clay to their Cherry Orchard Works, apparently assisted by a much older Simplex.

Acknowledgements

A particular debt is owed to Ken Scanes for his maintaining a record not only of new locomotives built by Alan Keef Ltd but of every locomotive that has ever passed through my hands, even if it has been only for a few days. By any standards this is no mean achievement and something I could not have managed myself. I was never a train spotter! My sincere thanks, Ken, for allowing that record to be included here and I hope you do not think I have been too drastic with the editing. Also thanks to my youngest daughter Alice for preparing all the drawings that go with this book. It has taken a considerable amount of her time when she should perhaps have been earning a crust for Alan Keef Ltd. Thanks also to those who have read the manuscript and for their comments thereon.

All the photographs are either mine or Patrick's except where otherwise credited. My thanks to those who have allowed their pictures to be used. There is one name that I have not managed to contact; you may realise who you are and I hope that you have no objection to my using your photograph.

Thanks are due to Steve Benton of the Tramway Museum Society for information on Milnes Voss & Co., to Andrew Nkusi in Tanga for checking my history of the Tanzanian sisal industry, to the Rev'd Elaine Goddard for checking the facts of Chapter 15, to Michael Greensmith for assistance in certain legal matters and to Michael Crofts for clarification of the Portuguese *débâcle*.

One of the problems of pontificating about railways is that there is always someone else out there who knows about a particular aspect of the subject in far greater detail than most ordinary mortals can ever hope to attain. This is fundamentally an autobiography so the thoughts and opinions expressed are mine and the inevitable mistakes are mine also.

Finally, thanks must go to Black Dwarf Lightmoor for taking on publication. I hope that it will prove to have been worth their while.

Most locomotive works plates give the year of manufacture but the one on this Baldwin, No. 44656, also gives March 1st 1917! Built for use behind the Western Front in the First World War, it spent most of its life hauling sugar-cane in India. It is seen in steam for the first time after a complete rebuild which included a new boiler, new tanks and cab and literally stripping down to last nut and bolt.

1

Prehistory

I lay no claim to being a railwayman born and bred, nor, for that matter, even to being an engineer. My father and grandfather did not work for the Great Western or the Lancashire & Yorkshire or whatever. However, having said that, railways of a sort go back a great deal further in the family than with many of those who make the claim to having railways in their blood.

Legend has it that Victorian children suffered a very strict upbringing and there is probably no doubt that some did. Some still do. It is certainly true that the whole ethos of life was more strictly regulated and that the process got worse as the Victorian era progressed. But listening to my grandmother talk gives the lie to all that. As a passing example, I have a book in which guests were asked to state their preferences on various topics such as music, games and so on. Under the heading 'Most Enjoyable Occupations' one writes 'walking home from work' and another, 'kissing a pretty girl'!

Where do railways come into all this? My great-grandparents lived in some style in a large house called 'Mortimer Lodge' that was set in some twenty acres of its own land on the edge of Wimbledon Common and which included its own farmery to provide the household with milk. Alas, it suffered a direct hit in the Second World War. It was here that my great-grandfather installed a 2ft gauge railway for the enjoyment of his children. The garden railway is nothing new!

Information on this is largely hearsay, aided by about three photographs. The only fixed dates I have are 1894 when there is a picture of my great aunt sitting on The Tram on the occasion of her engagement, with her fiancé standing alongside in true Victorian style. Again in 1895 there is a less formal photograph of my grandmother and presumably her fiancé. The situation is complicated by two sisters marrying two brothers. My grandmother was born in 1866 and on this basis the best guess is that it was installed in the late 1870s. This railway was apparently about 100 yards long and dead straight, sandwiched between the shrubbery, the tennis court and a paddock. Later, a curved downhill section of unknown length was added. The track is believed to have consisted of some very light rail, perhaps 12lbs/yd with the extension in something even lighter; 9lbs/yd was available at that time.

Rolling stock consisted principally of the rather splendid wagon known as The Tram, shown in the photographs, which was complete with spring suspension, screw brake and seats. There was also another home-built wagon that my grandmother said was apt to fall to pieces when at speed on the curved downhill section! Perhaps this set a trend for her as in later years she was a considerable investor in railways, with shares in many British lines and also overseas such as the Denver & Rio Grande and the Canadian Pacific.

Above: Engagement pictures on The Tram seemed to be *de rigeur*. This is my grandmother's sister Alice on the occasion of her engagement to Herbert's brother George Keef on 24 January 1894. Note the neat little sprung wagon with screw handbrake and very light rails.

Right: The Mortimer Lodge Tram. My grandmother plus dogs, probably on the occasion of her engagement to Herbert Keef in 1895. The tennis court is to the right. It has to be one of life's sadnesses that The Tram never came into my family's possession, especially as it would have been possible.

My father and his brother had an extensive 0 gauge model railway at Framfield, Sussex. A Bassett Lowke 0-4-0 Peckett-style tank engine named *Dido* hauls a train of mixed home-built goods rolling stock. In those days it was clockwork powered but in my childhood this locomotive was converted to third rail electric.

Motive power was presumably child power or perhaps the occasional gardener was roped in to push. There is a family legend that the eldest brother had designs on a locomotive but no details survive. It may have been no more than a pipe-dream. This leads one to the possibility that the whole scheme was inspired by Sir Arthur Heywood, but if there was a direct connection one would have expected 15in. gauge. I have reason to believe that the Mortimer Lodge Tram survived, unused, with a distant relation living at Boxmoor, Hertfordshire, until the late 1950s. In the light of later developments it is more than surprising that my father made no effort to recover what was, after all, a family heirloom.

Moving on a generation, my father, Michael, and his brother, Dennis, were railway enthusiasts as we would understand the term today. My father was at school at Malvern College where he soon

The brothers' tour of minor railways took in the Welshpool & Llanfair and their few photographs include this one of the *Countess* shunting the station yard at Welshpool on 4 September 1929.

discovered that the merit of being in the lowliest cricket team was that it played alongside the main line railway. My uncle Dennis was at Rugby, which could hardly have been more central to the nation's railway system. Between them they built up quite a substantial 0 gauge garden railway using equipment from a variety of manufacturers. I think the division of labour was that Dennis did the track work whilst my father hand-made most of the stock. Neither was very mechanically minded and the locomotives were perhaps the least satisfactory part of the exercise, the exception being a standard Bassett Lowke 0-4-0 clockwork Peckett saddle tank. A cousin had an even more considerable gauge 1 railway.

They also did a fair amount of travelling in order to take in some of the country's more abstruse railways, such as the Bishops Castle. Railways were not the sole motive for these expeditions; they were also walking holidays *per se,* with the further objective of including as many as possible of the country's cathedrals into the itinerary. Unlike today's walkers they were able to travel light by, in the morning, sending their bags on to the next stopping point by rail to be there for the evening. In addition most pubs provided accommodation. There is a family failing of not keeping a proper record, indeed any sort of record, of these sorts of expeditions and, apart from a small number of photographs and a recently made diagram of the model railway, I am relying on hearsay again.

Living in what is now East Sussex, the Colonel Stephens railways in that area were treated as an everyday occurrence and I think the model railway was very much based on these. The more far-flung ones, such as the Shropshire & Montgomeryshire, made a greater impression. Indeed, the Bishops Castle Railway, although not a Colonel Stephens line, made an impression which lasted my father to the end of his life.

These jaunts all came to an end in the late 1930s when they both were married and their respective wives did not really get on with each other. Added to this, the Second World War was about to break out and, although neither would fight in it, their lives were directed in very different courses.

2

History

I was born on the 18 December 1941 in Blandford, Dorset, reputedly in the middle of an air raid and named Alan somewhat by default in order to have me registered onto next week's ration cards. That was more important than actually registering the birth! I have to say that I have very few memories of Dorset, railway or otherwise. We moved away at about the time of my fourth birthday to a house at Eaton Socon in North Bedfordshire which was large enough to be split into two to form one house for us and another for my grandmother and her crippled daughter. As a young child I was brought up on the Beatrix Potter books, *The Tale of Peter Rabbit*, and so on, hence the title of this book.

During the war my father had been directed labour in the forestry industry or, more particularly, in the sawmilling and timber production end of it. With the cessation of hostilities, through a friend he obtained a job with a semi-governmental organization, the Rural Industries Bureau. This still exists under a different name and was set up to bring the benefits of what was then modern technology to rural workshops: gas cutters and arc welders to blacksmiths, machine tools to woodworkers and so on. A further part of his job was helping people to start new businesses, and he used to recall going to see two young men who wanted to start making hand power tools, Mr Black & Mr Decker! He covered the area of Bedfordshire, Hertfordshire and north Middlesex. Going on his rounds with him was an intrinsic part of my education for the next ten years or so.

The 0 gauge model railway had two reincarnations here, both of which were basically done by my father with, probably, my amusement as the *raison d'être*. The second was the more interesting, as it involved conversion to third-rail electric. None of us knew much about this and a highlight was a visit to Bassett Lowke's establishment in Northampton and a return armed with a transformer, controllers and a motor unit to be installed in the Peckett. This line was set up round a large greenhouse and was intended to go outside in a form of balloon loop. In common with many full size railways, some of the earthworks were made, including a tunnel under a path, but very little track laid. I have never been quite sure why. Other railway activities at this stage were fairly mundane: the occasional trip to London, a memorable excursion to Brighton involving a rail-tour through West London and a first introduction to the Leighton Buzzard Light Railway. This latter happened to involve seeing more or less a complete sand train derail beside Vandyke Road.

At about the age of seven I was taken by my mother to see my maternal grandmother in Montevideo, Uraguay. In those days it was the R.M.S. *Andes* – 27,000 tons and a fortnight each way. It is unfortunate that I was really too young for an adventure of this nature and most of what I genuinely remember has to do with railways. Shunting locomotives on the dockside in Le Havre and Lisbon, the cable car up the Sugar Loaf in Rio de Janeiro (for me possibly the highlight of the whole trip and the most terrifying for my mother), trams behind the beach in Sao Paulo, trams again in Montevideo and a seven-hour rail journey up country to see my uncle and aunt at Mercedes. A visit to the ship's engine-rooms was also high on the list. My being scared stiff of the 'crossing the line' ceremony is best forgotten.

My education up to this stage had been patchy, to say the least. Looking back I think my mother was perhaps a bit snobby and did not want her son going to the local village school, which, in the end, was where I wound up and well behind everybody else to boot. My father had hopes that I would get to Christ's Hospital, which – subject to a means test – was free, with Bedford School as second string. At the critical moment he had a small salary increase which ruled the former out and so it was to Bedford that I was headed.

This was patently not achievable from the village school, good though it was. In consequence I was sent to a crammers at Aspatria, near Carlisle, for about six months. Goodness knows why so far away but I believe there was some connection with a revered aunt. So at the age of ten I was put on the Thames-Clyde express at Kettering and told to get off at Carlisle where I would be met. I was not. I remember sitting on my trunk in the station forecourt for about an hour until someone turned up! Perhaps this has made me unworried about travelling in strange places ever since.

The whole experience was not an entirely happy one but it achieved its intended objective of my being one of only three who got into Bedford School in my particular age group in that year. The more astonishing thing was that

En route to Uruguay, my mother and I rode the cable car up the Sugar Loaf in Rio de Janeiro. After a major childhood tantrum elsewhere on the trip it is a wonder my mother allowed this expedition of which I think she was absolutely terrified.

The ex ice-breaker, *Princess*, as found by my father sunk below the top locks at Marsworth on the Aylesbury arm of the Grand Union Canal.

the establishment did not have electricity, so lighting was candles and oil lamps and heating by paraffin heaters. How we never set the whole place alight I shall never know and I cringe at modern attitudes to these things.

I made the trip each way several times, the journey in itself was interesting and I became appreciative of the scenery on the Settle and Carlisle line. I was also aware of the turntable at Hellifield, by then surrounded by a sleeper palisade, which was the origin of the Rev'd Audrey's tale of James spinning round on a turntable. Delights in Cumberland included walking a derelict branch railway near to the school and the occasional trips by train and bus into Carlisle to have one's hair cut. Again, both were done entirely on one's own.

There then followed what is best described as a watery interlude that lasted until I was eighteen. This requires description in some detail, being interesting in itself and having a bearing on later developments. I will cover it *in toto* here even though it covers the whole of the period up to my leaving school. Neighbours of ours at Eaton Socon acquired themselves a boat on the River Ouse and, being friendly with their son who was my age, I did spend a weekend away with them on it. I doubt if it was only this, but something inspired my father to have a boat as well. I think it must have been while I was in Cumberland that he found and bought an old iron ice-breaker from British Waterways. Being my father, it was not quite as straightforward as that. The boat was sunk at the time and had been for many years!

In fact the hull was sound, it had simply filled with rainwater over a period of time. So for £30 he had a boat and for another £5 it was raised and lying at the British Waterways depot at Marsworth. Reputedly they merely brought in a sufficiently large pump that took the water out faster than it could run back in again. My father and a friend then proceeded to bow-haul the boat eleven miles and seven locks to L.B. Faulkner's yard at Leighton Buzzard.

He then set about converting it into a canal cruiser and, in fact, must have been one of the very first to do such a thing. He did all the woodwork himself mostly using old deal furniture as a source of wood (partly because timber was then in short supply and partly to save cost) and left the fitting of an engine and such like to others. We still lived at Eaton Socon and I have memories of his returning from Leighton Buzzard, the better part of thirty miles, with a poor little Ford Anglia car loaded with waste wood from the boat.

In due course the *Princess* (believed to be her original name) was launched and there began a remarkable journey from Leighton Buzzard to Eaton Socon *via* the Grand Union Canal

to Northampton, the River Nene to Peterborough, the Middle Level Navigations to Denver Sluice and then the River Cam, Old West River and the River Ouse to St Neots. This was done over a series of weekends and as the Middle Level in particular was near derelict it was quite an exercise.

I did not do much of the outward journey but a couple of incidents from the return a year or so later will give flavour of what was involved. At Whittlesea, on the Middle Level, *Princess* jammed hard on an underwater obstruction of some sort and we pulled her over it with block and tackle. Only my father would have had a set on board! Later, on the River Nene we encountered a temporary bridge across a lock to carry heavy plant across. This left a space just too short to take the boat. The stern engine room was made of steel so we put it under the bridge and filled the lock, thus jacking up the bridge and allowing us to proceed. I would love to have seen the foreman's face when he came back on Monday morning and, oh! for some photographs of these things.

Again, exactly what prompted my father I do not know, but he then proceeded to move into the canal carrying business. I was about twelve and he, in his late forties, still had and kept his job. Obviously a meeting with Robert Aickman — who had by then founded the Inland Waterways Association — and one or two others made him think there was a future in it. He was not alone. Several small firms and No. 1s (individuals who lived on and operated their own boat, or pair of boats if they were married) came into the business at about that time. This prompted a move from North Bedfordshire to Linslade, now part of Leighton Buzzard but then a separate local authority in Buckinghamshire, where my father was lucky enough to find a canal-side property by the name of Bossington Gardens. It extended to about three acres, had been a nursery cum orchard and had also been dug about for sand. Its prime advantage was at least 300 yards of canal frontage of which he managed to persuade British Waterways to concrete-pile about a third.

In conjunction with Lord Geoffrey Percy, a younger son of the Duke of Northumberland, who, I presume, put up the money, he bought two pairs of canal boats from John Green & Co. of Macclesfield. Thus Wyvern Shipping Co. Ltd was born. These were all wooden boats — two motor boats, *Benevolence* and *Victoria*, and two butties, *Duchess of Athol* and *Duchess of York*. These were shortly followed by *Heather Bell*, a motor boat, and an ex-Grand Union Canal Carrying Co. steel butty which was renamed *Elizabeth* in honour of my mother.

These boats were interesting in themselves. The John Green motor boats were fitted with Petter single-cylinder semi-diesel engines which, unlike the more common Bolinder engines, were not self reversing but fitted with a reverse gear-box. This was of massive proportions and was open so that one could see it all spinning round. They were hot-bulb start which entailed heating a peg on the cylinder-head with a man-sized paraffin blowlamp until it and the head were red hot. One then pulled out a spring-loaded peg in the flywheel, pulled it smartly upwards against compression, when it rebounded giving the flywheel enough inertia to go back the other way over compression, fire and start. Not infrequently it fired on the initial pull and was then running backwards! The procedure then was to let it run to become nice and warm, stop it and start again. Being semi-diesel they used almost as much oil as fuel. As a measure of their longevity I remember another one being broken up and it was said a pencil would fit between piston and cylinder wall!

I remember going to see *Heather Bell* moored in the stub of the Stroudwater canal at Saul Junction. She had been built in the late thirties for a family in Stourbridge who used her basically as a pleasure boat, but with a difference. They used to come down to Gloucester, Sharpness or beyond and pick up a cargo for the Midlands as and when they felt like a spot of boating. For this type of usage she was reputedly fitted with an extra plank of depth to allow her to negotiate the lower River Severn to Avonmouth, a forecabin to provide extra accommodation for visitors and a Lister 2JP engine with air-start thus allowing the ladies to start the engine. For a single boat this was a powerful engine but would have been needed for a boat working independent of tugs and towing in those waters. She had latterly belonged to, and been used by, the Severn River Board primarily on bank protection work.

For those not aware of the system, canal boats at that time were usually worked in pairs with an entire family living on board in the two cabins, one on each boat and each about 6ft 6in. × 8ft 0in. inside. A family of six or seven children, sometimes more, were brought up in this space. The butty was always 'home' as the motor boat cabin tended to smell of diesel and oil. Boatmen and their families were usually clean, at least by the standards of the time, but the boats themselves tended to be alive with fleas and bedbugs. For this reason, if none other, I never achieved a cherished ambition to make a round trip on a working boat. When in for repair, the first job was to fumigate the cabins and a large tin of cyanide was kept for the purpose – probably enough to kill off most of Leighton Buzzard!

Any canal carrier depended entirely on the boat crews for their success or otherwise. Wyvern Shipping was only marginally successful in this respect, probably because all the best crews already had jobs elsewhere and their employers wanted to keep them. I do not remember them all but some stick in my mind. The problem was that they were on their own and the temptation of a better paid day or two's casual work shovelling sand or ashes somewhere was always a temptation. Thus an extra day waiting to load was claimed, a feigned engine breakdown or 'the wife having the flu bad like', being all a bit uncontrollable.

The Rice family (I think there were about six of them) possibly stayed with us longest and were good reliable people who did all that was asked of them. Ben Johnson and his wife became a family joke ever after. He always got on 'steady like' and managed to take an extra day on every trip and would often miss his turn to load. He was not devious, just slow. Billy Graham I remember more by his going than his activities. They were paid by a complicated system of cargo, tonnage, distance, waiting time and expenses. Read and write they might not but all could calculate their wages to the last farthing. There was the most stupendous row with Billy Graham on this subject and he went.

So the company had its boats and its crews and was after work for them. Initially, and in reality thereafter, this comprised sub-contract work for the principal carriers on the Grand Union Canal. Basically this was British Waterways themselves, the Samuel Barlow Coal Co. Ltd from Braunston and S.E. Barlow Ltd from Tamworth. In practice this was largely coal from the East Midlands coal field to John Dickinsons' paper mills and other users on the lower Grand Union with backloading from Brentford to Birmingham.

The Canal showing Church, Blisworth.

A postcard view of *Princess* in Wyvern Shipping Co. days heading south past Blisworth church. This must be about 1956 or 1957 in the earliest days of the hire cruiser business, but surprisingly it is believed to be Frank Arnold steering.

Unloading coal for Leighton Buzzard Co-op at Brantoms Wharf. My father wielding the shovel, Fred Rice beside him and his son on the planks. Note that the loaded boat could not get nearer the bank because of silted mud. The motor boat is *Heather Bell* with one of the Duchesses as butty, the latter having already been unloaded.

Coal was, and still is, a cut-price commodity but the cargoes out of London were more interesting and, I believe, a little more lucrative. They comprised such things as aluminium ingots and timber to Birmingham with grain to Whitworths at Wellingborough. There was also a spell of working for British Waterways out of Runcorn docks on Merseyside, again to the Midlands. This included such esoteric loads as imported tomatoes! About the only regular job that the company had in its own right was two loads of coal a month to the Leighton Buzzard Co-op. The snag with this was it had to be unloaded by hand which was already becoming an unwanted job.

Even with the aid of a rail strike the carrying business became depressingly unprofitable. The balance between profit and loss on a trip was so fine that the slightest delay or breakdown upset the system. An extra five tons on every load would have made the difference but lack of dredging prevented this. A severe winter effectively shut the canal network.

My mother is always credited with the comment, 'Couldn't we let the *Princess* out to holiday-makers in the summer, in order to help things along?' My father went to see British Waterways about a rate to do just that and got the comment, 'Oh, there's no future in that but you can run for a summer free if you want to try it!'

A few advertisements in *Motor Boat & Yachting* and the *Daily Telegraph* and the boat was let from May to September with the exception of one week in July! By the standards of the time *Princess* was well equipped. She had electric light, interior sprung mattresses and a pump-out loo instead of the inevitable Elsan toilet of the day. Even so, two of the traditional boat cans, about five gallons, was considered enough in the way of water. This is not as minimal

as it sounds; I know from later experience that with not too much washing one can cope adequately on a gallon per person per day. Ask anyone who has had to carry their water! However, it did require a certain amount of expertise to actually find water. Taps tended to be at the back of pubs or lock keepers houses and at Braunston top lock the supply was simply a pipe sticking from a bank out of which water always ran. The professional boatmen, of course, knew all this from their childhood.

Those early hirers must have been quite an adventurous lot. Many had already been on the Thames or the Norfolk Broads but many had not. To most, locks were something of a mystery and meeting a pair of loaded boats round a sharp bend was a source of panic. So far as Wyvern Shipping Co. was concerned, the die was cast. The future, indeed rescue, lay with pleasure boating.

For the next season *Princess* was re-engined with a new Lister FR1 engine (still hand-start) and *Benevolence* was converted into a pleasure boat. This latter was done very much on a shoe string and almost entirely done by my father in the spare time from his regular employment. She was fitted out as a 6/8-berth canal cruiser and the original Petter engine was removed. Adventurous they may have been, but starting one of those beasts would have defeated even the above-average hirer! It was replaced by a radiator-cooled Ferguson tractor engine belt-driven to a marine gearbox. This was still a fairly fearsome arrangement especially with the changeover required from petrol to paraffin, not mention the engine room being like a sauna.

There was logic in these apparently circuitous arrangements. Traditionally canal boat engines were, and often still are, cooled by using the canal water, but it has to pass through what was known as a mudbox in order to filter out the worst of the mud, weed and other debris in the water, and there was a great deal more then than now. The professional boatman always had one eye on the water outlet to see that water was flowing and that a blockage had not occurred. When it did there was a messy unpleasant business of cleaning the filter in the mudbox. All this was too much to expect of hirers. In addition, they inevitably tended to steer all over the canal without a thought to underwater obstructions and the belt drive offered some protection to the propeller, gearbox and transmission.

I have no record of the order of events, but memory suggests that at this point the ex-tug *Tyburn* was purchased and converted into a cruiser. It was renamed *Perseverance* which seemed appropriate and went well with *Benevolence*. Originally fitted with a twin-cylinder Kromhaut semi-diesel of monstrous proportions it was re-engined with a single-cylinder Petter, again belt-driven to gearbox and propeller. It suffered from quite deep draft at three feet, but made a fairly successful cruiser. I have very few memories of this boat except on one occasion the accumulated oil in the large horizontal silencer catching alight and producing a smokescreen the Royal Navy could have been proud of!

To further augment the fleet the butty *Duchess of Atholl* was cut in half and each half converted into a four-berth cruiser. The stern half became the *Lady Flora* after Geoffrey Percy's wife. Those less experienced in canals may not realize that a butty, or towed boat, is very similar – that is, sharp – at both ends and so doing this was not as daft as it sounds. With the benefit of hindsight, what was daft was that the cut ends, as it were, were boarded across and a propeller stuck out the back with no thought given to water flow with the result that when tried, the propeller just churned without driving the boat. This was overcome with a great deal of midnight oil being burnt by inserting two large tubes diagonally on each side to provide a flow of water in the right direction. It worked! More importantly these two boats were fitted with then-new Lister SR2 air-cooled engines complete with gearboxes and these sounded the death knell of any other oddities. They became the standard for us and many, many other canal users until very recent years.

There was always a demand for a two-berth cruiser and for one season there was a converted lifeboat to cater for this demand. However this was just as much trouble as the larger boats without the compensating revenue so the idea was not continued. At some stage in the proceedings Geoffrey Percy's own boat *Canada Goose* came into the fleet. This had been converted for him to live on permanently and boasted a hot water system and a bath. Luxury indeed.

The two motor boats, *Victoria* and *Heather Bell*, were kept in use by being let relatively cheaply to parties of Boy Scouts and similar organizations who used them as a mobile camping ground. It was a fairly crude type of holiday but it served a purpose at that time and it kept the boats in use. Nothing damages a boat quicker than abandoning the use of it.

The other butty, *Duchess of York*, was used as a horse-drawn trip boat whose principle object was probably to provide a use for the horses that my father loved to keep! These were generally booked parties of Women's Institutes and the like. In reality, to have done the obvious and used one of the motor boats was not feasible because that involved Board of Trade licensing for vessels to carry more than twelve persons. This was not only impractically expensive for the

amount of use envisaged but also involved meeting requirements more appropriate to sea-going vessels such as carrying a prescribed size of anchor! A horse-drawn boat, being always attached to the bank, was not subject to these regulations. However, on occasions, as we shall see, a chance was taken and a motor boat used.

Thus my father, to his eternal credit, turned a near bankrupt carrying business into a pioneering and profitable hire cruiser business which he was able to sell to a Major Griffin who had recently retired from the army and was looking for an interesting occupation. That he found it so, and that it continued to be profitable, is evidenced by the fact that his sons still run Wyvern Shipping Co. Ltd and I recently had the privilege of attending the fiftieth anniversary of the company.

The sale of the business happened about the middle of 1960 just as I was leaving school. It was precipitated, and not surprisingly, by a mighty row with his employers and he had to chose between his job and Wyvern Shipping. It was always my mother's wont to play safe and I suspect she encouraged him to remain in a nice secure job which, to be fair, he did enjoy. Again, I think he would not have liked the way the canals have developed into a decidedly artificial image of what they used to be. I also regret that the business was sold but it was not my decision and I suspect I would have had the same problems as my father. More to the point I would not have met my wife and that has been compensation enough.

Railways were not absent during this period but before returning to the main theme some reminiscing of canalling in what now seem those high and far off times may be of interest.

I think it must have been fairly early on in the Wyvern Shipping Co. saga, in fact before the family moved to Leighton Buzzard, that I went as crew with Geoffrey Percy for a trip on the river Nene. I think the intention was that I joined *Canada Goose* at Peterborough, we all had a trip down to Wisbech and then, all young and enthusiastic, I was there to wind up all those guillotine gates back to Northampton. It did not quite work out that way.

The party on board was, in its way, quite a celebrity one including Robert Aickman, founder of the Inland Waterways Association, Peter Scott (later Sir Peter Scott), already a celebrated naturalist, and, conceivably, the authoress Dorothy L. Sayers. I have memories of a lady reading from *The Nine Taylors*, which was of course appropriate for that area, but I think she was reading it because she was the author.

Having left Peterborough we locked down into the tideway at Dog in the Doublet lock and proceeded downriver towards Wisbech at a fair clip with the tide. About halfway the gearbox failed and left us without power. I do not remember anyone being alarmed although it must have been quite alarming. I suspect the visitors were oblivious to the possibilities anyway. Somewhat to my astonishment, Geoffrey Percy produced an anchor and rope with the idea that this could be used to slow and stop us at an appropriate point as we passed through Wisbech. Wisely he decided to experiment in advance. Over went the anchor, out ran the rope with the classic mistake of not attaching the end of it to the boat! More recent experience with tides suggest that we were probably moving much faster than was apparent and the rope would probably have broken anyway. So on we went with the tide, waving goodbye to any chance of stopping in Wisbech.

The river banks were remarkably steep preventing the possibility of beaching the boat on them, but with the last bridge at Sutton

Bridge (and very nearly the North Sea) in sight the tide eased and then turned and our headlong flight was over. We were then able to bring the boat to the bank and let her rise up it as the tide made. Assistance came in the form of a cockle-fishing boat of 1914 vintage with an engine nearly as old. We were towed to a derelict jetty and there moored to a floating pontoon. Interestingly the cockle boat's only means of stopping was also to throw over an anchor but theirs was an old engine block which did not dig in but merely dragged along the bottom.

Sutton Bridge was an interesting place. The former Midland & Great Northern Railway and the road, both being single track, shared the swing bridge which opened at high tide to allow shipping to and from Wisbech. A few hundred yards downstream was the remains of a grandiose railway dock scheme which had collapsed, literally, when the surrounding earthworks moved under pressure when the dock was filled with water. An 0-6-0 tender locomotive is reputed buried here following that collapse. The top of the walls of the entrance lock remain visible to this day although the rest is now an industrial estate. The derelict jetty to which we were moored was probably part of the scheme. In due course the gearbox was repaired and we returned to Peterborough – the party being by now thoroughly bored and, indeed, I think some of them had left before then. Certainly I left at Peterborough and went home by train and I believe Geoffrey Percy worked the boat back more or less single handed.

When the cruiser business started there was a need to move boats for docking and underwater repairs, usually to Walkers yard at Rickmansworth, always, of course, in the winter. This was about a day-and-a-half's journey with the night spent either at Marsworth or Cowroast (both near Tring). I often used to do these trips with school friends acting as crew. I always enjoyed having to work to a tight schedule and found, and still find, it hard to comprehend the idea of soozling from one pub to the next. There was also the regular Saturday chore of showing hirers how to work a lock and generally handle a boat. The Linslade base was very conveniently situated for this with Leighton lock less than half a mile away and the canal curving round so that hirers could be taken a good mile but only a quarter of a mile walk back!

Passenger carrying was done – but in a slightly clandestine manner in order to avoid the regulations. Two of these trips in particular tend to raise the hair on the back of my neck even now. One was with the motor boat *Victoria* for a twenty-first birthday party for a farmer's daughter who lived alongside the canal at Willan, now part of Milton Keynes. My father ran this one and I was only crew but the entire party had had more than enough to drink before they started, never mind by the time they got back. Our principal memory was of an accordion player walking into the canal and out again without missing a note! It must have been successful as we received Christmas cards from the family for many years afterwards. The second was a one-way horse-drawn trip with the *Duchess of York* for about three miles from Leighton Buzzard to Three Locks. At sixteen, I was in charge and the girl with the horse was thirteen. We started off fine, but after about two and a half miles the passengers started complaining that there was water round their feet! In fact the boat was sinking and quite rapidly. Shortly before our destination I beached the boat on a mudbank and the passengers walked the last quarter mile to their waiting coach. Fortunately they all thought it was a huge joke and the best day out in a long time, otherwise

the consequences could have been serious, even then. What had happened was that being a wooden boat she had dried out in the summer sun and putting forty people on board had been enough to put her waterline over the next plank seam so that the water came in. I rode the horse home and commandeered the local grocer in his delivery van to take me back armed with a suitable pump. Happy days.

I did two of what might be called official trips by actually hiring a boat with a party of school friends. The first of these was a one-way trip to Llangollen in North Wales with the half-boat *Duchess of Atholl*. We were able to arrange for the subsequent hirer to bring the boat back. An interesting sidelight on this was that only one of us was over eighteen and had passed a driving test. This person was very small and slight and always carried his driving licence when we were pub bound, the rest of us were all under-age but at six feet and a bit, did not bother!

This was a fairly straightforward trip but it had some memorable times. We travelled from Lapworth to Kings Norton through the Stratford Canal, which was near to derelict at the time. This was of course long before the Lower Stratford Canal was re-opened to Stratford on Avon. That was completely derelict. To say that we struggled is something of an understatement. The canal was choked with weed, there were numerous obstructions in the form of personal bridges across it and the locks were only just watertight. We spent a night by a pub along the way and were in sore need of its beer. This place brewed its own so whether you ordered bitter, mild or light ale it was all the same. We each had a pint and were gently ushered outside by a regular who advised that a pint was quite enough unless used to it. He was quite right as finding the boat later in the dark proved quite difficult!

Birmingham was black and smelly and the Shropshire Union wide, straight and boring. The next excitement came with the Llangollen arm itself. In the flight of three staircase locks at Grindley Brook we got our synchronization of lifting paddles wrong and landed the boat firmly on the bottom of the middle one! The biggest features of this canal are the aqueducts at Chirk and Pontcysyllte. The former is rather overshadowed by the adjacent railway viaduct but Pontcysyllte is awe-inspiring with, on one side, nothing but about an inch and a half of cast iron between you and the cricket ground 118 feet below! Added to this there was then a large notice on each end saying 'No Pedestrians, Towpath Unsafe'! In practice I suppose a boat on it adds no extra weight. The Llangollen canal is curious in other respects; it is very wide and deep where it crosses Whixall Moss, and a single track ditch with passing places for the last few miles from Pontcysyllte to Llangollen. It also has a fairly steady current along it as it is used as a feeder of water from the upper reaches of the River Dee to Chester.

The second of these trips was the following year, when we were all over eighteen, and involved the open boat *Victoria*. I am not sure why this was but it may have been the only boat available or simply that it was cheaper. This time we did a circular journey up the Grand Union to Crick, through the Leicester Section to Market Harborough and Leicester, down the River Soar and up the River Trent to Burton on Trent, into Birmingham and back. Added in was a quick return trip to Worcester because I wanted to see someone there!

Memorable parts of this trip were the Leicester section being very unused although not as bad as the Stratford Canal the year before. However three locks in Leicester were, by some quirk of history, the property of Leicester Corporation and we had to take out some of our floorboards to block up the holes in the gates to make them sufficiently watertight to be used! The River Soar was wide, deep and, with an empty narrow boat, fast; sufficiently so that turning upstream into the River Trent caused a notable slowing down. Burton on Trent was full of beer and railways and I had a short exploration of these – the railways, my companions were more interested in the beer. I promised myself a return visit one day but never made it before the lot was swept away.

We arrived in Birmingham on Sunday night only to discover that it was actually Monday night! It took us a long time to work out where we had lost a day. The journey down to Worcester was memorable for its speed. In terms of casual labour, a trip to Worcester was reckoned a good day's work, which with fifty-two locks in some seventeen miles seemed like hard work indeed. We set out to prove how possible it was and in fact it was actually quite easy. These were the only locks I knew so fitted, but the kissing post of the single top gate of each lock was extended up like a bollard. As a consequence one could enter the lock at almost full speed, drop a line around this bollard as one went by and thus stop the boat and shut the gate at the same time. Whoa betide one if one missed, the boat nearly went over the bottom gates! I saw my friend in Worcester, of which more anon, and my friends started the return trip. I met them at Hatton Locks and so have never actually travelled the whole of the Grand Union into Birmingham.

So back to the railway scene which, as I have said, was never wholly absent from my life. I was at Bedford School and whilst from Eaton Socon I could easily go daily on the bus, Leighton Buzzard was less handy. For a couple of terms I went by train leaving on the 7.18 and changing at Bletchley on the way. Bedford St Johns station was the opposite end of the town from the school so this daily journey also involved about a mile walk at each end. It was a deal of fun as a large number travelled to the Bedford schools by the Bletchley train and a good time was had by all on that leg of the journey. Bletchley, then very much a steam junction, could be fascinating with everything from the 'Princess Royal' Pacifics and 2-10-0 freights to Jinty shunters and an aged ex-LNWR 2-4-2 which periodically hauled our train.

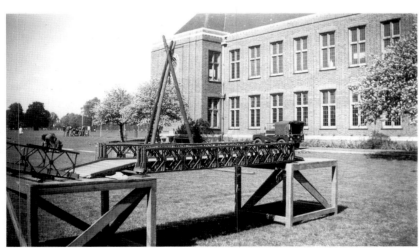

Once past the 'square bashing' stage the Bailey Bridge was my forte in the Engineers Section of the Bedford School CCF and we had this very fine model upon which to train. It must have served its purpose because the real thing presented no problems on field day.

With O levels approaching this was not a good arrangement and somehow my parents arranged for me to become a weekly lodger with the Colman family at St Mary's Rectory in Bedford. This lasted about a year and was not wholly satisfactory either, as I got waylaid into bell ringing with a tinned-foods salesman who also lived there, so homework, and thus schoolwork, suffered badly. An extra bonus was that the house had a large Hornby Dublo railway layout that proved a further disincentive. After an appalling end-of-year report I was shunted off to another establishment where temptations were less and which overlooked the school grounds. The penny more or less dropped and I did get on with a sensible amount of work. This arrangement lasted until I left school, with my returning home at weekends, which at least kept me up to date with the Bletchley railway scene.

Thanks largely to the Harpur Trust, who ran most of the private schools in Bedford, education was a major industry in the town. Bedford School, which I attended, was the oldest having been established in 1552. The Bedford Modern School, which then occupied much older buildings in the middle of the town, is generally better known. Slightly surprisingly, Bedford School itself has not produced a clutch of famous names but has, hopefully, produced its quota of worthy citizens. Both schools have their corresponding girls' schools, Bedford High School and the Dame Alice Harpur School respectively. All these schools were also unusual for their time in that they catered for day pupils, who lived in the town and went home for lunch, day boarders, who came in from the country and stayed for lunch, and full boarders who came from all over the country and, indeed, from all over the world.

This all had the inestimable advantage that the schools were not enclosed and inward-looking establishments like so many public schools then and now. Although there were fairly strict rules about behaviour and dress outside school premises, there were inevitably no restrictions about where one went or with whom. This also included girls from the other schools and so one had a much broader and more catholic adolescence than many of my age group. After all, one could have been a day boy cycling home to tea with his sister or a day boarder catching a train or bus home to who knew, or cared, where. In any case the further one went away from school the more relaxed became the rules and regulations.

Because of this I think the day boarders, a status to which I clung even when living in Bedford, were a bit of a thorn in the establishment's side. They tended to be sons of farmers and local professionals and perhaps, because of their necessity to commute daily by public transport on their own, were of an independent turn of mind that did not suffer school authority gladly. There was a sizeable booklet of school rules and it used to be my boast that I had broken all of them with the exception of the one about not bringing firearms into school!

In fact I went up the school in a fairly rough crowd of which I was on the fringe. After one almighty trouble, about what I cannot remember (I really cannot!), in which parents were called in, one of my masters complained that I had an instinct of knowing just when to leave off and thus avoid certain retribution. I was caned several times but usually for skipping games or some such. We were up to all sorts

My first insight into narrow gauge railways proper. Uplifting some of the last remaining track of the Welsh Highland Railway off Madoc Street in Portmadoc. Myself in front on the left. The removal of this rail by *Prince* was just about the last time a Festiniog train crossed the Britannia Bridge.
N.F.Gurley/Festiniog Railway Archives

of pranks in between times, some of them dangerous but nobody seemed to get hurt, even when letting a rocket off along the floor of the corridor of a crowded train! This all explains why a number of my age group were either expelled or asked to leave: one of the former immediately after bringing live .303 ammunition onto a CCF field day – and using it. In all honesty it was a miracle nobody was hurt or worse on that occasion.

All in all I quite enjoyed my school days although it has to be said that the day of leaving was a red letter day indeed. Academically I did not shine, in retrospect primarily because I was lazy. I could probably have gone on to university, which from Bedford, meant Oxford, Cambridge or Sandhurst, with Durham or Trinity College, Dublin, as a lesser achievement, if I had wanted and been willing to put in the work. I was not, so I did not and I have no regrets. School reports, perhaps in search of something to praise, consistently described me as of good character, intelligent and nice to know. Over the years I think that has stood me in just as good stead as the now obligatory qualifications.

Train spotting was all the rage at that time, and to be interested in trains but not a train spotter was simply incomprehensible to most people. (I once met somebody who had 'spotted' every locomotive

of British Railways bar four, which, by any standards, has to be no mean achievement.) The school library was pretty useless being full of ancient tomes and a few improving works, but the Bedfordshire County Library was excellent both in its lending and reference sections. It was here that I lighted upon *Narrow Gauge Rails to Portmadoc* by J.I.C. Boyd and this book set the scene for all that follows. Subsequently I have come to know James Boyd very well but he will accept no blame for all this!

It is difficult to decide how to deal with all the various facets of my life over the period of about five years in which we lived at Leighton Buzzard and which coincided with my last years at school. The school bit and the waterways bit have both now been covered but the railway bit had various manifestations. It is hopefully more satisfactory to deal with these in sections rather than to try and be chronological even though they all happened over more or less the same period of time.

The house at Linslade, Bossington Gardens, had a small brick-built stable-type building with a loft over. This was about twelve feet square and was just suitable for a further re-incarnation of the 0 gauge railway. This time I did it all myself and it was quite successful although scenery was conspicuous by it absence. I spent most of my time constructing overly massive baseboards and laying track and used almost entirely the rolling stock from my father's day.

This railway had a further new lease of life as an outdoor line. In exchange for doing some gardening (never my scene) I was allowed to excavate the garden to form a garden railway. This was to be a narrow gauge line obviously inspired by Welsh practice but built to my own designs to suit its supposed purpose. The inspiration for this was in part the aforementioned visit by boat to Worcester to see Allan Pratt who had an extensive 16mm scale garden railway which was very definitely North Wales. Like many light railways a good deal of earthworks were excavated, some track laid, some rolling stock built, a locomotive part built and the scheme foundered. Reason? In this case the sale of Wyvern Shipping Co. Ltd and a move of house. In addition, again in true prototype form, the scheme was probably too ambitious for its own good. And to carry the simile even further, some of those earthworks are still there forty-five years later!

Turning now to real railways, James Boyd's book inspired me to join the Festiniog Railway Society and a battle with my parents ensued to allow me to go to Portmadoc as a volunteer. My mother, in particular, was terribly protective of me which may have been the way of the world at that time or simply that I was an only child. The usual reaction to any unusual idea was 'No', although she usually came round to it in the end. Finally I went under the aegis of the London Area Group in company with a friend who, to my joy, dropped out when it was too late to change anything. I travelled on my own by 'The Welshman' from Euston to Pwllheli and Portmadoc, the train splitting at Afon Wen Junction. A route that is hard to believe if one goes to those parts now.

The year was 1958 and the FR had just reopened to Tan y Bwlch that year. Going with a group was actually quite a good idea as they knew the ropes and were not there to work solely on the railway. Somebody had a car and we made expeditions to the derelict Welsh Highland Railway and the Nantle Valley which was then still very active in the slate business. There was a further day out to the Talyllyn and the Vale of Rheidol. There was also a mixture of tasks undertaken which included lifting the last remains of the Welsh Highland Railway off Madoc Street and loading them onto wagons behind *Prince* on the Britannia Bridge; probably the last time an FR locomotive was there.

I went twice more on my own account and travelled Great Western by the Cambrian Coast Express, the route of which – if not the train – still exists. Both these trips involved me primarily in permanent-way work, first near Plas Tan y Bwlch and secondly in the new bridge at Minffordd installed in conjunction with the Trawsfynedd nuclear power station. On the second occasion I took Peter Arnold with me, of whom more shortly. Lack of a vehicle

Black Hawthorn locomotive *Kettering Furnaces No 2* at Kettering ironstone quarries. I never saw as much of the ironstone railways as I should or could have done but these were an inspiration and I should really have bought one when the system closed. Compare with *Trixie* in Chapter 6. *Eric Sawford*

prevented much travelling further afield on these occasions, but the derelict upper Festiniog Railway and the Croesor Tramway were walked. Peter and another friend arranged a brake van trip to Bala and a visit to Oakley Quarries both of which I missed, but to have telephoned Blaenau Ffestiniog 2 from Penrhyndeudraeth 1 has to have been something of an achievement!

Peter Arnold lived 100 yards up the road from us and was the son of Joseph Arnold of sand quarry fame in Leighton Buzzard. He also went to Bedford School, as a boarder, possibly because I did. He is a few years younger than me and, as is the case at that age, I did not have a great deal to do with him at school. However he arranged for me to visit the sand pits and see the local narrow gauge scene. Through him I also embarked on the idea of an article for *Railway World* about the Leighton Buzzard Light Railway. *Per se* this never saw the light of day but some of the research was used by others in books on the light railway and my description of the line in 1960 was finally printed by Rod Dingwall in *Narrow Gauge Tracks in the Sand* in 1997.

Perhaps the most remarkable omission in all this, especially in view of what was to happen later, was that I never registered the existence of Motor Rail Ltd, more commonly known as Simplex, in Bedford, and that despite getting on and off the train within sight of their works for years. Hockliffes in Bedford was an excellent bookshop. Here I came across a copy of *Ironstone Railways and Tramways of the Midlands* by E.S. Tonks and this opened up another railway world with much of it within easy striking distance of Bedford. The systems at Wellingborough, Kettering and Cranford were visited by train and bus on afternoons when I could avoid games and the occasional whole day that could be available during O and A level exams. Some of those slightly further away were visited as an excuse for somewhere to go when I was learning to drive. These included Scaldwell and Charwelton. To my regret I never reached Eastwell Quarries.

Model railways took very much second place when my father bought a complete railway from the just closed brickworks by the station at Woburn Sands. He sold the Lister locomotive, wagons

and the best of the track to ME Engineering Ltd in North London and kept sufficient for us to carry on the family tradition and have a garden railway. In practice this was primarily used as a means of moving a fair quantity of earth in connection with some building works and again providing a use for his horses. Total length was about sixty yards and we used the one remaining set of points largely for the fun of it. With this railway, which would in fact have been too lightly laid, I made a determined effort to obtain the Bagnall steam locomotive *Pixie* which was sleeping quietly in its shed at Cranford Ironstone Quarries outside Kettering. I had seen it, but only through the crack in the door. However I think that without doubt a clerical collar pulled rank and it went to the Rev'd 'Teddy' Boston at Cadeby Rectory! It could not have gone to a better home.

Little steam locos were there to be had at this time. I was subsequently offered the Kerr Stuart *Lorna Doone* and sent a picture of it in steam – price £120. In the same league were the two 6in. Bagnalls with the Birmingham, Tame & Rea District Drainage Board at Minworth. I was offered these, one with current boiler certificate, for £30 each! Unfortunately I was at that stage in life when I could find the £60 but not another £60 to get them home. One of these and *Lorna Doone* wound up in the Birmingham Museum of Science and Industry. However all these good ideas came to a grinding halt with the sale of Wyvern Shipping Co. Ltd and a move to Woburn some six miles away. Here my father in his true style had bought the redundant vicarage from the Bedford Settled Estates in near derelict condition and set about rebuilding it.

This also coincided with the summer of my leaving school and moving into the big wide world of work. These were the formative years of my life and I have covered them in some detail because, if I was to be philosophical about it, they were just that. They set the scene for what came later. I have also found that I must have been very well educated even if I did not make the most of it at the time. It was possibly the mixture of a good basic grounding, variety and freedom of movement that has meant that I tend to take in my stride problems that seem to floor many people.

Narrow gauge railways come home. About the only picture of the line at Bossington Gardens with flat wagon, horse Rocket and my father. The horse's harness is actually that used for pulling boats but was equally suitable for pulling our one and only wagon.

3

To Work

Leaving school was, as I suppose it is for everybody, a landmark. I was looking forward to it and was, I think, ready for it. The question of what job I was going to do became a bit of a problem somewhat at the last minute. In those days there was no question of having a year off or doing one's own thing for period. One went to work.

The troubles were two-fold. First, and anyone who is an only child will appreciate this, my parents did not want to lose me. They were not as bad as some I have come across since, but they were protective and did not want me going off to a strange job in a strange place. Second, for a number of years I had been determined that I was going to be a Church of England priest and it was only about a year before I left school that I decided I would be more use outside the Church than inside it. Only history and God will know if that was the right decision. To give them credit, Bedford School had realized that this was probably only a teenage infatuation and had not allowed me to change from the science courses to something more suitable.

Looking back, having decided on a change of direction I then did very little about it. True, I made a few enquiries of the country's locomotive builders but it was a bad time and the only one offering anything was Ruston & Hornsby, and then only a trade apprenticeship. Not unreasonably, my parents felt that having struggled to pay for my education they deserved better than that. I was strongly put off the Army although there was military tradition in my mother's side of the family. I think I could have enjoyed the Army although I might have proved too much of an individualist to fit satisfactorily into its ordered lifestyle. I did seriously think of going to sea and if I could have my life again that would be my choice. Therefore, how I wound up as an articled pupil in a chartered surveyors office remains a bit of a mystery, even to me! Probably my father had a hand in it in two respects; partly that he found me a job, almost any job, near to home and partly that it was the sort of job he would enjoy and therefore so would I. He was not totally wrong and I have no real regrets.

So it was that I started work with Stafford, Rogers & Merry of 17 High Street, Leighton Buzzard in September 1960 as an articled pupil to Mr Arthur Wells. I think it is likely that I was one of the very last genuine articled pupils although I did not realise this until a few years later any more than I realized the privileges to which I could have laid claim. The system was that my parents paid Mr Wells £202, in return for which he would show me his profession of Chartered Surveyor and Land Agent. He would not necessarily teach me – the passing of professional exams was up to me – but he would point me in all the right directions. As some recompense for my labours he would return the premium paid at the rate of 10/– per week over four years. My parents had to continue feeding, clothing and financing me the while which may have suited their

objective of retaining control. In the twenty-first century this all seems somewhat archaic and it was even then. When you read that Nigel Gresley was a premium apprentice at Doncaster works, this is the system he would have worked under. My problem was that I did not know the system and, for obvious reasons, Merry's were not going to tell me. I thought I had a job and treated it as such with due deference to my superiors and so on.

In fact I was only really answerable to Mr Wells and, in truth, not even to him. Correctly I was a free entity and could have come and gone as and when I liked. Obviously in order to give some semblance of continuity and to learn the profession, I needed to put in a significant number of hours but I did not have to be beholden to it like any other minor clerk. Similarly I did not necessarily have to put up with the other somewhat abrasive partners in the firm. There would, no doubt, have been hell to pay if I had stood on my dignity, even though I would have been within my rights to have done so. In any case in those days neither I, nor anyone else of my era, would have dared. Maybe an earlier generation, like today's, would have been more forthright. However, be all that as it may, it was an interesting job. It was very rare to spend an entire day in the office and, true to his word, Mr Wells took me almost everywhere with him. The experience gained with all sorts and manners of people in all sorts of situations has been invaluable ever since.

More specifically, Stafford, Rogers & Merry were auctioneers and surveyors of the old school. They did sell houses but were apt to consider it slightly beneath them. They were based primarily in Bedford, where they ran the cattle market all day every Saturday, and Leighton Buzzard was a branch office. There was also an associated office of Foll & Parker in Woburn Sands whose principal business seemed to be auction sales of the contents of houses. There were two Merrys in the firm, father and son, but what happened to Messrs Stafford and Rogers, and when, I have no idea.

There were five partners in the firm; the aforementioned Merrys who could be decidedly prickly to deal with and a Mr Scott, all of whom were based in Bedford. The latter drove fast cars and had a most explosive temper. If nothing else he taught me that when dealing with his ilk, always give a straight answer even if it is wrong, prevarication he would not have. These I tended to meet only on market days or at large farm dispersal sales. At Leighton Buzzard there was my Mr Wells who was pretty normal and Mr Leggett who had a complexion that must have cost a pile of money and who was often the worse for drink. I remember him one sunny afternoon standing in the front office and commenting on how it was snowing outside! For all that he was a darned good auctioneer.

In reality, the whole set-up was the end of an era and in retrospect I cannot but not think that the world is poorer for their passing. They were all characters, doing their own thing more or less in unison and it was only later, come the amalgamation with Brown &

Co. from Tring, that partners' meetings and any sort of co-ordinated management became the order of the day.

So, what did we do? A large portion of the Mr Wells work was reports on property for building society mortgages, often two or three per day. These involved visiting the property, measuring room sizes and also providing a thumbnail sketch plan of the outside. The valuation bit was usually simply a case of filling up a form and agreeing that the purchase price was reasonable, in other words, that the building society would not lose out if it had to foreclose. My part of the exercise was doing the site plan, which was usually straight-forward. Every now and then something unusual would turn up in this bread-and-butter type of work; I once found death watch beetle in the roof of an otherwise immaculate property! Allied to this was work for local solicitors simply preparing a more accurate plan of a property, particularly if one was being split up. I really enjoyed these and it could be quite astonishing how properties had been divided up in the past. I remember a row of terrace houses where the gardens behind were two plots out of step with the houses. Boundary disputes could also be interesting, such as trying to convince a Pakistani with limited English that he was not allowed to put a fence down the middle of a three-foot-wide access passage!

Occasionally we carried out full structural surveys of houses for buyers. These were often larger properties and for people who did not have to bother with mortgages. A great deal more care had to be taken with these, not least because the fees were substantial, but also because the surveyor was, even then, liable if he got it badly wrong. Again, we would periodically be retained to supervise restoration and building work as appropriate. In the same vein, I did all the drawings for at least two new houses. Nothing to do with us, but it is worth mentioning a local case of a new house where planning and building permission had been obtained, the construction put out to general tender and when the selected builder reached first floor level somebody realized that the staircase had been omitted entirely! It was added on the outside and looked a real feature.

On the agricultural side it was often rather similar work, sorting out boundaries, layout plans for new barns, planning applications, pegging out land to be sold or bought and all sorts in between. We also carried out the land agency work for all the sand quarries around Leighton Buzzard. This primarily covered negotiations with tenant farmers when the quarry needed to be extended, taking away a bit more of their land, but it also included ground surveys for both existing and new buildings. Possibly the most significant of these was the new Eastern Way screening plant for Garsides which included the railway connections into the Leighton Buzzard Light Railway. On one of these occasions I had something of a minor triumph. I had been out to measure up some new field drainage work for a subsidy claim and when I got back to the office my measurements simply would not 'tie' together. On the basis that if everything else is right the unthinkable must also be right, my conclusion was that the position of a pond on the Ordnance Survey plan was wrong. Mr Wells grumbled mightily at having to go out with me to check my figures, 'which I should have got right the first time', but I was proved correct.

For those who may not be aware of the significance of this a few words on the Ordnance Survey may be in order. The task of measuring the country was started in the early part of the nineteenth century. On the grand scale this was done by trigonometry and locally by actual measurement. Most people are aware that in a triangle, given one length and two angles all other sides and angles can be calculated. On this basis a line some seven miles long was set up on Salisbury Plain under as carefully controlled conditions of temperature as was possible. From this a series of triangles was built up across the country finishing with a test line approximately five miles long beside Lough Neagh in Northern Ireland. This was found to be only five inches different from the calculated length! No mean feat in those days. Most Ordnance Survey plans come at 1:2500 scale but the office had some at 1:500 for the centre of Leighton Buzzard dating from 1881 and the detail on these was quite remarkable, including such things as the layout of gardens, principle trees and the obligatory privy in the back gardens.

Auction sales were enjoyable, although I remember a few best forgotten, generally on account of the weather. Farm dispersal sales, often following a retirement, could be fascinating. I preferred being outside organizing lots and such like rather than being stuck in the office – usually the cleanest of whatever buildings happened to be available and, equally usually, as cold as charity. Items sold included everything from prize cattle to literally the kitchen sink. I still have a very splendid walnut dresser bought at a farm sale for the princely sum of 32/6d (£1.65).

Interspersed with all this were, of course, professional exams. Studying was done on a correspondence course from a college in London and I joined at least one residential course with them. Exams were taken in London at the Examination Halls in Southampton

My first locomotive as first seen in a disused chalk pit of Houghton Regis cement works near Dunstable. I was given it if I could take it away! This Baguley (Bg760 of 1918) locomotive was one of fifty built for use on very light track in the trenches of the First World War although most of them ended up with Canadian forestry battalions.

Row. I took the three stages but failed the finals – but, in something like a repeat of school days, I had changed course and rather lost interest by then.

I was only peripherally involved in the rebuilding of Woburn Old Vicarage, indeed my father may have been beginning to feel his age because he employed part-time labour far more than previously. I did however re-lay the 2ft gauge railway there and it did a achieve a full circle around the place, distance about 180 yards. In the process of demolishing and rebuilding the house it was used considerably for the transport of building materials to and from storage in the shrubbery. It was at this stage that it acquired its rolling stock in the form of a half-cubic-yard tip-wagon and a flat-truck, both from Little Haddam Limeworks in Hertfordshire. There was also a home-built hopper-wagon for delivering coal to the central heating boiler situated in the old cellars. Motive power was by hand pushing or occasionally by horse if there was enough to do to warrant harnessing up.

A locomotive was obviously a requirement both for use and for fun but it had to be light as most of the track was only 14/16lbs/yd rail at best. By this stage I had come across the Birmingham Locomotive Club booklets giving details of industrial locomotives past and present in most parts of the country. To my surprise, Bedfordshire turned out to be a surprisingly happy hunting ground but, even if I was not too late altogether, the majority of what might have been available was too heavy. In the end I approached Blue Circle Cement at Houghton Regis about a Baguley locomotive which was in a flooded clay pit once part of their operations. Imagine my surprise when they said I could have it if I could take it away! There is a snag to all things that are cheap or free, in this case it stood in about five feet of water but why should one let a little thing like that deter one? In practice the cement company went in with a bulldozer when the water level was down a bit and simply dragged it out. I was then able to remove it. Quite by chance I happened to phone home one day and my mother said something had arrived for me. I was expecting some exam results with some trepidation but it turned out to be a locomotive – much preferable. Thus Bg760 of 1916 came into my possession, the first of many many locomotives.

This locomotive was one of a batch of about fifty petrol-engined locomotives made by E.E. Baguley Ltd of Burton on Trent in 1917 for use on the Western Front during the First World War. In fact they carried the maker's name of McEwan Pratt, a firm that Baguley had taken over in 1912. Originally intended to work on very light 9lbs/yd rail, they were not particularly successful and were largely relegated to use on forestry lines and in base workshops where they were able to serve a useful purpose. Technically they consisted of a Baguley-made twin-cylinder petrol engine – which by today's standards was unusual in that the cylinder head and cylinder block were all one casting – that drove through a cone clutch into a two-speed reversing gearbox with jackshaft drive to the wheels. The change speed was by open gears, the larger of which carried the crankpins for the rod drive. Engine cooling was by a large water tank and the whole thing had a striking similarity to a steam locomotive which was probably deliberate.

This is proof that I did get the Baguley to work even if only fairly briefly. Here it is beside the paddock in the garden of the Old Vicarage at Woburn. Shades of the Mortimer Lodge Tram perhaps?

In common with most enthusiasts, I set about dismantling the machine to chip off the rust and get some paint onto it without giving sufficient thought to the overall scheme of things. I made an immediate decision that the engine was useless and gave it away to a friend who was a stationary engine enthusiast. This was a mistake as it turned out that the layer of chalk/clay covering everything had acted as quite a good preservative and things came apart remarkably easily. Knowing what one does now, I am sure the engine was probably retrievable and a complete original locomotive could have been a possibility. The gearbox was persuaded to work by some considerable belabouring with hammers and, whilst not perfect, certainly did what it was supposed to do. The wheels were profiled, axle-boxes and rods fettled so that in due course I had a rolling chassis. So far as the engine was concerned I came by a very elderly Citroën car out of which I robbed the engine and gearbox. Again this should have been preserved, not least because it had the accelerator peddle between the clutch and brake pedals. The engine from this along with its radiator was fitted into the locomotive and the whole lash-up did work, quite well too. The frame-work of a body was made but, like echoes from Wyvern Shipping days, other things were in the wind that brought most of this to a standstill.

At this time my grandmother, by then about 95, and her disabled daughter were living with us and for whatever reason my parents acquired a Swiss girl as an *au pair* to help out. (As a complete aside, Brigitte, for that was her name, had been told to be prepared for the fact that the English talked only about the weather. She said that by the time she had been in England a month, she knew why!) Anyway, at some stage my parents reciprocated an invitation to a Mr and Mrs Hobourn, the local churchwarden, county councillor and so on, and as he could not come Mrs Hobourn brought her daughter, Susan. A while later Brigitte was invited to the Hobourns to meet their daughter and I happened to make the comment that it would be much more to the point if I was invited to meet her daughter.

By some devious means this did indeed happen and it is inscribed in family lore that on this occasion I ate chocolate cake which is something I cannot abide! I had occasion to return the compliment with an invitation to the Hunt Ball of the pack of beagles I had

The Red House at Aston Clinton in 1964, at about the time we moved in. The Aylesbury arm of the Grand Union Canal is in the foreground with the lock under the bridge. The road passes in front of the house and the triangular piece of ground between road and canal was once a wharf.

been involved with at school. And so, as they say, one thing leads to another. Susan, who is always nervous of being driven by strangers, told me much later that any future for us had depended on how carefully or otherwise I drove that evening. Evidently I came up to scratch. Upon such things does one's good fortune depend!

People cope with having their girlfriend or boyfriend hundreds of miles away, but living in a relatively small place has its problems too. Which parent was going to be offended if we were both not there for tea on a certain day? Both families were staunch church people, so on which side of church and thus with which family did we sit? Fortunately perhaps, Susan was nursing at the Middlesex Hospital in London at the time and I came to know the West End extremely well which has stood me in good stead ever since. This did at least allow us to be on our own although running the gauntlet of the hospital nurses' home could be a bit daunting. Once engaged, life became easier in these respects although the build-up to the wedding itself put years on both of us, but then it probably does for everybody. On the plus side, having to steer a path through two lots of fairly determined parents may have been a good omen for the years to come. It is true to say that we have never seriously argued over anything.

With about two years from meeting to marrying, Susan at least found out about my passion for oddball railways and was subjected to visits to ironstone railways and the like. Neither of us are gregarious by nature so organized visits were never a part of the scene. Such visits were often fitted in with the mandatory visits to relatives which all fiancées suffer – thus I caught a glimpse of the Modern Tramways setup at Eastbourne and the first season of Bicton Woodland Railway. In any case, Susan was not totally inexperienced as her brother had, and still has, a passing interest in railways which had involved her sitting and watching the trains go by on the main line at Leighton Buzzard – ironically, from about the same spot that I usually sat and ate my lunch.

The question then arose as to where we should live. I was still with Merry's so it had to be within striking distance of Leighton

Buzzard. I put the word around and it was the Tring office which came up with The Red House at Aston Clinton. This had been a pub and stood beside a lock on the Aylesbury arm of the Grand Union Canal. I did remember it from a deliberate trip to Aylesbury and back in Wyvern Shipping days but now it was derelict. Not just derelict, it was a wreck. All the windows had been knocked out, part of the roof was off, some of the floor boards were gone, as was the staircase (how?), and there was no drainage although it did have water and electricity. Added to that it was a mile down a dead-end road and 500 yards from the nearest house. In other words, a typical Keef project! We bought it with quarter of an acre of equally derelict garden for the princely sum of £1,500.

First efforts to board it up met with resistance from the local lads but we persevered and in reality did not have many problems once it was obvious we meant business. Partly because of us moving in, the son of a local farmer decided to move into a caravan at some farm buildings across the field opposite. Tony Evitt proved a good neighbour when he was there which was not always. We did most of the initial clearance and the first stages of making the place habitable again ourselves. However it was patently obvious that we could not do it all and, after some initial work by a part-time bricklayer of my father's, a small firm of builders that I had used with Merry's was called in. Thus the job was done, but a snag was that whilst I was at liberty to go off and see what the builders were doing when Merry's were supervising the job it was not so easy when doing it for myself.

Amongst all this was a wedding to be arranged and, although the bridegroom's principle function is simply to be there on the day, one does tend to be involved in the run-up as well. Again the problems of living too close to one another came to the fore and have certainly given us talking points ever since. The wedding itself, on 19 September 1964, was a fairly grand affair. St Mary's church Woburn is like a small cathedral and lends itself to a certain amount of pomp and circumstance. The Rev'd Robin Osborne, although not having been there very long, was well loved and, along with both our families, liked to see things done properly. And indeed they were. Susan's home backed up to the church and, somewhat to the disgust of my parents, she walked to church and we were both able to walk back through the trees after the ceremony to the reception in her parent's garden. This was a very typical English family wedding with all the appropriate relations and friends involved.

We made off to Flitwick station and those that tried to follow us went to Luton instead, for reasons that have never been apparent. We spent a night in London and then crossed to France and Paris whence we took the night sleeper to Brest in Brittany for our honeymoon. The destination was also a little bit of a merging of interests. We had decided to go abroad, which in those days meant the near continent, and France was the

The traditional wedding group photograph. From the left; my parents Elizabeth and Michael Keef, best man Alistair Simpson, myself, Susan, bridesmaid Connie Martin, Susan's parents Bernard and Evelyn Hobourn.

obvious choice as school French at least gave us an inkling of the language. The traditional beach/sea orientated holiday did not, and never has subsequently, appealed to either of us. Brittany became the choice because of the similarity of the coastline with that of Susan's beloved Pembrokeshire and for me the chance to sample the metre gauge Réseau Breton system. In reality we probably saw more of the former than the latter but it was an enjoyable and memorable time for us both.

The original idea had been to try to stay in Camaret sur Mer which was a terminus of the Réseau Breton within the vast natural anchorage of Brest Roads, but that was not bookable from England so we stayed in Brest itself. In due course we went to take the ferry across to Camaret, only to find it had broken down. As it was an advertized service, we found ourselves bundled into the back of a large

Citroën van and driven about 100 miles round the head of the bay to Le Fret and Camaret. We certainly saw some additional scenery that way! The coastline and hinterland came up to expectations and we almost became commuters on that ferry. One day was spent 'doing the Réseau Breton' with a trip from Camaret sur Mer to Carhaix, the hub of the system, and on to Guingamps with return to Brest by standard gauge. The narrow gauge section was just under 100 miles, something which is virtually inconceivable in England. All regular passenger services had by then been taken over by a selection of diesel railcars but there was an apparently thriving goods service which was all steam worked and I did have a chance to see the odd Mallet at work. As always, my photographs are minimal but I do have the memory, which is more important to me. The whole set-up was very impressive, not least the main workshops and loco sheds at Carhaix, both of which were easily seen from the main line. I have no particular memory of anything out of the ordinary so I guess the trains must have run as timetabled and without fuss. One interesting thing we did see was gravel being unloaded from what appeared to be a coastal sailing vessel into Réseau Breton wagons at Le Fret. This must have been some of the last traffic on this short branch. Even if it was inevitable, it never really occurred to me that this solid and substantial system had only another three years to live. There may be slight compensation in that part of it was converted to standard gauge and the locomotive sheds still house and repair the replacement buses. Would that some of it could have been preserved as a functioning railway, but railway preservation was then very much an Anglo-Saxon pastime and had not yet been exported to the continent. Also to its detriment was that, in common with many other narrow gauge lines, the Réseau Breton was very much out on the limb on the Brittany peninsula.

Brittany was our honeymoon destination, and who said that the Réseau Breton had anything to do with the choice? Although passenger trains were entirely worked by diesel railcar there was still steam to be seen, and this Mallet 0-6-6-0 epitomises this once great system.

4

Muck but No Money

And so we returned from our honeymoon to a state of married contentment that has continued these many years since. I went back to working at Merry's but in truth my heart was not in it by then. Although by now I was actually being paid, in an effort to make this significant so that I could get married I had moved into the estate agency part of the firm. In retrospect this was a mistake. Merry's ideas on estate agency were very laid back and almost anyone could have done better.

However, the estate agency business was beginning to become the thrusting cut-throat business it has become today, and that was really not for me. In due course all this came to a head and it was only a question of time before they kicked me out or I left. I pre-empted the former – just.

I think it was during these remaining nine to twelve months with what had now become Brown & Merry that I came to the conclusion that I wanted to work for myself and not for anybody else. I remember walking away from Merry's on my last evening and, for almost the only time in my life, feeling lonely. From now on it was me against the rest of the world, I had made my bed and would have to lie on it. The possibility of being my own master was greater now, as Susan was, as she always has been, very supportive of what I wanted to do, whereas my mother always viewed the nice steady job somewhere as the best thing in life. Various options were looked at in greater or lesser detail, joining with some friends to set up as estate agents in Winslow, joining forces with a local builder, even taking over a large but run-down furniture shop in Leighton Buzzard.

As a foretaste of things to come I gave serious thought to taking a lease of the Leighton Buzzard Light Railway with the idea of turning it into a tourist attraction. A letter to Mr Fred Arnold at Arnold's London office, where the registered office of the light railway company now was, brought that idea to an abrupt halt. However it may perhaps have sown some seeds because it was not long afterwards that the Iron Horse Railway Society achieved the same objective. Maybe I was just too soon.

In the event it was something that was more conventional and about which I certainly knew more at that time, even if that knowledge was somewhat limited, that took the prize. I turned to pig farming. My market experience had been largely with pigs and I had a number of friends who appeared to be making a living out of them in some fairly ramshackle buildings on allotments and the like. I had had some experience of keeping them and this was added to by a short course at the local agricultural college. It is necessary

to wind the clock back to my Woburn days for a moment. In truth this all started at the annual church fete. I managed to win a pig in the Bowling for a Pig competition! Yes, a real live one, even if it was only the runt from a litter. I think everyone was a bit surprised when I actually took it away. Anyway, I put it in a small summerhouse, fattened it up, and in due course it went to Bedford market. I then built a proper sty, bought a couple of weaners and did the same thing again. Several times.

In the middle of the fields behind The Red House there was a set of derelict farm buildings and, after a lot of pestering, I managed to obtain the use of them in return for repairing and making them usable again. I would have dearly loved to have had a lease on the twenty-five acres or so in which they stood but that proved impossible, which, again with that glorious benefit of hindsight, was probably a good thing. So when the crunch came with Merry's I was all set to move on to, hopefully, greater things. Amongst what I had been taught at the college was how to approach a bank manager for a loan to buy stock, etc. It worked. I suppose because of the articled system under which I started work I had never had the opportunity to accumulate any money so I had to go that way in order to make a start at all. It started an association with overdrafts and bank managers which has been with me ever since!

Writing this in the changed circumstances of the new millennium, it would seem the daftest thing to have done, but in those days it was quite possible to make a living – not a fortune, but a living – from twenty sows and what they would produce. It was also considered quite feasible to start with half that number and build up to it. The bank manager certainly did not poo-poo the idea, which must have meant something. So I used his loan to go out and buy some very nice Large White gilts (in pig or ready for their first litter) and we were off. A firm was dismantling and selling prefabricated bungalows erected as temporary housing during the war and one of these made an excellent farrowing house, or maternity ward if you prefer.

At least I thought so, but maybe my pigs did not, as I had endless trouble at farrowing time with sows suffering mastitis and lying on little pigs. In the end I had to be with my sows throughout farrowing until they settled down. Many a night I spent there with them; at least it was warm and comfortable. Similar pig problems prevented my getting to my grandmother's 100th birthday which always has been a regret. Obviously keeping pigs on this scale was not a full-time occupation and I had adequate time to earn money elsewhere. Indeed this was part of the overall plan, if there was such a thing, to build the herd up. To this end I spent time repairing a cottage for an erstwhile colleague, assisting a couple of local farmers at haymaking and when they were on holiday and, most interesting of all, working part time for Peter MacKinnon who specialized in church roof repairs.

Opposite: The Red House, *circa* 1966. The proximity to the lock on the Aylesbury Arm of the Grand Union Canal is clear. The building at top right is the farrowing house for pigs and Susan's efforts to create a garden are evident. Under a sheet in front of this building is the Baguley 760 and to its right the frame of the de Winton *Kathleen*. No permanent track has yet appeared.

I honestly think that he was one of the cleverest people I have ever met. His business was a three man band affair but he would quite happily take down a completely rotten church roof and build another in its place. I remember him going out to buy an extending ladder which reached to 56 feet, and we needed it! Having measured up he would go out into the surrounding neighbourhood and pick the oak trees he wanted for the main and lesser beams. He would fell them, bring them back to his workshop, saw to the basic sizes and shapes, carve in all the mouldings and decoration, cut the dovetails to fit the wall plates and erect same onto the church walls. Bear in mind that some of these beams were 25 feet long, 12 inches thick, 30 inches deep and had to be placed 50 feet off the ground – it was no mean achievement. Admittedly it was all done with the timber green which made it easier to work and it subsequently seasoned *in situ*. I learnt a great deal from him, such as that for this sort of work he would buy a new 100-foot steel tape for each job and that all significant measurements for that job were made with that tape and no other – there could then be no problems with stretched tapes. It was all wonderful experience, and having to move a heavy lump of something with limited means at one's disposal has never presented a problem for me.

Possibly at my father's instigation, but no doubt aided and abetted by me, he installed a short railway to move sawn timber away for stacking and seasoning and for its return when required. This was basically U shaped with a siding into his workshop and was of 1ft 8in. gauge. Whilst primarily hand worked, he subsequently acquired an Orenstein & Koppel diesel locomotive from the closed lime-works at Barton in the Clay. This did work but I am not sure that I ever saw it used. 1ft 8in. or 500mm gauge was a common continental gauge and, together with O&K locomotives, was marketed in this country by William Jones of Charlton.

At this stage railways remained very much a hobby, but I met (or they found me) a number of people who would be significant in the

years to come. I put down a few yards of track in the garden at The Red House although there was never enough to call it a railway; efforts to make use of it in conjunction with the buildings across the fields were frustrated by the landlord. An unusual wagon by W. & J. Howard of Bedford was tidied up and the Baguley brought from Woburn. Although I had heard from him previously, I had a visit from Rich Morris of subsequent NGRS and Gloddfa Ganol fame who had acquired a similar Baguley to mine. He was at the beginning of starting what subsequently became a huge collection of narrow gauge locomotives. His Baguley was missing its gearbox and he offered to swap the de Winton locomotive *Kathleen* for the gearbox out of mine. I shall never be able to decide who had the best of that deal!

Kathleen looked like a de Winton in that she had wheels, boiler, water tank and bunker in the right places but she was impossibly incomplete, especially bearing in mind the facilities that I then had available – basically nothing. There was a pair of cylinders, badly worn, and a few other odds and ends but that was it. I think it must have been advertised somewhere but somehow I came to hear of another de Winton but of 3ft gauge, *Llanfair*, ex Penmaenmawr Granite Quarries, which was for sale at Llanwrst in North Wales. My father and I took the train to have a look at it and I bought it for the princely sum of £30 with an old Clayton steam wagon boiler and a steam winch thrown in for good measure. It was rusted solid but the theory was that the bits could be used to make *Kathleen* work. Ignorance is bliss! I did not then know that every de Winton is different from every other de Winton.

So Tony Evitt, our neighbour, and I went to Llanwrst with a van-load of blocks, jacks, winches and the like and loaded it onto a lorry which in due course re-appeared in Aston Clinton. I had hoped to ramp it off onto the ground but lorry drivers are always in a hurry and we finished up dragging it off onto a pile of sleepers from where I subsequently jacked it down to ground level. I thus became the proud owner of three narrow gauge locomotives none of which worked and of which two still do not forty-plus years later, although it has to be said that they have not been mine for many a long year.

Another person who passed my way at that time was Alf Fisher, justifiably proud owner of *Chaloner*, the only de Winton to survive in working order. He bought it from Pen yr Orsedd slate quarry at a time when steam locomotives were still in use and redundant ones could be bought at, shall we say, reasonable prices. He had obviously heard of this strange person who had acquired a couple and lived more or less on his doorstep. Many years later I copied *Chaloner* in some detail when building *Taffy* but more of that anon. This was 1967 and the moment in time when the Leighton Buzzard Light Railway finally ceased to serve its original purpose as a sand carrier

A very youthful me on the de Winton *Kathleen* at The Red House. This locomotive is preserved insofar that it has not been scrapped but forty years later it is no nearer to being a working locomotive than it was then.

Of the very few pictures of the 'pig railway' at Cote Farm, this is the only one which shows any pigs. Note the portable turntable to allow a muck wagon to reach within shovelling distance of the source of same.

and entered the era of railway preservation with the formation of the Iron Horse Preservation Society. The original intention had been to develop the light railway along an American narrow gauge theme, in particular after the style of the 2ft gauge railways of Maine. In this they were way ahead of their time and it ultimately took a private individual to achieve anything like what they had in mind some thirty-five years later. In due course this scheme died and the railway went off in an entirely different direction. As did I, and for that reason never had very much to do with the exercise until much later and then in a totally different capacity altogether.

The pig business along with additional work from elsewhere was just about, or just not, making ends meet. The arrangement by which I used two lots of buildings 200 yards apart but over which I had no effective form of tenure was not satisfactory and if growth was to be achieved then better and more extensive premises were called for. In addition, in November 1966 our first child, Patrick, was born and there was thus going to be another mouth to feed, clothe, educate and so on. There was a lone property advert in the Pig Farmer which caught my eye for a property in West Oxfordshire and thus we came to move lock, stock and barrel to the hamlet of Cote, five miles from Witney, Oxfordshire. The removal date was to be 24 January 1968. As one could in those days, I went out and bought a lorry from a local roundabout firm in Leighton Buzzard so that I could move all the sundries myself leaving only the furniture and the animals to the professional. This was a Ford Thames Trader which, unusually for its size, had a six cylinder engine. According to the name still painted on the side it had belonged to a firm making hair shampoo, which is no doubt heavy,

and was first registered in Derbyshire, which is hilly, so this may have been the reason.

This was going to be the business! Railways were to take second place and money was going to be needed. Thus the two de Wintons were sold and I used the lorry to deliver them to a man in Pershore who intended to restore them in the manner that I had in mind. He never did and the sale was actually a mistake. The money realized was, frankly, insignificant but the principle was commendable.

The immediate problem that became apparent was that I needed something better than a wheelbarrow to remove the endless supply of muck created by pigs to somewhere away from the point where they created it. I did not have and had not intended to buy a tractor and trailer for which, in any case, Cote Farm was not really suited. The alleyways between the buildings were not quite wide enough for convenience but on the other hand they would satisfactorily take a railway! Thus the railway which we had had was put back to some sort of commercial use. It should be mentioned that following our marriage my parents had sold the Old Vicarage at Woburn and bought a derelict farm house in Heath and Reach on the outskirts of Leighton Buzzard. Here my father had installed part of the railway for the movement of building materials. The initial railway at Cote therefore consisted of a U-shaped layout with our one and only set of points leading off to a dungheap. The track was all very light, being mostly 14lbs/yd rail at best, and was entirely hand pushed.

This was all very fine, but by the time one had shovelled out a pen-full of soggy muck or slurry into even only a half-yard wagon, pushing it away uphill onto a tip became hard work. Motive power was obviously required. This led to some interesting correspondence with both R.A. Lister of Dursley and Motor Rail Ltd of Bedford as to the likely cost of a new small locomotive. This could never

The Lister locomotive with its rudimentary cab in the form of a lean-to wooden shed was a bonus when feeding pigs in the rain! Unusually, this locomotive was fitted with a Ruston & Hornsby engine.

have been justified or afforded but it was a good excuse! I still have the replies and was quoted £736 and £1,030 respectively. More to the point was a general writing round to existing users of Lister locomotives to see if they had anything for disposal. I was lucky, and struck gold with the Southern Gas Board at their Poole works where they had two locomotives and some hopper wagons for disposal. One loco and two wagons were currently for sale; in due course they were bought and I duly winched them into the lorry and brought them home. This collection was a lesson in trying to be too clever. I knew the locomotive was a runner but I took a spare starting handle with me just in case its own was missing. Would it start? No. It was not until I got it home and looked more carefully that I realized that the engine ran opposite rotation to normal and I had been trying to start it backwards! Use its own handle which was there all the time and it started first swing.

And so I came to have a proper railway with real locomotive power. In the fullness of time this actually became quite sophisticated. I fitted my lorry with a tail lift and when some pigs were ready for slaughter, moved them out in a container on the tail-lift board and so into the lorry. Narrow gauge containerization – on a small scale! The hopper wagons were passed on to the Festiniog Railway where they may still exist, but the very heavy wagons on which they were used were effectively Lister locomotive frames minus the power units, and in due time these were broken up for the wheels and axles and sold. Not long after this the second locomotive and wagons at Poole gas works came up for sale. Purchase of this necessitated the sale of the first one to ME Engineering Ltd in North London from whence it eventually wound up with Boothby Peat Co. Ltd near Carlisle. The second one was slightly different in that it had an overall roof, I will not call it a cab, very much more like a lean-to garden shed. At least I was now in the dry when using it. Again the hoppers went to the Festiniog Railway.

At about this time I came across a Ruston locomotive in a showman's yard (I often seem to be on the periphery of their industry) in Swindon. This I bought without any real intention of keeping it. It turned out to be a 13DL, something of a rarity, and to have been operated by Devon County Council at Beacon Down Quarry, Parracombe – more renowned for their fleet of Kerr Stuart 'Wren' class steam locomotives. I got this to go, repainted it, and in due course it too went to ME Engineering. The very few photographs of the 'pig' railway in operation manage to feature this locomotive.

The pig business was simply not making ends meet although it was not as apparent as that at the time. In any case profit from pigs is very cyclical, usually on a six- to twelve-month cycle. The reason for this is that from conception to slaughter takes about eight months depending on the market being served. As a consequence if there is a dearth of pig meat and prices are high, people start breeding pigs again, or large organizations increase their production, with the effect that six months later there is a glut and prices fall again. 'Pigs is either muck or money'. A lot depends on how long the cycles are and whether you can survive the hard times. Added to this, inflation was beginning to make itself felt in the British economy although it was to be a few years before this became really serious. A few years later it was possible to see what happened. As stated previously, it had been quite possible to make a living out of twenty sows and what they would produce. Due to inflation and other pressures this number had to increase in order to achieve the same result. Indeed,

by the time I finished with them one needed double that number. I was thus never able to grow the business out of its own resources to achieve the desired result as I genuinely believe one could have done five years previously.

In an effort to help the situation I needed a job, any job, and it happened to be with Brazil's, subsequently taken over by Bowyer's, who made pork pies, sausages and bacon in Witney. This was in what was euphemistically called their meat selection department and was an evening shift starting at 4.30 p.m. In reality it involved cleaning up after the day shift in the room (all departments were rooms – sausage room, bacon room and so on.) where meat was boned on piecework, and generally having everything ready for the next day. The next day's meat would arrive during this shift having been bought at Smithfield Market during the day and it was part of my job, with others, to unload it. It is no good being squeamish when presented with a 5-ton van-load of loose pigs heads! It was also my first encounter with trades unions which were almost ruling the country and certainly trying to run British industry at that time. The shop steward was a bit put out when he asked me if I was a member of any other union and I said, 'Yes, the National Farmers Union.' 'Huh, that's a bosses union.'

It was obvious that the pig business could not go on and, reminiscent of my departure from Merry's, I managed to sell out just before the bank forced it upon me. I can still remember the stillness and quiet of the yard after they had gone. This fortuitously coincided with my applying for and getting a supervisor's job at Brazil's. My mother was delighted! Security at last. Again this was initially for the evening shift, starting at 4.30 p.m. to cover a part-time shift of seventy to eighty people, mainly women, who worked 6 to 10 p.m. In reality I could finish any time between the official 1.30 a.m. and 4.30 a.m. I think an evening shift is probably the worst of all possible worlds to work regularly. One cannot have an evening out or keep up with television, one tends to be out when one's children are at home and whilst I was left with part of a day in which to do other things it always seemed to be the wrong part. Anyway, I had a job which involved maintaining production, arguing bonuses with women on piecework and generally trying to maintain control of a fairly unruly bunch of the opposite sex who, whilst obviously needing to work, were in it as much for the sociability as for the money. Something of a baptism of fire. Anyone who has done anything similar will know what I mean. Forget about the gentle sex!

Not very long after I started this the manufactured meat trade took one of its downturns and most of my 'women', some sixty in all, were made redundant. The night they left was a night to remember. They finished up pushing each other round the yard in meat trolleys and I cleared up something like twenty empty wine bottles and fourteen of spirits after they finally went! Following the inevitable reorganization I wound up as one of two night supervisors. The job entailed seeing through any final production

and, when necessary, persuading somebody to stay on for a few more hours into the night to finish it; also seeing the delivery vans loaded for the morning's sales-roundsmen and keeping tabs on those who came in very early, from 4 a.m., to get the wheels turning for the day shift. I have to say that I thoroughly enjoyed working night shift, the staff were generally more responsible, there was none of the internal friction and infighting common to the day staff, one was very much one's own master and had to deal with the problems oneself as they came along. It was also a straight eight hours, 10 p.m. to 6 a.m., meal times included.

Just a flavour of some of those problems. An Italian employee came to me one day saying he had been underpaid. He was always very willing and would do any odd thing asked of him and it turned out he had worked through continuously from 6 p.m. one evening to 8 a.m. the morning but one after, so he had been underpaid by 24 hours! A man came ringing on the yard bell one night, could he use the phone to call a doctor, his wife was in labour and he could not find a phone box that worked. We sent a heavily-loaded hired bulk lorry off to a London depot one night. That particular depot was entered through an archway and, when they had unloaded it, it would not come out! I think they let the tyres down in the end. The police used to call for a chat occasionally and it was policy to provide them with some bacon or sausages to take home which was reciprocated when the police were needed. Nobody abused it and no harm done. I was walking along the loading dock one night and a man fell through a door across it, out cold at my feet. He had stretched the patience of the only black man on the shift one step too far. Both were good reliable employees, admitted their mistake and all was forgiven with a good dressing down. Sometimes we used to get some most spectacular moths about in the early morning, usually around the ladies lavatories! Otherwise it was a good steady job which left me quite a chunk of each day and especially all day on a Monday to do useful things with railways.

It was at this stage that Cotswold Light Railways appeared on the scene and that deserves a chapter to itself. As a consequence I left Brazil's for the summer but conveniently for both of us they were pleased to have me back the following winter. In fact I only worked about four months of that as railways were taking over, but that, as they say, is another story. My mother was not impressed!

Life at Cote deserves a section on its own, and here is as good a place as any to say a few words before the whole railway business became serious. The life of self-sufficiency has been epitomized by the television series *The Good Life* and whilst with us the reason for it was entirely financial the process was remarkably similar. The financial problems stemmed of course from the collapse of the pig enterprise and the start of the railway business with, as a consequence, no capital left to speak of. This was exacerbated later on by our very conscious decision that our children should be privately educated and it is possibly not so far from the truth to say that that is still being paid for. However I know that we, and I think they, have no regrets on the subject.

Cote Farm *circa* 1971 with the first and very simple railway installed for pigs. This used equipment from Linslade and Woburn. The position of the muck heap varied and track was re-laid accordingly. *Scale 1:500*

A lot of fun was had on the railway at Cote especially at children's birthday parties. Note Cote Baptist Chapel to the left, Jemima the house cow and Murray the dog drinking from the water trough in which a goldfish lived for about eight years despite being frozen solid in the winter and dried out in summer!

and live happily out of doors all year. Like all beautiful ladies they can also be very temperamental! A sizeable vegetable garden, not to mention a soft fruit cage, completed the picture. We also had some chickens but a source of trays of cracked eggs made them uneconomic.

Holidays were not non-existent, but Susan's mother had a flat in Exmouth, Devon, and we always went there for around ten days in the summer. Exmouth has excellent beaches and Dartmoor is very close, so a great deal of fun was had by all. The compensation to the children for not having the foreign holidays that were then just becoming the vogue was that they always had space around them. There was a pond to play and get filthy in, the whole of one summer was spent building a 'house' which then had to be 'opened' by a much embarrassed neighbour, we had

We had pigs, so they were in themselves a source of food and we had a delightful character who used to come and slaughter them for us. He was a licensed slaughterman and his two loves in life were killing animals and singing in the church choir! Because there was no facility to scald the hair off a pig he used to set the carcass up in a shower of straw and set it alight which imparted a flavour all its own to the pork. We also used to sell this meat to our friends and neighbours. Six acres of land also needed tending so we had a cow, Jemima, and later Elsie as well, to provide milk for the house and also to raise calves which were either sold or slaughtered for veal, or better still as 'baby beef' which is another delicacy unheard of in the normal way. We never gave names to animals we knew we were going to slaughter. We did make our own hay but usually had to buy some in as well. A cow to milk seems an awful liability and to a large extent it is, but one kept for the house can be kept fairly casually, only needing to be milked once a day. I used to milk ours in the field which can be a bit trying if it is snowing! For all their apparent delicacy Jerseys are very hardy

dogs which were part of the establishment, Patrick had his own locomotive to rush around on and he also used to come on my travels with me. When they were older we used to rent cottages in various parts of the country which provided a change of scene for all of us. Even if money was a bit short it was indeed a good life.

The crowds are out for the first season of Cotswold Light Railways at South Cerney. The Hunslet locomotive from Brian Goodchild's garden line is seen with the two carriages from Trevor Barber's Woburn railway at the one and only station.

5

Cotswold Light Railways

Once again I am going to deal with this *en bloc* and return to the main story in due course despite there being an obvious overlap between the two. This may become confusing but hopefully all will be revealed. Cotswold Light Railways began as an idea for a retirement occupation for my father and, in theory at least, started off as being his brainchild. It rapidly turned into me doing the construction and subsequently running it. It again goes back to the idea that the only way to make any money out of railways was to have one somewhere and run it as a passenger-carrying operation. Being based where we were, we looked around for a suitable site on which to put and operate a railway that was not too far away and yet had, we hoped, potential. We looked at several places and wound up with the Cotswold Marina at South Cerney, near Cirencester. It was always hoped that this might be one of a number of such railways, hence the title of Cotswold Light Railways, plural.

Gloucestershire County Council had an ongoing problem as to what was to be done with the many worked-out gravel pits in the area between Cirencester and Cricklade, mostly centred around the village of South Cerney. To this end they produced an extensive document setting out a whole raft of possibilities and designating the whole area the Cotswold Water Park. Needless to say, most of the suggestions were for water-based leisure activity whilst continuing to allow gravel extraction to take place. To give credit where it is due, the concept was very far-sighted and the Council were willing to back suitable proposals within the area.

Thus we came across the Cotswold Marina. This was operated by a subsidiary of Hills of Swindon Ltd, the gravel company, and was a means of doing something productive with their own worked-out pits in the area. Again it was commendable and had considerable potential. Whilst they also used some of the lakes for water sports of various sorts, the one with which I was concerned was intended as a day-visitor attraction. The lake (for which read old gravel pit) was shallow and sloped gently into the water on two sides and, as lakes go, was not very large. Thus there could be swimming and boating in the lake, together with other more land-based attractions. There was adequate space for car parking and also for touring caravans and such like. You could even park your car at the water's edge, rather like a ringside position at an agricultural show. A new spine road had been built into the area largely to make egress for gravel lorries easier but also to make access for visitors better. The new site was in charge of one Mike Warren who also had charge of the other leisure activities of Hills.

Here we encountered difficulty number one, in that Hills did not really know what they wanted to achieve from the site. They also had the naive idea that the site was for the benefit of 'nice' people only. Thus they overlooked, or did not know, that middle England is only the way it is because it does not spend money lavishly on its entertainment. This particularly applies to people with caravans who tend to be either retired or hoping for a cheap holiday with their children. It is the so-called masses who are unconcerned about how much a 'good day out' costs them. However, be all that as it may, the actual layout of the site was changed several times, fortunately before I started track-laying, although I did have to move my materials at least once. The site also included a gravel washing plant although the life expectancy of this was finite and short. It was something of an eyesore and noisy when in operation but the plus was that there were always machines around to do a bit of earth-moving for me and the offer of a ready supply of gravelly ballast when needed.

Thus for the beginning of the 1971 season I had laid about 500 yards of track together with some sidings. I was able to rent, and subsequently buy, the two carriages used by Trevor Barber on his Woburn Abbey railway and latterly at Overstone. Motive power was initially provided by a variety of diesel locomotives but passenger operation centred round the Hunslet locomotive acquired from Brian Goodchild at Leamington Spa. The track was a mixture of 20lbs/yd Jubilee track and rails spiked to wooden sleepers. Initial operation was to pull the train out and push it back again. Happy days! Such things just could not be entertained by our present litigious and safety-conscious age.

Hills provided refreshment facilities from a caravan, car parking and a reasonably decent entrance from the road and we all opened for business. This was to be the beginning of what is now called a learning curve and although it was not steep, it was salutary. In retrospect, considering the low-key approach by one and all, it is perhaps surprising that there were any visitors. As much as anything it may have been that most of the other activities in the Water Park as a whole were for members only. Here people could do legally what many of them had done illegally for years and that was to swim in the lake. The salutary aspect was how long it takes for any wholly new tourist venture to 'take off'. Since then I have seen this many times and even well-known names underestimate just how long it will take before their new venture achieves its designed potential.

Having said that, I did carry some passengers, at least enough to consider the effort justified and to continue with it. A number of people beat a path to my train in order to see what it was all about, the most notable of whom was Joe Powell who ran a 10¼in. gauge line at Ashton Keynes about a mile from the site. I am not sure whether it was right at the beginning, but from very early on a young lad by the name of John Matthews appeared on the scene with his parents and somehow or another became part of the furniture. He was always willing to help lay track or drive trains, other than passenger ones. He stuck with it right to the end and I still see him occasionally. You will notice that I keep saying 'I' – my father, for whom it was all intended, really had very little to do with it either in the building or in the operation.

Left: After the conversion of the railway to metre gauge, Fowler locomotive *Dinmor* with a well loaded train of tramcars ex Charleroi in Belgium. The re-gauged railway followed the same route as the previous one.

Right: Although this picture was taken in the 1990s, it is from scenes such as this that the business started. The owners were going to bury the four locomotives in this picture! I bought them, sorted them out and, except for one that was scrapped, sold them on to other users.

As already related, I went back to Brazil's that winter, at their request, on the definite understanding that I would need to be off again the following summer. The next year's season began to show good promise and we persevered with it largely on a weekends-only basis with some outside assistance to drive trains during the week for the school summer holidays. Cotswold Marina themselves had also done a good deal of work to improve the place, most notably spreading a large quantity of sand at the water's edge to form quite a respectable beach. They also diverted some of the gravel-washing plant's water so there was a decent flow of water through the lake to keep it fresh. I extended the track a little but otherwise kept things much as they were, not least because there was no overall plan for the site development and ideas changed regularly.

My, our, ideas also changed around this time. In those days one foresaw a steam locomotive as a vital adjunct to that type of railway and I had hoped to acquire one from Portugal. For various reasons that came to naught. But with this idea in mind we (and this is how my father came into it again!) bought a large quantity of surplus rail from the closed Norden clay mines at Corfe Castle in Dorset. This line was originally of 2ft 8in. gauge and then re-gauged to 2ft to take *Russell* of ex-Welsh Highland Railway fame. This rail was of 35–40lbs/yd and of very mixed vintage and type but was a major step forward and a necessity if steam locos were to be considered. With this material to hand a start was made on re-laying with heavier rail, and then everything changed. At about the same time I bought a 3ft gauge Fowler 'Resilient' class diesel locomotive from Dinmor Quarries in Anglesey. This was quite a beast. It weighed 8 tons even though it was only 45h.p. but unlike most small diesel locomotives of that power it looked the part, had a good-sized cab in which even I could stand up and was a sensible match for suitable 2ft gauge carriages. To convert it to 2ft gauge was not impossible as the type had been built to that gauge. It also had electric start! Up to this point the official locomotive used was the Hunslet, which was quite attractive, along with a variety of locomotives that passed through my hands. The present carriages were OK but not ideal and something better was sought.

I am not quite sure how it all came about but I think it probably emanated from my parents having a holiday based at Barcelona in Spain where they came across a derelict roadside tramway of metre gauge at Sitges on the Mediterranean coast. This had some delightful balcony cars built by Falcon of Loughborough sometime in the nineteenth century. It was considered feasible to convert these to 2ft gauge, although I now suspect it would not have been that easy. He also looked at a complete 2ft 6in. gauge railway that in practice would have been a better proposition altogether, but the gauge put us off. My father had the benefit of my mother having Spanish as her second language. The upshot of it was that we decided to convert the whole railway to metre gauge. It was not as daft as it seems – it would be different, we had suitable rail, we had a locomotive more easily converted to metre than 2ft and we hoped to have some very attractive and unusual carriages. A small metre gauge steam locomotive from somewhere was a possibility, surely.

In the event the Sitges trams were all sold off locally to be 'plinthed' and have by now probably disappeared altogether. Again I am not sure how, but my father was once more on the case and ran to earth some tramcars at Charleroi in Belgium. Once more my mother's knowledge of French, almost as good as her Spanish, came into its own. This started off with us being offered some motor cars but when he went to look at them he discovered that there were trailer cars available as well and that these were much more suitable for our purposes as well as being cheaper. The down side of either of these was that they were not attractive vehicles – indeed some would say downright ugly! However, they had been the latest thing in their day, about 1939, when they were rebuilt from earlier, more typical Edwardian tramcars of continental style. Reputedly they had been rebuilt just before war broke out and had survived unscathed in a warehouse for the duration of hostilities. If nothing else, at £300 each they were cheap underframes upon which to do something else if one wanted.

And so the 1973 season was one of all change. Shades of 1896 with a gauge change, albeit in the opposite direction and in midsummer. The 2ft gauge equipment was sold, the carriages going to Jo and Barry Curl of Hampshire Narrow Gauge Railway Society fame at Durley, the locomotives and track being distributed to various customers of my burgeoning railway supply business. The new railway and its equipment was, I think, treated with some astonishment by the patrons of Cotswold Marina but from my point of view it had many merits. Even if it needed a little coaxing,

a locomotive with electric start was a bonus particularly if using labour other than oneself. The all-enclosed tramcars gave one peace of mind when carrying numbers of children, who otherwise tended to have a death wish by hanging out of the open carriages in all directions. I also had an increased passenger capacity which at times was needed. The season turned out to be good, encouraging one for the future.

That winter the track was considerably extended although a complete circuit had not yet been achieved. For 1974 I also took over the boats and crazy golf and the train was offered free to all those coming into the place, for which I took a percentage of the gate money. This turned out to be the best year of the whole exercise and we all really thought that the place was going to 'go'. There were large numbers of people coming in and they seemed to appreciate what there was for them; admittedly not that much but it was a cheap day out, especially for families.

On the railway front, apart from steadily extending the track, the only major change was the introduction of a 50h.p. Hunslet mines locomotive that I found in a scrapyard in Greenwich. This emanated from the explosive stores inside the Rock of Gibraltar and we thus named it *The Rock*. It was something of a brute to handle but it had the merit of having air brakes which in turn could be connected to the tramcars not only to work their brakes but also to operate the air doors as well! The Fowler, named *Dinmor*, again after the place whence it came, rather became spare engine although both were used. Operation continued to be on a pull out, push back basis but on very busy days a loco was used at either end of the train. The tramcars were remarkably suitable for this purpose, they rode well and negotiated the sharp curves easily despite being only four-wheelers, but I suppose they were street cars anyway!

1975 turned out to be a disaster but through no fault of mine and, in fact, spelled the death knell of the whole Cotswold Marina enterprise although it was a couple of years in the dying. With a view to having an improved year like the previous one I took on Henry to operate my side of the show. During the week there was time for him to let the boats and handle the crazy golf together with running some trains when required. He lived on site in a small caravan that I provided and this also helped with any security problems. Susan and I and family helped out at weekends. This

was the year that Hills finally demolished the gravel washing plant and built a sensible entrance into the place. It was also the first of two exceptionally hot summers. 1976 was hotter and even produced a Minister for Drought! The problem came in July just as the school holidays were starting. The lake became foul and the local environmental health officer closed it for swimming. This contretemps was created by the removal of the gravel-washing plant which had produced a flow of water through the lake and out into the adjoining brook, and without this the water just stagnated. Too late, Hills pulled themselves together and started pumping water through from a huge adjoining lake. In fact it was only closed for about a fortnight but, as is always the way with these things, the local papers had banner headlines when it was closed and a short paragraph somewhere in the middle when it was re-opened. In the public eye it was no longer a place to take one's children. The following year Hills did start pumping in a more timely manner but I think they lost heart, or interest, or both at about this time and it was downhill from here on. I used, in vain, to grumble at them about smartening the place up and trying to make it a little less like the disused gravel pit that everybody knew it had been. Money seemed to be the problem but there were many simple and fairly cheap things they could have done which would have helped – for instance to buy a white smock coat for all the sundry part-time employees just to make them look as though they belonged.

Despite all this we had not given up ourselves and presumed that 1976 would bring a return of the improving times. The track circuit was finally completed with some fairly tortuous curves and a level crossing across the main entrance. This made train operation much simpler and easier for less skilled staff. Whilst Hills improved their catering facility from a caravan to a 'Portacabin' type building, they also decided to franchise it out. This may not in itself have been a mistake, but the people they got in did not seem interested in making a go of it. They also had a very rough and ready appearance and that is not a good image to have in the catering business. From my point of view they had the merit that they would run the train for me on a commission basis during the week, which was fine so far as it went, but again there seemed to be an inability to present a professional image. With Hills apparently no longer concerned, anything went and the end of the season was the end of the Cotswold Marina.

Anyone would be entitled to ask why I did not gather the reins into my own hands and take the whole thing on and run it the way I knew it should be run. There is an easy answer; by now the tail was wagging the dog. The railway supply business – which had been intended to keep me occupied, rather than necessarily earn me a living, during the winter months – had become a fully-fledged occupation in its own right. It now had two full-time employees as well as myself and a part-time secretary. Alan Keef Ltd had also been formed with an outside director and the prospects were generally looking good, not to mention a great deal better than the small income then derived from Cotswold Light Railways. In addition, with Alan Keef Ltd now employing most of my weekday energy I was less than enthusiastic about spending all of every weekend at South Cerney.

6

Making a Start

So what was I doing in between running Cotswold Light Railways? Fundamentally I was creating a surprise for myself which to a large extent subtends to this day. If anyone had said that it was possible to start, run and expand a business dealing in light railway equipment and nothing else in this day and age I would have laughed at them and the world would have laughed with me. Nevertheless that is what I have achieved. It still comes as something of a shock that I am still at it nearly forty years later, that I seem to have made a name for myself which is recognized as a good name to do business with, that I can maintain employment for a dozen or more people, indeed that I should be in a position to write these words at all. For example: a few years before this goes to print Alan Keef Ltd's turnover reached the magic million pound mark, and at a church meeting recently the chairman was asked to point me out to somebody as that person had read about me in the railway press and wished to be introduced!

The business has always been fairly well documented for a variety of reasons. Firstly, the railway enthusiast fraternity have always kept close tabs on what I have been doing, the number-crunchers always wanting to know which locomotive came from/went to where and when. Second, in the hope that either this account would be written or simply that somebody someday might like the information, I have consistently kept all my sales invoices which give quite a good chronological record of what went on. Third, and for me the most important, at Cote I did not have planning permission for what I was doing and it might therefore be necessary to prove that I had carried on business there for the requisite number of years to have acquired the right to do so.

Dealing in second-hand equipment was the name of the game in the early days and we still do it to this day as and when the opportunity arises. One of my earliest deliberate 'deals' was to buy some badly bent rail from Trevor Barber at his Woburn Abbey Railway, straighten it all out and subsequently sell it back to him! Forgive me Trevor, but I have done similar things elsewhere over the years. For the benefit of Cotswold Light Railways I had bought a complete railway from Brian Goodchild at Leamington Spa. This comprised a Hunslet locomotive, a Simplex locomotive, a bogie wagon, various other wagons and several hundred yards of largely Jubilee track. (For those not familiar with the term I should perhaps explain that Jubilee track is something akin to Hornby track but in full size. It is usually 20lbs/yd rail and of 600mm/24in. gauge but not always. The idea is that it is easily portable.) Having bought this I then removed it to either Cote or South Cerney, all being done single-handedly, including the lifting and loading. I also loaded and delivered a fairly historic Baguley locomotive which had been bought by Richard Morris. Doing this became quite a useful sideline to the main business. So what to do with what I did not want for the South Cerney project became the question.

I think I advertised it in *Contract Journal* and that is how Mixconcrete Aggregates of Northampton came to buy the Simplex locomotive, some of the wagonry and another Simplex I had bought from a scrap merchant in Wellingborough. This latter had been at Bedford waterworks and I had tried to buy it whilst at school! As I was still working nights I remember having to get up in the middle of 'my night' in order to demonstrate it to them! But I suddenly realized that I had made a profit, or rather that what I kept had cost me very little. Maybe there was some sort of business to be done here. Certainly it was enough to make me change my box-van type lorry intended for pigs to a Bedford TK flat-bed which was much more useful for the way things were going.

Opposite: Cote Farm, 1971. By this stage all is quiet and the pigs have gone, but the railway business has not really started. However it has begun to stir as there are some stacks of second-hand rail about and a locomotive lurking inside what became the workshop. What we always called the 'Big Barn' stands in front of the house with the kitchen garden in front of that. At the extreme right are two of the large elm trees that succumbed to Dutch Elm disease a year or two later.

Right: The beginnings of a business. Two Simplex locomotives unloaded off my lorry in London docks for shipment to Singapore. At that time there was a seemingly insatiable demand for small locomotives, especially Simplex, for logging operations in Malaysia.

Part of the group of six steam locomotives purchased in Portugal for resale in this country. Seen here is the 0-4-0 Orenstein & Koppel, in steam at the front, followed by a big 0-6-0 and the pride of the bunch at the back, a First World War 0-6-0 Hudson. Only the middle one reached England.

This was 1971, and when I look back at the records everything seemed to be happening at once and I wonder how I coped. Cotswold Light Railways was just starting, I was spending some of my time at Brazil's and I was also buying up derelict locos and even complete railways around the country. Not to mention my elder daughter Florence being born in November 1969. There was a whole string of purchases of which the biggest was seven locomotives – six Simplex, one Hibberd – from King's Dyke brickworks near Peterborough. My father helped finance this purchase and in later years told everyone that of course he helped me get started. True, but only marginally so!

Again I am not sure how I made the initial contact, but A.R.C. Motor Co. Ltd bought four of these locomotives for export to Singapore for use in the logging industry in that part of the world. This was to be the first of many sales made through them. However they were only interested in either Simplex or Ruston locomotives, any other makes had to be sold through other agents. Locomotives had to be in good running order for this customer, cleaned, painted and ready to go to work. The specified paint scheme was black frame and wheels, dark green engine and orange bodywork. Horrible, I thought. But when done it actually looked quite good and thus it became my house colours for new industrial locomotives. There was the added advantage that when these things became a concern, orange was deemed to be a safety colour.

The purchase of a pretty derelict Simplex 32/42 from a scrap yard in Bedford started a type of work which continues unabated to this day. This locomotive was ex London Brick Co. Ltd and was of their common gauge of 2ft 11in., not the handiest to resell to somebody else. However I sold this locomotive to Pleasurerail Ltd who were just setting up their railway at Whipsnade Zoo and for whom Trevor Barber was now manager. Pleasurerail Ltd was a consortium of Bill McAlpine (now Sir William), Major Monson and Commander Lassels, whose intention was to indulge their interest in narrow gauge railways by building passenger lines in various parks and stately homes. Whipsnade was the first of these. This line was 2ft 6in. gauge as it utilized equipment from the Bowater's paper mill line at

Sittingbourne in Kent. Ignorance is bliss! I had no real idea how wheels were fitted to axles except that they were pressed on and I knew even less about that. I dismantled the loco and took the wheels to a local heavy engineering firm who had a press of supposedly suitable size but to no avail. They suggested British Rail Engineering at Swindon and this in turn became a regular job. They re-gauged them without turning a hair although I think they had never seen 'locomotive' wheels so small. Thus was a locomotive re-gauged and sold to a customer. I shudder to think how many I have done since. For the same job I supplied a couple of tip wagons which I again re-gauged from 2ft by welding a piece into the axles and stepping the frames out each side to suit.

Late in 1971 I was approached by Michael Crofts from Leiston in Suffolk with the idea of a joint venture to import some 600mm gauge steam locomotives from Portugal. They belonged to the Empresa Carbonifera do Douro, a coal mine in the Port wine region, and it was to be my job to find homes for them in this country. They were an interesting collection: five Orenstein & Koppels – an 0-4-0 at 5 tons, four 0-6-0s, two at 7 tons and two at 13 tonnes – and, pride of place, an 0-6-0 Hudson of First World War vintage. All were in reasonable condition, probably steamable if you were brave, and certainly the 0-4-0 was used to pull the others out of their shed for inspection, photographing and to make a final steam journey along the line.

Thus began what was to be a long drawn out saga that took some two and a half years to resolve. Between us we put up some money and with relative ease I managed to sell the 0-4-0 to Trevor Waterman for his Creekmoor Railway at Poole and the Hudson to Pleasurerail, with them wanting an option on one of the 0-6-0s. This would cover our costs and hopefully leave a fair profit in the sale of the others when back in this country. In my case the profit would be one of them for South Cerney. In due course Michael went out to Portugal, bought them all, obtained a valid export permit and had them transported down to the docks at Oporto. Bingo! The local newspaper ran a front page headline that we were removing Portugal's heritage and even going so far as to suggest that one of them, the Hudson (and the most valuable), was the oldest locomotive in the world, etc. etc. All very largely nonsense, especially the last, but sufficient for the customs authorities in Lisbon to revoke the export permit. In later years I have become sanguine about how long it can take to achieve simple things on foreign soil, but then it seemed an eternity. The upshot was that a year or so later they released the two 7-tonners, *Fojo* and *Sao Domingos*, and one 13-tonner, *Pedemoura*. After much negotiation the former went to Trevor Waterman and the latter two to Pleasurerail.

But the Portuguese government was quite adamant that they were going to keep the remainder. They stood on the dockside for a number of years, not improving in condition and incurring huge quay rental fees. Their ultimate fate I do not know except that the Hudson is in a museum somewhere. Michael went out to Portugal again and was paid some small compensation for them. This was paid to him in cash with, he thought, the expectation that it could be removed from him as he left the country, under some currency regulation or another. All credit to him that he made a bit of a fuss about having to catch a certain flight the next day and then caught the first available flight out of Portugal which happened to be going to Madrid, a direction he was not expected to take!

One person who appeared on the scene at about this time – and who was to become a long-time friend, and especially so to Patrick in later years – was John Hall Craggs who was just laying out an extensive 9½in. gauge railway at Brightwalton, near Newbury. I sold him a quantity of light rail that came from a pipe works formerly operated by Hills at South Cerney and I also made my first set of points on an experimental basis for him.

Something of a coup for this era was the purchase of two locomotives from London Brick Co. Ltd at Peterborough and their subsequent sale to Blue Circle Cement at their Sundon works. Again this involved re-gauging, this time from 2ft 11in. to 3ft, and also fitting new wheels to one of them. The usual other work was required to bring them up to the 'good second-hand condition' in which they were offered. This was the first time I had come across a Simplex 60S weighing in at 7 tons and it stretched my methods of handling locos to the limit. However the deal was done and all parties were happy. I took a Simplex 32/42 in part exchange and it languished in the yard for years until the remnants were finally scrapped.

Amongst the locomotives that came from Flettons at King's Dyke was a Simplex, Works No. 8882, for which, out of all the spare parts that were part of the deal, there were insufficient to make up a complete engine. I bought an engine of the same type out of a Priestman digger locally and although the two, both Dorman 2DWD, were markedly different, I wound up with a complete machine. My son Patrick, aged five, was much involved with this exercise and he knew the completed locomotive as 'Digger'. The name stuck. Shortly afterwards I sold it to A. Waddington & Sons Ltd of North London, the first of about six sales and subsequent

re-purchases that I made with that particular locomotive, and it has become something of a pet and acts as works shunter, now officially called Digger.

Waddingtons' at that time had a major contract installing a main sewer at Farningham in Kent. This was along a valley bottom and they laid an extensive 2ft gauge railway alongside in order to minimise disturbance to the landowners. It was not continuous but there were in total about one and a half miles. I supplied at least four locomotives and Richard Morris tried out a 'steam tram' – in reality a Lister locomotive converted to steam – there. I had considerable further dealings with Waddingtons' and was sorry when they were swallowed up by a larger company, as they were very light railway orientated. I also used to supply odds and ends to Fred Watkins Ltd of Coleford in the Forest of Dean, mostly light track, wheelsets and so on. On one occasion I supplied a complete railway – track, turnouts, bogies and all made up to fit the site – to go into what appeared to be a bacon factory. As always when one deals through somebody else one never knows who and where the end user is – another little mystery. When the company moved to The Lea, a one-man-band haulier who used to collect from Cote for Fred Watkins found me again and did a considerable amount of work for us until he retired.

Gary Stevens and Graham Morris of the Island Narrow Gauge Group from the Isle of Wight also appeared on the scene about now. I think they were then recently out of school and were trying to start a narrow gauge/transport museum on the island. Graham is well known nowadays as a designer of boilers but also as the justifiably proud owner of the peripatetic steam locomotive Peter Pan. This is to be seen at many railways, both here and on the continent in the summer months. Gary was, and is, something of a character and I employed him for some time as my wandering platelayer, more of which later. Sufficient to say that only Gary, driving my van, could have been hit by a riderless motor cycle! The rider had come off about 100 yards previously but the bike was still going. Similarly, his wife rang up on one occasion to ask where Gary was, he was late for his tea. I had just sent him off for two weeks in Scotland!

When the Humber bridge was built – it was then and still is the world's longest suspension bridge – I hired some track and bogies to carry materials along a jetty to the base of the off-shore southern tower. Here is one of the useless bits of information one picks up; the tops of the two towers are theoretically one inch further apart than they are at the bottom due to the curvature of the earth. That is assuming the contractors could build that accurately! In the same area I supplied track, bogies and a locomotive for the extension of an oil terminal jetty at Immingham but, to the chagrin of the railway enthusiasts, the locomotive disappeared without

Typical of the early days of the business was this contractor's railway at Farningham where a railway was used to carry materials on a pipe-laying contract in a very wet valley. Although in separate sections, there were about one and a half miles of this line.

trace. It either landed up in the North Sea or, much more likely, was cut up at the end of the contract. I still get asked about it!

This was the time of the beginning of the loose partnership between Richard Morris, Peter Nicholson and Michael Jacob. We knew them as 'The Merry Men'. Largely in the name of the Narrow Gauge Railway Society, they set about acquiring a large amount of narrow gauge equipment, being given, or virtually so, a great deal of it. I collected a goodly amount of it from various parts of the country and went to some fascinating places in the process. Equally, I acquired the more useful items in exchange for the transport costs, which in turn were sold on. Eventually this led to a parting of the ways when I found I was becoming just another storage point for their material which they had little intention of restoring or doing anything else with.

In some respects a foretaste of things to come, I supplied a railway to Roy James at The Seahorse public house at Leysdown on Sea, on the Isle of Sheppey. I do not wish to offend the good people of Leysdown but at that time it really had very little to commend it. The railway ran for 100 yards or so on a piece of ground behind the pub and consisted of a Simplex and a Ruston locomotive and some four-wheel carriages he had picked up from somewhere. I spent a lot of time there sorting out track and repairing locomotives. Despite appearances, there was serious money in the place and he never ever queried my costs. Once when he came to see me he pointed his Jensen car down the M4 at 100m.p.h and was in Chippenham before he started looking where he was going, having overshot Oxfordshire by about fifty miles! He was reputed to have a Rolls Royce hidden away somewhere where the Inland Revenue did not know about it.

In reality, one was coming to the end of an era in these matters. Railways had gone completely out of fashion both as a national means of transport and as an internal means of moving materials. The rubber tyre and the great god Motor were approaching the peak of their powers. It was also a time of high inflation, and smaller firms that had been able to exist by cobbling together their own machinery found they could no longer survive. Larger firms were viewing railways askance as they tend to be labour intensive and no-one seemed willing to thoroughly modernise a light railway system in order to review the lifetime costs of the operation. As has tended to be the case ever since, the longevity of railway equipment was being sacrificed to the short-term cost advantage of other means of doing the job. Added to this, what has become the health and safety industry was just beginning to raise its head and make life difficult for the railway user.

All businesses have major turning points in their histories and mine had now reached its first. I received a telephone call from John H. Rundle Ltd of New Bolingbroke, Lincolnshire, asking for a 7-ton Ruston locomotive for pleasure use. No more than that. If I could help they would send me a photograph of something along the lines of what they wanted. As it happened, I did have just such a locomotive in the yard, albeit a slightly oddball one. It turned out that this was required for Butlin's holiday camp at Ayr in Scotland and was to be the beginning a long and fruitful relationship with Butlin's. Indeed, without putting too fine a point on it, their work changed me from being a dealer specializing in light railway equipment to an overhaul and manufacturing organization in its own right. I had by this time taken on my first employee, a general fitter by the name of Clive Wall who had served his time in Swindon works. His only problem was that it seemed most things that he had made must have been wholly jigged as I almost had to teach him how to use a ruler. Not that long afterwards I took on his brother Martin who was a welder and equally well trained.

Before the locomotive was delivered to Butlin's I was introduced directly to them by Rundles and first met their Keith Palmer at Minehead. The problem there was the track on their Peter Pan railway. These railways were 2ft gauge and had individual cars on them powered from an electric third rail. As originally laid they had curves as sharp as 4-foot radius. We set to and re-laid the track with new sleepers and pick-up rail including re-routeing it to get rid of the worst curves. This apparently simple job was of huge significance as it was the start of contract track-laying work which remains a major part of the business to this day. It was also where my early training as a surveyor and my experience with Cotswold Light Railways paid their dividends. I had

Locomotives and wagons were supplied for the rebuilding of the pier at Bournemouth. A Simplex 40S wends its way amongst the girders as the new structure takes shape in 1979.

The Ruston locomotive *Sue* at Butlin's holiday camp at Ayr in Scotland. This was really an unsuitable locomotive for that particular railway but it was what they asked for and at that stage I was in no position to advise. Otherwise, it was the start of a long-term business relationship with Butlin's.

built and operated a passenger carrying railway and I was also capable of properly laying out any alterations or new works. Butlin's had become part of the Rank organization and they quite obviously had a mandate to put their house in order after the haphazard days of Sir Billy Butlin himself. This was just as well as H.M. Railway Inspectorate was just about to gather all these little railways under its wing. This was probably a good thing, but they were apt, and still are, not to understand fully the difference between a main line train to get one from A to B as quickly as possible and the park railway setting out to give visitors a train ride. Perhaps Butlin's knew this was coming, I do not know.

With my new-found contact directly with Butlin's I then went to their camp at Ayr where the Ruston, *Sue*, was due to run. I was more than a little horrified by what I found. My first and principal worry was that the line was laid in only 20lbs/yd rail which was really much too light for a 7-ton loco. However the track was well ballasted and utilized half ex-BR sleepers that were largely in good condition and I, at least, had not recommended the locomotive. I realized afterwards that the locomotive that Rundle's had previously supplied had gone to Pwllheli where the track was of 30lbs/yd rail. However there was worse to follow. It was this sort of situation that had caused the entry of the Railway

Inspectorate on to the scene, and one can only say 'Quite right too.'

It is necessary to digress slightly to explain a little about the trains principally used by Butlin's. In the days of Billy Butlin himself, he was apt to decide quite arbitrarily to do or buy something and then it was up to the local staff to make it work. This had happened with his railways. The original railways had been supplied by Hudswell Clarke in 1938 and there was later post-war 2ft gauge equipment from Baguley, but apparently on a whim whilst in the USA he had bought two complete train sets from Chance Manufacturing Co., Wichita, Kansas. These were, and are, very beautiful and surprisingly rugged but are of a very odd design. They are a modelled on a 4-2-4 switcher which in itself must have been unique. They had petrol engines and drive through the bogies with the 'driving' wheels floating on radius arms to allow the locomotive to follow the track. The big snag with the earlier ones was that the wheels are scale profile as well and the track has to be spot on to allow them to run at all. The carriages had similar bogies to the locomotive and were prone to breaking axles. The bogies at Ayr had been replaced by some made locally.

These had obviously also suffered derailment problems so the wheel flanges had had rings welded onto them to help stop this. However these were now too deep and were knocking the fishplate bolt heads. So, out with the gas cutter and cut the heads off the

Much more typical of Butlin's was this locomotive built by Chance Manufacturing of Wichita, Kansas, USA. Despite the unusual 4-2-4 wheel arrangement and somewhat flimsy appearance, these locomotives have stood the test of time and most of the Butlin ones are still in use. This one is at Skegness *circa* 1975.

A complete Chance train at Butlin's Filey in 1978. The railway here simply encircled the boating lake except where it crossed it on girder bridges. The first two carriages are of my manufacture and the third is original Chance with a deeper valance below the frame. All are running on my bogies. *Dave Holroyde*

bolts! Then they wondered why the track was falling to pieces. Added to this they had also found that the track was narrow in the gauge in places; so again, out with the gas cutter and cut the head of the rail away! When *Sue* was delivered we all went too and carried out some emergency repairs to the track to make it possible to run trains in reasonable safety.

Jumping ahead a little, this was the beginning of major work for Butlin's to re-habilitate all their railways around the country. Not only was it to be excellent work in itself but it was good recommendation for anybody else. The first move was to re-bogie the Ayr carriages and here, quite by chance, I had a design that Trevor Barber had thrown at me on one occasion. As designed it was too precise for railway work but modified it has proved a wondrous bogie with a well-deserved reputation for giving a comfortable ride. I built no less than forty-eight of them for Butlin's alone and overall I must have built many hundreds to the same basic principle in all gauges from 12¼in. to 3ft. Some of them are travelling 12,000 miles and more each season!

It also turned out to be a year of getting Butlin's out of trouble. They suffered a calamity with an elderly Baguley locomotive at Clacton and I was able to hire them a Simplex for a few weeks while Rundles put it right. That created an embarrassing moment when I arrived with a good replacement locomotive, unloaded it, ran it half way round the track and it stopped! What had happened was that transporting it there had shaken up all the dirt in the fuel tank which had then gone down the fuel pipe and blocked it. Clean it out and all was well, and my red face could subside. This happened to me at least once subsequently. At Filey the railway ran over some fairly sharp curved bridges and these were playing havoc with the carriage wheels. They were wearing out wheel flanges in weeks rather than years. It was incredible to see, but with some advice and minor track alterations the situation was contained although Filey was always to suffer this problem more than anywhere else.

Life was not entirely Butlin's, although it seemed like it at the time. Whilst on holiday in Edinburgh, and having left my card at a small peat bog at Newmains, I was contacted by Boothby Peat Co. Ltd at Brampton, near Carlisle. Slightly to my surprise I was asked to go to their peat moss at Boltonfellend to advise both them and Scottish Agricultural Industries (SAI) on how to improve the

operation of the moss railway. It was my first introduction to the peat industry and I was on a steep learning curve so far as understanding their operation was concerned. Anyway, they paid for my going and there has been good business to follow over the years right up to the present. It started with my building some all-steel peat wagons which they subsequently copied in quantity. On the same trip I also made contact with Caledonian Peat based in Larbert and their irascible director, Ken Whammond, with whom I always got on very well but whom many in the industry could not abide. These are both names which will appear again but both are now part of William Sinclair Horticulture Plc.

This trip to Scotland also enabled me to visit the site at Foyers on Loch Ness where Reed & Mallik were digging a lengthy tunnel through rock in connection with a hydroelectric scheme. Following my experimental set for John Hall Craggs I went on to make a fair number of turnouts for the tunnelling railway on this scheme. Hindsight tells me that I must have been on something of a wing and a prayer with these as I had no real idea of the geometry of points and crossings and simply made what looked right. However they worked and the customer was satisfied. I also supplied three 7-ton Simplex 60S locomotives for this contract, all of which came from various sources including London Brick Co. Ltd.

There were sidelights to this contract, the first of which was to become the story of my business – getting paid. Reed & Mallik were not good and I often added the cost of a solicitor's letter to their quotations as this was normally required to obtain payment. The second was more amusing: both Mr Davidson of Reed & Mallik and Mr Dobson of A.R.C. Motor Co. sounded very alike and very rumbustuous on the phone but neither would announce who they were. I got it wrong once and Mr Dobson was quite offended. However that was where the similarity ended. Mr Davidson was indeed a large character who had spent his life in civil engineering plant maintenance and would regale me with tales of how it was the norm for him and a gang of men to jack up and load 0-6-0 standard gauge shunters sideways into railway well wagons at the rate of two a day. On the other hand, the first time I met Mr Dobson I nearly died of surprise. I found a little old man with thick glasses sitting behind a desk with a pencil in his hand recording his every phone call and conversation in a large book.

The new city of Milton Keynes was just starting and my invoices supply an endless record of selling 20lbs/yd rail to T. Kilroe & Sons who appeared to be digging all the main sewerage tunnels. A totally Irish organization, with everyone from the telephonist upwards being from across the water, they grew into a large outfit and just as suddenly died away. Such is the way of the contracting business. I think Timmy Kilroe was one of the few Irishmen who did not spend every penny he earned on riotous living and thus was able to build a large business from scratch.

1975 was the year of the cancellation of the first, or rather the second, attempt at a Channel Tunnel, the first being in the 1880s. For this I built a pair of rail-carrying bogies and prepared to supply three second-hand locomotives of 3ft gauge to Taylor Woodrow who were part of the consortium building it. Having seen the equipment used and been marginally involved in the successful effort to bore a tunnel under the Channel the mind boggles at the idea of buying second-hand locomotives and odd wagonry from me at that stage of my business. Anyway, the government cancelled the project and I was paid out for the work I had done and got to keep the locomotives and anything else left over. Such a situation has not happened since but I realized afterwards that I had not claimed enough for the inconvenience factor of having the equipment left on my hands.

The invoices suggest a year heavily involved with Butlin's: tracks were re-laid at Minehead and Skegness and carriages endlessly refurbished and fitted with new bogies. The Chance carriages were something of a trial until we got used to their foibles. First we fully dismantled them. We then found that although apparently all the same, they were not and that even seat ends were not drilled in the same positions let alone the hole positions for the wooden seat slats. After this each seat end and seat slat was marked for position! Added to this the cast aluminium seat ends had a Red Indian's head complete with feathered head-dress cast into it which had to be painted-up in five colours – just tedious. The seat end also had cast

into it the date of 1863 for which it took me a long time to find the reason. I knew it was not the date of the completion of the American Transcontinental Railroad, but I eventually identified it as the start of the building of said railway. In reality the volume of work for Butlin's was too great and was a worryingly high percentage of my turnover but it all worked out well enough in the long run.

This is as good a point as any to cover the subject of *Trixie*, the first brand-new locomotive with which I was involved and which I have always classed as AK1 of 1974 in my locomotive build list although purists might argue the point. I think Trevor Barber always had ideas of getting back into the railway operating business on his own account and worked out some good ideas of how to get the longest possible railway into the smallest possible land area by the use of earthworks and similar devices.

As mentioned with Cotswold Light Railways, the thinking of the time was that any such railway should be steam operated at least for some of the time. Two foot was seen as the right gauge but the supply of small second-hand steam locomotives had dried up even at that stage. Importing them from, say, Portugal was a possibility but finding them in the first place, transporting an unknown quantity home and then restoring it was an expensive process. (In 2000 this was done on a grand scale with some twenty-two locos coming back from Mozambique. The importers even shipped out their own lorries and crane to provide transport to the docks!) With all this in mind, Trevor felt that he could design and build a new locomotive at comparable cost and it would have the great merit of being new, not just a rebuild. At that time traction engine prices were just beginning to rise out of the price bracket of ordinary mortals and it was thought to be only a question of time before small steam locomotives did the same. This is true up to a point but it has taken thirty years and we are not there yet! For the third time I have seen the same mistake made in 2006 with some Hunslet steam locomotives.

Seen here in 1980, the railway at Butlin's Pwllheli was the only one that actually served a purpose by carrying passengers out to a beach, and because of this trains there had four carriages instead of the usual three. The chairlift in the background went further, right out to the headland. Judging from its condition, and the track as I remember it, the Chance locomotive could be brand new. A young lad seems to have talked himself into a footplate ride! *Peter Knottley*

Trevor Barber brings *Trixie* and train into Llanuchllyn station on the Bala Lake Railway, looking justifiably pleased with the performance of his creation. Despite being built for this railway, the sale never went through and *Trixie* has had a chequered career ever since.

boiler and Hackworth valve gear which he borrowed from the Kerr Stuart 'Wren' design of similar size and power, and as such it worked very adequately. Needless to say there were some complications. Trevor ran into problems with boiler design and it was built far more heavily than necessary, which meant that the loco was tail heavy and should really have been an 0-4-2. The springing had to be adjusted as a consequence as well as adding a heavy ballast weight on the front. A good many people did not like the weatherboard/cab but Trevor's and my answer to that was, 'Well, you never saw the 0-4-0s at Kettering Furnaces!'

I managed to arrange a sale to Bala Lake Railway and for this reason she was initially fitted with side buffers to match their rolling stock. The sale was subject to her performing satisfactorily when delivered. In due course I delivered the completed locomotive to Llanuchllyn and Trevor came to put her through her paces. She worked well and could pull virtually anything put behind her, although admittedly that line is nearly flat. In common with most marine boilers on locomotives, *Trixie*'s had a habit of sulking when steam raising. This happens just before steam first appears and can be embarrassing. It happened in a big way once at Bala and maybe had something to do with putting George Barnes off the loco. Anyway,

Howsoever, that was the logic – now to the practice. Trevor was to build the locomotive and I was to sell it. That was the basis of our agreement, plus my lending moral support and what assistance I could. The design was based very much around the 6in. Bagnall design and *Pixie* in particular (the one I had tried to buy from Cranford ironstone quarry). Trevor was to play tricks with *Pixie* – hence the name. In reality the locomotive turned out to be a fairly straightforward 0-4-0 saddle tank with 6in. × 9in. cylinders, a marine

Trixie heads a train back to the Merion Mill terminus of this short-lived line. Ken Whittaker is driving. The two Baguley carriages were subsequently re-gauged to 500mm for the Chemin de Fer Touristique du Tarn, near Toulouse, France.

at this stage Trevor wanted to increase the price, as I am sure it had cost him more than he had expected, and I am equally sure that this was the excuse being looked for to back out of the deal.

There was then something of a panic to sell *Trixie* and that one fell to me. *Trixie* moved on from Bala to the Centre for Alternative Technology which was then just setting up in the old Llyn Gwern quarry which originally had its own branch from the Corris Railway. She really had no connection with alternative technology except insofar that an attempt was made to burn sawdust compressed into something resembling pig feed nuts. I think the reality was that they wanted something a bit showy to transport the Duke of Edinburgh for a few hundred yards when he visited the centre. Trevor, as driver, was introduced to His Royal Highness whilst I stayed fairly well in the background. It was one of the first of the strange meetings and events with which my business has peppered my life and which have made it all worth while.

The spin off from this was that *Trixie* was seen by Raymond Street who owned a woollen mill at Dinas Mawddwy. Meirion Mill was situated in what had been the terminal station of the long defunct Mawddwy Railway and Mr Street thought that to recreate some sort of railway interest on the site might be good for his business. In due course, and for totally different reasons, this had a profound effect on my business. Sufficient to say that he bought *Trixie* (at the price originally asked of Bala Lake Railway) and, with some other equipment I found for him, set up a short railway with the intention that it should ultimately extend further along the old trackbed. All this came to naught largely because it was discovered that despite the euphoria of steam railways they tend to be a dirty smoky sort of thing that did not sit well with a high-class woollen mill. Although the railway brought more people to the establishment, as was intended, they were not the sort of people who wanted to spend money on a limited range of high class goods. So after a season or so *Trixie* was on the move again.

This time the move was more permanent. I sold her to the Rail Rebecq-Rognon in Belgium. This was a new venture in the usual mould of building a railway along an old standard gauge trackbed. It included a fairly spectacular viaduct and was intended to run through the street in a way that was possible on the continent but not here. I also sold the railway half a dozen of my carriage bogies as well as various other items. *Trixie* served them well although for reasons I never really understood they had fearful problems over boiler insurance. I saw her much later in 1992 when I went there with the engineers from de Efteling in Holland for whom we were negotiating the building of a new steam locomotive. She was tucked into a corner and looking decidedly woebegone. She was subsequently sold to 'somewhere in France' and has since surfaced again in the last few years on the Chemin de Fer des Chanteraines in Paris where I hope she will be put to work once more. She does, however, still carry my name and the significant 'No. 1'.

Pleasurerail were building a new 15in. gauge railway at Blenheim Palace that spring and this brought a small amount of work initially on a railway which over the years has produced plenty. They were having what are normal problems with the Duke of Marlborough who is always apt to want everything instantly and would like one to build a railway without disturbing the grass! At the end of the year I re-engined the Guest 2-6-2 locomotive *Tracy Jo* with a second-hand engine from a Bedford lorry, in which guise it ran for many years. Based on the Vale of Rheidol locomotives, this machine

was unusual in having been built as a steam locomotive complete with proper cylinders and motion, but has always been internal combustion powered. She ultimately became a steam locomotive on the Bure Valley Railway in 1996.

On the Butlin front, *Sue*, at Ayr, put a connecting rod through the crankcase mid-season which caused a panic to provide another loco to pull trains and also to put the engine right. A new crankcase was unobtainable, but I found a firm in South London who were able to weld it all up and rebore the crankshaft mountings, drill out the oil ways, etc, etc. Very clever people, but they had obviously suffered over the years with one-off customers not paying them properly so it was cash only, real cash, on collection!

It is worth recording my one and only sale to Joseph Arnold & Son at Leighton Buzzard – some sleepers for the New Trees Quarry extension. A 'Jim Crow' is a hand-operated device for bending rails and I started a fairly regular purchase of these in Birmingham and onward sale to Locospoor of Den Hague in Holland who in turn sold them on to Bord na Móna in Ireland. Locospoor sent me their catalogue which was a real gem; it included Jung steam locomotives and Planet diesels, but is still a useful reference work to this day.

Trixie's moment of glory when the Duke of Edinburgh opened the Centre for Alternative Technology at Machynlleth. Although I am standing almost behind His Royal Highness in my sheepskin coat we did not speak! *Trixie* had no real connection with the centre or its aims but was used primarily as a centrepiece for the event.

Simplex 60S locomotive on the northern approach ramp to the Dartford Tunnel. Two of these locomotives were hired to this project and keeping them running became an ever-increasing nightmare. Note that, from the name on the side, this was before the days of Alan Keef Ltd.

In the latter part of 1975 I embarked on the hire of two locomotives to Balfour Beatty for use on the second Dartford Tunnel. These were two Simplex 60S locomotives which I had left on my hands after the aborted Channel Tunnel exercise and which had been to Reed & Mallik in Inverness previously. They were put into good running order and delivered to the site at the northern end of the tunnel. Although this job started well and was to go on for something like eighteen months it became an absolute nightmare. The tunnel – being under the Thames and, I gathered, fairly shallow – was worked under compressed air which meant that everything going in or out had to pass through an air lock. The locomotives were used to haul the trains of muck from the air lock up what was to become the approach ramp of the tunnel to the disposal point on the surface. This involved a standing start and then continuing to haul on a gradient of about 1 in 30. Although the Simplex 60S was capable of this the Achilles heel of these locomotives in my experience has always been the clutch and it required reasonably skilled and careful driving to avoid ruining it. Both of these qualities tend to be lacking on construction sites and especially so at that time.

The consequence was a continual string of breakdowns and I became adept at changing clutch plates in the half dark. Whilst the Simplex is a very easy locomotive to work on, the clutch is its worst part as it invariably means lifting the engine out after having removed all the bonnets and so on. On one occasion they rang to say that the gearbox had fallen into two halves! I think the driver had tried to change down a gear going down the slope and had managed to get into two gears at once which jammed the gearbox solid. Before parting company with itself it had almost sheared a 2in. × ½in. key lengthways! In the end I could stand this no longer and agreed to hire them the locomotives at a much reduced rate and they maintain them.

Now back to Merion Mill. Whilst Mr Street was the instigator of the scheme, it was very largely co-ordinated by Ken Whittaker who was a management accountant who worked part-time for Meirion Mill. He had opted out of the rat race and was living in a cottage nearly on top of a mountain close-ish to Dinas Mawddy. He was a fairly knowledgeable railway enthusiast and, to cut a long story short, I asked him to join my business in order to take advantage of his accountancy abilities, a subject about which I have never been knowledgeable. Thus was born Alan Keef Ltd. Not only because there was a stranger in the business, but with increasing trade came increasing risk and thus a limited company became essential. It was progress – it was 1976, but in some respects the problems were only just beginning.

This is my first new locomotive (AK2 of 1976), built to the requirements of Richardson's Moss Litter Co. Ltd. The 'works' were subsequently transferred on to a new frame at 2ft 6in. gauge which became AK3 of 1978. The frame left over from this conversion became *Skippy*, our mobile ballast skip used for track-laying work: see Chapter 11.

7

Alan Keef Limited

So I was now limited company. So what? Well, in reality it did not change very much. One still did the same things, had the same customers and the same problems, possibly more of the latter because there are rules to which one has to adhere. It does lessen the ultimate risk of something going sour and one losing all one's personal possessions in a bankruptcy. In 2007 we came very close to just that happening, and would then have been grateful for the protection thus afforded. However, if one trades with an overdraft, as most businesses tend to, then the bank usually has matters so well tied up it makes little difference. But hope springs eternal and that is never going to happen, is it?

Indeed life went on as usual. Without being endlessly repetitive, it is difficult to convey to the average person how much my business was built on the strength of the work I did for Butlin's. It was by this time that I had built up a rapport such that about the beginning of September each year I would go down to their head office in Bognor Regis to meet Keith Palmer and Neil McCullough and discuss any particular plans for the coming winter so far as their railways were concerned. This would be followed by a tour of all their camps to inspect the railways, discuss any problems with the local managers and write a report on same. This also included estimates for the work to be done. More often than not I would simply get a phone call to say 'Get on with it.' Alternatively there might be a rearranging of priorities to suit the budget but basically it would all be done in the end.

So when I casually say that half the track at Ayr was re-laid and the Peter Pan fitted with a new centre rail, it represented perhaps twelve weeks' work for my track layers and also eight or ten trips to Ayr for me to be sure that all was going according to plan. These trips, to the outside observer, might always have seemed ludicrous and at face value they were. I would catch the night sleeper from Cheltenham to Glasgow, breakfast in Central Station, train to Ayr, taxi to site, arriving about 10.30 a.m. I could well leave again by one o'clock and reverse the process so I had been travelling for thirty-six hours to be on site for a couple of hours. However, these trips were vital: they ensured that my men knew I would be coming but not necessarily when, I was in contact with Butlin's people on site, and if there ever were any queries about what was happening I could say, 'Well I was on site on such a date and all was well then.' In practice, of course, I would often have an initial load of materials to deliver and could often combine visits to other customers at the same time. It also made for some interesting railway journeys such as the time I bought a ticket out of the signal box at Hummanby – the nearest station to Filey – to Kilmarnock (the signalman never batted an eyelid!) with bus on to Ayr. It also involved some fairly close liaison with the Railway Inspectorate who wanted to see all that was being done; and meeting either Les Abbott or, occasionally, Major Olver around the country was all part of the service. In their way Butlin's

railways were quite something even if they did treat them as just another ride.

So in the winter of 1975/76 the railway was re-laid at Minehead in an end-to-end much-shortened run, the first of much moving around of railways at Minehead, and walkways with handrails were provided on the bridges at Filey together with some re-laying. The first new carriages built by myself but to the overall appearance of the Huntington carriages were also supplied. Altering the layout of their railways and moving them around became a habit. This ranged from the major alterations such as carried out at Minehead, of which more in due course, to, unbelievably, altering a Peter Pan layout so that the gardeners did not have to clip the bushes!

At one time Butlin's had a camp at Mosney in Ireland, some twenty miles north of Dublin. It did not have a miniature railway, as they called their 2ft gauge lines, but did have a Peter Pan track which, as usual, required the centre pick-up rail renewing. This was the occasion when I proved the Irish joke to be true. These centre rails were made of one inch diameter steel bar welded together and to a steel plate on each sleeper. I suggested that it would obviously be cheaper if they supplied the bar from within Ireland rather than my shipping over a relatively small quantity. Fine. Quantity required? 600 feet. The question came back, 'Did we want it all in one piece?' Neil McCullough said he had visions of them looking for a long thin van to fetch it in!

This was a year in which a number of people who were to become long term customers appeared on the scene, and indeed some of them still are, thirty years later. Such names as the Longleat Estate; Doug Skinner, of whom more anon; Commander Francis, who was operating the Wells Harbour Railway but was shortly to embark on his much more ambitious project of the Wells & Walsingham Railway, the country's longest 10¼in. gauge railway; John Crosskey, a private preservationist of ex-North Wales slate quarry railway equipment; Croxden Gravel Ltd, who had just taken over the peat moss formerly operated by Richardson's on Chat Moss at Irlam, and the Leighton Buzzard Narrow Gauge Railway Society, who had taken over from the Iron Horse Society and were just getting into their stride.

One profitable and amusing deal was when I got wind of a quantity of Ruston wheel castings in a scrap yard at Newton-le-Willows. At that time Ruston & Hornsby had become part of the English Electric group and the locomotive spares business had been transferred to the old Vulcan Foundry works at Newton-le-Willows. Obviously they had had a clear out. There was an enormous pile of wheels there and I did a deal with the man for six tons of them at a tonnage price delivered. In due course these turned up at Cote but not what I ordered – the entire heap, eighteen tons, in the back of a tipper lorry! At least they were easy to unload even if the yard was completely blocked. In fairly short order I sold them to the Festiniog, Talyllyn, Llanberis Lake and Leighton Buzzard railways, a few privately, and there were still the odd ones left ten years later when I moved to The Lea.

Along with one of *Digger*'s return trips to my ownership came another good Simplex which I re-engined with a Deutz conversion kit bought from Simplex. I really thought I had arrived when I could be as lavish as this. The loco was subsequently sold to White Moss Peat Co. at Kirkby on the outskirts of Liverpool. One point I did not fully appreciate at the time was how much this exercise reduced the locomotive weight and I had to subsequently add some very heavy Ruston buffer blocks I happened to have.

The railway at Longleat House had been installed and operated by one Les Anderson, who in due course moved on (maybe his lease ran out, I do not know) to set up a company called Minirail Ltd with the intention of re-opening the Lyme Regis branch of the old LSWR as a 15in. gauge railway. This scheme foundered for a variety of reasons, I think partly a few vociferous

Because I made a new frame for it, the enthusiast world has included *Redgauntlet* from the Romney, Hythe & Dymchurch Railway as having been built by me although it carries no works number. In fact it was originally built by Michael Jacot and is here seen upon return to its home railway in 1976.

objectors and partly the timescale of pursuing it became more than Minirail could stand. Either way, the company went into liquidation and I was asked to value the assets and assist in their disposal. Here my experience at Merry's came to the fore and I set up an auction on site. This took place on 7 November 1976 and raised a grand total of £18,140.47 which was slightly over my valuation and very close to the sum needed by the liquidators. However there were some very strange goings-on in the background of this because although I got my commission and expenses for the sale (I deducted it!) I never received any pay-out on the sums owing to Alan Keef Ltd.

As might be imagined, I spent most of the previous week at Combe Pyne setting up the sale, getting everything lot numbered and so on. I returned home on the Friday before the sale to find Bill McAlpine on the phone and wanting to go and have a look at what was for sale. For whatever reason, he wanted me to be there when he inspected and I reluctantly said I would turn tail to be there for Saturday morning but I had to leave in time to be back for a long-standing lunch date. 'Oh, no problem,' he said, 'we will pick you up with the helicopter about nine o'clock and you'll be back for lunch!' And indeed I was, but I did feel a bit of a lemon standing out in our field, all dressed up, carrying a brief case and staring into the sky at 8.45 on a Saturday morning.

Looking through the invoices, it was also a year of hiring out equipment. Mostly small jobs, a few yards of track and a couple of bogies. What they were all for, the records do not tell, but they included Balfour Beatty (apart from Dartford), CJB pipelines and a locomotive to Boothby Peat Co. One Saturday I was just about to drive out of the gate and a man appeared asking, in a strong Australian accent, if I was Mr Keef. 'Yes,' I said. He said that he had come all the way from Australia to see me. No advance warning or appointment or anything like that. The upshot of it was that I made about a dozen sets of points for, I believe, a children's home near Melbourne in both 20lbs/yd and 13½lbs/yd rail. I subsequently

sold them a large quantity of fishplates and bolts, but curiously I have never heard or read anything more about the place since.

This was my first truly international sale, but one slightly nearer home was the sale of the first of two Baguley carriages to the Chemin de Fer Touristique du Tarn and their subsequent conversion to 500mm gauge. These were the carriages from Merion Mill. Jaques Daffis, who came over to see the work in progress, was in England rather longer than he intended after he turned back onto the wrong side of the road following a wrong turning and collided with another road user.

I first met the redoubtable Major Olver of HM Railway Inspectorate at Hythe Pier where updating of the near-non-existent braking system was required. The *raison d'etre* of the railway was to transport people to and from the ferries across the Solent to Southampton. At that time this was a remarkable outfit where time seemed to have stood still. They were virtually self-sufficient in everything they did and had the staff to maintain the boats, the pier and the train. Typically there was a man there who painted everything, point him at it and he painted it! I fitted an air brake system to the train but it was never wholly successful as the staff did not want it and had no intention of allowing it to work. Ultimately it was quietly abandoned. General Estates who owned the place had a habit of operating this kind of facility. At one time they owned Selby swing bridge, the right to construct which was granted by Royal Charter and it was exempt from all forms of taxation, much to the chagrin of the Inland Revenue, VAT and local authorities. At a much much later date I happened to be on the end of Hythe pier and witnessed the take-off of the only remaining air-worthy Sunderland flying boat which was on a demonstration flight prior to sale. Needless to say I did not have a camera with me!

A major contract was the re-laying of the railway at Doddington Park, near Chipping Sodbury. Also included were six carriage bogies and a pair of drop barriers where the track crossed the exit road-way between two high walls with absolutely no sight lines at all. The brain was also exercised by having to make a curved set of points. One is often asked how some of the more abstruse rail gauges materialized. Doddington is a classic case in point. Possibly on my suggestion, but unbeknownst to me, they took the wheels out of one of their locomotives and took them to Swindon Works for re-profiling. Swindon of course asked what profile they wanted on them. Blank faces all round and when shown a selection of profiles they opted for one that said GWR on it, on the basis that that should be all right. I only came to hear of it when Swindon dropped a sizeable clanger by forgetting to put the template in the wheel lathe and removing one flange altogether! When I got there and saw the massive standard gauge profiles put on these wheels I realized that we had another problem. The wheels were now 24½in. gauge as well as one being altogether flat. It would have been no trouble to have re-laid the railway at 24½in. gauge and made the bogies accordingly, but we should have wound up with an odd-gauge railway of no use to anyone else and unsuitable for any other second-hand equipment. So I persuaded my good friend Mr Pinnegar at Swindon to re-do the wheels to a sensible profile and got him off the hook of the flangeless wheel with one of the Ruston wheels from Newton-le-Willows. He reciprocated at a later date and got me out of a corner!

Possibly a portent of things to come, I made a new frame to go under the locomotive *Redgauntlet* for the Romney, Hythe and Dymchurch Railway. This locomotive had been built privately by Michael Jacot and served a useful purpose for the RHDR, but the frame was not up to serious railwaying. A useful job, obviously successful as it is still at work and something which I was by then able to take in my stride. For want of any better yardstick, the industrial railway fraternity classify whoever built the frame as the locomotive's builder. As a consequence, *Redgauntlet* tends to find itself included as a locomotive built by Alan Keef Ltd, which is far from correct in this instance.

John Hall Craggs had me collect some fairly derelict 9½in. gauge equipment from Severn Beach which was put into useful order and delivered on to him. One of the locomotives was a rather unsuccessful diesel electric machine that I ultimately rebuilt as a successful diesel hydraulic locomotive some twelve years later.

The major work of 1977 was something of a coup. Quite how they found me remains, as so often, a mystery but I supplied a complete railway to the Imperial Iranian Navy. (This was the days of the Shah.) The Navy had a major naval base at Bandar Abbas at the southern end of the Persian Gulf and they planned to use a ship that they had bought in Italy as additional barracks. This was to be moored at the end of a 700 yard long jetty and the train was required to carry personnel to and fro. Delivery was required pretty quickly and it was perhaps a measure of the state of British industry at the time that everything I wanted was more or less immediately available and the entire railway was delivered in eight weeks!

As luck would have it I had had a letter shortly beforehand that Simplex had some stock locomotives for urgent and immediate sale. Two of these provided the motive power and I set to and designed some carriages distilled from my experiences at Butlin's and elsewhere. These were quite sophisticated in their way as they were required to have electric lighting and cushioned seats but only a canvas awning for a roof. My standard bogies came to the fore again. I specified that the train should be fitted with air brakes, which caused raised eyebrows at Bedford as a 40S Simplex had never been so fitted and their attitude was, typically, that it could not be done. I had a good firm of air brake suppliers in Oxford who saw no real problem and between us we managed a successful system which has been repeated many times since. The track was straight-forward 20lbs/yd Jubilee track with a few turnouts to go with it.

The question of shipping it all to Iran was the next headache as the Naval Attache's office at the Iranian Embassy, with whom I was dealing, could not make up its mind what it was doing. Initially the urgency was such that they were going to fly it all out, rails included!

This was not actually as silly as it might sound as the Iranian air force had the planes and the pilots; it was to be treated as just another exercise using a little extra fuel. Bear in mind that RAF Brize Norton was only five miles away. In the end they decided against that but insisted that it be shipped in an Iranian ship. This was done and the ship ran aground in the Red Sea. I always regretted that it did not sink altogether and then I should have had the job to do a second time over! To add to their problems the barracks ship was impounded in Naples for debt. Anyway, it all got there in the end and I believe served its purpose adequately.

Open days have always been a bit of a tradition when I

Locomotive and one carriage of a complete railway supplied to the Imperial Iranian Navy. The locomotive is a new 40S Simplex with additional bodywork and the carriages of my own design and manufacture. Air brakes, electric lighting and cushioned seats made this quite a sophisticated train. A note on the back of this picture states that the complete trainset, including 1,000 yards of track and five turnouts, was supplied in just eight weeks!

have something to show off, and the one for the Iranian order was probably the first. It produced some good publicity and explained to the locals just what I did. This latter has always been a bit of a problem as most people seem to think it is not really a business at all but just an overgrown hobby. The reverse is nearer the truth! A quirk on all this occurred around twenty years later. A friend with no railway interest came across a small locomotive in Damascus, of all places, and he was absolutely insistent that it had my nameplate on it. Unfortunately he did not take a photograph but almost the only possible contender for this honour has to be one of the locomotives supplied to Iran.

At a more mundane level, trackwork continued for Butlin's with work at Filey, Minehead and Ayr. The track at Filey surrounded the boating lake and when it was not in use children used to take a great delight in throwing the ballast into the lake. The consequence was that every year or so some extensive re-ballasting had to be done. Good for my business and good for a local contractor who, about every five years, had the job of dredging the lake!

This was also the year when the Glasgow underground, or subway, suffered one of its rebuilds, something that happened to it about once in forty years. It had originally been built (to 4ft gauge) in 1896 as a cable operated underground railway and was, as a consequence, roughly circular in plan with a track length of six and a half miles, double track, and trains hauled round it in opposite directions. This was electrified in 1933, in part using some of the original cars and, from my own experience, was on its last legs. The cars had longitudinal seats and when braking the back of the seat moved differently to the seat upon which one was sitting. The decision had been made to close it for rebuilding but this happened rather more suddenly than expected due to problems with part of the tunnel. Reputedly the trains stopped running and staff had to tell passengers waiting on platforms to please come back in two year's time! The old railway was literally two circles of track and no more. The cars, and for that matter maintenance vehicles, were lifted on and off the track up a shaft directly into the Govan works, and I once had the privilege of seeing this happen.

For my part I supplied three 60S Simplexes to Taylor Woodrow who were the main contractors. Amongst these were the ubiquitous ones that I had had for the aborted Channel Tunnel. They were converted to 4ft gauge by welding outrigger channel frames to the sides and fitting longer axles with associated bits and pieces. They were also fitted with air brakes and air sanding gear. Following a runaway due to lack of air this was later changed to fail-safe air braking, something I do not normally fit to locomotives, only the train.

If you are squeamish do not read this paragraph! The old trains on the Glasgow subway had open doorways with concertina metal barriers; after all, they never went outside so there were no problems with the weather. Work on the tunnels included cleaning the muck of the last eighty years off the tunnel walls and this proved to have a distinctly unpleasant smell. When analysed it was found to consist largely of a mixture of grease, human skin and human hair. The detritus of well lubricated trains carrying millions of passengers over the many years!

1978 saw me making a seat for the local village of Aston to commemorate the Queen's Silver Jubilee and also supplying another 500mm gauge carriage to the Chemin de Fer Touristique du Tarn. This was also the year that Butlin's re-gauged the railway at Pwllheli from 21in. Its splendid Hudswell Clarke 'Princess Royal' Pacifics had already given way to a rebuilt Ruston and this in turn gave way to the standard 24in. gauge Chance trainset. I also built new carriages on this occasion, utilizing and re-gauging some 30in. gauge wheelsets which Butlin's just happened to have in a store at Littlehampton. Goodness knows where they originated from. Butlin's also re-laid and extended the railway at Ayr which involved some fairly major earthworks and curves down to a 25-foot radius. Once again my surveying skills came in handy. Once pegged out everyone swore blind that I had got it wrong but I stuck to my guns and, sure enough, as the earthworks developed I was proved right. What a relief!

I took the old carriages from Pwllheli in part exchange for the work being done and these have a minor claim to fame. They were

Left: Another much altered Simplex locomotive. This is a standard 60S (11004 of 1955) converted to 4ft gauge for use in the rebuilding of the Glasgow Underground. The 'outriggers' were fitted to carry the axleboxes so that the wheels did not interfere with the frame. It has been fitted with air brakes, painted in Taylor Woodrow colours and is ready to travel north.

Right: Hunslet locomotive *Cackler* in steam in the yard at Cote in 1978 before going back to Cushings Steam Museum in Norfolk. Note an early, and only partially successful, attempt at a steam air compressor on the footplate. *Ivo Peters*

too long for my lorry and would have wasted a lot of space on a 40-foot trailer so I shipped them back by rail. This involved taking them into Pwllheli and then collecting from Swindon, both short trips that one hoped the law would not notice. As such, this was the last consignment by rail out of Pwllheli before the goods facility was closed.

On the overseas front, I supplied another couple of Ruston locomotives to Singapore – but this time direct to Bian Huat Hardware as ARC Motor Co. had ceased to exist in the meantime; also some sets of points and, in the course of the year, no less than 6,000 sleepers to the ultimately abortive 12¼in. gauge line built by John Ellerton on a small part of the Réseau Breton. John Ellerton could be fairly abrasive at times and by all accounts did not hit it off with the locals, who retaliated by calling in their friendly saboteurs from Algeria who quietly removed rails in between trains.

The ex-Dinorwic Quarries Hunslet locomotive *Cackler* came in from Cushings Steam Museum at Thursford in Norfolk to be stripped off, have a boiler test done and air brakes fitted. Steaming her afterwards brought a visit from the redoubtable Ivo Peters and I have one of his excellent photographs to record the event. Two carriages were built to go with the locomotive, based on those built for Iran.

Two Simplex 40S locomotives were supplied to Richardson's Moss Litter at Carlisle, one of them being fitted with a Perkins engine and automotive-type clutch. Simplex only ever built three of this type, very much as an experiment, and it causes much head scratching to this day if certain types of spare part are required.

Just as the previous year had been a year for hiring out rail track, this was a year of selling it. Amongst many others, customers included Great Row Colliery at Stoke on Trent, Cumberland Moss Litter Industry at Kirkbride and Richardson's on several occasions. On a grander scale, I supplied the complete trackwork for a new railway at Lightwater Valley Park, although curiously have had

virtually nothing to do with the place since. On a more permanent front I supplied and laid track at the West Midlands Safari Park for Severn Lamb Ltd. This may sound surprising as, in the leisure market and as the brand leaders in the industry, Severn Lamb tended to be my principal competitors. However, over the years I have laid a good number of railways for them and also continue to maintain others upon which their trains operate.

This particular railway included some quite considerable earthworks. One embankment, some six feet high, was done in midwinter with the ground frozen solid and I fully expected it to sink all over the place when it thawed out, but no, all was well. I employed a couple of lads to do this job who could never have been classed as my best track layers and they managed to let the ballast wagon run away and crash into the back of Severn Lamb's brand new locomotive. Whilst it cost a good deal to repair the back of the tender, the only consolation was that the damage would have been much worse if it had hit the front.

The latter part of 1978 was spent refurbishing carriages for Butlin's at Skegness and Clacton together with some re-laying work at Pwllheli. Following the Iran job I fitted fail-safe brakes to the train at Longleat in order to comply with Railway Inspectorate requirements. This was to be the first of many such jobs and was closely followed by similar work for Ray Beardow on his railway at Woburn Abbey.

Doug Skinner had for a long time been an occasional customer for bits and pieces for a private railway. He then came by a job as a landscape architect for Telford Development Corporation and as such became responsible for putting into practice their ideas for a steam railway at Telford. For this, a steam tram had been designed and very largely made 'by committee'. By this I mean that the wheels and axles had been supplied by Allens of Tipton, the frame made by a local firm of steel fabricators, Kierstead Systems Ltd, and a Peter Bridges of Oundle was to supply the vertical boiler and single-cylinder steam engine which was to propel the beast. Yours truly was to do the bodywork, finish it off and generally make it work. A similar situation existed with a carriage. Because of the system described for *Redgauntlet*, Kierstead are classed as the official builders!

I said it would never work successfully but had to eat my words! It did, and remarkably well, although considerable driving skill was needed to achieve the desired result. It was named *Thomas* – after Thomas Telford, the redoubtable civil engineer, which was appropriate – at an official naming ceremony by the Rev'd W. Audrey of 'Thomas the Tank Engine' fame – which was rather less so. In reality only a few hundred

yards of track were ever laid and the whole scheme ultimately foundered in apathy and financial cutbacks. A rather splendid photograph was taken which could have been almost anywhere in Belgium or France in the previous eighty years or so. Perhaps more surprisingly it was remembered some twenty years later and led to a major contract in Argentina, of which more in due course.

Two more Simplexes were sold to Singapore and an ex-Butlin's Baguley to Derek Preece at Callington, Cornwall. Another Jim Crow to Locospoor, presumably for Bord na Móna, and no less than five tons of dog-spikes to Australia to go with the points and other bits and pieces already supplied. It is also worth mentioning that I did a surprising amount of work for one or two local firms and farmers, in particular Burford Laundry and Miss Gauntlet who farmed a large farm in a remote corner beside the River Thames.

My contacts with Railway, Mine and Plantation Equipment (RMP) led to the making of sixteen turnouts in 2ft 6in. gauge which ultimately went to the Royal Ordnance Factory at Bishopton outside Glasgow. These were part of a much larger order for at least twice this number that their normal suppliers, Taff Wagon Co. of Cardiff, could not complete in time. On a lighter note, I sold a second-hand Ruston locomotive to Nobels Explosives for their factory at Wigan. This had been on a pleasure line and came complete with a rudimentary steam-outline body and a clown's face on the front. They positively refused to allow me to return it to industrial condition!

Back in 1976 I had been approached by Iain Richardson with the idea that I should build a small diesel locomotive to replace the ageing Lister locomotives they used on their peat bogs. This was exacerbated by Hunslet having taken over the Lister designs and charging exorbitantly for any spares required. Thus was born, a year or so later, the K.12 design that was to be my first entirely new diesel locomotive. I had a lengthy session with Iain and his chief fitter Eddie Bouch as they had some good ideas as to how it might be done. The prototype had a very light frame, a Lister engine and a gearbox made up from the components of a Bobcat skid-steer loader. I built it to 2ft gauge for trial purposes and it was rebuilt with a heavier frame at 2ft 6in. gauge once it had proved successful. The original is with us still in the form of *Skippy*, our much travelled ballast truck used for track-laying purposes. It has had two more engines and three different gearboxes since then and is convertible to various gauges. It has travelled the length and breadth of the UK, been to Ireland and even as far afield as southern Germany. It really should carry GB plates!

So in one respect 1979 was a landmark year in which what might be termed the first production locomotives were built. These were two K.12s, built in quick succession, one each for Country Kitchen Foods at Wilmslow and Croxden Gravel Ltd for their works on Chat Moss, both being on the fringes of Manchester. The former was quite sophisticated

by the standards of the time with electric start, lights and wipers and incorporated an American single speed reversing gearbox that was robust and incorporated a clutch effect with which to take up the drive. As peat operations go, Country Kitchen Foods was unusual in that they wanted wet peat upon which to grow mushrooms at the parent factory. This was the moss in which Lindow Man was discovered, a 2,000-year-old body perfectly preserved in the peat, together with a second body a few years later. The Croxden loco was identical except that the engine was hand start and the cab door on the opposite side. It is a measure of the way in which this type of equipment was treated that when I went to photograph it on the day after delivery they had managed to bend the corner of the cab roof and had been pushing loose rails against the back of the cab. So much for our efforts in painting it!

A railway for which I did a number of jobs over the years until it closed was a line behind the butts at the National Rifle Association at Bisley, Surrey. This consisted of a short, largely straight, line a couple of hundred yards long, a Lister locomotive and a few wagons and was used for carrying targets out to the range; one of the many odd places my business has taken me to. A couple of wagons from here made an appearance at a new private railway twenty-five years later with my name on some of the axleboxes.

I had carried out one successful auction sale at Combe Pyne and now another came my way. Trevor Waterman who, it will be remembered, had bought the O&K steam locomotive *Fojo* from Portugal for his private railway at Poole, had in the meantime moved to another farm at Maiden Newton, near Dorchester. For whatever reason this had not worked out and he decided to sell up his railway collection. I had been asked to give a valuation beforehand and I breathed a sigh of relief at the end of the sale when the total came to pretty well exactly the figure I had given. I had, however, sweated during the sale as the major items had not sold for as much as I expected, or indeed they were worth, but the difference was made up by higher than expected figures on the railwayana of which there was a great deal. *Fojo* was bought by a private customer, subsequently resold, dismantled and sadly has yet to work again.

It may look careworn in this picture but this is the first production K.12 (AK4 of 1979) and my real *entrée* into the world of locomotive building. It is here seen at the peat moss of Country Kitchen Foods at Wilmslow. This is the peat bog in which 'Lindow man', a preserved 2,000 year-old body, was later found.

Bulrush Peat Co. Ltd, a subsidiary of a Danish peat producer, were just starting operations in Northern Ireland and bought a considerable amount of equipment from the Waterman auction. As a separate deal I also supplied three second-hand 40S Simplexes which originated from Minworth Sewerage Works. As usual, these were sold as being in good second-hand condition which meant in good running order, repainted and so on. One day Robin Thompson, the manager, phoned to ask how I was getting on, to which I replied that one was painted and the other two progressing well. 'What colour?' he enquired. 'My standard colours of black frame and orange bodywork' I replied, to which the immediate response was, 'For goodness' sake paint them any other colour than orange!' I was not, until then, wholly aware of the significance of orange in Northern Irish lore.

I had also sold *Digger* along with track and bogies to Christiani & Neilson for a rebuilding contract on Bournemouth pier. There were four locos from Minworth, and in due course I sold the other one to Bournemouth where Christiani's had got fed up with swinging the handle to start *Digger*.

Peter Howard from Maidstone asked me to go and have a look at a Jung steam locomotive from the Cameroons that was lying in a barn in Tavistock. It was in reasonable condition and he subsequently bought it, when it fell to me to put it back into running order. There was nothing seriously wrong and it was primarily a case of stripping the boiler and having it certified for use in this country. It is now on the Bredgar & Wormshill Railway in Kent. At the same time I regauged two of the Butlin's carriage underframes from Pwllheli to go with it.

Left: The steam tram, a locomotive seemingly built by committee, on its original site at Telford. At the time I doubted whether this machine would actually work but had to eat my words! This timeless photograph led to a substantial order from Argentina over twenty years later.

Right: AK5 of 1979 for Croxden Compost Ltd on Chat Moss, near Manchester, was identical with the K.12 for Country Kitchen Foods except that it did not have electric start for the engine and therefore no lights. The cab roof has been bent despite the locomotive having been on site for less than 24 hours when this picture was taken!

8

Rhyl, *et al.*

The exercise known simply as 'Rhyl' amongst the family was a total and unmitigated disaster and, by all that is right, should have brought the company down – indeed, it might have been better if it had and allowed me to start again from scratch with a clean slate. Having said that, there were good reasons for it, and even with the benefit of hindsight those reasons were sound – they just did not work out.

Just where the enquiry came from is lost in history, but evidently early in 1978 I must have had an enquiry to rebuild the 15in. gauge miniature railway at Rhyl on the North Wales coast. This had been one of the very early miniature railways in the country, having been built in 1911. It was originally laid out by the redoubtable Henry Greenly and constructed and operated by Miniature Railways Ltd, a subsidiary of Bassett Lowke Ltd, using that company's standard 'Little Giant' Atlantic-type locomotives. Maybe I should have been warned by the fact that Miniature Railways Ltd went into liquidation two years later, although that was probably not the fault of Rhyl.

The railway was then taken over by a local amusement group and rebuilt in the 1920s with new 4-4-2 locomotives built by the manager, Albert Barnes, and included such luxuries as an all-enclosed station. It then went from strength to strength but, I would presume, started to languish in the 1960s. It was finally shut and the track pulled up in 1969 when the lease ran out. The whole area of the Marine Lake around which its mile of track ran became increasingly run-down and something of an eyesore in a town that is not particularly beautiful anyway. I have memories of seeing it over the intervening wall when I travelled to Portmadoc *via* the North Wales Coast.

The local council – by then Rhuddlan Borough Council – who were the owners of the Marine Lake, had made a small start on improving the lake with the introduction of some boats, a cafe and other amusements. They then proclaimed that they were wanting the railway to be rebuilt as the centrepiece of the rejuvenation of the area. They were prepared to provide and lay the track and then lease it to someone to operate the trains. Shades of the subsequent privatization of British Rail! Their estimates were that 200,000 people would ride the trains.

Whilst we did not believe the latter figure, looked at from Alan Keef Ltd's point of view there were attractions. Historically the company was, and to a lesser extent still is, short of work in the period July to October each year. This is because the leisure customers are all using their equipment at that time of year and do not want anything other than breakdown repairs until the autumn, when they start thinking about the next season. At that time our other major work component was the construction industry where a similar situation applied; both were taking advantage of the good summer weather. So something that would provide an income through the summer months had to have attractions. In addition there was a sizeable and worthwhile contract to be had to lay the railway for Rhuddlan Borough Council, not to mention repairs, overhaul and ongoing work for the new railway.

Just to complete the arguments in favour, if the council were going to refurbish the whole area it would obviously draw people to that end of the town, especially on days when the beach was not attractive. A sizeable portion of Rhyl's holiday clientele came during the Lancashire wakes weeks which usually fell outside the normal British holiday season, and a further plus was that the main coach setting-down point for the town adjoined the Marine Lake. Whilst 200,000 passengers *per annum* was plainly ridiculous, somewhere in the region of 80,000–100,000 was possible. On this basis, the railway was definitely profitable and would do what was required of it. Added to this, Ken Whittaker lived, whilst not close, close enough to be able to manage the concern, thus giving him a more active part in all our affairs. Whilst the company did not have money to throw around, it had done well out of the Iranian Navy contract, and although the project meant additional bank borrowing, the potential seemed to be there to pay it off fairly rapidly. It might have been better if Barclays Bank had dug their toes in at this stage rather than later.

So on the strength of all this a subsidiary company was formed, Keef Railways Ltd, who would be the operators, and Alan Keef Ltd made a deal with the council to lay approximately one mile of 15in gauge track more or less along the old route around the Marine Lake. This was tricky in places as new buildings and roadways had been built which created some fairly sharp bends. However, a route was finally agreed with both the council and the Railway Inspectorate although there were problems over what we considered excessive fencing required by the latter. As part of the deal the council were going to provide some of the labour force.

In the spirit of the exercise Alan Keef Ltd bought the Barnes steam locomotive *Michael* from Entam Leisure Ltd, who had it stored along with some of the original carriages in the amusement park opposite. An 0-4-2 steam-outline diesel locomotive along with a rake of three carriages was bought from the railway at Dudley Zoo. This line was dying by inches from having been one of the more successful railways of its type. As had always been part of the grand scheme, Alan Keef Ltd overhauled all this equipment as part

Opposite: Cote Farm in 1985. One of the carriages for Peatlands Park is being assembled outside the workshop. To the right are a selection of second-hand locomotives including *Old Sparky* from Butlin's Pwllheli, and two Simplex U series from Ireland. In 3ft gauge are the two ex-Isle of Man carriages, one at the end of the house and the other beyond the workshop, with the ex-Peters Marland wagon at the end of the 3ft gauge track. Heaps of track materials and other re-saleable items are to be seen in all directions. The white on various roofs is frost!

of its normal business. The original carriages were interesting in that according to the axleboxes they were built by Milnes Voss & Co. of Birkenhead, who were one of the very early firms of tramcar builders and went out of business in 1913. In due course all this material was delivered back to Rhyl and we were ready for business.

Whilst building the railway I necessarily made many trips to Rhyl, and whenever I did not have anything to take I went by train as it was a fairly easy journey. On one such occasion I helped a woman off the train at Rhyl who was obviously not far from producing her next baby. I sympathized and said my wife was in the same state after an eight-year gap and we were not quite used to the idea. 'Oh,' she said, 'that's nothing, it's fourteen years since I had the last one!' And so, in due course, in March 1978 our second daughter, Alice, was born.

It was decided to operate the railway in the opposite direction to previously as subsequent road works had created a significant gradient near the river bridge and the Barnes 'Atlantics', whilst excellent little locos, were not noted for their haulage ability and they would thus run downhill at this point. They had been designed for a flat easily curved railway and initially would not go round the sharper curves now existing, but an easing of the bogie pivot block solved that one. One of the original employees was taken on as driver.

The railway was reopened with a reasonable fanfare of trumpets on 1 July 1978 as planned, and then organized disaster struck. Rhuddlan Borough Council, not unreasonably, had their amusement rides inspector inspect the railway. I am not saying that he had been got at by anybody but he condemned it outright. Some of his comments displayed a chronic lack of knowledge of railways that was hard to credit and I only hope he knew rather more about the other rides he inspected. I was fortunate in being able to whistle up Major Olver of the Railway Inspectorate to come and give his opinion, and he discounted most of what the man said but found some more problems of his own! But at least these were legitimate railway matters. The upshot was a long wrangle with the council and whilst all this was being resolved they forbade us to run. Just what one needed with the summer season upon us. However, more

by sheer cussedness than anything else, we did open for a few weeks and the results were not encouraging.

Back at Alan Keef Ltd it was a case of survival with the additional millstone of the Rhyl operation around our necks, and we all hoped for a sensible season in 1979. As a consequence there was a minimum of winter maintenance done and another wrangle with the council about the state of the track before we opened at Easter. In the meantime they had done absolutely nothing to improve the Marine Lake or the surrounding area that winter; if anything, the general appearance had become worse and even more run-down. Before the high season came it had become patently obvious that passenger numbers were going to be nowhere near our expectations, never mind those suggested by Rhuddlan B.C. It became possible to calculate that we needed around 55,000 passengers to at least partially achieve our objective whereas the actual figure was about 35,000 which just about paid the operating costs and no more. It was obvious we had to get out – and fast.

I made some enquiries of various of my customers for someone to take it over and one man, at least, was sufficiently seriously interested to go and look. The figure we were looking for was not high and would have got us off the hook with the Bank but in the event it was a local haulier who crept out of the woodwork with an offer of about 75 per cent of what was needed. And even then we had to take an Austin Maxi car with a lost log-book as part of the deal! We had no choice, and were, frankly, glad to get out of the local politics with their own agenda that had by then probably achieved their objective.

As a footnote to history, almost exactly twenty years later flood relief works in Rhyl necessitated the removal and subsequent re-laying of part of the railway and Alan Keef Ltd did this for the contractors in the normal course of business. Virtually nothing, but nothing, had been done to the rest of the railway in the meantime, despite its having been to greater or lesser extent operational during the intervening period. So much for the great concerns for its safety at the opening: proof of the old adage about it not being what you know, but who you know.

Ken Whittaker drives the Barnes 4-4-2 locomotive *Michael* on the inaugural train on the reopened Rhyl Miniature Railway. Sadly, despite apparent enthusiasm, local vested interests achieved their objective of ensuring that this project was not a success.

So it was back to the core business with its wild fluctuations in our fortunes between winter and summer, added to which was now a very twitchy bank manager. It did not help that 1980 brought a collection of jobs that never happened (see Chapter 13 for details). I cut the workforce to one man and even then some of the earnings were gained from the installation of a mobile home for my mother-in-law. At this time I became good friends with the Oxford County Court bailiffs and visits from the 'black-back brigade' at the Inland Revenue became the order of the day. This was the point at which I was strongly recommended to put the company into liquidation and start again – just not possible, because all too often there was only one supplier and to go bust on them was going to cause untold problems for the reincarnated company. So survival at any price became the name of the game, and was to remain so for a long time to come – indeed it was to get frustratingly worse before it got better.

At the end of the year matters improved with some major track rationalization work for Blackpool Pleasure Beach. This railway had been built in the 1930s using the splendid equipment built by Hudswell Clarke & Co. of Leeds. The precursor of this had been the 1ft 8in. gauge equipment at Golden Acre Park, Leeds, and the North Bay Railway at Scarborough. For reasons lost in the mists of time the Blackpool line was laid to 1ft 9in. gauge, as were the subsequent lines for Butlin's. The details of this equipment will appear later, but suffice it to say that the Pleasure Beach Express comprised two trains of eight carriages, a 4-6-4 Baltic tank engine, a fair replica of the 4-6-2 *Flying Scotsman* (not to be confused with the one at Kilverstone Wildlife Park) and a monstrous but very beautiful 4-6-2 'Princess Royal' Pacific like the Butlin's ones. All these locomotives had been built as diesels with a torque convertor transmission, but had been rebuilt with a hydraulic system that worked perfectly satisfactorily.

The snag with all this was that the railway itself was very convoluted with extremely sharp curves and an impressively complicated station layout. The first job was to remove the badly worn turnouts and replace them with the best of the remainder by a process of simplification. This involved the removal of no lesser a thing than a diamond crossover. A good deal of re-sleepering and re-railing was included with this work. I discovered much later that Hudswell Clarke had quoted a minimum radius curve of 50 feet, meaning absolute minimum for sidings and so on, but that the Pleasure Beach had taken them at their word and designed the railway with all curves of that radius. It created a problem that exists to this day.

The big *Princess Royal* was the real problem. There was, and is, one point in the track circuit which terrifies me where the line forms a curve (50 foot radius) of some 200 degrees with the edge of a lake just about on the sleeper ends. To get the *Princess Royal* to negotiate this curve demands that it be driven full tilt at it as with anything less she will jam in the curve! To help ease the problem I suggested that it was quite normal practice to remove the centre flanges on six-coupled locomotives and perhaps this should be done. Having some knowledge of the subject, 'the boss' agreed. So I did. The loco did go round the corner easier except that the curve is so sharp that middle wheels fell off the rails on the inside! I just could not believe it was that bad. This was where I called in the favour that Swindon Works owed me and Mr Pinnegar found a couple of HST wheels with cracked centres out of which they machined two tyres to suit and fitted them. Serious red faces all round, and serious repercussions down the years despite the fact that the reinstatement was entirely at my cost. In addition to all the above, the air brake system on the trains was modified, upgraded and made to work again.

The principal driver of these locomotives was a delightful character who was a dwarf and just the right height to fit in the loco cabs. He used to keep his house keys on a long chain in his pocket and would complain bitterly that the chain had to be that long to reach the lock of his front door but if they fell out of his pocket then he tripped over them! He certainly had no time for today's political correctness of being vertically challenged.

This was the time of the restoration of the Basingstoke Canal where an extensive 2ft gauge light railway was used along the towpath for removal of dredgings, repair of banks and general supply of stores to working sites from the nearest road access. Whilst they had their own locomotive, I hired them a Simplex and also supplied a few other bits and pieces. I also supplied the Droitwich Canal restoration project, largely with engine spares.

1981 was the first time we exhibited at a major exhibition, in this case the International Construction Equipment Exhibition (ICE) at

Until the Internet took over we used to attend exhibitions on a regular basis. This is the first time at the National Exhibition Centre, with a K.12 on show together with a set of points and an 18in. gauge mine tub. The locomotive (AK7 of 1982) had been built for Richardson's Moss Litter Co. Ltd.

the National Exhibition Centre in Birmingham. I think we have exhibited at something almost every year since until the Internet took over from this style of advertising. This type of exhibition is an expensive pastime, especially if one makes an exhibit to put on the stand. However it does put ones name in front of a large number of people. I have always consoled myself with the thought that it would cost me that much to go round and see all the people that I know who come on to the stand and one might just pick up something completely new. Experience dictates that in my type of business it is quite rare to be able to pin any particular job on any particular exhibition, but it has happened. The other side of the coin was that if one did not attend the sort of exhibitions where one was expected to be, possible customers were apt to think one had gone out of business and one never heard about what they might want. On that first occasion I took a K.12 locomotive

This 2ft 6in. gauge K.12 (AK6 of 1981) is brand new in Richardson's workshops and is being 'armour plated' to protect it from the rigours of working on a peat bog! See also Chapter 16, when this machine had been preserved.

which was subsequently sold to Richardson's Moss Litter at Carlisle, albeit after conversion to 2ft 6in. gauge. Mr Richardson came to the show to see it but unfortunately not until the final day, so I could not put up a sold sign until the last minute! A set of points also exhibited subsequently went to Drusilla's Zoo near Eastbourne. I always enjoyed exhibitions, it added a little bit of glamour to the scene even if being on a stand all day could be jolly hard work!

There was also a flurry of activity on the carriage front, with some ex-Dudley Zoo units going to Lightwater Valley. Some new bogies were supplied to Bicton Gardens and to the Cotswold Wildlife Park. Also at the Cotswold Wildlife Park I carried out an overhaul of a Dorman engine in a Simplex loco which had 'stopped'. When I took the cylinder head off it became apparent that somebody bore somebody a grudge, as a handful of assorted small nuts had been tipped down the air inlet. The effect was that both inlet valves were bent and there were the remains of several nuts on top of the piston which, to say the least, had an interesting pattern on it. I also carried out a gearbox overhaul of a decrepit Ruston locomotive at Woburn Abbey. This had a dilapidated, wooden, supposedly steam-outline body that people thought was marvellous but the whole thing was in the late stages of being totally worn out.

A couple of 40S Simplexes were sold, one to Jones & Bailey Ltd for a contract job in South Shields, and another to Norritt Klassman Ltd for a new peat operation near Penicuik, south of Edinburgh. An unusual Co-Bo locomotive built by Guest Engineering of Stourbridge was initially hired and subsequently sold to Blenheim Palace. In common with all Guest internal combustion locomotives this used a military-surplus Daimler Scout Car petrol engine as the power unit. These had a pre-select gearbox but no reverse gear so a means of making it go backwards was essential and tended to be the Achilles heel of an otherwise excellent machine.

So ended a very dull year, in which we probably made a thumping loss and left me looking for an injection of capital in some form in order to survive. To this end I wrote an appraisal of the company as I saw it and what might be done. It makes quite interesting reading.

So what became of all this? I think I showed it to a number of different people but nobody came rushing to press money into my

hands – probably because I wanted to keep control of the business and run it my way, which had patently not made itself a fortune up till now. Why should it change? Why indeed?

However a good deal did come to pass, but over a longer period of time than the plan envisaged, and in general terms the business continued to grow as the opportunities arose. The financial problems eased only to come back again much later. On the positive side, after a couple of false starts I did acquire a good workshop manager who was perhaps not quite as versatile as I would have liked but did produce quality work. I did acquire a wheel press but it put the lie to the antiquated machinery bit – it came from Crewe works and was listed in the tender forms as ex LNWR, pre 1900! It is capable of producing about 350 tons pressure and is still doing yeoman service.

On the development and order front I did develop the K.30 diesel hydraulic locomotive, the prototype of which went to Norritt Klassman's new peat operation at Pencuik. It was fitted with a Lister engine and Poclain hydraulic transmission and as a design has proved successful insofar that of the nine built all except one are still in commercial use. Only two were built for peat bogs but two others wound up in that usage. I never attempted the National Coal Board, although occasional work was done for them after the Simplex take-over. With the subsequent demise of the British coal industry that was probably a good thing. When the Channel Tunnel actually happened the equipment requirements were way outside my league although two ex-NCB Simplex T series locomotives were sold to them. The mechanical handling bit has to some extent come to pass but not at all as anticipated, but more of that in due course. Of the overseas business mentioned, the enquiry from Singapore was genuine and in lesser forms has occasionally reared its head again ever since.

As suggested in the report, there was the possibility of a major job in the Gulf and this did indeed happen. It was a first in more ways than one. It was probably my largest single order to date. It was the first to involve significant overseas travel and it was the first to involve working overseas. I was approached by George Wimpey Ltd, the civil engineering contractors, as to whether I could

Alan Keef Ltd
A Case for Expansion?

1. The Company

Alan Keef Ltd was formed in 1975 to take over the business then run as Alan M. Keef operating on a sole trader basis. It is a private limited company with £13,500 paid up of £15,000 authorised share capital. Of this, the writer, A.M. Keef, holds £8,500, the remainder being held equally between Mrs S.E. Keef and Mr K.W. Whittaker, the latter being company secretary and accountant. It has thus been in business for a period of about 10 years.

2. The Business

The company's business is that of light railway engineers to the leisure, industrial and contracting industries. As such, this ranges from miniature railways in customer's gardens, through the construction and maintenance of leisure railways such as those in Butlin's holiday camps to the provision of complete railways used by contractors on such jobs as tunnelling and pier repairs. Technically it covers all gauges from 10¼in. to 4ft and the provision of track, locomotives and rolling stock. The peat industry, particularly in the North of England and Scotland, is a fruitful source of business and there is a small trade in the hiring out of equipment.

3. Keef Railways Ltd

This is a subsidiary company which was formed in 1977, largely on the strength of the Iranian contract, to operate a pleasure railway at Rhyl in North Wales. This turned out to be a total disaster. Sufficient to say that at the beginning the company had an overdraft of around £5,000 and after the sale of the operation in 1980 this stood at £17,500.

However there was a sound reason for becoming involved and this was that historically Alan Keef Ltd's business suffers a very low turnover in the late summer, August to October, and it was felt that a summer orientated exercise would provide much-needed revenue at this time.

4. The Present Situation

The business is currently turning over about £90,000 per annum and has been for about three years. Of this, about 20 per cent is accounted for by Butlin's Ltd. In the past this turnover has been sufficient to have an employee in each principle trade, fitter, turner, welder, with additionally lorry driver, painter, carpenter, etc. as required. The turnover has not increased with inflation and the present staff consists of myself, a turner/welder, a good labourer and a part time platelayer in the winter months. It is perhaps a conclusion of this that £100,000 is the limit of turnover for the present style of business, largely UK orientated.

Fundamentally the business is profitable even if the day to day finances are beset with cash crises and bedevilled with never having enough capital other than that provided by the banks on the security of property. Over the last six months the overdraft has been reduced to £12,500 together with an improvement in the debtor/creditor situation. If the workload can be maintained over the coming slack period then this improvement can be maintained.

It is a custom of the trade to give at least 6/8 weeks credit although as much as twice this is taken from creditors.

5. Premises and Equipment

The company occupies what were, and are, farm buildings belonging to myself without the benefit of planning permission. With judicious use of existing buildings and care not to upset neighbours there is no reason why this situation should not continue and allow some room for expansion. The company does not pay any rent but it adapts, improves and maintains the buildings at its own cost and also pays my rates, electricity and telephone and I am quite happy for it to continue thus.

With the exception of a heavy duty wheel press it has all the equipment it needs for the present scale of business, albeit some of it is more than a little antiquated.

6. The Need

Without wishing to appear to be blowing my own trumpet it is my opinion that the business has been built largely on my own personality and the ability to provide the right goods at the right time and at the right price. From a personal point of view I enjoy, and am therefore probably best at, either doing the work on the shop floor or being the man in personal contact with the customers who produce the ideas that can then be put into practice. Because I do not wish to lose control of a business which I enjoy and which is partially built for the benefit of my children I have, therefore, a choice open to me:

i) To return to the state of being a sole proprietor and doing what work I can myself. Although there are times when this is very tempting and could be just as financially rewarding I do not think I want this.

ii) To carry on as at present taking what expansion comes my way. I am quite prepared to take this course.

iii) To go for a deliberate policy of expansion aimed at making the whole operation more efficient and less harassing. If there are not too many strings attached, this is perhaps the most attractive option.

To achieve option (iii) requires that I largely divorce myself from the minutiae of management and concentrate on new ideas and selling them to the customer. To employ others to do what I shall thus be unable to do is immediately going to increase overheads and it would appear that a turnover of around £250,000 would be required to cover these additional costs. Obviously this will increase the labour force which in turn can be better balanced than at present which in its turn should make the whole outfit more efficient. It is my view that the company's prices are at, or even slightly over, the limit of what the market will bear especially in the field of what is fundamentally steel fabrication.

The prime requirement to meet this target is an exceptionally versatile works manager who is going to be very difficult to find. Additionally someone to take over the office and the day to day accounts, and also possibly a design draughtsman although conceivably this could be done on contract at home by someone retired. Additional workshop staff can be recruited as required and in any case would be paid for by the work in hand. Good second-hand additional machinery is likely to be adequate and its capital cost can very probably be written off against the first few major jobs for which it is used.

The additional work would have to come from increased sales in the UK and overseas, principally the Far East. So far as the UK is concerned the additional markets would appear to be:

a) Develop a 30h.p. locomotive particularly for the peat industry.

b) Break into the larger mining concerns and particularly the NCB, which latter might prove extremely difficult.

c) An increase in the right kind of civil engineering activity such as the Channel Tunnel.

d) New markets altogether such as materials handling generally and agriculture for animal feeding and muck shifting. These would require some prior professional market research.

There are already a fair number of specific enquiries from overseas which, if finalised, could achieve the required additional turnover in more or less one jump and might be easier to achieve than, say, breaking into the NCB.

e) An enquiry from Singapore for up to 70 units per year of a 30h.p. diesel locomotive.

f) An enquiry from Indonesia/Philippines for bagasse-burning steam locomotives with which to replace diesel locomotives.

g) An enquiry from the Gulf for an inspection railway underneath an oil jetty. This may happen anyway and appears to be worth about £90,000.

h) Possible retrieval of an enquiry for K.12 locomotives for Tenerife.

i) An enquiry for mine cars for South America.

7. Ireland

In the past, agent's commission and the strength of the pound have been stumbling blocks to overseas trade and very preliminary enquiries suggest that it might be possible to operate a plant in Eire for the manufacture of new equipment only. This would take advantage of the low level of the Irish pound. In practice this is always going to be lower than its English equivalent.

There is also the possible spin off from this in the fact that Bord na Móna, the Irish Turf Board, are very large users of rail equipment (they literally buy locomotives by the dozen) and they might prefer to buy equipment made in Ireland provided price and quality are the same. A turnover of at least £200,000 per annum for this plant on its own would be needed to make it viable.

8. The Achievement

It would not, in my view, be too difficult to achieve the required turnover if even only a few of these straws in the wind can be grasped but it will take 12 months or more. Additional capital is primarily needed to pay for the management staff for that period, to stabilise the cash position in such a way that the company can hold greater stocks of material such as rail and develop such things as its diesel locomotive design. In short, to leave it in a position to take advantage of all work offering as the recession lifts.

supply an inspection railway for an oil jetty in the Middle East. It sounded simple but when we got down to details it turned out to be *underneath* a gas jetty in Qatar, a small Arab state which sticks up like a sore thumb on the western side of the Persian Gulf. Added to this the customer was understandably twitchy about fire risks as not long previously that establishment had had what was then the world's largest land-based insurance claim for a fire at the attached refinery. The jetty comprised a concrete deck, carrying roadway and pipes, standing on splayed steel piles and was about 800 metres long. The railway was required primarily for an initial inspection and report on its condition and for the repairs required following that inspection. If it was available for subsequent maintenance that was a bonus because it was reckoned that the railway would cost less than having to scaffold the jetty twice (for inspection and subsequent repair).

On the basis of drawings and photographs it was possible to come up with a basic concept and cost of what could be done, and this being acceptable the next move was a visit to Qatar. The object of that first visit was to carry out a detailed survey of the jetty and to decide how the railway was going to be fixed to it. In principle it was simple enough – cross-girders would be fixed to the piles with gigantic U bolts and light-weight girders would be suspended between them, with rails clipped thereto and on those would the trolley run. In addition to inspecting and working on the main deck, the ability to work on and around the piles was also required. All this sounds quite simple, especially with my surveying abilities, but in practice was not so easy. Despite the water being one of the few relaxations for ex-patriots in the Gulf, finding a small boat and boatman caused Wimpey considerable problems.

Following survey, a detailed plan was prepared, the quote adjusted and an order placed. When one reaches this stage it suddenly dawns upon one that one actually has got to do all the things one has said are possible! The final outcome was a trolley on 7ft rail gauge which was hand wound along a fixed wire laid up the jetty. The trolley itself was in three sections – the front and rear of which could, again with wires, be wound out to surround the piles and give access to the extreme width of the jetty. When this was being done the trolley was clamped to the girders. The rail was 20lbs/yd and the whole thing was galvanized, another first. This was done by Painter Brothers of Hereford who were later to become useful customers of Alan Keef Ltd. I subcontracted the manufacture of all the structural steel-work, together with on site erection, and designed and manufactured the trolley myself. The whole job went remarkably smoothly except that upon arrival some of the girders got bent and some rails went missing. Fortunately the steel erectors managed to sort out the girders and some more rails were road-hauled out from the UK. This led to some outlandish additional cost claims by said steel erectors but, perhaps fortuitously, both they and the steel fabricators went into liquidation very shortly afterwards. I went out to Qatar to commission the whole thing and it did all work remarkably well. Wimpey carried out their survey, which was the object of the exercise, but they did not get the contract for subsequent repair as they had hoped and what happened to my masterpiece I know not. Its remains are probably still there.

And so after this little escapade it was back to normal working. As an adjunct to the work done for Blackpool Pleasure Beach I had bought the 1ft 8in. gauge Hudswell Clarke locomotives and carriages from their park at Morecambe. These comprised the 4-6-4 Baltic tank locomotive *Robin Hood* and the 4-6-2 tender locomotive *Flying Scotsman* together with four carriages. There were another two carriages but for some reason they wanted to keep these for use with a water slide. The mind boggles! Included in the deal were all the track materials, mostly very well worn. The whole lot was in a very sorry state and I only bought it to prevent it being scrapped, which possibility seemed extremely likely. I felt it could languish in my yard and somebody might like it someday.

As chance would have it, that somebody appeared on the scene much sooner than expected. Michael Ann from Drusilla's Zoo mentioned to me that Lord Fisher of Kilverstone Wildlife Park, near Thetford in Norfolk, was considering the possibility of a railway as an additional attraction in his park. One thing led to another, as they say, and the upshot was that the ex-Morecambe equipment was sold to Lord Fisher. The fact that it was an odd gauge did not matter in this instance as it was to be used on its own without reference to any other railway. A fairly short railway, some 600 yards or so, was designed and laid which gave passengers an interesting ride but with a fairly quick turnround time. Being the better of the two locomotives, *Robin Hood* was completely rebuilt and the two best carriages refurbished. The work and cost involved in the former were considerable and more than either of us had expected but the end result was very satisfying. It was a pleasure to see this rather splendid locomotive working again. It was fitted with a pre-production prototype of a Lister engine that ultimately never went into production. It has proved to be an extremely good engine remaining in regular use until *Robin Hood* itself moved into preservation. Obtaining such spares as have been needed has been

The inspection trolley for the gas loading jetty in Qatar was the first overseas contract involving overseas travel. The principle of the 7ft gauge trolley is demonstrated on the track suspended underneath the landward end of the jetty.

interesting, but all the suppliers seem to know all about the engine. Apparently there are two others, both still at work.

To my mind the carriages were very much less satisfying as at Morecambe they had had very tall vaguely 'Wild West' roofs fitted to them that were anything but in keeping. I wanted to lower them and make them more in line with the locomotive but 'Lordie' would have none of it. *Flying Scotsman* and the other two carriages were left to be done at a later date by local contractors. Lord Fisher's own staff laid the track under my supervision and a very fine job they made of it. At the same time as doing this we were also re-laying the railway at Pwllheli for Butlin's and I was driving to Thetford, on to Pwllheli and home. It was probably 700 miles of the worst motoring in England. I seriously thought of buying a helicopter!

Due to the amount of work that had to be done to *Robin Hood* in particular, it is doubtful if this contract was at all profitable, but dealing with the Fishers was delightful and was, maybe, some consolation. Lord and Lady Fisher always insisted that when I went there I should stay with them as a house guest. The kitchen was usually additionally occupied by some small animal in need of tender loving care. Lady Fisher had, I think, a sloth as a house pet and his Lordship usually had copies of Hansard or the proceedings of the House of Lords lying about on the coffee table. They always seemed very happy for their guests to participate in the drinks cupboard and generally to make themselves at home. I continued to deal with them and keep an eye on the railway until they retired and their son took over. It was not long after that that the park closed altogether but *Robin Hood* & co. did not pass out of my life as will become apparent.

Allied to both these jobs I ran a railway operating course at Pwllheli, primarily for Butlin's amusement park managers but one or

Left: The prototype K.30 (AK8 of 1982) was sold to the new peat workings of Norritt Klassman at Penicuik in Scotland following trials on site. This was a surprising sale as Klassman are manufacturers of peat harvesting machinery in their own right and are possibly the largest of the German peat producers.

Right: Rebuilt *Robin Hood* at Kilverstone Wildlife Park. Although around fifty years old at the time, these Hudswell Clarke diesel locomotives were built in the true traditions of steam locomotive engineering and are a tribute to the men who built them.

two others were there as well, including Lord and Lady Fisher for whom I think Butlin's was a complete eye opener! Talks were given by Les Abbott from the Railway Inspectorate and Butlin's own safety inspectors. The paperwork I provided for it has continued to turn up in unexpected places for many years afterwards. It must have done some good.

The Hunday tractor museum near Hexham in Northumberland had bought the complete 2ft 6in. gauge railway from The Dalmunzie Hotel in Scotland with the idea that it could be used as an attraction in their largely agricultural museum. However, for Hunday Museum it was perhaps less than useful. The rail was exceedingly light, 16lbs/yd at best; the Simplex locomotive of 1920 vintage still had its original petrol engine, and the two carriages, also of Simplex manufacture, were in deplorable condition and in any case only seated eight people each. Added to this, or because of it, they had bought an ex-military Hunslet mines-type locomotive of some 8 or 9 tons weight. This promptly destroyed such of the ex-Dalmunzie track as had been laid. That was being rectified but more suitable carriages were required and to this end the museum had bought some ex-National Coal Board knifeboard manriders. I was asked to make some presentable carriages using the wheelsets from these. This I succeeded in doing, although the resulting vehicles were slightly incongruous. For all that they ran a number of years at Hunday Museum and many more on the Isle of Wight.

Still in the north of England, it was at about this time that I built a batch of mine tubs for Swales Bros for a private coal mine on the edge of the Keilder Forest. Like so many small mines it was in an inaccessible clearing in the forest although in fact not far from the Keilder Dam. Despite being a drift mine it disappeared down a hole that appeared to be not far short of vertical. The most astonishing part was the haulage gear, which consisted of a Bedford lorry on blocks chained to some adjacent trees and with a large drum built onto one of the back wheels. Mr Swales then used to sit in the cab and 'drive' the lorry thus pulling tubs out of the mine! He let the empties back down again on the foot brake. The Achilles heel of the operation was that the building of the dam had raised water tables all around and it was rapidly becoming uneconomic to pump the mine clear of water. It closed not very long afterwards.

This period of 1982/83 was to be a time largely concerned with industrial railways. I air braked a Simplex 60S locomotive at the NCB's Wheldale Colliery for Simplex. There was supposed to be a second one to do but it never happened. With the benefit of hindsight I suspect that the Simplex locomotives themselves, despite their rugged construction, were not really up to the brutal treatment meted out to them in the coal mining industry, especially in Yorkshire. This was followed by the making-up of 3ft gauge test track for Thomas Hill Ltd at Rotherham for the testing of a prototype manrider train which they hoped to sell to the NCB. I do not think they were ever successful.

This K.30 (AK9 of 1983) was built with a stand-up cab so that the driver could see over the train of peat wagons. Originally built for an entirely new peat operation near Ballyshannon in County Donegal, it subsequently moved to Midland Irish Peat Moss Co. near Mullingar where it is seen with a train of empty peat wagons.

The next major contract also came right out of the blue and this was for a complete railway for a new peat bog being opened in the hills behind Ballyshannon in County Donegal, Ireland. The man concerned had gone to London, I think to see RMP, and had picked my name out of a directory he was idly leafing through in his hotel room. The upshot was the supply of a K.30 locomotive, ten bogies upon which he then made his own bodies and a wagon tippler together with about a mile of new track which did come from RMP. The wagons were ex-MoD ammunition wagons from RAF Fauld, lengthened by about two feet. The locomotive was a bit unusual as it was built for the driver to stand up to drive. The scheme was, perhaps, an exercise in obtaining grant money as it closed down about four years later and appeared to have dug very little peat. The whole area has now been planted with trees. I was involved in the subsequent sale of the railway equipment to Midland Irish Peat Moss Co. Ltd, near Mullingar, and monies received were paid to some unusual places but, as far as I was concerned, it all worked out well.

There were some considerable storms on the East Coast that year and at Clacton Butlin's suffered substantial damage. An easterly wind with a spring tide could very often flood the camp at Clacton. Next to the miniature railway was a large steel tank, for what purpose I do not know, and on this occasion the flooding was so severe that this tank floated and somehow one of the carriages got underneath it and thus was largely destroyed when the tide subsided. At the same time, the track, being on wooden sleepers, also floated away. The tank had to be cut up and a new carriage body made using the existing bogies which had survived. I was told that the night gateman, the only man on site, finished up sitting on his chair on his desk in the gatehouse to keep out of the rising waters!

Following this, a further K.30 was built for Milton Hall Brick Co. Ltd of Southend-on-Sea. This was a brickworks where, instead of digging a deep pit as was usual, the clay came from the top six feet or so of the surrounding fields. As a consequence the railway became quite extensive as it reached further and further from the works. This loco was followed up a year or two later with a rebuilt Ruston locomotive using the same hydraulics as the K.30. In due course this company and its successors were to become major customers of Alan Keef Ltd. The K.30 locomotives are fitted with 19in. wheels for the simple reason that I had bought a largish quantity of brand-new tyres of this size in an NCB disposal sale. These were extremely hard and, I would think, almost everlasting. I sold four to British Rail Engineering at Swindon – whatever for I have no idea although they may have gone to Leafield Mine at Corsham.

Drusilla's Zoo had a very sweet steam-outline locomotive built upon a Ruston frame. The old Ruston engine had been replaced with a more modern unit but, as happened on several occasions, those who did it failed to allow for the increased speed of the new engine and the input drive to the gearbox would not take the extra revolutions. As a consequence we fitted a new Petter engine with a permanent reduction box between it and the gearbox which has proved very satisfactory. Unusually, this was done in midsummer. Also supplied at this time was a Lister locomotive, re-gauged from 15in. back to 2ft, wagons and 2,300 metres of Jubilee track to Midland Irish Peat Moss Co. Ltd who were just opening a new peat bog near Mullingar in the Irish Midlands. This again was the beginning of a long relationship that goes on to this day.

The highlight of the year was the securing of an order for the Treasure Island Railway at Thorpe Park, near Staines outside London. This came through, of all unlikely sources, Bassett Lowke Ltd, the model-makers of Northampton. Severn Lamb had been asked but said they could not do what was required. The criterion was to be able to transport a maximum of 1,500 people per hour through Treasure Island which was an island in an old gravel pit (the whole lot being converted to a theme park) connected to the 'mainland' by a narrow causeway. Gradients of 1 in 40 together with 40-foot-radius curves were the order of the day and the line ran through the middle of a fibreglass galleon! Two trains of four 30-seat carriages were provided together with two K.60 locomotives, basically the K.30 with more

weight and larger engine. However, Thorpe Park said they would fit steam-outline bodies to the locomotives themselves and that suited me as I thought their expertise in these matters would produce something spectacular. Not a bit of it – I think they dragged some bits of rusty old steel out of the lake and made the bodies with that. I was thoroughly ashamed to have my name attached to them. The system worked for a number of years and at its height was reported to be carrying some 10,000–12,000, yes, thousand, people per day. A sidelight on this was that at the beginning the gravel pit was still a functioning operation and a steady stream of gravel barges passed by Treasure Island between the working area and the screening plant. All in all this was a very successful job which kept us going for a whole winter although there were of course all the usual small sales of rail, fishplates and so on.

And so we come to 1984 which, apart from the Thorpe Park job completed for Easter, was a very dull year and financially was the beginning of a downward trend that was to culminate in the move to Herefordshire. With the benefit of hindsight, whilst at the same time looking forward a little, the business had never really recovered from the Rhyl fiasco but had up until this point managed to contain its problems. The effect of a dull year's trading was therefore to exacerbate a bad situation. One is, of course, never aware of quite what is happening at the time and I have always tended to have a bad habit of not laying off staff soon enough. The ensuing couple of years, as will be seen, produced some interesting and prestige jobs but these were never enough to cover the intervening lulls. One has to question whether these jobs were even profitable and I think I have to accept that they were not. The nature of the business is such that it tends to have very high overheads brought about by the amount of travelling to see customers and so on. If times are hard this gets worse as one tries to drum up more business. Added to that I had also almost certainly been taking too much out of the business to pay for my children's education, a subject about which I have no regrets.

On the track-laying front, the entire railway at Woburn Abbey was moved to a new site in the Animal Kingdom, now Woburn Safari Park. Although only about 450 yards in length, the owner operated it on a shoe-string and the cost of moving had to fall in line. As a sign of the times, it was also the beginning of a major rationalization at Butlin's, with ultimately the closure and sale of some sites and the devolvement of maintenance to local management. Not good for me! Similarly, this period is peppered with hire contracts, some of them quite substantial, but obviously the contractors concerned were not out to spend their own money. Hire contracts are very useful business but care has to be taken that the job is going to pay for anything that has to be

A more conventional K.30 (AK10 of 1983) at Cherry Orchard Brickworks near Southend-on-Sea. This is the only K.30 so far preserved; the rest are still at work at the time of writing which must say something for them.

The train on Treasure Island at Thorpe Park descends through the fibreglass galleon on its tour of the island. Although relatively short lived, this line was designed to carry 1,500 people per hour up 1 in 40 gradients and round 40-foot-radius curves! The park made their own bodies for these locomotives (AK11 and AK12 of 1984) and initially made a very poor job of it.

bought; or, if it does not, at least the residual value will equal the second-hand sale value. The snag also is that having provided all the material it is a month before one can invoice anything and probably another two before one is paid. Indeed, one large contractor, who had better remain nameless, took ages to pay a number of very modest invoices of about £100 each. When I finally threatened legal action I was sent a wad of cheques and remittance advices, they having drawn the cheque each month but not having actually sent it! And I thought I was the only person who did things like that.

I have a record of a sale to New Zealand of a Ruston locomotive and two carriage underframes and know nothing about its ultimate use although it was obviously for a tourist railway of some sort. The locomotive, which emanated from Billing Aquadrome, had already had a quite reasonable steam-outline body fitted to it and, judging from the price, the underframes were new. An odd sale overseas at this time was four ex-Butlin's Chance carriage bogies to a railway enthusiast in Austria who appeared to be building a 2ft gauge model railway to a high standard and for his own amusement in a castle on a mountain peak near Vienna.

At Butlin's the carriage bogie mountings and wear plates were modified to utilise a ball roller arrangement. I was always a bit sceptical of what the long term effect of this would be, fearing that the point loading on the balls would wear into the wear plate and create greater problems than they were trying to solve. In practice, Butlin's closed most of their railways before this could be fully ascertained. I think it was at about this time that one of my tracklayers backed my car hard into a pillar at Barry Island, so much so that it must have stripped some teeth in the reverse gear system. I subsequently drove the car for some 5,000 miles with no reverse. To say the least, this required forward planning, particularly where parking was concerned!

Llanelli Borough Council had taken over what had once been a munitions factory at Pembrey between Llanelli and Carmarthen. Upon abandonment it had been sold to a scrap merchant who spent the next several years stripping out everything that was removable and saleable and in his turn abandoned it again. There was a good deal of 2ft gauge track left on site, most of it set in concrete and therefore

not worth the scrap merchant's while removing. To install a narrow gauge railway was therefore an obvious thing to do and I spent a good deal of time with the council discussing possibilities and likely costs. It was and is a huge site and the initial idea was to make the railway do something useful, but in the event they merely laid an oval of track about 500 yards long around which the train crawled, and I mean crawled, at about 2m.p.h. They bought a defunct railway from further along the coast at Pendine Sands which included one of only two locomotives built by Robert Hudson Ltd, of wagon and track components fame. These locomotives were singularly unsuccessful, being built for use in the Woodhead Tunnel and sent back – having the axles individually hydraulically driven it was quite possible to have the wheels turning in opposite directions! The whole project was carried out under various unemployment schemes and as far as it went was successful. In the short term it meant the sale of a good deal of track materials and a carriage underframe. At later stages, overhaul of the locomotive and the building of a complete new carriage also came my way. At a later date still, the local model engineering society installed a 3½in./5in. gauge track and this became much more attractive to the public and its operation was not the local authority's problem. As a consequence, the 2ft gauge railway was initially mothballed and ultimately closed, which is a pity as it is an attractive site that deserves better in the way of a railway.

It was quite a busy time on the industrial railway side as well. Two Simplex 40S locomotives, second-hand from Severn Trent Water at Minworth sewerage works, were sold to Richardson's Moss Litter and, more remarkably, a BEV battery locomotive of 2ft 6in. gauge for their Fannyside Moss near Airdrie. Simplexes were hired to Redland Bricks at Nutbourne Works near Godalming but this ultimately resulted in their buying a new K.30 locomotive with some of their scrap locos in part exchange. Norritt Klassman at Penecuik ordered another K.30 with a Deutz engine supplied from the parent German company, but before I could start making it cancelled the order and had a completely rebuilt Simplex 20/28 instead using the same engine. A spare wheelset was supplied to the K.12 at Country Kitchen Foods, Wilmslow and I suppose that a railway supplied to Cheltenham also classes as industrial. This was the hire of a locomotive, wagons and track for contractors building a tennis court in the back of a very smart garden in an equally smart part of Cheltenham. The Jubilee track was laid on scaffold boards across the lawn and through the flower beds, one machine was taken in on sheets of plywood and everything, but everything, else went in or out by rail. It was the forerunner of some useful business to come.

The next big job was a complete railway for Cricket St Thomas Park for the Taylor family. The main house and some of its surroundings subsequently became well known as the setting for the television comedy series *To the Manor Born*. Although they could be infuriating, and who cannot, I had to admire John and Stephen Taylor. I may be wrong, but I have the impression that at a relatively young age they decided that they were going to do whatever it took to live the life of country gentlemen and they succeeded in doing

Pembrey Park, near Llanelli. This attractive 450-yard-long railway was all that materialized of a much grander scheme to provide a transport service in what turned a disused munitions factory into a country park. This picture is from much later when we had a steam-outline Simplex locomotive there on long-term hire.

carriage bodies ex Fairbourne and a quantity of 20lbs/yd rail. An initial survey was carried out to prove the practicality of the scheme which, although satisfactory, was not quite as good as could have been wished. The preferred route, decided by existing fences, woodland and estate roadways, left one terminus well below the zoo and the other well above the heavy horse centre but I guess the two short stiff climbs with a train ride in between was better than a steady uphill half-mile walk. Added to this, the railway ran down the opposite side of the valley from the main house and the zoo. This involved the building of a very spectacular steel arched bridge some twenty feet above the water to carry the railway across the valley. John Taylor did tell me that this cost more than the rest of the railway put together and as my bill was £26,000 …! It is, in fact, very much taken for granted and should really be one of the wonders of the narrow gauge world.

Patrick and I went there to do one of the initial surveys and the Taylors failed to tell us that one of the paddocks contained a large and irascible stag who appeared over the hill pawing the ground and breathing eternal damnation upon railway builders. 'Ah. You met Wapiti', was all the sympathy we got! In a sense things got worse. Having re-engined the loco and made new bogies for the carriages, and they having laid the track, we in due course delivered. The carriages were articulated and the roof clearances to the next carriage were a bit tight on the curves, so what did Stephen Taylor do? He took a chain saw and cut the corners back! So much for all our care in manufacture. Cricket however, and despite the problems, remains an ongoing customer

just that. By and large, John did the management and Stephen did the work but it seemed to work out for them. The park sloped down the valley from a zoo near the main house to a heavy horse centre in what I guess had been either the estate workshops or the home farm. Visitors, especially elderly ones, were apt to saunter gently downhill to the farm and then have trouble getting back. The railway was to help overcome this problem.

It so happened that I had some 15in. gauge equipment to hand, notably the Guest double bogie locomotive from Rhyl (known to us as the 'Ice Cream Van' due to its one-time colour scheme), some

The bridge across the valley at Cricket St Thomas Park should, by rights, be classed as one of the wonders of the 15in. gauge railway world. Here a train is seen crossing it in recent times with the train being driven from the driving trailer towards the camera. When built, the bridge was reputed to have cost more than the rest of the railway put together!

Left: This is a publicity shot by Petter Diesels of the prototype and only K.20 (AK15 of 1984) at the bottom of the field at Cote. This locomotive was not highly successful, later had a cab fitted, and was periodically hired out before being exported to Pakistan.

Right: AK13R of 1984 was a rebuild of a Ruston locomotive (RH452280 of 1960) with a hydrostatic transmission. Originally for the Solva contract but later converted to 15in. gauge and sold as a spare locomotive to Littlecote House, Hungerford, where it is here.

Right: The Hydrotip wagon was a good idea that failed to catch on. The theory, and it worked, was that a driver could tip the wagons in his train one at a time back from the locomotive and then right the wagons to return for another load. Two are seen on hire to the Solva sewerage works contract.

Left: Framed by the excavator arm, a standard K.30 (AK14 of 1984) loads clay at the Nutbourne works of Redland Bricks. This pit was unusual in that two different types of clay were loaded into each train for blending. This locomotive later went into passenger service at Billing Aquadrome.

Right: It is perhaps only the lights at the very top that give this picture away. We did all the trackwork for the 'underground' scenes in the James Bond film *A View to a Kill* at Pinewood Studios whilst the outside shots were filmed at Amberley Chalkpits Museum.

to this day, and will continue to turn up in this narrative.

On occasion I have been involved in legal actions relating to small railways where someone has been hurt. One of the first was at Drusilla's Zoo where a child had obviously jumped from the train as it approached the station and tried to race it into the platform. The claim was that the train had stopped so suddenly that he had been thrown out and it had then run over his foot. This seems something of a contradiction in terms!

A glamorous and prestigious job was the track work required for the studio shots for the James Bond film *A View to a Kill* being filmed at Pinewood studios. This was laid out in the field from the drawings provided, so that when delivered it only needed tweaking into position. Various alterations were called for at very short notice and thus considerable cost but that is the way of the film industry. The 'outside' filming was done at Amberley Chalk Pits Museum and I think they got the railway credits on film!

It was, however, a fascinating insight. For instance this was the first film to be shot in the new 'Big Studio', wherein a polystyrene forest had gone up in flames shortly beforehand and I was told that the steelwork for the new building was ordered whilst the fire brigade were still on the premises! Certainly the builders were still on site. Fibreglass tunnel walls were supported by genuine 12in. × 12in. baulks of timber as being cheaper than doing that in fibreglass as well. Joinery and set painting of superb quality is seen for a few seconds on the final film and then scrapped, literally. Another film was in production at the same time and for this the set, the cast and everyone else was waiting around for the antlers of reindeer to grow to a certain point!

There are always occasions when one perceives what seems like a good idea but when the crunch comes the world does not want to know. I had two at about this time. The first was that, having built a fairly successful diesel hydraulic locomotive, the K.30, and sold some into industry, it seemed logical to use the hydraulics to tip the wagons to unload the train. So I built some and, after a fair amount of jiggery pokery, the system worked well. The principle was that a slightly modified side tipping wagon was fitted with hydraulic rams at each end and these were actuated by the engine hydraulics. The system was so arranged that the first wagon back from the locomotive moved first and when this was fully tipped the train could be moved forward and the next one tipped and so on. Once the whole train was tipped the wagons were then returned to normal in any old order as the system chose. The second of these ideas was the building of a K.20 locomotive to fill in the gap between the little K.12 and the K.30. So a 2-ton loco was built with a Petter engine and Sauer/Sunstrand hydraulic transmission. It was deliberately intended to be cheap. The snag was that it did not work very well, primarily due to pump control problems.

These were overcome in the end with reasonable success and this and the 'Hydrotip' wagons were put to some use together.

Susan and her family have always had a great love for St Davids in Pembrokeshire, and to have some work down there was something of a bonus. Just before one reaches St Davids there is an inlet from the sea and the small village of Solva. This has a sewerage works on the opposite side of a bluff from the harbour and the only access was through a very constricted tunnel that had a 2ft gauge railway already concreted into its floor. Shellabere Price had a contract to rebuild the sewerage works and the only regular access allowed was through this tunnel. They were willing to hire the K.20 and wagons for the duration and both were exhibited at the International Construction Equipment Exhibition in Birmingham beforehand, which was hoped to be good publicity for both of us. In principle it all worked and indeed I rebuilt a Ruston locomotive with hydraulic transmission in order to give them a second train so they could have one with skips and one with flat wagons.

The building of all this equipment and then hiring it out was technically commercially successful but it stretched my slender finances to breaking point, especially as there appeared no ready market available once the job ended. The wagons were never used again and the K.20, being really something and nothing, hung around for several years until after the move to The Lea before being exported. One consequence was that we took to factoring our invoices. For those not conversant with the principle, one's debts are taken over by a finance house, in our case a firm called Manson Factors, and when a customer was invoiced we received 80 per cent of the invoice value from them by return of post. The balance was paid to us as and when the customer paid, less Manson's charges. They did the statements and chased the money (something I have always detested) and only passed it back if it got to the point of going to court for collection. The big advantage is that at the point one takes it on one receives a lump sum equal to 80 per cent of one's invoices outstanding at the time which, I guess, is usually used to reduce bank borrowings. It was with me anyway. At that time I think it was perhaps a bit unusual although nowadays a fair number of our suppliers use the system. Although, and in fairness to Manson, the system worked well, it did later cause some serious problems and I would not recommend it to anyone. If you can get by without, do so. The snag is that getting out is not easy as one has to find again that lump sum that has been provided. Again in fairness to Manson, they would take any customer to whom I was willing to offer credit terms, unlike, I think, some of their competitors. They were also quite happy for me not to send them each and every invoice.

1985 was a year of building quite a number of locomotives. A foray into 10¼in. gauge was an 0-6-0 petrol locomotive for Commander Francis for his Wells–Walsingham line. He provided a Ford car engine and gearbox and I effectively cleared up the yard and built a locomotive out of all the bits. The result was very successful. As he turned locomotives at each end there was no need for more than the car reverse gear – this is always a problem with automotive cast-offs. It could travel as fast as you dared drive it and worked for many years until rebuilt as a diesel hydraulic, by which time I imagine the original engine was worn out. In 2005 we built an almost identical locomotive, in appearance at least, in 12¼in. gauge for a private customer.

Whilst this was happening a major re-lay of the railway at Butlin's Minehead was also going on that was different in several ways. The railway itself was fairly straightforward although fitting into some places was quite difficult. The Chance locomotives beloved by Butlin's did not have a full range of speeds in reverse because, like the Wells and Walsingham locomotive, they used an automotive gearbox and therefore it was always necessary to turn them at the end of each journey by some means or another. This was usually done by taking the whole train round a turning-circle – but space was short near reception and we overcame the problem by using a triangle and reversing the train round it after the style of American practice. The line then had to cross a barriered level crossing on the entrance into the main car park. This was normally manned. It then ran in a dead-straight line for some 800 yards between the car park and the camp, where it was crossed by numerous pedestrian crossings, then to bear left to a station and a very tight turning-circle by the new flats. The materials from the existing railway were used in its construction, together with additional new rail and sleepers as required. The carriages were refurbished and fitted with canopies, and an additional vehicle was made for the transport of guest's luggage.

The new railway opened in August of that year but never really realized its potential. The idea was that it should act as what is nowadays called a people-mover for those staying in the flats that were getting on for half a mile from the main entertainment areas of the camp but …: it did not open until 9.30 in the morning, the staff all went off for lunch for an hour or so in the middle of the day and, most ridiculous of all, it shut at 5.30 p.m! What can one say?

I did offer a diesel railcar to operate on it which would have been much more sensible and, being fully enclosed, would have been much more suitable for purpose; but it was not to be, and when, as mentioned earlier, management was devolved to the camps, it all became too complicated and Butlin's one real attempt at making their railways useful closed.

Cote Farm with the track shown at its greatest extent shortly before the move to Lea Line. This was generally laid in heavier rail although the quality deteriorated the further one went from the centre of operations!

Scale 1:500

and far-reaching consequences. It was followed by an enquiry for two locomotives of 2ft 6in. gauge and 4 tons weight for use in the same works. At that time, with the possible exception of some military establishments, this was the largest industrial narrow gauge railway system in the country with some twenty-two miles of track and about a dozen locomotives in regular use. The mainstay of the fleet were seven Barclay locomotives and it transpired that the buffers were required because the drivers had been playing dodgems with them together with loaded trains of explosive! (To my knowledge they were never fitted but that is incidental.)

As a consequence, the specification for the new locos was fairly tight and, in particular, they had to be limited to 8m.p.h. They also had to be fitted with spark arresters, soundproofed fully-enclosed and heated cabs, with quite a complicated electrical system that could be isolated in sections. I took them to see the prototype K.30 at Penicuik and their Mr Stanford came to Cote to look at my facilities. He was a fairly dour Scot who one could imagine being a pillar of his local kirk and when I took him back to the station there was a bit of time to kill so we repaired to the buffet bar. He had a beer but I refused one on the grounds that I had to drive back, although in reality because I do not like beer. Rightly or wrongly I have always felt that it was this gesture that got me the order for two locomotives!

These were quite sophisticated by the standards of the time and I was proud of them. When it came to delivery and commissioning, first I took them into Richardson's Moss at Gretna in order to show them what a modern locomotive could be like, but they did not rush to buy. Second, being close to Butlin's at Ayr, Susan, Alice and myself booked in there for four days whilst I did the commissioning. It was quite an eye opener to see Butlin's from the other side of the counter as it were. We did all sorts of silly things like play bowls, ride the roundabouts and enjoy the excellent entertainment.

Simplex had also quoted for these two locomotives and had obviously lost it to me. It was not very long thereafter that they approached me with the request that they were now going to concentrate on the fork lift attachment side of their business and if, by some fluke, they received an order for a locomotive, would I build it for them on sub-contract? The answer was, of course, that I would be delighted. However it was to be the following year before anything positive came of it.

Because of the urgency to get this railway built I had four men working at Minehead, who, unusually for Butlin's, were accommodated within the camp. Finding suitable people was something of a problem, but phoning around produced one Chris Gorman, from Shaftesbury in Dorset. Chris obviously took to the job like a duck to water. He has always been totally reliable and although often driving somewhat disreputable vehicles has always been in the right place at the right moment. He will reappear in this narrative with monotonous regularity!

Earlier in the year I had sold five second-hand Ruston buffer blocks to ICI Nobels Explosives for their Ardeer Works at Stevenston, not far from Ayr in Scotland. These were supposedly for fitting to their Barclay locomotives which had some broken. This apparently small sale started a chain of events that was to have entirely unexpected

There was also a down side to the ICI Nobels sale, and that in some way related to Manson Factors. The invoice was passed to them and was paid in the usual way but somehow or another a chunk of it seemed to disappear. I have never understood this and neither did my long suffering bank manager at Bampton, especially as this was one of the rare occasions when I had actually back-checked and found that I had built the locos at a profit. In reality I was almost certainly in the classic scenario of over-trading without having a firm hand on what was happening, but it was very strange nevertheless.

Of equal or greater significance for the future was the building of an 0-4-0 steam-outline diesel locomotive for the Cotswold Wildlife Park. This was based on the 3ft gauge Peckett at Shanes Castle in Northern Ireland and I borrowed some of the original drawings from the Lord O'Niel in order to get the proportions right. It was powered by a Perkins 4.108

This 10¼in. gauge 0-6-0 petrol locomotive (AK16 of 1985) for the Wells and Walsingham Railway was built by gathering together a collection of useful components and building a locomotive out of them. This shot is at the Wells-next-the-Sea terminus in 1990. It is still in use but with a new engine and transmission and steam-tram-engine type bodywork.   *Dave Holroyde*

engine with Linde hydrostatic transmission and was the forerunner of a considerable line of generally similar locomotives. Effectively on its own it ran the railway at the Cotswold Wildlife Park for some eighteen years until, in 2003, a new, bigger and heavier locomotive was built which can regularly haul a fourth carriage, thus giving increased capacity and allowing the old lady to remain as a standby. In this context it should be borne in mind that this quite lengthy railway carries some 150,000 passengers in a season.

The rest of the year was spent on the usual type of work with one or two jobs of minor interest. I profiled wheels and supplied some new wheelsets for Wadsworth Becker lifts for what was then the RNAD at Monks Park Mine at Corsham in Wiltshire, and carried out a fairly major overhaul on the dreadful Ruston locomotive at Woburn. This again involved gearbox work and I said that it was the last time that I would tackle a Ruston gearbox, which I think it has been! The Hudson locomotive at Pembrey Park was re-tyred and two locomotives sent to Bian Haut Hardware in Singapore. A memorable, but best forgotten, exercise occurred at the end of the year. The ICI Nobels locomotives had, at their request, been fitted with lever handbrakes for which I had used an articulated-trailer handbrake unit. This had not been wholly successful and it had been decided to fit a conventional screw-down handbrake. I made up new units just to bolt in place and Tom (a fitter) and I left with a car-load of tools and bits and pieces to fit them and spent the night in Carlisle on the way. Just about as we got there we realized that whilst we had all the tools, we had managed to leave the actual brake units behind! Panic! Susan and Patrick, who happened to be home from school, God bless them, packed up the units, took them to Cheltenham station, saw them onto the night sleeper train to Scotland and I got up at 5 a.m. to collect them off the train in Carlisle. ICI were none the wiser!

In January 1986, the Taylors from Cricket St Thomas reappeared on the scene wearing a different hat. Peter de Savery had bought Littlecote House, near Hungerford, and they were acting as consultants for its opening to the public. A railway was required and I was used to design a layout, carry out the necessary survey work and see it built. It was, in fact, quite a challenge as the difference in level was considerable not to mention having to avoid various watercourses, ancient garden walls and a Roman floor – it being one of the rare years in which the latter was uncovered. They had also bought a collection of rolling stock from the Fairbourne Railway that was then undergoing its transformation from 15in. gauge to 12¼in. gauge, and this all had to be refurbished. By comparison the track was straight-forward. The carriages were all fairly run-down, especially where bogies and running gear were concerned, as a result of having been run for all their lives in their own local sandstorm on the beach at Fairbourne. The Taylor's could not understand why I insisted on replacing all axle box bearings and some of the housings as well. In addition they had to be fitted with full air-brakes, as the Littlecote line was fairly precipitous. With the carriages they also bought one of the Guest 2-4-2 steam locos, at that stage given an American look and renamed *Sydney*, but I had nothing to do with that. For a diesel shunter and spare loco I sold them my rebuilt Ruston which had been used at Solva, now re-gauged to 15in. All in all, between us we produced a very attractive railway that was quite spectacular as well. In the longer term either de Savery lost interest or the project was not as successful as hoped, but after five or six years Littlecote House returned to being a private house and the railway was dispersed.

Remember that the year is 1986, because the Littlecote job was followed by an interesting one that had repercussions many years ahead. RMP were approached by the Department of Environment in Northern Ireland for the supply of track and rolling stock for a railway on a peat bog being turned into Peatlands Country Park. They were anxious to sell the track materials – there was to be a mile or so of track – and were happy to act as my agents in the provision of the rolling stock. The concept had an interesting history. The bog in question was near Dungannon and was a very large one. It had had a 3ft gauge railway on it for peat haulage and uniquely this was electrically operated by overhead wire using basically street-tramway-type equipment. Latterly this had given way to diesel locomotives of which they had both a Diema and a Planet. The use of bogie wagons was also unusual on this type of operation.

So Ray Coventry of RMP and I went to see what it was about. The bog was to be turned into a park, in part to promulgate the idea of how bad a thing it was to cut peat, but also to allow the public to see how it used to be done and to create a nature reserve at the same time. The track was to follow a roughly circular route around a mile in length with a spur line to some existing buildings, which added nearly another quarter of a mile. The carriages were to be modelled on the remains of the old bogie peat wagons using rough-sawn boards in slatted sides, cut up to give doors for access. There were to be three of these, together with a van that was to act as either a tool van/travelling mess room during construction or a mobile instructional unit in the finished product. In addition there was a hopper wagon for ballasting the track. RMP sold them all the track and I took a load of old rail in part exchange. We were told that if the water in various ponds was blue in colour it signified that explosive had been stored there – after all, we were in Northern Ireland!

It was altogether a very nice and fairly straightforward job. I had quite a chunk of design work to do but was able to use my standard bogie design widened to 3ft gauge and modify some existing wheelsets for the 4-wheeled vehicles. The van was subcontracted and built entirely in wood and as such was wholly satisfactory. Except for the ballast wagon, all the stock was air braked and equipment was supplied for the customer to fit air brakes to the old locomotives. Patrick had just left school and, although it had not been the intention for him to join the firm straight away, a spasm of high general unemployment meant that he did just that. He started in the workshop with the building of this order and I think he had a fairly hard time of it.

Another relatively small job which provided valuable experience a good many years hence was the laying of a track for Ibstock Bricks at their Laybrook works. This was sixty metres long and of 2m rail gauge and had to laid within 3mm of level in all directions. No mean requirement. It was achieved by using flat bar sleepers which were bolted into the concrete with jacking screws and thus each one could be individually adjusted for level. Within 6mm was achieved

using a good quality builders level but I had to hire a laser to tweak it the final little bit. On it was to run a rail-mounted forklift truck that reached up to about twenty-five feet to feed wet bricks into drying ovens. No wonder it had to be so accurate!

As always it is the side issues that make life so interesting. Laybrook works made London stock bricks (the yellowy ones with black speckles) and traditionally these were clamp burnt. This is possibly the oldest method of burning bricks and involves stacking the wet bricks in a precise manner with layers of straw and coal between them, and then setting the whole lot alight. Old brickyards very often have what is apparently a heap of old bricks but is in fact where the wind changed and fused the whole stack into a one solid lump. But at Laybrook they put a quarter of a million bricks into one heap and fired it! Admittedly it was under a shelter, but the stack was so large that they could be placing wet bricks at one end and taking burnt ones off at the other.

It must have been in the first half of this year that I was driving to South Wales to look at a possible railway project and for whatever unknown reason took the A40 through Gloucester instead of the motorway over the Severn Bridge. Between Gloucester and Ross on Wye was a large warehouse-type building with a 'For Sale' board on the gate. On the way back I stopped to have a look although I was very unsure just where I was when I first saw the place. It consisted of a large corrugated iron building, which the agent's particulars in due course told me was some 7,000sq.ft together with a substantial brick office and a useful chunk of yard and land. The modified farm buildings at Cote were rapidly becoming on the small side for the amount of work we were handling. This looked to me like a good opportunity, although the prospect of moving ourselves and a complete business was daunting in the extreme. Susan and I mulled it over for some time but the more we thought the better the idea seemed. Because of our desire to live on the premises however, a lot hung on our being able to obtain planning permission for not only

The first two (AK18 and AK19 of 1985) of four K.30 locomotives built for ICI Nobels Explosives. These were a new generation of locomotive with soundproofed cabs, sprung buffers, spark arresters and a generally high standard of finish.

AK20R of 1986 was a rebuild of Ruston 30DL locomotive 283513 of 1949 for Cherry Orchard Brickworks at Southend-on-Sea. It was fitted with a Deutz F3L912 engine and a hydraulic transmission based on that in the K.30s whilst retaining its original cab and bonnet work.

Whilst all these decisions were being made business had to go on. The invoices record a remarkable amount of repair work for local farmers, particularly Miss Gauntlet at Chimney. Butlin's was very much as usual with some emergency track repairs at Minehead in mid-season because of damage caused by people driving cars over it. By this time they had disposed of the camp at Filey and it was being operated by one Trevor Guy. He wanted to hire a train for the first season and I built him a couple of carriages, adequately but cheaply, and set up the little K.20 to haul them. They were duly delivered and within two weeks of opening he went bust. I managed to prove they were mine and retrieve them but it did not exactly help the cash flow!

Among the final jobs at Cote was the building of a replica ballast hopper wagon for the Festiniog Railway so that Leeds Industrial Museum could have one of theirs to help their collection of Hudson wagonry. Also at this final stage Simplex came up trumps with an order for a 60S locomotive. This was started at Cote but finished at Lea Line and was of 3ft 6in. gauge for Ghana Bauxite Corporation.

a change of use for the main building but also to build a house on the site as well. A major attraction was also to be able to cash in on the Cote property and thus, hopefully, solve the financial problems. These matters being satisfactorily resolved, thus came about the move to Lea Line, Herefordshire.

The history of the place was that it had been built shortly after the Second World War by a Mr Day for use as an animal feed warehouse. It had then been used for storage and making pallets by a local firm of packers, from whom we bought it. It had been empty for three or four years and small trees were beginning to grow in the yard. It stood on two acres of land that included a stretch of cutting on the old Gloucester to Ross railway. The local village is The Lea of which Lea Line is a small part. People will tell you that the Line refers to the part of the village through which the railway line runs but in fact the name is much older than that and probably refers to ley lines. It has to be said that we were lucky to be able to do what we wanted and to move into the edge of what I consider to be the most beautiful part of England.

After this it was wind everything down. The surplus machinery and the crane were sold off and some thirteen 40-foot-trailer-loads of everything were moved to The Lea along with goodness knows how many pick-up-loads of smaller items.

9

All Change

Indeed the move to The Lea was all change in every sense of the word. Not only did we have to get the business set up and running again, but I also had a house to build for the family to live in. To a point, the business was fairly easy. Positions of machines and suchlike had been decided in advance and the building rewired accordingly. I had bought another crane, a Rapier of 6 tons capacity, which made handling easier. The work; well, that we brought with us. Due to major redundancies in the area labour was not a serious problem and Alan Bremmer, who had been my workshop manager at Cote, decided to come too and, initially at least, to commute from Witney.

The immediate need for somewhere to live was overcome by being able to rent a house in the village that was normally let as a holiday home in the summer. Our arrival in November meant that this was available to us until required the following summer. All our furniture and belongings including Susan's mother's mobile home were stored in the workshop building, suitably covered and protected, but we still had a house to build. Planning permission had been obtained for the land immediately behind the workshop – a lovely site with an extensive view across the valley to Lea Bailey and the Forest of Dean. However this land was covered by a larch spinney which had obviously been planted to screen the building for the houses the other side. I found somebody to fell part of this so that a house could be built; 'What about permission?' he said.

Apparently, despite having been given permission for a house, we still needed a further permission to fell the trees on the site. Now the trees had never been properly thinned and as a consequence were about thirty feet high and eight inches in diameter. The planners were anxious to leave some in place but to leave any sort of screen was totally impractical as on their own these trees would have fallen over, never mind being blown over. Anyway, in due course planning and forestry officers arrived to discuss the matter. The latter walked round the corner of the workshop, took one look and in a deep voice said, 'Fell the bloody lot!' At least somebody knew what he was talking about. So we did just that, although we did leave about a third of the area afforested, partly as a wind break and partly as a small spinney to be ornamental and a source of firewood. The felled timber was sold and we had a stupendous bonfire of all the lop and top leaving a clear site upon which operations could commence.

The house itself was, perhaps surprisingly for this country, bought out of a catalogue! Somewhere we had come across a firm called Design & Materials from Worksop, whose business was the supply of the design and all the materials with which to build yourself a house. And very good they were too. They produced a not-too-glossy brochure with a multitude of house designs in it from which one could take ones pick or not. It sounds daunting, but in reality it was fairly simple to shortlist down. For instance, we did not want a bungalow, which cut out one whole section; we needed four

Left: The first steam-outline diesel locomotive I built (AK17 of 1985) for the Cotswold Wildlife Park at Burford, Oxfordshire, a few miles from Cote, and its bigger sister *Bella* (AK68 of 2003), built some eighteen years later to cope with heavier trains and nearly year-round usage. This railway carries around 150,000 passengers per year.

Right: The premises at Lea Line in 1986, before we moved in, looking very uncared for. The access to the site for our new house was to the left of the office building and new track had to be laid in the yard and into the workshop.

3ft 6in. gauge Simplex 60SD757 stands in the yard at Lea Line awaiting the fitting of ballast weights and couplers before shipment to Ghana Bauxite. This locomotive was built on contract to Simplex and as a consequence carries their works number not AKL's. The yard tracks have not yet been laid at this time.

Our new house at The Lea has reached first floor level and another couple of pallets of bricks are being delivered by the K.20 locomotive No. 15 – which by this time had acquired a cab. Larch spinney behind house and workshop to the right in this scene from 1987.

bedrooms, which restricted matters further, and so on. Having settled on something near to what we wanted, we then played with bits of cut-out card on an enlarged plan to make sure that our furniture, some of it rather large, would fit into the rooms and thus we came up with a design which has proved extremely satisfactory to live in. The kitchen could have done with being a couple of feet longer but one cannot win them all. Despite our looking at and approving the plans, and Planning and Building authorities doing the same, one staircase half-landing goes straight across the middle of a window, but at least it gives light to both floors! Perhaps the most surprising part was that Design & Materials were quite happy for me to buy bricks from the local yard and second-hand slates off the old brewery in Ross. Externally the house is not as elegant as we might have wished but the internal convenience and the outside view compensate for that.

One snag with deciding to build a new house in a new area is that one has lost one's previous supply of sub-contractors and suppliers whom one can trust and one has to start again from scratch. We were lucky in finding a young man, John Turner, who had just started out on his own with a very-second-hand JCB doing groundwork and concreting. He had previously re-floored part of the workshop and he did the site levelling and the footings for the house, some of it in the snow. A bricklayer and his mate were perhaps the least satisfactory of the sub-contractors but they did effectively build the house. Carpenters, electricians, plumbers and plasterers were all good and some of these, including a much better equipped John Turner, are still working for us twenty years later. In the early stages the weather was bad and access was not good down what was to be our driveway. As a consequence, and to the astonishment of most concerned, a railway was laid down said drive and materials brought from the yard by rail. A few bogies and the K.20 did yeoman service.

Come the middle of May we had to move out of the house we were living in, but were again lucky in that there was another house three doors away available for a further month. As anyone who has done it will tell you, building a house is a deceptive business: once the main structure is up and the roof on, one thinks it is finished – but in reality one is only half-way there. Another month was not enough in which to complete the house to what most people would consider a habitable state. Susan was quite determined she was not going to go through the rigmarole of moving into yet another house; she was going to move into our own, whatever. At this stage the house had walls, roof, floors, staircase, windows; but no doors, water system or electricity and only plaster on part of the second floor. We moved in, to the considerable surprise of the plasterers. As most of our own furniture was still stored and not easily got at we found people lending us furniture as though we were either poor newly weds or some sort of refugees! Anyway, with the aid of a long pipe for water and an extension lead from the workshop we made ourselves fairly comfortable. The water supply was interesting, shall we say. The property was on a private supply and this worked somewhat intermittently. I did have a grumble to the local farmer who operated it and received the classic comment, 'Ah, you don't want to worry about that, it's very cheap!' True, it was, about £3 per year, but we would have liked some water. In due course we fitted a very large tank so that we could last three or four days without any incoming water, but ultimately the state of the supply became so bad that we had to go onto the mains. But at this early stage the snag was that, having heated large quantities of boiling water with which to have a minimal bath, there would then be no cold to put with it. Another problem was that as the plaster dried, it dried out into our bedding and clothes which were then thoroughly damp; not nice. We also used mother-in-law's television but thought that when we went out we should perhaps take it with us as there were no doors on the house. In the end we decided it was probably safer in the house than, literally, rolling about in the back of the car. At any other time of year but midsummer we could not have done what we did but we all survived very well and it has been a talking point ever since. The house was finally properly finished with all the carpets down just in time for Patrick's twenty-first birthday in November.

Having done it, I am not sure that I would recommend anyone to build their own house as we did. Undoubtedly one gets much more house for one's money, which was the object of our exercise, but the frustration is considerable. Probably the most annoying bit is the habit of sub-contractors to suddenly ask for something, which one then runs round in circles to get, only to find they do not need it immediately. For instance, the brickies would tell me that they needed more cement and I would go into Ross, get another ten bags and then find they still had four.

Times it happened. Similarly, I think self-builders are deliberately given a hard time by building inspectors; we had endless trouble with a young man who really did not appear to know his job. All sub-contract building workers take on more work than they can properly handle (indeed, do not all businesses?) and one just thinks that good progress is being made with, say, fitting out the kitchen, and they disappear for a week trying to keep someone else happy. I finished up doing a large part of the second-fixing myself as the carpenter suddenly announced he was moving to North Wales with his new girlfriend. However, on the plus side, it is fun to go looking at things and being able to buy them there and then when you see them. We bought a bathroom suite out of a showroom at a knockdown price and were almost given a dishwasher because it had a dent in the side where we would never see it anyway.

I am sure the business suffered because of all these distractions but we won through. The building work went on for another year or so anyway as we sorted a garden out of a building site and generally got the place into the sort of shape we wanted it to be, but most of that could be done at evenings and weekends. As inferred, we did of course bring a fair amount of work with us, notably the 60S locomotive for Simplex and two more locomotives for ICI Nobels Explosives. For the latter we even put some 2ft 6in. gauge into the new track at the works in the hopes that there would be more to come. The Simplex was completed first and in due course went to Bedford for onward shipment to Ghana. The two K.30s were in most respects the same as the previous pair but had slightly increased speed and a few other very minor changes. Five articulated 15in. gauge carriages were built for Cleethorpes Miniature Railway and all this made a good start to a new year in new premises. The lesser work was holding up too, with such things as the sale of the locomotive *Sue* (ex Butlin's, Ayr) to a private individual who

AK21 and AK22 of 1987 for Nobels Explosives were almost identical to Nos 18 and 19. All of them were later repainted in ICI grey and blue as in this shot of No. 21, and very smart they looked too.

Simplex 40SD530 ex-works at The Lea was again built on contract to Simplex and carried their works number even though the take-over of the Simplex business happened whilst it was in build. This locomotive was subsequently re-gauged and raised to clear the electric pick-up rail on Volks Railway at Brighton.

subsequently had it re-bodied and fitted with air brakes for use on the Teifi Valley Railway.

Matters with Simplex were looking good too when they obtained an order for a 40S locomotive from what became Butterley Brick Co. Ltd for their Star Lane Brickworks, near Southend. As agreed, we started building it although they actually made the frame. When it was about half complete the second major turning point in this business occurred. I had a phone call from Martin Everritt, the managing director, asking to come and see me. The upshot was, in six words, 'Did I want to buy Simplex?' In principle at least there was only one answer! In practice we were only interested in buying the locomotive side of the business; others were going to take on the fork lift attachment work which would be primarily spares only. Susan and I took a trip to Bedford to try and see what sort of deal we might expect and also to see what we might be going to get for our money. I, quite obviously, had enormous enthusiasm to take it on; it perhaps meant that Alan Keef Ltd had finally arrived on the railway scene. Martin Everritt and especially his accountant, Cyril Trupp, had equally obviously done their homework and they quite rightly saw us as possibly the only buyer. Between them they had worked out a deal by which I bought the business effectively on hire purchase. The story was that the lease on the Bedford premises had nearly run out and the parent company did not consider the business sufficiently viable to make it worthwhile renewing. Simplex Mechanical Handling Ltd was to remain in business to receive payments from me and to act as a buying house for the Wemys' family tea estates in Africa. The purchase price was £100,000, of which £70,000 was to be paid off in monthly instalments over ten years.

For that we got all the drawings, manufacturing records, patents, the jigs and fixtures for manufacture, all the spare parts currently in stock, fifty-two boxes of nobody knew quite what which had

been going to be exported in South Africa but never was, the gear-cutting machinery, foundry patterns, the choice of any staff who would make the move and, finally, anything that we liked to buy in the disposal auction. All in all it added up to another eight 40-foot-lorry-loads to the works at The Lea! On the staff front, John Palmer, who was assistant design engineer, came permanently – at last I had a properly qualified engineer on the strength. Peter Cross, who probably knew more about Simplex than anyone then living, came for a period of about three months to teach us how the spares system worked and one of their machinists came for a week or two to teach us about gear cutting.

It was all very impressive but there was one ingredient missing which I did not immediately realise, indeed did not properly appreciate for some years. There were no customer records. For the last twenty years or so most of their production had been sold through agents, of whom Railway, Mine & Plantation Equipment covered the bulk of the globe, although there were a few others such as Wigglesworth in East Africa (see Chapter 10), Carl Strom in Sweden and Glastra in Argentina, but Simplex themselves kept no records of the end users. Thus we were unable to do a mailshot to wave the flag and say, 'Here we are now, we can supply any spares or new locomotives that you need.'

It all worked something like this. Simplex kept records of their locomotives by works number and in about three different systems. The drawing office had the technical and build details together with any variations from standard, sales kept a record of type and some basic information such as engine number and the accounts people kept detailed customer and financial records. All this was then paraphrased onto a record sheet that included customer – normally the agent only, except for the UK where they did deal direct – basic details of type, weight and rail gauge, how it was despatched and, of all things, the shipping marks. The latter did at least tell one to which country each locomotive went to, but precious little else. When RMP effectively collapsed a year or two later, by slightly devious means I came by their records, which were something of an eye opener. They kept a similar card index that again detailed their agent as the customer and, in turn, often, but far from always, the agent's customer. Even then it was usually very brief, such as Kalimantan Timber Co. or Benguela Railway. It looked good but in practice was not. The most astonishing part was that although RMP were always most insistent that they should be sole agent for a particular country they themselves were quite happy to deal with two or three different agents within the same country and occasionally deal direct with the end user as well. However none of this helped us greatly even if it made fascinating reading.

To complete this story it is necessary to move forward a year or so to the point where RMP, quite suddenly, ceased to be the firm they were. Again it was said to be a case of a lease running out on their sophisticated offices in Finsbury Square. Again I took advantage and took into my employment Dennis Wilby, whom I had known for many years as I had, latterly at least, bought most of my new rail through RMP – this being easier than dealing with either Raine & Co. or British Steel. I had long thought that to employ somebody to promote and handle sales would be a good thing as I just did not have time to get round my customers as I felt I ought. In addition, more sales were needed to carry the additional costs of moving, Simplex, better premises, and so on. In the event I was proved wrong; either Dennis was the wrong person or my type of business does not lend itself to being 'sold' by anyone other than a principal. In reality there must have been some of both but I think more of the latter. He was with us for about two years and we all parted amicably enough. A bonus he brought with him was the UK agency for the sale of the German MFD re-railing equipment which was excellent equipment and was much used by the MoD, British Steel, British Rail and a number of other large rail-orientated companies. It was useful business but could get a little fraught with the large sums of money involved in a business my size, something Dennis was not used to at all. It was an interesting comparison to those who came from Bedford who were completely unfazed by financial crises!

The Simplex business meant that we now had to start despatching spare parts around the country and around the world on a regular basis, which was something entirely new. Not only that, we had to make or obtain the parts first. Patrick very largely took over the organization of this with the sure guidance of Peter Cross. This was an excellent situation as it meant that having had a longish spell at the sharp end in the workshop he could move on to doing and organizing his own part of the organization without having to work in my shadow. This, I am sure, has something to do with how father and son manage to combine so well to run the show, something which is not always the case in family firms. For UK delivery we had to find a carrier and the first we used – Ailey Parcels, who were conveniently close in Mitcheldean – charged, as all carriers do, on weight. The snag was that they did not have a set of scales so the guesswork was considerable! For overseas shipment we started to use, and still do, MSAS Cargo International in Bristol, now part of the DHL group.

On the locomotive front, the first Alan Keef-built locomotive changed hands from its original customer when we bought the K.30 from Redland Bricks at Nutbourne when rail haulage ceased there, and resold it to Billing Aquadrome complete with a balloon stack chimney to give it a sort of steam outline. At about the this time we completed the Simplex 40S originally ordered from Bedford, but for the railway enthusiast this creates the anomaly that, because this and the Ghana Bauxite loco carried Simplex works numbers, we have built two more locomotives than our works numbers suggest. RMP came up with an order for two second-hand locos for Singapore for which we supplied a Simplex 60S and a very elderly 32/42 but what they were for we were, of course, never told. At the end of 1987, the much travelled K.20, No. 15, was sold to Whessoe along with some new track and one of the carriages built for the abortive park at Filey. Whessoe had been carrying out a major refurbishment of the irrigation canals in Pakistan, of which I believe there are something like 7,000 miles, and they needed some VIP transport for the official re-opening of a dam. There already was some 2ft gauge track on the dam which merely needed refurbishment and extending to the nearest point that could be reached by the official limousine. I suspect it was all used once and that was it, but it was a good sale, so who were we to argue! Through all this there was a considerable flurry of Simplex spares activity which all boded well for the future.

It is worth mentioning that shortly after the move to The Lea I acquired a regular book-keeper/accountant in the person of Bert Raven, who initially kept my books on his own computer at home and subsequently on ours when we moved into the computer age. He was good but dour with it and I probably did not take as much notice of his comments as I should have done, but at least he could produce monthly figures which was good for the bank and gave me some guidance as to what was going on. With his assistance and some good and well-paying orders I was able to give up the use of Manson Factors which in itself was quite a major achievement. As explained, it meant that I had to absorb all the money owed by my customers for a couple of months until they started paying direct. It was well worth it though, simply to have control of one's own destiny.

So onward into 1988, which was a year of large spares orders, building and rebuilding locomotives, together with the usual array of smaller orders. There was a large Simplex spares order, £10,000-worth, from Wigglesworth presumably for Tanzania, and another for Centramin in Peru. A continuing supply of spare parts started for Fiji Sugar Corporation which is about the most far-flung of our customers; one cannot get much further away before one starts coming back! One contract that came with Simplex was a quarterly maintenance contract on two T series locomotives at the Hem Heath colliery of the National Coal Board near Stoke on Trent. These were on surface stockyard work and were reasonably well cared for, not to mention being kept in a very good centrally-heated shed so that working on them was a pleasure. Later in that year we carried out a complete overhaul of one of them, 101T 023, to bring it back to something approaching pristine condition.

I have no record of the precise date, but it was about now that Richardson's asked if we could help with some Planet locomotive spares. F.C. Hibberd Ltd, whose brand name was Planet, had been taken over by the Butterley Company at Ripley and enquiries of them disclosed that they were not interested in a small spares order. I then asked the question as to whether they would lend me the drawings so that I could make the parts for my customer and obviously pay them a commission for the privilege. They were not interested in that either, but I could have the entire Hibberd/Planet drawings if I wanted! Again there was only one answer, even though they ultimately decided that they wanted £500 for them. Thus we made the bits for Richardson's and also a few spares for other people. One of the problems with these drawings, quite apart from being absolutely filthy having been stored in collapsed plan chests over a machine shop principally machining cast iron, is that the drawings are all we have. There is no locomotive register and the drawings often do not refer to locomotive type, are muddled and have some missing. To be able to help I have to have a part number and then can usually trace what is needed. However they are fascinating to look at – Hibberd, a bit like ourselves, were obviously willing to have a go at anything and there are drawings for narrow gauge double bogie locomotives and coke-car locomotives which were actually built, conversions of steam locos to diesel and bucket excavators which were not, tow tractors in many different sizes and configurations, etc, etc.

There came a major rebuild of a 3ft gauge Simplex 40S for Fisons that included a large quantity of new spare parts. Later in the year this was followed by an even more drastic rebuild of a Ruston LB class loco, *Simba* by name, which was fitted with Simplex wheels, K.30 axle boxes and hydrostatic drive. On the new locomotive side, an order was obtained for a steam-outline diesel locomotive generally similar to the one built for the Cotswold Wildlife Park. This was for the East Hayling Light Railway who intended to build a railway on the seafront at Hayling Island – in practice this did not happen then, although it did come to fruition many years later – and a 'temporary' railway was built in Warner's holiday camp. Due to very long delivery from Perkins at the time, this was fitted with a Ford engine that initially gave endless trouble and was eventually replaced under guarantee. Despite this it warranted an article in the Ford industrial-engine house magazine.

This steam-outline locomotive (AK23 of 1987) for the East Hayling Light Railway was very similar to the one built for the Cotswold Wildlife Park but with more in the way of brasswork. It is seen here alongside Patrick's *Woto* (WB2133 of 1924), which had just arrived from a scrapyard in Romford.

Following on an original Simplex enquiry we received an order from Patterson Simons of London for two 10-ton Simplex U series locomotives for a coal mine in South Korea, which were the first Simplex locomotives to carry Alan Keef works plates and numbers, Nos 24 and 25. Having six-cylinder Deutz engines and hydrostatic drive they were fitted with massive hydraulic pumps from Commercial Hydraulics Ltd. These were very good but suffered from having external settings and adjustments. The Koreans had an unstoppable habit of trying to 'tweak' the system to obtain, as they thought, better performance. The result was that having gained it in one place they lost it in another and then could not rectify the position. John Palmer went to South Korea twice, accompanied on one trip by a Commercial Hydraulics engineer, in an effort to get the locomotives to work properly. It seemed that this was perfectly possible, even easy, to achieve, but within days problems started to arise again and in the end we all abandoned any attempt to get the Koreans to operate them properly. There is often an amusing side to these things and on this occasion it came with booking flights through a firm of Korean travel agents to whom I had been recommended. The conversation went something like this:

AK: I believe you can book an employee of mine onto a flight to Seoul?

Agent: Yes, when do they want to travel?

AK: Is Friday possible? (It was then Tuesday.)

Agent: Yes.

AK: (Surprised) O.K. And how much will it cost?

Agent: (Long pause) Not more than £700.

And it did not, and it all worked fine, even on the second trip when John came back *via* Hong Kong and for the same price! In practice, the flight was a Jumbo

Simplex U series locomotives (AK24 and AK25 of 1988) at Kyung Dong coal mine in South Korea. We had to go out to these twice under warranty largely because we could not stop the local engineers 'fiddling' with the hydraulic pump settings.   *John Palmer*

jet with less than half the passenger space fitted out as such and the rest carrying freight.

A further locomotive built later that year was again a Simplex, but a 40SD, for Butterley Brick Co. at Southend for their Starr Lane works. On this occasion we upgraded the very cramped cab of the proper 40S by giving it a frame more akin to the old 20/28 design which allowed a fairly presentable cab to be fitted.

Not so much a contract as a dealing exercise was the purchase, dismantling and subsequent re-sale of the track from the railway at the Stoke on Trent Garden Festival. There was about a mile and a half of this all laid in new 30lbs/yd rail on half main line sleepers together with several very fine sets of points, all of which had only done one season's work. A large proportion of this material went to the East Hayling Light Railway mentioned above but it was fairly liberally distributed about the country to such organizations as the Great Bush Railway, Blagill Colliery, Groudle Glen Railway and most of the remaining sleepers to Bulrush Peat in Northern Ireland. As the site was to be flattened, Susan was also able to acquire some very high quality plants, particularly azaleas which we still have. Despite having been destructive with this railway we were nevertheless able to hire equipment for the building of the rail track at the forthcoming Glasgow Garden Festival, although Severn Lamb bagged the order for the trains.

Dennis Wilby obtained a very large order for new track and turnouts, including a diamond crossover, from Stork Amsterdam B.V., all of which was made by Hocking in South Wales. As with so much of this type of order the regret is that we never get the slightest idea of where it is ultimately going. More useful was a new gold mine being opened by Ulster Minerals at Gortin in Northern Ireland where we supplied a large quantity of rail and turnouts and gained a commission from Wingrove & Rogers on the sale of a BEV battery locomotive. We also had a similarly large order for rail to Bulrush Peat, but were unable to handle a second potential order due to cash flow problems. The margins on selling rail tend to be small and because we had to pay on delivery we simply could not handle too many large orders at once. However, we had plenty of work in hand: the year had started with a spate of wheel work for various customers followed by our carrying out a major restoration-type overhaul of what was the first 60S that Simplex built and which was slightly different from all subsequent ones. This was for Chalkpits Museum, was sponsored by Ibstock Brick and painted in their colours.

Back in Woburn days I had been somewhat amazed to spot what appeared to be a monorail in use on a bridge site when Laing's were building the M1. I did not investigate it at the time and in fact simply squirreled it away as one of the more unusual things I had seen. When the railway business came into being I came across this equipment for real and was occasionally asked for it but never had any. It was originally developed by a firm called Road Machines Ltd of West Drayton for concrete placing which is, I guess, what it was being used for near Woburn. In essence it consisted of track sections, straight and curved, which latched onto legs with the whole being very easily assembled and moved about. On this ran a power car with a tipping bucket of about half cubic yard capacity to which could be added a couple of trailers. The whole thing could be set off and stopped automatically with pegs set into the track sections. In due course Road Machines sold their business to Metalair Ltd with whose business it did not really fit, and they in turn offered this part of it for sale. We were quite interested and I went to have a look. We came to the conclusion that the monorail business would have been worth having, but they insisted on including powered wheelbarrows and the like in the deal and we had no use for that. In the end Rich Morris bought it all and it was hidden away in North Wales, although it does come out on show occasionally. Indeed he has built a steam locomotive to run upon it which is definitely different.

The upshot was that as there appeared to be a market we developed our own version with an effort to simplify some aspects of the original, not least so as not to infringe any patents there might have been. The original was sold for a great many uses other than concrete placement, particularly into sewerage works for removal of sludge from settling tanks, a use for which many narrow gauge railways were also built. Also, apparently, large quantities were sold to the Danish military for troop transport. We, in fact, only ever sold one set, probably because the cost of bespoke manufacture was too high but also because the market had largely disappeared. This was used on a site in London and then bought by a gardening contractor, a Mrs White's Gardens with an address on the Chelsea Embankment, and has never been heard of since. For all that, we have two sets and about 400 metres of track and it has been hired out relatively consistently over the years.

The monorail moves some of its own track components forward to help build a tennis court in a garden in Cheltenham. This was the type of work for which it was designed and built.

An event of some note at this moment was the purchase of the Bagnall steam locomotive *Woto* by Patrick. There were a pair of these, the other being *Sir Tom*, of 3ft 6in. gauge that had worked for British Insulated Callender Cables at Erith, Kent, and which had wound up in a scrap yard in Romford, East London. Both were in remarkably good condition and were even complete with all their undamaged boiler fittings, gauges and so on. Perhaps having spent the last twenty years half buried in old cars had actually done them a favour! The snag was that the man would only sell both of them together and by chance John Quentin was looking for a steam loco as well and a deal was struck. There was much discussion as to who should have which, with Patrick being a bit restricted on price but obviously having the better facilities for subsequent overhaul. John Quentin changed his mind at the very last moment, literally as they were being unloaded from the lorry, but my opinion has always been that Patrick had the better half of the deal.

Thus commenced a five-year slog for him that resulted in a first class restoration effort. *Woto* will reappear in these pages, but in the broadest terms the rebuild involved not only the usual strip down and refurbish but some major works such as cutting the frame in half longitudinally and welding it together again in order to re-gauge from 3ft 6in. to 2ft 0in. This in turn required the making of new axles and re-tyring was required anyway (an un-machined set of tyres came with it). The boiler was remarkably good and needed virtually no work, but for modern usage she had to be fitted with air brakes and the original oil firing converted to coal firing. The painstaking work which Patrick carried out on *Woto* is a tribute to his methodical nature and has stood him in good stead for the quantity and quality of steam locomotive building and restoration work that has been his stamp upon the company.

It was at this point that the Simplex purchase began to pay off on a reasonable scale with spares being supplied to Zambia Consolidated Copper Mines (ZCCM), long time users of Simplex locomotives, particularly the U series. ZCCM was a nationalized company and had a buying office at Ashford, Kent. Over a period of years they bought every conceivable spare part for the U series Simplex from complete wheelsets through driveboxes to hydraulic hoses. The major snag with ZCCM was that their ability to pay depended on the world price of copper. If the price fell then the Zambian Government did not sell copper and there was no money to pay for what they had bought. When they did sell they then went on a buying spree again and so the cycle started once more. In fairness, they always paid in the end, often with interest added, but it could be nail-biting along the way.

Steady sales for a while, again for U series, were spares for the nickel mines of Canada and although this dropped off completely, possibly due to the demise of the agents involved, they have since come back on a small scale some fifteen years later. More significant, and to be a recurrent theme in later chapters, was the supply of spares for T series locomotives in Tanzania – initially supplied through an agent in Hampshire although at the time I do not think we knew where they were going.

January 1989 saw our first introduction to the Woodhead Tunnel, a site that will also become a continuing theme. The background of this is that the Sheffield, Ashton-under-Lyme & Manchester Railway, a constituent of what ultimately became the Great Central Railway, built two parallel single-bore tunnels each some three and a half miles long under the Pennines between Dunford Bridge and Woodhead on their line between Sheffield and Manchester. When, in the 1950s, this railway was electrified, a new double-track tunnel was built alongside and the original tunnels taken over to carry electricity cables. To install and service these a 2ft gauge railway was built beside the trough carrying the cables through one of the bores. We first became involved when Balfour Beatty wanted to hire a locomotive for a repair contract in the tunnel. At the time the only available and suitable machine was a 60S Simplex which, to add to its other peculiarities, had once been a standard gauge shunter at Fort Dunlop in Birmingham. However one of the problems at Woodhead is the limited clearance beside the cable duct. To overcome this problem we set this locomotive 6 inches off-centre on the track, which only made it look strange if you viewed it from the end!

North Gloucestershire Narrow Gauge Railway Society at Ashchurch, near Tewkesbury, had three 2ft 6in. gauge wagons which originated from the Bowater's railway at Sittingbourne. These were of massive construction to carry ten or twelve tons of paper and therefore eminently suitable, in theory at least, for 2ft gauge carriages. In fact they were rather short and had rather high couplings but nevertheless we re-gauged all three as required and at a later date lengthened and added balcony ends with steps together with lowering the couplings on one of them – this one will reappear later – and the other two were sold to Leighton Buzzard who did not use them. In the fullness of time we bought them and converted

them to 3ft gauge, fitted air brakes and sold them to the emergent West Clare Railway in Ireland who fitted their own bodies.

Spares and odd sales were good and on the locomotive front we rebuilt 60S Simplex 11111 for the Teifi Valley Railway – with stand up cab, air brakes and so on – where it now rejoices in the name of *Sammy*. This was followed by a rebuild of the 9½in. gauge double bogie locomotive for John Hall Craggs. As recounted, this emanated from Severn Beach and the only good thing about it was a new twin-cylinder Lister engine. John was persuaded to spend a not inconsiderable amount of money to have a 'proper' hydrostatic drive fitted using a Linde variable swashplate pump and a motor on each bogie chain-driven to the wheels with fairly simple bodywork and a cab large enough to get into easily. It has proved a good and reliable workhorse on his railway. Although the bogies (heavily rebuilt) and engine were original, we did make a new frame for it and thus it qualified as a new locomotive and carries works number 27.

We also overhauled and hired a Ruston LB series locomotive to Butlin's at Minehead for the season. This was painted black with wasp stripes each end and named *Mavis*, being sort of like her namesake in the 'Thomas the Tank Engine' books. I subsequently discovered that this caused consternation amongst those asked to drive the machine! What is in a name, one might ask? At season's end this locomotive was sold to Knebworth House. A much more major exercise was involved in the purchase and subsequent overhaul of two T series Simplex locomotives for Transmanche Link, more usually known as the Channel Tunnel. These were two of three locomotives that had been worked to death by the NCB at Ledstone Luck colliery, the third of which was incomplete and ultimately scrapped. They were delivered to site in May and July of 1989. Later, both of them had the 6DA Dorman engines reconditioned and additional air compressors fitted because again they had to work hard for their living, primarily moving wagons through the wagon maintenance shop.

Butterley Brick Co. came up trumps for a new 40S Simplex and, as No. 28, this was delivered to Southend in June with a stop *en route* for a visit to a Simplex gala at Leighton Buzzard. One is being

a bit *blasé* just passing off a new locomotive in a couple of lines but it was followed by what I have always considered to be one of my more remarkable sales.

Some years previously I had sold a locomotive to a man who had a contract to supply stone for the rebuilding of the spire of Salisbury Cathedral. I had to go to court in an effort to get paid but the bailiffs would not reclaim the locomotive because the quarry, actually a mine, was within an MoD site. In the end I think he went bust and the loco disappeared from view. In an effort to overcome these problem the cathedral itself started to subsidise the operation. The effect was that I managed to sell a locomotive to the Dean and Chapter of Salisbury Cathedral itself and they paid for it in six instalments! I went to see the Clerk of Works and he had an office in a Portacabin on the cathedral roof of all places. The locomotive in question was the one returned from hire at the Woodhead Tunnel and it was also returned to being central on the track.

Also in the line of oddball locomotives was a Simplex sold to William Blyth Ltd for clay haulage at their tileries virtually underneath the Humber Road Bridge. This had been fitted with a Lister HA3 engine which stuck out of the side by about a foot. It has a certain claim to fame as being the last traditional industrial narrow gauge railway of this type in the UK. In similar vein were two 20/28 Simplexes rebuilt for Midland Irish Peat that were fitted with three-cylinder Deutz engines and Lipe automotive clutches rather than the traditional Simplex type, and in which the engine also stuck out one side but in this case only by about one inch. One of this pair was fitted with solid rubber tyres on the wheels. This was something that Midland Irish had already fitted to one of their existing locomotives and found very satisfactory (the locomotive in question is one of only two Ransomes & Rapier locomotives still in existence and is a museum piece in its own right). Somewhat surprisingly, fitting rubber tyres not only increases haulage ability on dry rail but also does it on wet rail too. Midland Irish have to renew the tyres about twice a year but seem pleased with the loco's ability. The idea did not catch on generally, although conversions were tried by both Richardson's and SAI.

Left: This is has been the monorail's more usual application – construction work in confined spaces. In this case the clearance of a stream with a public footpath alongside which had to be kept open. The track had one leg on dry land and one in the water.

Right: Helping Big Brother with pit alterations inside Neville Hall Depot, Leeds.

Monorail afloat. For clearing vegetation from a Norfolk fen the monorail is crossing a watercourse on an inflatable support. The 'land' here was so wet that each track leg had to be supported on an inflated car wheel.

at Ardeer were despatched by rail as wagon-load traffic from a private siding to which it was transported by the internal railway system. British Rail in their infinite wisdom decreed that they would collect only a minimum of twelve wagons from any private siding. The Nobels siding possibly would not even take twelve wagons, so that was the end of that. The other, and similar, event was that at least an equal quantity went out by sea from their own wharf. This was the opposite side of the river from what had been Irvine Docks. As part of a regeneration scheme a new swimming pool and sports centre had been built in the docks area. It was then realized that large quantities of explosive were being loaded only a few hundred yards away from said sports centre. No prizes for guessing which had to close.

The business has always had a measure of professional consultancy work attached to it and there were three of these in quick succession. The largest was an inspection and report on the condition of the entire 2ft 6in. gauge railway system for ICI Nobels at their Ardeer Works. Although somewhat reduced in size, there was then still some twenty-two miles of it and the family described it as my walking holiday in Scotland! I walked the entire thing and inspected all the 150 or so sets of points included with it. Parts of it had been derelict for a long time and were well overgrown although I was told that the storage bunkers served still had explosives in them. This also included a separate but shortish length of track that had wooden rails and served the area where black powder, the traditional gunpowder, was still being made. Indeed inside most of the bunkers or buildings into which wagons went the rails were wood with a bronze strip on the top – the possibility of sparks and explosives do not go together. I also had entry into an area that was very hush-hush where propellants were manufactured which was also handworked with no locomotives allowed.

Whilst this report, in common with all other reports for a similar purpose, inevitably highlighted the problems with the rail system, it may or may not have been used as a lever to close the system down. Although even that is not strictly true, as a very small part of it is, at the time of writing, still working. More likely are two other non-connected events which happened at about the same time. A high percentage of the explosives made

Totally unconnected to this, I had recently been into a military establishment where the British Rail scenario had also closed their private siding and ammunition was now being delivered by road. Thinking that this was all highly unsafe I went to one of my local MP's surgeries to raise the matter. However, one is certainly not supposed to know what goes on military premises and possibly not at Ardeer either. Knowing that I could speak to him about anything without fear of retribution if we were in the House of Commons I asked if Parliamentary Privilege was possible under these circumstances. Without the slightest hesitation he asked if I

One of two Simplex T series locomotives (101T 018 or 020 of 1979) supplied to the Channel Tunnel project. These locomotives were originally part of a batch of three built for the National Coal Board's Ledstone Luck Colliery and, after conversion from 2ft 6in. to 900mm gauge, were primarily used for shunting wagons through the repair and maintenance workshops. Looking decidedly care-worn, they have returned to our yard and await resale elsewhere.

wanted it in writing. Worth knowing. In fairness he did take the matter up and I had a detailed explanation from the Ministry of Defence.

But to return to professional matters. At about the same time I was asked to appear as a professional witness for the defendant in a Health and Safety Executive prosecution relating to an accident on a 10¼in. gauge railway at a nursery near Stirling. Whilst this was a very simple little railway running round in a fairly small circle it was very much subsidiary to the main enterprise. My only grounds for contention were that following the accident somebody who actually knew about railways, preferably HMRI even though 10¼in. gauge is technically outside their jurisdiction, should have been called in rather than just the local HSE inspector. What I did not know until I got into court was that despite somebody having been hurt in the derailment, the owners simply put the train back on the track and carried on as before and in full view of those who had been hurt. I had to admit that that was not best practice but I did feel that a criminal conviction was a bit over the top.

At about the same time I carried out a survey to ascertain the various possibilities for extending the railway at Kilverstone Wildlife Park for Lord Fisher. My own opinion was that the railway was fine as it was; to extend it was simply going to extend train turnround times without being able to charge accordingly. However his lordship was adamant, so the survey went ahead and then in due course the railway was extended. On the original layout Patrick had helped me with the survey work whilst he was still at school and on this occasion Alice, also still at school, was the surveyor's assistant. Some of the work was in a paddock containing a large billy goat and she made the classic mistake of turning her back on him and got well bunted from behind. I am not sure she has forgiven me yet!

Left: One of our rare essays into something smaller than commercially sized 10¼in. gauge equipment was this 9½in. gauge double bogie diesel-hydraulic locomotive (AK27 of 1988) for John Hall-Craggs. This has proved a stolid workhorse over the years and one of its first jobs was spoil removal during the excavations for a new engine shed.

Right: The first public steaming of *Woto* in 1992. This was a private open day for friends, family and those who had been involved in its rebuilding to 2ft gauge. It was thus a precursor to the many open days that have followed.

AK29R of 1989 was a rebuild of a Simplex 60S originally built for East Africa (11004 of 1955) and was one of those locomotives that passed through my hands several times. After being used on the Glasgow Underground it was further modified to 3ft 6in. gauge and fitted with pockets for subsequent fitting of Nigerian Railways couplers. It was, and maybe still is, used for shunting a private siding at Kaduna, northern Nigeria.

Wigglesworth came up with a large order for 1,000 metres of track, ten wagon turntables and ten side-tipping mine skips all for a mining operation in Tanzania, and Dennis Wilby sub-contracted most of this to what was left of Hudson's in Leeds. On a much smaller scale we supplied track materials, including a symmetrical turnout of 745mm rail gauge, and an aluminium boat trolley for a Col. Aylward who had an ancestral castle on an island in a Scottish loch with a small boat being the only means of access.

We attended an exhibition at the NEC in 1998 which was without doubt the biggest flop of a show we have ever attended. There were very few visitors and the exhibition was too large for them to see it all. However a man with whom we had lost contact found us again and came up with an order for a locomotive for shunting

3ft 6in. gauge main-line wagons in Nigeria. For this we rebuilt a Simplex 60S and subsequently built another one for the same customer. More interesting was a later order for an 85S for shunting in Port Harcourt docks for the same concern. This was the first and last locomotive of this type to be built since the 1950s. All these locomotives were supplied without couplers, these being fitted on arrival having been taken off scrap rolling stock. We have supplied some spares since, but from what one hears of the state of Nigerian Railways generally they are probably no longer in use.

The following year started with a sale of some 2ft gauge track and a battery-powered skip frame to Parry People Movers Ltd in Cradley Heath. This was an offshoot of J.P.M. Parry Associates who made hand-operated concrete block and tile manufacturing machinery for export to third world countries in which I think they were, and are, reasonably successful. The Parry People Mover was, and again is, intended to be an environmentally friendly form of urban transport because its motive power is drawn from a large flywheel which is driven up to high speed from a static source and from which the power is subsequently drawn. Despite claiming numerous grants for innovation this is not a new idea and indeed Sentinel built a shunting locomotive using the same principle between the wars – it was not successful.

Having converted said skip frame to flywheel power and run it around their office building I was persuaded to build a more substantial underframe and to be paid in shares in the company for which privilege I became a director. That lasted about a couple of years until somebody came along with better environmental pretensions than myself and paid very good money for my shares with which I bought myself a boat! Later we built a test track for the first serious flywheel drive vehicle at Himley Park. Having said all that, in 2006 a Parry People Mover was authorized for use on

Before I took up sailing as a pastime I built *Taffy* in my spare time as though I had nothing better to do! Its number and date, AK30 of 1990, are somewhat arbitrary as the project took about five years to complete and that was about the halfway point of construction. This portrait was taken much later at Leighton Buzzard alongside the original de Winton, *Chaloner* of 1877. The cylinders, some of the motion work and a few other odds and ends are original, the rest is new.

the Stourbridge branch where it is used for off-peak and weekend services. We supplied K.40 wheelsets and drive box for this vehicle which has an LPG engine on board to power up the flywheel, although this does regain energy when used for retardation when going downhill.

When we bought Simplex they told us that we could expect, roughly annually, at least one very large spares order which would make it all worthwhile. In 1990 it did actually happen in the form of a whole string of orders from Fiji which totalled some £35,000. The year was good in respect of other spares supplied as well, including Ghana Bauxite and £3,000-worth sold to agents in Paris for Madagascar. In similar vein, we sold some Jubilee track to the Crown Insolvency Agency for delivery to a company in Frome. Why and what for? The two Simplex T series locomotives at Hem Heath colliery were completely overhauled including reconditioned engines and torque

Above: AK36 of 1990 was almost identical to 29R except that it was new throughout and had a different logo on the headstocks. Mounted on skids, knocked down, wired to a container flat and partially shrink-wrapped it is now ready for shipment to Minna in Nigeria.

Left: For the same customer and destined for Port Harcourt docks is this 10-ton Simplex 85S (AK37 of 1990). This was the first of this type of locomotive to be built for some thirty years, and almost certainly the last.

Below: The exception that proves the rule. One of our few excursions into standard gauge locomotives was the supply of this Ruston 88DS (RH46625 of 1962) to the Docklands Light Railway. Due to our having a full workshop at the time the overhaul was subcontracted to Esca Engineering Ltd of Wigan and is seen on the low loader ready to leave their works in 1991.

convertors, fitting new cab heaters and so on. The first true steam-outline diesel locomotive that I had built at Cote – for the Cotswold Wildlife Park – was also in for a major overhaul.

On the steam locomotive front, new axles were made for the Orenstein & Koppel, *P.C. Allen*, at Leighton Buzzard and a new boiler designed for both *Chaloner* and my own de Winton, *Taffy*. This stage of progress with the latter settled the official year of build, being roughly half way through. Also, we made wheelsets for four 15in. gauge locomotives being built by a consortium headed by Brian Gent with the idea that the members would have one each. These were based on the Heywood design *Katie*. In the event, financial and other problems got in the way and ultimately only one has ever been completed.

Although not track-laying in the accepted sense of the word, over the years we have made up and laid several ghost train tracks. Essentially these are a single guide rail with a round bar electric pick-up rail alongside, the

Swee' Pea (AK31 of 1990), an 0-6-0 10¼in. gauge locomotive for Hastings Miniature Railway. When delivered the chimney was fractionally too high for the engine shed doorway, but a sledge hammer (to the doorway) soon solved that problem!

locomotive built low with a dropped driving position and flame-protected engines. Whilst the latter were not flame-proofed as understood by British Coal they were to a recognized standard for flammable areas of operation. There were no electrics in the accepted sense; recoil starters were fitted, hand klaxon horns and the headlights were fully enclosed, unswitched and only worked when the engine was running. These were being bought on Letter of Credit to RMP and delivery of the Perkins engines was tight for the due-date required for shipment. RMP was made very aware of this and given the opportunity to extend the L/C as they saw fit. In fact the engines came through as planned and the locos were ready for shipment on time. No ship available! Thus RMP had let the Letter of Credit run out and had to go back to Nigeria for an extension which the Nigerians were under no obligation to give. Because of the L/C arrangement we had not been paid anything along the way – RMP reluctantly paid us £40,000 on account a month later, I think only out of fear that we might go broke and they could thus lose their locomotives altogether. They were finally shipped three months later, we got paid and after a struggle also got some interest on the money as well. It nearly broke us. The only further surprise with these locomotives is that we have never heard anything about them since. No spares enquiries, no reports from anybody, nothing.

former acting as a guide for an electrically propelled car around a short track in a dark room in which various 'ghostly' events occur. I always worked these out most carefully on paper first with all the curves, usually all the same radius, and straights calculated so that when on site it was simply a case of fixing to the floor. The first of these was at Whitley Bay, near Newcastle on Tyne, closely followed by one for Flamingoland at Malton, Yorkshire. Over the next few years these were followed by similar installations at Drayton Manor Park, Sandy Bay Park, near Exmouth, and at Yarmouth Pleasure Beach.

No. 31, our first 10¼in. gauge steam-outline diesel locomotive, was built for the Hastings Miniature Railway. Patrick Talbot, who runs this railway, is the last person one would think able and willing to buy a new locomotive and, indeed, buy subsequent spares and service for it as required but nevertheless he has been. This is perhaps an unfortunate little line; it has great potential but the local authority who own the site will not give him any security of tenure so he is obviously unwilling to spend any more than he has to. Some ten years after this event the council had plans to revamp the whole railway, extend it, and make it serve a useful purpose. The snag was that they wanted whoever then took it on to spend about £200,000 altering the seafront. Not surprisingly there were no takers and Patrick soldiers on from season to season as best he can. On a lighter note, yours truly measured the height of the tunnel cum engine shed but when delivered the chimney was just too high. So it was out with a sledge-hammer and knock a chunk out of the lintel to give clearance. Shades of Stephen Taylor at Cricket St Thomas and his chain saw! He wanted the locomotive named *Swee' Pea* after the daughter of Popeye and Olive Oil in the cartoon series. However he did not know just how it was spelt and as she only appears very occasionally in the series I spent a happy afternoon in a shop dealing in second-hand comics until I found a reference to her. All in the name of business, you understand!

Then disaster all but struck. RMP obtained an order for two K.30M locomotives for Nigeria Coal. These were basically a K.30

10

World Traveller

In 1988 there started a spell of travelling the world, for myself primarily and, to a lesser extent, Patrick – both in search of, and because of, overseas business. As will be seen, this has tended to be to the less well-known countries, many of which have been, or still are, well down the so-called Third World list. Most were part of the former British Empire or were very closely allied to it. The experiences have been fascinating, have not always brought the business expected, but overall have probably paid for themselves well enough. We have both been very lucky in meeting and being entertained by people in these countries who were willing to take the trouble to make us at home and tell us about the local way of life. Ex-patriots, British or otherwise, were, I think, always pleased to see a face from 'the Old Country' with whom to talk about something different from their daily grind. It is said that foreign travel broadens the mind and opens the bowels. It can, but one survives!

Prior to this, my first overseas trip of note had been to Qatar in the Persian Gulf, and some first impressions of foreign travel were interesting. Being a Muslim country there was no alcohol, which does not bother me, but there was red and white grape juice available with meals, which was very nice, together with a water waiter always at one's elbow. Avenues of trees are planted along the dual carriageways, but these have to be watered on a daily basis. The traditional Arab souk is a glorious place where you can buy literally anything, but must not worry about the smells. I went off the oil-rich ex-pat Brits when somebody's wife told me, in all seriousness, that she did not like coming back to England as she could not shout at the shop assistants. Never drive into a camel – its body is at just the right height that it will fall onto you and invariably crush you to death. In the event of a road accident nobody does anything at all until the police arrive. In Qatar you are only allowed to sound your horn if there is somebody walking in the road – but as there is *always* somebody walking in the road the cacophony can be awful! Added to all this was the 1982 winter in England – I just managed to get to the station, Heathrow and away as the snow came. I sat in the sun and saw it all on television whilst the family were having a horrendous time with frozen pipes, milking not only our house cow but another one along the road as well. I'm not sure I've ever really been forgiven for going at that moment!

The real start of overseas travel was to Tanzania, shortly after the Simplex take-over. It was instigated by J. Hugh Leslie of Wigglesworth & Co. who had been Simplex agents for East Africa. Once again I was lucky to be introduced to the country by somebody who had spent half a lifetime there and who introduced me to people who in turn became generous friends. The idea was to try and reinvigorate the Simplex connection, although in practice it was probably too late for reasons which will become apparent. It does not stretch the point too far to say that Wigglesworth *were* the sisal industry in East

Left: The multi-gauge set of points in our yard gives a straight run through at 2ft gauge and 2ft 0in., 2ft 6in., 3ft 0in. and 3ft 6in. on the curve into the workshop. By the chance of rail sizes, the 3ft/3ft 6ins rails give 10¼in. gauge as well. This also gives a good head-on view of one of the K.30M locomotives protected and ready for shipment to Nigeria.

Right: Two K.30M mines locomotives (AK32 & 33 of 1990) for the Emulu Colliery of Nigeria Coal. These were fitted with flame-protected engines with inertia starters and fully enclosed but limited electrical equipment. The curious part about this pair is that we have never heard anything about them since – or even if they arrived!

My introduction to Africa was sitting beside the pilot of a light aircraft from Dar es Salaam to Tanga, and here we are approaching Tanga airport. On arrival, when I enquired for a taxi I was directed to the control tower where they did indeed find one for me!

would be. It all sounds ridiculous but, had I not been, the whole trip would have been thrown into jeopardy and probably my credibility with it.

Before proceeding, and because Tanzania will become a recurrent theme from here on, it is necessary say a little of and about the country and its sisal industry which was my primary reason for being there. The country became German East Africa during 'The Great Game' that was the splitting up of Africa between the European powers. With the defeat of Germany in the First World War, it became the British Protectorate of Tanganyika until independence as Tanzania in 1966 (incidentally, the Great War lasted a fortnight longer in East Africa because the combatants did not know that the Armistice had been signed, and those who had the misfortune to fight in both places said they preferred the Western Front!). The island of Zanzibar remained separate until it became part of Tanzania in 1985. Until its abolition in 1807, Zanzibar was the centre of the East African slave trade to the Gulf states, India

Africa, particularly Tanganyika, now Tanzania. They not only were very substantial end users in their own right but also sold Simplex locomotives to all the other sisal estates to boot. According to Peter Cross there was a time when one loco in four went to East Africa – and in those days that meant one a week! This was one of the few areas where RMP were not Simplex agents although even then they did manage to sell a few locomotives there as well.

The arrangement was that I would meet Hugh Leslie and his wife at the Mkonge Hotel in Tanga on a certain date. So I had most of the available jabs and inoculations that are possible, started on the anti-malaria pills and took the KLM flight to Dar es Salaam. I had been well primed on the dire problems of Africa generally, and Tanzania in particular, by RMP and others, but most usefully had been given a name, Rajab, in Dar es Salaam, who would meet me at the airport and generally assist as required. And did I need it! In those days one needed to take US$65 in cash with one, any other currency being frowned upon, which was then compulsorily converted into Tanzanian Shillings at a ruinous rate dictated by the government. Rajab saw me into the Kilimanjaro Hotel which was in the midst of a power cut, so we had to climb the back stairs more or less through the kitchens to reach my room. Of course no power, so no water either, although as I later discovered the water could go off on its own independently of the electricity supply. A great introduction to Tanzania and what was then the best hotel in its capital city! I loved it.

Then arose the question of getting to Tanga by the following afternoon. The options: the train only ran on alternate nights and not that one; I was strongly recommended against the buses and anyway the overnight ones were all fully booked; the Air Tanzania flight the following morning was cancelled (experience would reveal that it nearly always was), which left the only alternative of a charter flight. After much haggling I duly left Dar es Salaam in a five-seat Cessna and $200 poorer. By not arriving at any recognized time there were of course no taxis at Tanga airport. To obtain one I was sent to the control tower and told to ask there! Indeed they found a taxi for me and I was at the Mkonge Hotel by the time I said I

This is sisal. The leaves are cut from the bottom up and crushed for the fibre inside them. Each leaf has a vicious point at its end. The plant has about a 10-year life before replanting is required.

and the Far East. As a consequence of this and the much inter-marrying that inevitably went on, the Tanzanians are not black in the true African sense but are more coffee coloured. They are not so tribally inclined, as are, say, the Kenyans. Also, and probably because of this interbreeding, they tend not to be concerned about colour and always have a smile on their faces, however hard life is. This was exemplified in Kenya on one occasion. When in Africa I like to ask for my coffee without milk rather than black but on one occasion in Nairoibi I forgot and the waiter reiterated a long drawn out *blaaackkk* in protest. When I tell this to my friends in Tanzania they hoot with laughter saying they would never be so silly. They would not, or maybe they are just having a dig at the Kenyans!

Due to this history, the country is also roughly equally divided between Christians and Muslims but they do manage to live in reasonable harmony with each other and have the benefit of having public holidays to suit both religions! At about the time of my first visit the country's official language changed from English to Swahili which is spoken by most of the population anyway so it was no real change. English was, and remains, the language of business. Swahili is supposed to be an easy language to learn although my efforts have not been at all successful, but I think if one was there for six months or so one would soon pick it up. In my experience I have begun to understand a good deal in only a fortnight.

As African countries went following independence, Tanzania had a fairly benevolent entry into the international community under President Julius Nyerere. However, in the mid-1970s he produced something very akin to the Cultural Revolution under Chairman Mao of China. This was based on the theory of Africa for the Africans, that everyone should have their own shamba or small farm to work and should have as little contact as possible with the outside world. Everything of national importance was nationalized, railways, electricity, hotels and so on, including about 80 per cent of the sisal industry. Because Africans were not supposed to deal with the outside world the indigenous Indian population came into their own as middle-men, something they were and are very good at anyway; a sizeable Greek minority left altogether. By the time I reached Tanzania in the late eighties this proud country was on its knees, living on aid handouts from the Western world. I think it was so bad that the country was actually short of food, even in hotels frequented by Westerners. My view at the time, and I think history has born me out, was that the country had then just managed to change presidents from its founding father to President Mwinye without bloodshed. In Africa at that time this was no mean achievement, and thus Tanzania would recover its status in the world.

Having given a potted history of Tanzania it is probably

My first visit to a sisal estate railway saw this Simplex 32/42 with a train of bogie wagons delivering rail for a new track to reach the area where newly cut sisal was just becoming available. In many ways the operation was similar to peat operations in the UK where temporary tracks were laid to the current point of operations.

My tour of sisal estates on behalf of the Tanzania Sisal Authority saw some Simplexes which required very little to make them operational. Indeed I think this somewhat battered 60S had been used occasionally until very recently. This particular estate, unusually, made carpets from sisal in their own on-site factory. The material in the background is the waste from doing this.

necessary to say something of sisal and the sisal industry itself. Sisal is a plant best described as looking like a giant pineapple with long stiff leaves growing from the stem, each with a murderous point on the end. The nearest English lookalike is the yucca plant. It is these that are cut and crushed to extract the inner fibres which in turn are spun to produce sisal string, rope and even carpets. The leaves do not regenerate and are cut from the bottom up. As a consequence it is necessary to clear and replant every ten years to maintain production. This replanting has major organizational, labour and cost implications and it was not doing this that crippled the Tanzania Sisal Corporation and many of the smaller growers. In addition, it was at about the same time that polypropylene appeared on the scene which in turn took away

most of the market for rope and baler twine. Sisal is not indigenous to East Africa, and it all started prior to the First World War when 1,000 seeds rolled up in an umbrella were smuggled out of Mexico, where it is. These were planted in Tanzania by one Alfred Hirdock, who thought the climate and soil might be about the same. Of these only sixty-eight grew to fruition, but on those sixty-eight was built a considerable part of the economy of Tanganyika/Tanzania and a chunk of Kenya as well.

And so I came to be introduced to Amboni Ltd – by far the largest sisal producer in Tanzania with the exception of the nationalized Tanzania Sisal Authority itself. Kurt Klien was their chief engineer and I travelled with him and Hugh Leslie to visit a couple of sisal

estates and their main workshops. The latter were something of an eye opener as they were well capable of doing literally anything required to their machinery of all types. This even included a temperature and humidity-controlled workshop for the overhaul of diesel injection pumps. Of the two estates visited, one had a railway and the other never had had. On the former, some elderly 32/42 Simplexes were hauling trains of sisal leaf over temporary track in a manner very similar to the British peat industry. This line also included a tunnel under the main road and it was not the only one I saw. I think this was, in fact, not a terribly big estate – others I went to later were huge and rail hauls of ten to fifteen miles and more were not out of the way. On a subsequent trip I

Left: Lugongo Estate. This is what a sisal railway and train should look like and the re-engining of two 3½-ton Simplexes was really our only success in the rehabilitation of sisal railways. Even this was ultimately abandoned following a change of management. This train is approaching the mill after a journey of possibly ten kilometres.

Right: Although nobody has yet bothered to paint it, this T series which is loading cane out in the fields has been rebuilt with a new Perkins engine, JCB gearbox and shaft drive to the wheels. I counted no less than 103 wagons in its train. The locomotive with it is a Simplex U series into which TPC themselves have shoehorned the transmission out of a metre gauge Simplex shunter! Note the snow-covered summit of Mount Kilimanjaro above the man in the red shirt. 1998.

Left: As with the 60S on the previous page, this Simplex 32/42 looks as though it only needs someone to swing the handle for it to be on its way. The estate near Mombo was in a truly spectacular location.

Right: TPC Ltd, near Moshi, operated a fleet of hydraulic drive Simplex T series locomotives. This one is shunting a train of sugar-cane backwards over the weighbridge to the mill in 1988. To give an idea of the scale of this operation the railway extends to some fifty miles and it is twelve miles from the main gate to the factory and offices!

visited their Vipingo Estate in Kenya about twenty miles north of Mombasa. This was another large set-up with railway matters ruled by an irascible Swiss who 'knew it all' and was busily modifying Simplex locomotives without a great deal of success. Many have tried this, largely unsuccessfully, but in the end he did buy some substantial quantities of spare parts. Even so, tractors and trailers were beginning to appear and the end was nigh.

Hugh Leslie also introduced me to Andrew Nkusi at Tanzania Sisal Authority, with whom I have had a great deal to do and who remains a good friend. Aside from the decline in the sisal market TSA had suffered particularly badly from being politicized. In absolute terms its estates had been plundered for short term gain.

Sisal acreage had not been replanted, rails had been sold off or stolen for fencing, locomotives and wagons had been run into the ground literally or the personnel who knew about them had left or died of AIDS. I made one memorable trip when I visited most of their estates to see what could be salvaged from the wreckage as far as railways were concerned. This took me to places in the back of beyond that no tourist would ever reach, where I saw something like 120 Simplex locomotives of which about twenty-five could be rescued at modest cost. There was one estate that had most of its rail system still there even if parts of it had been uplifted and just laid aside. In most of the others the overall system had gone but rail was still used to deliver sisal leaf into the de-corticator and often to take

wet sisal out to the drying grounds. These short lines were worked either by manpower or by tractor which destroyed the track and made a bad situation worse. The idea was to rebuild locomotives to work these, thus saving a tractor that was much more valuable elsewhere. Despite the efforts of myself and Andrew, there was never enough money or will-power to kick off even a pilot scheme.

One of the problems of the sisal railways was that they were all built very lightly, only 16–20lbs/yd rail and that laid more or less straight on the ground. This was fine when the system was set up with only 2½- or 3½-ton locomotives. But then the Simplex 32/42 appeared on the scene at around 4½ tons which could obviously haul more and with good maintenance the track would just about stand it. But then Simplex in their infinite wisdom replaced it with the 60S, weight five to seven tons, and whilst again haulage loads increased the track just could not withstand the extra loading. By this time maintenance was deteriorating and, as happened in England, anything that would do an apparently better job was acceptable. Despite these trends I did have one notable success and that was at Lugongo Estate, again in the middle of nowhere, some thirty miles north of Tanga. Visiting Lugongo was like turning the clock back. The whole place was immaculate, as I imagine they all must have been in the great days of the industry. Gates and fences were all intact, offices and workshops were well equipped (if a little antiquated) and even the stones beside the roadways were painted white! All this was ruled over by a Mr Tenga for the Dutch parent company. We provided two conversion kits for 20/28 Simplexes and Patrick went out to fit them. Although we never heard anything officially I believe there were, unusually, engine problems with these and they did not last too long.

My first trip to Tanzania, and indeed each subsequent one, has involved a visit to TPC Ltd at Moshi. This is a large sugar estate in the shadow of Kilimanjaro, which at nearly 20,000 feet is Africa's highest mountain, where they run a fleet of Simplex U and T series locomotives, and includes some fifty miles of 2ft gauge track. Twice I travelled from Tanga by train, in itself interesting. Trains left Tanga at 6.30 p.m. and nobody, but nobody, would give me an arrival time in Moshi, merely 'tomorrow morning'! The nearest I got was between 8.30 and 11.00. It was a sleeping-car train and cost the equivalent of £6 for 250 miles, so I suppose one could not ask for too much. Mind you, there was no glass in the windows and only a little electric light when they twisted the wires together between carriages! On one occasion my return journey to Dar es Salaam was equally interesting – the only available transport was a TPC lorry; it

took fourteen hours with a driver and mate, neither of whom spoke English; I even survived a Tanzanian lorry drivers cafe on the way.

I arrived in the last days of English management and was welcomed into a dying world of colonialism. Money was scarce and nobody had great enthusiasm – they were simply working their time out. But as always in Africa there were curiosities that I still do not understand; for instance, great effort would be put into sorting out old nuts and bolts for when one was wanted, but a new one could be bought quite easily in Moshi town – I saw them for sale. Whether money was really that tight or there was some sort of principle involved I shall never know. I was given a bungalow, very basic but it had a shower (cold only), and I ate in the visitors' canteen, but the whole ambience was from a different era. One outstanding merit was that I knew the water came direct from a 450-foot-deep borehole and was therefore drinkable, about the only place I trust in East Africa.

Over the years we have done a great deal of very good business with TPC, and fairly easily as well, which has largely and unobtrusively paid for my unrewarded efforts with the sisal industry. The big jobs came much later through a firm of German agents when we fitted new engines and transmissions complete with new wheelsets and drive boxes for the Simplex T series locomotives. John Palmer went out twice to see these fitted. Being an avid golfer he fitted in well as TPC have their own nine-hole course! These transformed the original locomotives and to see them hauling 100 wagons of sugar-cane is a sight to behold. I also sold them the prototype (and only) K.100 locomotive at a time when they were desperate for anything that would haul cane. This has proved a slight embarrassment as it is obviously not as powerful as the Ts but TPC will not be convinced of this and as a consequence it has suffered failures due to overloading. There's a moral there somewhere. At the time of writing, the estate has been taken over by Mauritians, who are big in the sugar-cane industry, and they have visibly improved the whole place and almost re-laid the entire railway system. It is there to stay

Brunei. I was supposed to be able to plot a suitable course for a 2ft gauge railway from this boat on the river! In the end I did get some maps with contours on them and was able to make sensible suggestions.

which is some consolation even if I have lost an order for a new locomotive to Schoma of Germany primarily because at the time I could not give a fast enough delivery.

A final snippet on Tanzania. The Mkonge Hotel was originally built in 1952 as the sisal growers' club complete with a hall for entertainment, dances and the like. In those days everyone travelled by sea and prior to its building dances and so on were arranged so that the public rooms of calling ships could be used for the purpose. This was fine until a ship was delayed and did not arrive on schedule. It gives a whole new meaning to being 'All dressed up and nowhere to go'!

I had a strange telephone call from a man in the Cotswolds who knew somebody in Turkey who was concerned with a railway in a bird park. All very vague and we got off to a bad start, or at least he did, because from something I said he thought I was a Freemason, which I am not, and so we should be brotherly and pally together. However, we went to Ismir and I met his colleague and was introduced to the proposed scheme for a railway in a wetland bird reserve. There was great fanfare of trumpets whilst they opened a new visitor centre and I found myself as honoured guest who had come all the way from England to advise on a railway system for this new park. The Turks had been shooting wildfowl across this area for centuries and I think the whole thing was a ploy to demonstrate how environmentally friendly they had become and could they now join the European Union please?

Adjoining the site was a salt works and somebody said they thought there was an old locomotive there and would I like to see it? But of course I would. I found a huge 2ft gauge system for handling salt from the evaporation pans to the works. Never mind one old loco, I lost count at twenty-six – all in running order! They were mostly either Diema or Schoma. More astounding was to see trains being loaded with a large hydraulic excavator from a bank of salt some thirty feet high and upwards of a mile long. I also found a small G series Simplex in a drift coal mine some forty miles inland from Ismir but that operation has since closed down.

The highlight of my trip was a visit to Ephesus. I had somehow never imagined a Roman city being so huge. In the town near the railway station it was sobering to walk around the ruins of the Basilica of St John to which Mary, the mother of Jesus, had retired after the crucifixion. I still have the very beautiful Turkish mat that I bought in a shop on the opposite side of the road. The man I went with was setting up a second home in the area and I went on some furniture buying trips with them. Some five or six years later I was involved as a witness in a court case when he and his wife parted company as to which of them had actually paid for the furniture. I had no real idea!

I happened to be in Turkey on the Sunday that was census day. Now in Turkey you do not fill in a form of how many people there are in your house on a particular day but you stay at home and are counted. Everyone, but everyone, stays put; there were a few taxis but otherwise no buses, no trains, no shops open, nothing moving in a city of several hundred thousand inhabitants. Being a visitor I could move around, albeit only on foot, and it was a most extraordinary sensation, like being the last man on earth. It was so quiet that a few children were playing football on the city's inner ring road! Except that you do not have to go to your home city to be counted, it was almost biblical and a re-run of how Mary and Joseph came to be in Bethlehem.

Although not strictly in order I had an interesting experience on the occasion of my first visit to de Efteling in Holland. Having landed at Schiphol airport I heard that dreaded announcement over the public address system, 'Would Mr Keef just arrived from Birmingham please go to airport information!' Well I did, where there was a message asking me to ring a certain number. The next problem was to obtain some small change because when converting currency one is always given the largest possible denomination notes and certainly not any coins. Not useful when one has to make a phone call. Eventually that was overcome and understanding achieved as to how a Dutch call box worked, to find out that Christian Fuller who was supposed to be meeting me had had a car accident on the way to the airport. Would I take a taxi? De Efteling would pay for it when I got there. The distance was about eighty miles! Well, I got there without problem, but when I did the taxi driver would not let me out of his sight until he was sure of being paid. I cannot say I blame him.

On a much later occasion, on one of my visits to Ravensburger Spieleland, I travelled back to de Efteling by train, involving the spectacular journey down the Rhine Valley. I stayed in a small hotel on the Dutch–German border that overlooked the Rhine and I was kept awake at night by the throb of hard working diesel engines pushing the continual stream of barges up-river against the current.

My next venue, as it were, for world travel was Singapore, when we had an enquiry for a railway in Singapore Zoo. I went out to discuss the possibilities and my instructions on arrival were to phone Mr Bernard Harrison to arrange actual time and place for our meeting. I did, and spoke to his obviously Chinese wife who had a message for me. Imagine my surprise when the man himself, with a name like that, turned out to be as Chinese as they come. In due course we won the order in front of Severn Lamb for which they have never really forgiven us. My stay in Singapore was enlivened by visiting a number of firms, such as Bian Huat Hardware, with whom I had been in contact over the years and to whom I had sold second-hand locomotives. It will be remembered that these were used for coastal logging operations, so imagine my astonishment when in one yard I found no less than forty-two, yes, forty-two, brand new Jenbach Pony locomotives and in another several hundred tons of new rail and literally hundreds of new wheelsets for these operations. Some of the Jenbach locos were original with a built-in single-cylinder engine and others had a Spanish twin-cylinder instead. At around that time an embargo had been placed on this type of logging so what happened to them all I do not know. I am a great lover of Chinese food and one of the joys of Singapore was being taken to the Chinese restaurants that the Chinese themselves frequent – something entirely different. Business-wise, a few spares sales to Indonesia came from it, and I always had a welcome at the Zoo when I passed that way again.

And pass that way again I did, several times. Because no business actually resulted the railway details will be dealt with later in Chapter 13, but I did several things in the course of looking at possibilities that other people actually pay money to do. The first was a visit to Brunei with a view to a railway into the hinterland to take tourists to a proposed lodge from which they could then walk into the rain forest. The intriguing bit was a boat journey in a local ferry. This was a covered boat perhaps twenty to thirty feet long with two of the biggest possible outboards on the back that took us to a small town from which the railway was due to start. From here we took a dug-out-type canoe (with only one outboard) onwards to the point roughly where the railway might finish. The river became increasingly fast flowing and shallow, with the effect that we had to get out and wade, partly to lighten the boat and partly to drag it over the shoals. From this exercise I was supposed to be able to judge the best place to put a railway! This trip was with a wild Austrian with a local wife, and another exercise he took me on was to rescue a couple of monkeys from the garden of a relative of the Sultan. The fleet of Mercedes and Rolls Royce cars in the garages had to be seen to be believed. But then, rescuing monkeys is all in a railway engineer's line of business!

I subsequently went back – Susan came with me on this occasion – and dealt with a collection of Chinese as my Austrian appeared to have disappeared. In fact he had not and was very cross that I had seemed to go behind his back. Hence, I think, no business. Foreign travel seems very glamorous and can be fun but it can also, as on this occasion, be damned hard work. Due to a flight delay we arrived in Brunei exactly twenty-four hours after leaving Heathrow and I was immediately bounced into a meeting with half a dozen Chinese that I had never met before, this was followed by dinner for both of us with the same and a few more of their colleagues. For good measure they then insisted that we should go out with them to see the illuminations! We were just about dead on our feet. More interesting was breakfast the following morning when we were taken to a Chinese eatery where whole families obviously went for breakfast. There was oriental food such as one has never seen before, and added to that was trying to make polite conversation whilst at the same time attempting not to make too many mistakes or offend.

The illuminations we were taken to see were in fact Jeradong Park, a theme park of no mean proportions. We had had a stray enquiry for a railway supposedly for the entertainment of the children of one of the Sultan's wives. That came to nothing so far as we were concerned, but the idea had developed into a full blown theme park for the use of the children of the entire country which, it has to be said, is not large. The big thing was that everything was free! This sounds great but in my opinion it actually put something of a blight on the place. There was no excitement in the air, children just queued up, although that was rarely necessary, and got on any ride they wanted. They were just thoroughly *blasé* about it. It almost was not fun! From here we moved on to Mulu caves which, in reality, was only about fifty miles from where we were in Brunei. However getting there involved three separate flights. The first of these was international to an off-shore island which got us into Malaysia. The second was to the oil town of Miri on the north Borneo coast where we were put up in possibly the most gorgeous hotel I have ever stayed in; light and airy and running down to the South China Sea, it belonged to our hosts and we were treated accordingly. The third flight was inland to Mulu itself and is the only time I have been weighed onto a flight along with my baggage ('Please, to stand on scales with bags!').

Mulu caves are the world's largest and were only discovered relatively recently. The main cavern will supposedly take St Paul's cathedral five times over with room to spare. Its further claim to fame is that every evening some five million bats go out to forage over distances of fifty miles and more and then return the following morning. We were given a retired Ghurka as a guide for a rapid three-mile walk along raised wooden walkways to the caves which included a visit to the lesser caverns by weak torchlight because the power was off. We did see the bats and it was well worth the effort. Susan tends to be an unusually fast walker and on our return trip our Ghurka was distinctly out of breath!

At Chhatak Cement Works in Bangladesh, limestone is delivered by barge during the rainy season when the river is high. It is simply unloaded overside and when the river levels drop wagons are taken down tracks like this to retrieve it for use.

From here we returned to our host's base in Kuching, where we were lodged in the Hilton (no less) where there always seemed to be a flunkey to open doors when required. We also had the use of a chauffeur-driven Mercedes if required. I do not think they could quite understand that we actually liked to walk and to eat at the local Chinese food stalls. I should dearly like to go back to Kuching, which was once the base of the Brookes family, the so-called White Rajahs of Sarawak, who ruled the country as their own personal fiefdom for a hundred years or so until the middle of the twentieth century.

So we moved on to Singapore again, where hotel accommodation was not quite so lavish, as we

When Patrick went to Taggerhat Quarry, which was one source of the limestone for Chhatak Cement Works, they laid on this special train for him to collect him from the river jetty. He was the first European to go there for over seven years.

were now paying for it ourselves! Singapore had changed and many of the Chinese eating and shopping areas had been tidied up or swept away, with those that remained very much up-market and ridiculously expensive. It no longer seemed possible to sit on an upturned bucket in the street and have one's shoes repaired as I had done in the past. It was also that time of the Chinese year when moon cakes are the rage. My advice is to avoid them, they are the driest of dry sponge mix. The whole trip was lovely even if business did not result, but somewhat spoilt by Susan feeling extremely ill on the flight home.

It seems to be the oddball countries that I get too. The next was Bangladesh, where we had sold a K.80 locomotive to Chhatak Cement Co. and I went out to see it put into service. Because I did not realise I needed a visa I was not allowed on my booked flight and had to go the following day having gone into London and got one from the Bangladesh High Commission in the meantime. It had always been my fear to arrive in a completely strange country and have nobody to meet me or a hotel booked. This is just what happened, as they seemed unsure as to when I was actually going to appear. However a car hire man kindly let me use his phone to make contact at no charge to me (would that happen at Heathrow? I do not think so). So I arrived at our agent's offices and was left making polite conversation to a man who casually enquired if I played cricket. 'No,' I said, 'indeed I don't really find it an interesting game at all.' I then enquired if he played and, 'Yes, he did, quite a bit'. It transpired that he played for Bangladesh and when we went out for dinner that evening, complete strangers would come up and shake his hand with great deference. Oops!

The next day we flew to Sylhet which was the nearest airport to Chhatak Cement. It is also the centre of tea growing in Bangladesh and I have since seen it advertised as a tourist destination. However the cement works was some miles away and on the other side of a major river, indeed it seemed to be the opposite side of the river from all other forms of communication: railway, road, telephone, telex and so on. Having crossed the river in a small boat there was then a small fleet of pedal rickshaws to take one to the offices

or one's accommodation. As always, the people I was with were keen to accommodate me, show me round and explain how the place worked. The works were a little over a mile from the river, where limestone was brought by barge from the quarries. This was primarily done at the time of the monsoon when the river was at its highest and the stones were thrown by hand over the side into the water. As the water retreated they were then carried by hand up the bank to a storage pile from which they were then loaded, again individually by hand, into side-tipping wagons for the journey to the crusher in the works. Alternatively there were some tracks which led down into the water so that stone could be loaded from the emerging pile directly into wagons. I did not see it happen, but apparently our locomotive arrived by rail on the opposite side of the river, was unloaded into a warehouse, taken out of the other side, down a flight of some fifteen to twenty steps to be loaded onto a barge and in due course landed, presumably onto one of the tracks going down into the water on the works side.

It was in due course commissioned and everyone was very pleased with it and it was then that I got caught out with something which has never happened before or since. On the day I was due to leave it was announced that I would meet the general manager and then tell them how to get the best out of their new locomotive. 'Them' turned out to be the entire available works staff from the general manager down to the tea wallahs and of course most of them only spoke Bengali. So, a) I had to think pretty quickly of something to say to the assembly and b) speak through an interpreter which is quite difficult, firstly to keep what one has to say simple, secondly not say too much at once and thirdly to remember the thread of what one is trying to say whilst the translation is going on.

We subsequently supplied a second locomotive to Chhatak with a few minor design changes and Patrick went to commission that one. He, like myself, loved Bangladesh and came home laden with Marks and Spencer shirts bought at wholesale prices in the local market. In addition to commissioning the locomotive he paid a visit to Taggerhat Limestone Quarry whence a high proportion of the limestone for the cement works came. This came to the factory by barge and as he went there by boat it seemed that the only way of reaching the place was indeed by water.

This establishment was a turn-back of the pages of history. It was very much a stronghold of 60S Simplexes and masses of very small side-tipping wagons that were rope-hauled out of a large pit and then trundled along quite a lengthy line to the nearest watercourse. Upon his arrival there was a special train waiting to meet him at this terminal comprising a 60S and a very much home-made open 'carriage'. It transpired that he was the first European to visit the quarry for seven years so was quite a *cause célèbre*. A further claim to fame has to be that the quarry straddled what is now the Bangladesh–India border so the internal quarry line had a customs post on it! The works itself also had an aerial ropeway which crossed into India but whether this also had a customs post, I do not know.

Again a couple of snippets. Nearly everyone walked about with a neatly furled umbrella to keep the sun off in the heat of the day and the rain if it should be raining. Bear in mind that just over the border into Assam is the wettest place on the planet with something like 230 inches (twenty feet or six metres) of rain per year. More soberingly, I also saw women sitting in the sun breaking up large boulders for railway ballast. To many Western eyes this would not be a pleasant sight but at least they must earn something to help feed themselves and their families but with more respect than simply begging.

With our experience of TPC in Tanzania, I had long thought that there ought to be some business to be done with the sugar industry in Kenya, and in addition there were reputed to be some sisal estates around Voi which still had railways. With this in mind I opted to exhibit at the Britain in Kenya Exhibition in 1995 and see if anything could be made of it. I had previously looked at the Nairobi International Trade Fair (and also at the one in Dar es Salaam) but had decided that these held nothing for us. It was our first and last overseas exhibition and for once I did all the right homework to find out who the potential customers might be and to send them official invitations. Susan and I went to man the stand but also went to spend a few days in Tanga beforehand so that she could have the Tanzanian experience. Probably once was enough! Unlike British shows where visitors like to look at your stand without being seen to be doing so, the Africans would march onto the stand and then ask what you had to sell them! We were overwhelmed. The consolation was that I did see most of the people that I wanted to see but the resultant picture was a disappointing one. Yes, there were indeed large sugar estates but, without fail, my visitors told me that they had been very badly advised and, as so often in my experience, been told to take their railways out as there were better ways of hauling cane. They appreciated that to reinstate would be enormously expensive even if the long-term advantage could make it worthwhile. I did subsequently put

forward some proposals but, hardly surprisingly, to no avail. Of dubious merit, we were both introduced to President Arup Moi when he visited our stand.

For my next overseas trip I picked the short straw, although I would not have missed it for worlds. I went to the Sudan. In the same year Patrick went to Antigua and St Kitts, but more of that in a moment. Here one has to start from the simple fact that the Gezira Light Railway operated by the Sudan Gezira Board, all 800 miles of it, is far and away the largest 2ft gauge railway system in the world. A proving run for a newly overhauled locomotive is twenty-five miles each way! Its purpose is the transport of raw cotton from field to factory and it is situated in the delta between the Blue and White Nile rivers just south of Khartoum. It is a fairly compact system with the longest haul about 120 miles.

The genesis of my trip was that Hugh Phillips Engineering Ltd had rebuilt some Baguley locomotives from a cancelled order (which, incidentally, put Baguley out of business) for the Gezira Board. Half way through, Hugh Phillips had gone into liquidation and the customer was not very pleased with the locomotives anyway. Could I help with either new locomotives or with refurbishing old ones, some of which was part of that contract anyway? In the event, by the time I got there Hugh Phillips' agent had obtained a judgment in the Sudanese courts requiring the Gezira Board to proceed with the contract with Hugh Phillips' successors Red Dragon Rail Ltd. Certainly the Sudanese were not very happy with this outcome but there was little they could do about it. My hope was that we might be able to work out some other refurbishment deal that would be useful for all concerned.

Thus I arrived in Khartoum in the middle of the night and was taken to a hotel of sorts, as the one usually used by Europeans was full until the following night. A watchman asleep on the pavement was literally kicked into activity and I had a bed for the night. This was fine although there was a distinct lack of English. The next day saw me through the usual pleasantries and being taken to the

There were some twenty to thirty derelict locomotives, mostly Hunslet, in this graveyard of the GLR workshops at Marangan and some, at least, could have been economically rebuilt and modernized, which was the reason for my being there. Alas, internal politics have so far prevented their rehabilitation.

headquarters of the Sudan Gezira Board and their workshops at Marangan. The journey was eventful in that the driver managed to hit a donkey at speed and the effect might have been far worse had we not been travelling in a large Mercedes – although that was small comfort to the poor donkey. In company with a group from the British embassy who had arrived there at the same moment we were entertained to a publicity film for the Gezira Board which extolled the part the Light Railway played in its activities.

The workshops were interesting and well equipped in an old-fashioned sort of way and probably capable of doing almost anything for the railway. Trips to look at this or that were interspersed with frequent returns to an air-conditioned office to drink copious quantities of water, and this seemed to apply to my hosts from Khartoum as much as myself. The temperature was in the low forties centigrade but they said that next week it would get hot, that is, up to forty-five or fifty degrees! Once again I was tempted to wonder what it must have been like in the days before air conditioning; my erstwhile boss, Arthur Wells at Brown & Merry, had been in the Sudan, conceivably even at this self-same place and loved it. Unfortunately the ability to do anything constructive was being diluted by the fact that Sudan was teetering on the brink of Muslim fundamentalism and it was deemed more worthwhile to

Left: The world's largest 2ft gauge railway system at some 800 miles is that of the Sudan Gezira Board. It is a Hunslet stronghold and this locomotive coming out from overhaul will be given a trial run of some twenty-five miles each way. 1997.

Right: This Baguley Drewry was one of their latest acquisitions but was suffering badly from the perpetual very fine dust and insufficient engine cooling ability in a country where the temperature can reach 50°C or more.

Patrick had another private train laid on for him when he visited the 2ft 6in. gauge sugar-cane railway that encircles the island of St Kitts. He had been asked to advise on a possible tourist operation but in the event this was done by others. This has to be narrow gauge railwaying at its idyllic best.

winding the train up to speed and just letting it go. Whilst one hopes the drivers are not actually asleep, at least a modicom of comfort is called for.

The year that I went to Sudan, Patrick went to St Kitts. This was brought about as a consultancy exercise and we were paid for him to go. In addition we had had some contact with a man in Antigua who was thinking of a tourist railway there. The idea in St Kitts was to use part of the existing sugar-cane railway as a tourist line, especially as a new deep-water jetty was being built to allow ever larger cruise ships to dock alongside. The 2ft 6in. gauge sugar-cane railway encircles the island and is some forty miles in length. In places it is on high viaducts and the views are spectacular. This railway is another stronghold of Hunslet locomotives although there are a few Rustons and a very elderly Armstrong Whitworth diesel electric to provide some variety. Once again Patrick had a special train for his tour of inspection! Due to falling sugar prices the whole sugar industry in St Kitts is under threat: every year is predicted as its last, and 2005 may have proved to be such. However the tourist train idea was put into operation by a consortium from Alaska, nothing to do with us, and since the mothballing of the sugar mill they are at least using the whole railway in various permutations of operation. In Antigua the sugar railways, also of 2ft 6in gauge, have all gone, but if you know in which clump of bushes to look, and I joke not, there are the remains of several Kerr Stuart Brazil-class locomotives to be found. Most of the track, diesel locomotives and rolling stock went to St Kitts when the mills on Antigua closed.

be building a little mosque in the works yard than to be getting on with repairing a locomotive.

The Gezira Railway was probably built using equipment second-hand from the Western Front of the First World War and, although there seems to be little recorded about it, that would seem to fit with what I saw. However it must have had a complete rebuild sometime in the 1950s that carried on over a period of twenty years or so, in that it became a stronghold of Hunslet Engine Co. and presumably of Robert Hudson as well. They produced a series of 0-6-0 and, later, 0-8-0 diesel locomotives fitted with Gardner engines and Hunslet's own gearboxes which have proved to be almost indestructible. I spent a good deal of time, in between drinks, inspecting the scrap line of some twenty or thirty derelict locomotives with the idea of re-manufacturing them into something more modern. None had been seriously damaged but many had been cannibalized for spares, particularly for the more ancient of engines. There were also the remains of a few Schoma locomotives which were reputed to have been singularly unsuccessful.

After a drive apparently into the wilds of nowhere I then visited the main running sheds and the headquarters of the railway itself. Here at least was a fleet of operational locomotives and sidings full of literally hundreds of bogie wagons. Although locomotives obviously did not come here to die, a good many other things did, such as Wickham railcars, Hunslet railcars (the only ones I have ever come across), strange bogie home-built railcars and the remnants of a complete signalling system with lever frames and all. I also saw one of the Baguley/Hugh Phillips locomotives and was able to witness some of its problems at first hand. These related primarily to inadequate cooling, hardly surprising in the temperatures, and a very inadequate cab. By repute a good many trains run at night because it is cooler and, in view of the distances, it is a case of

My next destination was Argentina, which I discovered is an awfully long way away. The first time I went I flew Alitalia via Rome and glibly thought it would be about six to seven hours on from there. I nearly died when it was listed as thirteen and a half hours and then we were half an hour late as well. After that I swore that any flight over three hours I was going business class and somebody somewhere would have to pay for it! Anyway, I was duly met by Luis Gutierrez, who was something of railway enthusiast himself. He took me to see a friend of his, Georges Ricardes, the walls of whose office were lined with such a collection of tinplate and other railway models as to make one drool at the mouth. I gratefully accepted a cup of coffee and in due course there was a whooping of whistles and the coffee arrived on an LGB gauge 1 train running along a shelf on the wall! And I thought the English were crazy …!

The object of the trip was a possible railway at the Iguazu Falls National Park to carry visitors in from new car parks further away from the centre of attraction. Luis and I flew to Iguazu and were taken to meet Mr Sampracos who was one of the two people behind this scheme. He is an enormous man and quite a character. I could have blown the whole project in that first meeting because he sat expansively behind his desk and announced that he was Greek. To which, in a fit of madness, I said, 'Well, that's not your fault.' He looked at me for a moment, then roared with laughter and virtually climbing over his desk, shook me by both hands announcing that I was his friend. And he was right, because without his faith in us I do not think we would ever have won the job in the teeth of the considerable competition. The contract was to provide four train-sets to carry people over two separate railways about four kilometres long to different parts of the Iguazu Falls. Because it was in a National Park a major part of the project was to be environmentally friendly and as a consequence the locomotives were to use natural gas as fuel.

The Iguazu falls are situated more or less where Argentina, Brazil and Paraguay meet. The falls themselves are higher and carry more water than Niagara and form the boundary between Argentina and Brazil. In fact most of the falls are in Argentina but the best view of them is from Brazil. They have been a tourist attraction for many years and are remarkable in that one can walk along walkways on the very edge of the cataract with the water literally falling away under one's feet. The rebuilding of all these walkways was also part of my host's contract. Whilst there I was also taken to a cabaret run by Mr Sampracos' wife at Foz do Iguazu, a sizeable city on the Brazilian side. At the time I was unaware that Brazil speaks Portuguese whilst the rest of South America speaks Spanish, but by repute Mr Sampracos only spoke Spanish and his wife Portuguese yet they understood each other perfectly! He also kindly took me to the Itapu dam which is the world's largest hydro-electric scheme and retains a lake some 600 kilometres long. There are supposedly various quite serious ecological concerns, but the scale of the project is unbelievable. Sufficient to say that it provides 25 per cent of Brazil's electricity and 75 per cent of that for Paraguay, at the height of construction they were pouring enough concrete every twenty-four hours to build a five-storey block of flats, and that the overhead crane over each of thirteen turbines is rated at 1,350 tons.

My one regret in all this was that an elderly aunt (a stepsister of my mother's) was still living in Montevideo and as it worked out I could easily have taken the ferry across from Buenos Aires and perhaps seen her. By the time I came back to commission the equipment it was too late. Certainly the first time I went there was still some feeling about the Falklands War some ten years previously and there were posters around proclaiming 'Las Malvinas son Argentinas'. Argentina was very much a country to which to emigrate for earlier generations, my mother's family being a case in point, and there are many who look very British. I was introduced to a journalist who spoke not a word of English but whose ancestors had escaped the Irish potato famine to Argentina and he looked every inch an Irishman. It is truly said of the Argentines that 'they look like the Italians, dress like the French, speak Spanish but wish they were English!'

Apart from a trip to Lanzarote, a place I disliked intensely, and it is very questionable whether it comes under this chapter heading at all, that is the limit of my travelling. The one place I should like to have reached is Fiji for the obvious reason that it has the longest 2ft gauge railway system after the Sudan, not to mention Fiji Sugar Corporation being a customer of ours. It has always been just that bit too far away even when I have been in the Far East. The United States has become attractive, I am not sure why, but it is a very big place and it is difficult to know where to begin.

Patrick has been to India twice. The first time was another inspection job for a railway on a tunnelling contract at the Dul Hasti hydroelectric scheme in Kashmir and again we were paid for his going. Personally the trip was a bit of a disaster, not least because he was not aware that he was in the process of going down with glandular fever at the time. Neither did he appreciate being taken to the site in the ubiquitous Indian Ambassador car under armed guard along perilous dirt roads in the mountains of the lower Himalayas. He did, however, attend part of an Indian wedding in New Delhi and paid a visit to the Indian Railways Museum there that in turn may have led to his second and much more interesting trip to the sub-continent. This was to the Darjeeling Himalayan Railway, in connection with quoting for two new locomotives. Apart from seeing it as it really is and not as it is presented to the tourists, he had the opportunity to do some locomotive driving on that truly unique line. Like so many things, it ultimately came to naught – but how else could he have done that?

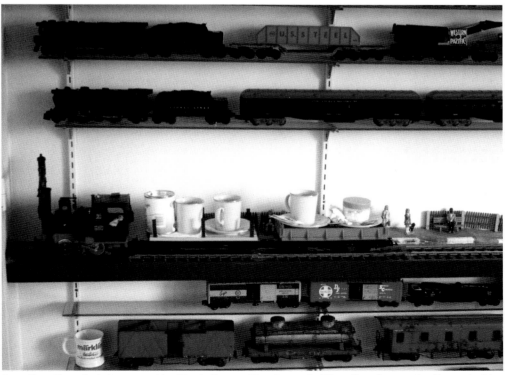

Argentina. On arrival at our agent's office in Buenos Aires I accepted the offer of a cup of coffee and with a mighty whooping this is how it arrived!

The 4-4-0 locomotive (AK35 of 1990) for Singapore Zoo was loosely based on the free train locomotive in Fiji. The engine and hydraulics are in the tender although the drive is actually to the driving wheels. *John Palmer*

Train on the Singapore Zoo Railway in 1994, headed by AK34 of 1991. The locomotives on this railway were originally fitted with petrol engines to avoid any possible pollution of the adjoining drinking water reservoir. The name is very original and translates to 'Red Choo Choo'!

Brand new steam locomotive (AK38 of 1991) for de Efteling theme park in Holland stands in the station headshunt whilst on trial at Leighton Buzzard. Despite the continental appearance there is a strong affinity between this and *Woto*.

11

The Naughty Nineties

As has been intimated, the 1990s proved to be a difficult time for the company although they started off with something of a bang. As had happened similarly once before, we obtained a major overseas contract which appeared to buck the national trend and lulled us into a false sense of security.

This was the contract for a complete railway for Singapore Zoo. This comprised two locomotives, eight carriages and the supply of rail and turnouts. They laid the track themselves having obtained the services of a professional permanent way engineer who was currently working on the then new Singapore Metro. The locomotives were an 0-4-0 similar to that at Hayling Island and Cotswold, plus a 4-4-0 tender loco based very much on the free train locomotive that used to operate in Fiji. Both were hydraulic drive after our usual style but were unusual in being fitted with petrol engines, in this case the industrial version of the Ford Fiesta engine. The reason for this was that the railway was beside one of Singapore's main drinking water reservoirs and it was felt that with petrol any fuel spillage would evaporate whereas diesel just might get into the water supply. It was evidently not a real problem as in fairly short order the zoo replaced the engines with Toyota diesels.

The carriages were quite a departure for us; firstly, being supplied in knocked-down form, that is, as components for final assembly on arrival, and, secondly, having aluminium floors with stainless steel stanchions and framing plus cushioned seats and drop-down side curtains against tropical thunderstorms. They turned out to be both rather narrow and short having been designed to carry as many people as possible whilst getting several at a time into a 20-foot container. However they are believed to be still working and giving rides to children as intended. They were in fact built on our underframes by a local firm who specialized in the manufacture of showman's living vans. This is a remarkable business and is possibly worth a history of its own but in essence they build super high quality permanent home-style living vans for the fairground industry. These include chandeliers, marble worktops, marble fireplaces, top of the range showers and bathroom fittings, decorative glass panels and so on, and are quite something to see, and at that time they had no less than fourteen in build together. Building our little carriages was child's play.

Woodhead tunnel was to the fore again with Taylor Woodrow carrying out major works there. As far as we were concerned this involved a Simplex with a Deutz engine conversion in it, a carriage to be used as a manrider and numerous wagons including two Hudson bogie flats bought from Festiniog Railway. Woodhead is a difficult place to operate in and most of the contractors who have worked there learn the difficulties by bitter experience, price the next job accordingly and therefore do not get it. As a consequence we are always dealing with a different firm. In this case the hire was prolonged because the hire was passed on to Pirelli Construction who were installing new cables. This was to some extent brought about by there being a cable fire in the tunnel when Taylor Woodrow were there (fortunately there was no-one in the tunnel at the time) which involved the replacement of some two and a half kilometres of cable priced at £5,000 per metre!

In addition to the Singapore Zoo job, another major coup of this period was the building of a brand new steam locomotive for de Efteling theme park in Holland. This was actually started off by Dennis Wilby who went there in response to a request by Christian Fuller, a Dutchman who thus became our agent for Holland and surrounding area. At the time he was making a tour of German and Dutch peat works. He and I then met the engineers from de Efteling at Rebecq-Rognon to have a look at *Trixie* as we thought that would be of more than adequate size for their operation. However they were adamant it was not and wanted something larger and thus was born a continental version of Patrick's Bagnall *Woto*. The line at de Efteling is some two and a half kilometres in length and the park sees some three million visitors per year, making it one of the world's largest. The railway is entirely steam operated using two Orenstein & Koppel locomotives and a Jung, the latter having originally been a fireless locomotive and later having had a boiler fitted. In this day and age it is slightly unnerving to see the drivers come on shift and take out the next steam loco, which is all ready and waiting for them, as casually as the postman takes out his delivery van. The original plan had been that when the new locomotive went into service the Jung, *Neefje*, would come back to us for a major rebuild with heavier frames in particular. However it seems that the new locomotive, our No. 38, *Tryntje*, was so good that *Neefje* has never been done.

The traditional British narrow gauge locomotive with its saddle tank, flared chimney and often abundant brasswork is not recognized for what it is on the continent. Their view of a narrow gauge loco is what might be called the 'Orenstein' style with well tank, stove-pipe chimney, no frills and more often than not painted black. We compromised on this and built a locomotive with side tanks, the stove-pipe chimney but with the Bagnall marine-type boiler and a brass dome. De Efteling were very sceptical of our using taper roller bearings in the axleboxes and insisted on our giving them a ten year guarantee on these; they are still running well beyond the ten year period. I went over to commission the locomotive which went smoothly and everyone was satisfied.

A somewhat incongruous job was the purchase of two Clayton battery locomotives from the then just still-operational Wheal Jane tin mine in Cornwall to be re-gauged from 24in. to standard gauge for Tilbury Douglas Construction, for a contract on the Waterloo & City line of the London Underground. This was achieved by making new axles that put the wheels outside the frames with substantial 'mudguards' over them. The water at Wheal Jane

Left: One for the model makers! An unusual view of No. 38 as it is loaded onto a lorry. Note the compensated brake rigging, drain cock gear and the amount of dirt collected in really very little running.

Right: *Sir Winston Churchill*, a 15in. gauge 0-6-2 steam-outline diesel locomotive (AK39 of 1992) on the railway at Blenheim Palace. This was the first of this type of locomotive to be built.

must be particularly corrosive as the frames were thick with rust accumulation such that even shot blasting had great difficulty in getting back to real metal. These locos did their job for the duration and I believe one of them remained on site until the next reincarnation some fifteen years later.

My visits to Tanzania/Kenya began to pay off with no less than £27,000-worth of spares orders from the Vipingo sisal estate near Mombasa. In addition, we provided new hydraulic pumps for two of the locomotives at TPC at Moshi. These Simplex T series locomotives were fitted with Dowmatic pumps that had become life expired. We provided new pumps and associated control gear from Commercial Hydraulics and John Palmer made his first trip to Tanzania to see them fitted. All went smoothly until he came to leave, when the general manager decided that he expected a large backhander in return for the business. I have always left these problems in the hands of the local agents, who in this case were a Dar es Salaam firm primarily making oil filters and other vehicle parts, and supposedly 'a very good friend' of said manager. As nothing was forthcoming he created a rumpus to the effect that the pumps were no good and had been incorrectly fitted and so on. This was overcome but the agents saw a market for their filters. They were entirely of the

wrong specification and collapsed internally with all the bits going through into the system and thus satisfactorily ruining the pumps. Very fortunately TPC attached no blame to us for this *débâcle* and this whole exercise was quietly dropped until they embarked on a much more radical scheme later.

Back in the UK we were approached by the Docklands Light Railway for a second-hand diesel shunter of some sort for occasional

Now on its home territory and named *Tryntje*, No. 38 stands outside the running shed at de Efteling. The shed arrangements here are unusual in that there are two buildings at right angles to each other to accommodate the three operational steam locomotives.

at about this time that Philip Kent joined us and he was initially deeply involved in this abortive exercise. He subsequently became workshop manager before moving into the design office with Alice and it is fair to say that without his encyclopedic engineering knowledge life would have been that much harder.

There were a couple of mystery jobs. The first was a substantial quantity of Simplex spares for RMP that we think went to Austria, but have no real idea. The second was a second-hand Simplex plus some wagons and track that were sold to a firm in Jersey for export to Angola, but for what, again we have no idea. In both cases we were paid without problem, so I suppose who were we to worry? More positive were ten metre gauge wheelsets for Guyana Sugar Corporation plus a host of smaller jobs which all helped to keep the wheels turning.

maintenance work and shunting cars in the depot when necessary. Somewhat surprisingly they, or rather we on their behalf, bought a Ruston 88DS shunter in Norwich. This was in good condition but was an antiquated machine to put amongst all their new automated and driverless trains. Because of the amount of work we had on hand we sent it to Esca Engineering Ltd at Wigan for refurbishment, not least because at that time they held all the Ruston drawings and spares know-how. This was a bit painful as they were an officially-accredited quality-controlled firm and every move had to have its accompanying piece of paperwork. Be that as it may, the refurbishment was reasonably successful although a number of subsequent visits were required both by Esca and us. It certainly did its job until a new purpose-built machine came from RFS Engineering at Doncaster, when it was relegated to spare. I suspect that this was really a case of money; the provision of such a machine had been missed from the original budgets and when the need arose there were no funds to buy one. A stopgap that could be paid for out of revenue had to be found until such time as capital budgets would allow buying the real thing. We have all done it!

Quality control has just been mentioned, and this became something of an obsession within industry of all sorts in the 1990s. Grants were available and various organizations set themselves up to provide quality assurance schemes for aspiring firms, BS5750, or ISO9000, being the golden grail of all this. It was supposed to particularly apply to those wanting work with local authorities and even reached the pitch of window cleaners having to be suitably accredited! We went a long way along the road and finally backed off, saying that we would live or die by our own reputation. The problem is that it is easy and appropriate to achieve the necessary paperwork with new work but it does not sit at all comfortably with our dealing activities or with refurbishment work where decisions are made as one goes along. Simplex used to hold a similar accreditation allowing them to do military work and many firms are so accredited, but not Alan Keef Ltd. We do not think it has affected us yet. It was

I had long had a basic design for an 0-6-2 steam-outline diesel locomotive in my mind for use on 15in. gauge. The opportunity to build this came with an enquiry for a new locomotive for use at Blenheim Palace. This locomotive followed the, by then, standard pattern of Perkins engine, Linde hydraulic pump and slow-speed motor under the cab floor with chain drive to one axle and the drive transferred through the side rods to the other driving wheels. It produced an attractive machine with a roomy cab and well able to do its job. History will probably say that it is one of our less successful designs although, to date, all those built are still working for their living. By the nature of the wheel arrangement and the type of railway they tend to operate on, they are prone to considerable flange wear and all have had to have the driving axle beefed up. Because the engine and 'works' are well boxed in they also have a tendency to overheat and this was overcome at Blenheim by fitting mesh into the side panels, not beautiful but it solved the problem. This particular locomotive has had to work unreasonably hard as the demand to use the railway is greatly in excess of its notional carrying capacity, this in turn being exacerbated by the railway being steeply uphill in one direction. A train designed to carry sixty-four passengers finds itself not infrequently carrying a hundred plus!

The winter of 1991/92 was a busy one with the building of the second of these 0-6-2 locomotives, together with a set of four carriages, for Haigh Hall Country Park at Wigan. This in itself was straightforward enough, but it was the obtaining of the order and its aftermath that was entertaining. I was invited to Haigh Hall to meet the council's Director of Leisure Services, Gilbert Swift, to discuss the possibility of a new train for the park's railway. I was fairly royally wined and dined in Hall's official dining room before we got down to business. We then hammered out a deal for what was needed and although I do remember some comment about where the money was to come from, he simply brushed this aside. He then sent for the park's official order book in which he wrote out an order for '1 train and carriages' and the amount – in the order of £45,000.

It is the one and only time I have received an order for that value 'just like that'! He was obviously a popular person and the locomotive was named after him as it was his parting shot before retirement. This was all delivered and was perfectly satisfactory except that the locomotive name was removed about a month afterwards and has never been replaced. Apparently it is best not asked where the money for its purchase actually came from!

Trackwork took on fairly major proportions with a major re-lay in the Woodhead Tunnel after Taylor Woodrow had finished there. This primarily involved re-sleepering where the sleepers had rotted in those places where the tunnel is wet. This was followed by track-laying at Himley Model Village in the West Midlands

0-6-2 locomotive AK41 of 1992 at Haigh Hall Country Park, near Wigan, stands at the platform with a rake of our articulated carriages. At this stage the loco still carries its nameplate *Gilbert Swift*, about which more is said in the text.

where Parry People Movers were installing a test track for their flywheel-powered trams. This was interspersed with a ghost train track at the West Midlands Safari Park. Very much as a favour and for old time's sake, I bought, and subsequently managed to re-sell, a funny little railway for an erstwhile friend of my father's. This had a gauge of 11½in. and appeared to have been built without reference to any accepted sources of knowledge. Known to us all as 'Mr Peacock's railway', it was battery electric powered and was really quite good for having been cobbled together at minimum

cost from whatever happened to be to hand. It had been built to fit into a small garden but gave a good deal of variety in the process. There were two locomotives, a passenger vehicle and several goods wagons. Fun for what it was.

More seriously, we had a series of large spares orders starting with the first of two from the Crown Agents totalling £20,000 for Simplex parts for Ghana Bauxite. In two parts were orders from Singapore Zoo that included substantial spares such as bogies and hydraulic pumps. A further retrofit pump kit was supplied to TPC along with Simplex T spares to Indonesia and wheels for ZCCM in Zambia.

Quite unknowingly, history was probably made in 1992 when we built a 60S locomotive for Guyana Sugar Corporation and at the same time supplied a retrofit Perkins engine kit for an existing locomotive. History says that in all probability this will have been the last traditional Simplex locomotive to be built. The development of the K series range which followed hard on its heels meant that we could build a better locomotive cheaper than the traditional Simplex which was by now very much individually hand built.

The development of a new locomotive design was often a sign that we did not have enough work to do to keep our workforce fully employed. It was hoped that doing this would not only produce a marketable product but also keep the workforce together until something more remunerative turned up. As it happened, the number series of new

This 60S locomotive (AK43 of 1992) will probably prove to be the last true Simplex locomotive to be built. It is of metre gauge and was supplied to Guyana Sugar Corporation in South America. It stands on temporary rails outside the works prior to despatch.

locomotives had reached around 39 so that this machine could be classified as K.40, be of 40 horse power and numbered 40 in the works list as well. The intention was to produce a locomotive that could compete with Schoma and Diema from Germany on price as well as specification. To do the latter it had to be shaft drive (no more rattling chains) and also simple to drive. At an exhibition to which John Palmer and I went we came across International Transmissions who are a subsidiary of JCB, the construction equipment giant, and who made all the latter's transmissions. Although they already sold a good many transmissions elsewhere, including to some of JCB's principle competitors, they were anxious to extend their market. Not only could they provide the transmissions but, with JCB being Perkins' biggest UK customer after Massey Ferguson, they could also supply the engines as well if we could use the standard specification. Around the transmission used in the 3CX backhoe excavator was developed the K.40.

Accordingly, John set about designing an axle drive-box which would match the ever reliable Perkins 3.152 engine (incidentally, originally put on the market in the 1950s) with the 660 series transmission and the requirements of an industrial locomotive. The prototype drive boxes were of fabricated design in order to save pattern costs at this stage, the wheels were probably some second-hand ones we had by us and the axleboxes were those used on the K.30. Something of a *tour de force* was the control whereby John achieved handbrake, service brake and throttle all in one lever which certainly made driving the machine idiot proof. Forward and reverse was made easy with electrical operation. The gearbox of the transmission unit was locked in one gear only – usually third – and the torque convertor was allowed to take up the drive. The locomotive was built at 3½ tonnes which experience had proved to be a more satisfactory weight than the traditional 2½ tons of an earlier generation.

On test in the yard it did all that was asked of it and the control was remarkable. It seemed to have a great ability to get the power to the rails, which is, after all, what it is all about. The proof of the pudding came with our being able to hire it to C.F. Donelon Ltd for use on a tunneling contract in Bristol. This had the advantage of not being too far away in the event of problems. They had instructions to break it if they could! In six months they did not, which was good enough for us. Although totally irrelevant, it has to be mentioned that this is the place where Patrick went to a booked appointment with the site agent who then proceeded to change his clothes down to and including his underpants whilst all the while continuing to talk business as arranged! This locomotive also went on trial to one of Richardson's peat bogs, but although it worked eminently

satisfactorily they could not get beyond the fact that it did not have a cab! It went on various hires for us and eventually was sold to de Efteling for use as a maintenance locomotive with us taking a very dilapidated Schoma in part exchange.

The early nineties were peppered with hire contracts of various sorts. Taylor Woodrow at the Woodhead Tunnel has already been mentioned but we also hired them a locomotive at their Isle of Grain plant that was making tunnel segments for the Channel Tunnel. Later, with the tunnel completed there was a Simplex on almost permanent hire to their plant at Southall even while we were building them a new K.40. There was enough of this business about to build another K.40 primarily for hire only. This and the original No. 40 went to a waste-water tunnel contract with Kier Construction at Mansfield. They got about 100 metres into the tunnel when it was discovered that 20 per cent of the water being pumped out was pure petrol! Apparently what had happened was that a garage, long since closed, must have had a leaking tank for years and the fissured rock below had absorbed and retained the petrol which started to flow out once the surroundings were broken into. This, understandably, brought the whole job to a standstill while the pundits decided what to do about it, and presumably who was to pay. We had to fit the locomotives with flame protection gear at very considerable cost to Kier and the tunnelling restarted. In the event after about a further twenty metres the ground was clean and all the effort was for not much.

We also supplied two locomotives to Dew & Co. for a dredging contract on the Rochdale canal where the track was laid to a much heavier standard than is usual for this type of work. There were also odd hires of bogies and jubilee track to various contractors. The monorail also had quite a spate of outings, with possibly the most glamorous being in the Neville Hall Depot of British Rail in Leeds.

Two K.40 locomotives, AK40 and AK47 of 1992 and 1994, the latter brand new on the left, on hire to Kier Construction for a tunnelling contract in Mansfield. The K.40 locomotive has proved itself a capable locomotive in many spheres of activity where locomotives tend to be abused rather than used.

Luxury cab on 3ft gauge, K.40 (AK44 of 1993) at Peatlands Park in Northern Ireland. This was the first locomotive we fitted with an independently mounted and soundproofed cab, something that has since tended to become a standard feature especially on passenger locomotives.

It was laid in the pit between the main line running rails for the removal of concrete being broken out in renovation works.

Possibly one of the first of a type of work that we now call railbound materials handling was to construct three small handbraked trolleys for Morrison Construction who were at that time converting the A74 between Carlisle and Motherwell into the M74. These, along with some associated track, were installed in culverts under the motorway in readiness for the day when the adjoining pipes needed replacing or repairing. The odd part about it was that because the surroundings were inevitably damp, if not actively wet, they insisted that the trolleys be galvanized but were quite unconcerned about the rail which in our opinion was likely to suffer much more. So far as we know they are there to this day, probably unused.

At Kilverstone Wildlife park there occurred some sort of family *débâcle* in which Lord Fisher retired very suddenly and moved away, leaving the park in the care of his son who ran a vineyard close by.

Over the years we have attended many exhibitions and one of the most consistent has been Leisure Industry Week at Birmingham's National Exhibition Centre. Here we have a 15in. gauge 0-6-2 (AK42 of 1992) on display. This locomotive was exhibited twice before being sold and carried whatever nameplate we happened to have available, in this case *Taffy*'s!

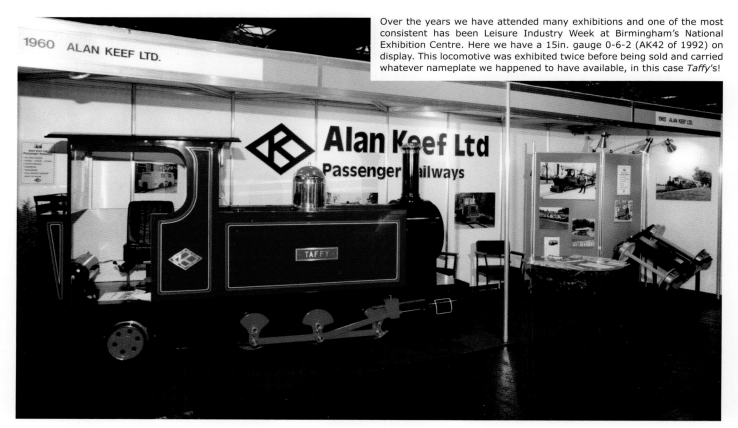

As though on cue, the locomotive *Robin Hood*, which had borne the brunt of the work over the years, decided to break a crank pin at this moment in time. The resultant damage was considerable and the process of repair highlighted a good deal of other repairs that had by then become urgent. Fortunately Lord Fisher had put *Flying Scotsman* back into operational condition and this was able to take over. *Robin Hood* came into the works and major work was carried out to restore it to good running order. Perhaps obviously, perhaps not, the new regime at Kilverstone could not last and we were a very long time being paid for this work. After perhaps another season the place closed completely, another example of one man's dream not outlasting him. It was also perhaps the first sign, unnoticed at the time, of the financial problems about to beset Alan Keef Ltd in the second half of the 1990s.

1993 also saw some very sizeable spares orders with no less than £75,000 worth going to ZCCM, mostly wheels and tyres. The year's mystery sale was a Simplex locomotive, four articulated carriages and half a mile of track to Trinidad. We also sold a Simplex to Ray Wright who operates Clearwell Caves in the Forest of Dean. This was for a proposal to re-open as a visitor attraction a gold mine less than two miles from our works. Here there is a tunnel that goes about half a mile into the hill that was opened in the 1890s as a gold mine. Whilst there was, and still is, gold in these hills it is not in payable quantity and the original project was unsuccessful. However the second project has not fared much better and although the loco is still there nothing much more has happened.

More prestigious was the building of a target trolley and about sixty metres of track for University College, London. This was installed at Holland & Holland's shooting grounds just north of London. Our environmentally friendly age had produced the concern that the use of lead in cartridges was creating lead poisoning in animals and birds that eat carrion which had been shot. Alternatives such as steel and titanium were in use but these had the snag that the pellets were inclined to ricochet and at least two people had died as a consequence, which makes me wonder where our priorities should lie. As a result, a research project was set up to fire different types of pellet from different ranges at a target on our trolley to investigate such things as spread, force of impact and so on. The man concerned sent me a photograph of the final setup with written on the back, 'The shape of pings to come!'

The year saw the delivery of two notable K.40 locomotives. The first was a 3ft gauge version for Peatlands Park in Northern Ireland. This was the first production K.40 and was special because it was the first locomotive to have an independently mounted and soundproofed cab complete with heater, demist and other such luxuries. Their other locomotives were indescribably noisy and the difference with this one, in which two people could whisper to one another in the cab and be heard, was remarkable indeed. The other K.40 was supplied complete with twelve-seat manrider to National Grid for use in the Woodhead Tunnel. This was unusual in that it was fitted with the Deutz F3L912W indirect injection engine specifically for underground use. This machine must have put up a great many miles service by now.

The carriages in use at Blenheim Palace had first been used at the Düsseldorf exhibition in 1937 and had come to this country along with the three Krupp 4-6-2 steam locomotives that had been built to go with them. These were heavy and quite elaborate carriages and the Duke decreed that if another was needed then it must be just like the old ones – even if the cost was going to be just under £11,000 for a sixteen-seat carriage body only, as they already had some spare bogies! The problem was that these carriages had a curved under-skirt not only at the sides but round the ends as well which were themselves curved rather than square. In addition, the seat framing was in tubular steel with special aluminium castings to fix them to the main frame. If building in quantity, as the originals were, all of this would have been all in a day's work, but for a one-off it simply became hours and hours of labour. Anyhow, a very fine vehicle was produced and everyone was satisfied. I will not go into details, but these carriages were originally fitted with a very ingenious fail-safe braking system which I have on occasions sought to reproduce but it has never been economically worth while. They are also fitted with a very neat form of buckeye coupler which one day we will reproduce, and as built this automatically connected up the air brake system. All well ahead of its time for this type of equipment.

At this time we also supplied two, indeed so far the only two, K.80 locomotives to Chhatak Cement Co. Ltd near Sylhet, in northern Bangladesh. The second one followed the first about nine months later with a few minor modifications. The details of the commissioning trip have been described, but these locos weighed in at 8 tonnes and were fitted with Deutz F4L912 engines of 75h.p. with which we had some trouble at the specification stage, because that had to describe the engines as being of 82h.p. at maximum engine speed, which we were not using. The transmission was the

AK46 of 1993 together with its accompanying manrider built for National Grid Plc for use in the Woodhead Tunnel. This three-and-a-half-mile ex main-line single-bore tunnel is used as a cable tunnel and has a 2ft gauge railway throughout its length for service and repair purposes. Being for underground use, this locomotive was fitted with a Deutz indirect injection engine and exhaust conditioning equipment.

K.80 locomotives (AK45 and AK50 of 1993 and 1994) are seen together hauling trains of limestone off the weighbridge at Chhatak Cement Works in Bangladesh. The newer of these two, on the left, has a slightly more sophisticated cab than the home-built version on the earlier model. At the time, this works seemed to be the opposite side of the river from all other forms of communication including the telephone!

same as in the K.40, but in this instance we arranged for two gears (second and third) to be used. On trial the locomotive hauled a test train of 46 tons uphill round a very sharp curve onto a weighbridge which meant a stop/start operation as each wagon was weighed. Everyone was satisfied.

In between times over the previous years we had built a stock 15in. gauge 0-6-2 locomotive which was in fact a hollow mockery as we never fitted it with engine and transmission due to cost. Nevertheless it went to at least two Leisure Industry Week exhibitions at Birmingham before being sold, along with some carriages taken in part exchange from Haigh Hall, to Derek Parnaby near Durham for a public railway in the grounds of his house. He had his own ideas about engines and transmissions and the machine was reasonably successful. The venture lasted only about a couple of years before the whole railway was sold to Vancouver in Canada where it is still operational.

In Ireland things were moving apace with the Cavan & Leitrim Railway at Dromod. The Kerr Stuart No. 1 was beginning to look seriously like a locomotive again, and rather reluctantly we re-gauged the remains – frame and wheels only – of a 5ft 3in. gauge (Irish standard gauge) railcar to 3ft gauge and fitted it with a Mercedes engine with automatic gearbox. We had not got enough length of track to try this out satisfactorily but it was believed to work. The 2ft gauge Kerr Stuart *Diana* also appeared on the scene. This belonged to a delightful man, Dennis Davies, who was intending to return it slowly to running order. It needed a new boiler, and this would have to wait until he retired and could cash in an insurance policy! As work started to dry up at this time it was a very useful job we were pleased to have, even if it was still in the works ten years later. 'Slowly' became the operative word! Although this was an extreme example, this has always been a problem and has created the need for us to have larger premises than are strictly necessary. Even quite simple overhauls can come to a grinding halt due to lack of available spare parts and a section of workshop is thus occupied while one waits for something to arrive. With private customers this can be exacerbated whilst waiting for them to decide on the next move or to find the money, or both. Such a one was when we re-gauged a

brake van for a man who was a postman who planned to pay for the work from his Christmas overtime – and then the Post Office reorganized Christmas so there was no overtime.

For many years we were on the National Coal Board's computer for one of their collieries for the supply of Deutz engine oil filters. It was probably the result of having once had a Simplex locomotive, but who were we to argue if they wanted to continue to buy them from us? Similarly, for a lengthy period we sold a certain size of fishplate bolt to Murphy's, the contractors, and subsequently sold them to a firm of nut and bolt suppliers in Brixton who in turn sold them on to Murphy's!

It is always surprising how being able to help somebody at a particular moment can pay all sorts of dividends later. One such was Alton Towers. We had a mid-season panic call from them to the effect that could we provide four (!) new steel tyres of 21in. diameter for their 0-6-0 locomotive? As it happened we could because the ZCCM business had gone very dead and we had some U series tyres in stock which were exactly that size. They sent the wheelsets down and we cut the old tyres off, re-machined ours to suit, shrank them on and returned them and everyone was happy. From this stemmed a complete overhaul of both their working locomotives, the re-wheeling of their eight bogie carriages and some considerable amount of trackwork. This was a particularly dull railway that worked as two parallel single tracks on an almost straight run along an old carriage drive completely enshrouded by trees. The only 'excitement' was a sharp downhill curve into the station at one end which ended in the buffer stops. On these we provided some specially-made Oleo buffers capable of bringing the train to rest from 8m.p.h. within the length of the buffer stroke, about twelve inches. These on occasion did get used, and I gather that the stopping effect was alarming but better than hitting a solid stop.

On a domestic note, the end of 1994 saw the infilling of the railway bridge over the cutting which formed part of my property, in order to allow 40-tonne lorries to use the road and also allow the traffic to travel more freely, that is, faster, past my gate. This latter was to have repercussions much later but I was sorry to see

Sally, prototype and sole K.100 locomotive (AK48 of 1994), with seventy-two wagons of sugar-cane headed for the mill at TPC Ltd, Moshi, Tanzania, with a jolly African crew all trying to get into the picture.

Sandy, AK49 of 1994, was a K.40 built for use in the tunnel segment plant of Taylor Woodrow Ltd at Southall, Middlesex. This works unfortunately closed before a second locomotive that had been provisionally ordered could be built.

the railway bridge disappear as it was unusual in that the arch was sprung directly off the rock on each side without any side walls. It also did away with an attractive walk used by many people. Because of this I then obtained planning permission to infill the cutting and use it as a licensed tip for inert waste. This was a big mistake. I got involved at steadily increasing cost with various supposed landfill organizations culminating in coming under the jurisdiction of the Environment Agency. It is hard to believe that one could run into something so autocratic and bureaucratic as that organization; it considers itself no less that the twenty-first-century incarnation of God – when all one wants to do is fill in a bit of old railway cutting. If I had known then what I know now I would have got on and filled it in and argued afterwards; the fine could never have been as bad as the ongoing costs have been.

We had an enquiry for a railway on the outskirts of Aberdeen which would have been 15in. gauge and which required enclosed carriages as it was to cross a golf course. At the same time as this was being considered, Cricket St Thomas Park wanted to increase the capacity of their railway, with their thinking working along the lines of converting the present 15in. gauge line to 2ft and, more alarmingly, turning it into a circular-type railway. This would have involved a high and long bridge over the lower lakes that would have put the present fairly spectacular bridge completely in the shade. It never reached the serious design stage but I guess said bridge would have been 250 feet long and fifteen to twenty feet high! In the event neither project went ahead but we did sell a complete new train set to Cricket St Thomas with

the option of selling it on to Aberdeen if the 2ft gauge railway came to fruition. Also unusually, the whole train was bought through a hire-purchase company, one of the very rare occasions when this has happened and, much later on, our finding that we were an approved supplier to a well known finance house.

The train consisted of our 0-6-2 locomotive and four articulated carriages, the end one of which was fitted as a driving trailer so that it could be used on a push pull basis. This worked extremely well and to this day I find it slightly unnerving to sit in the wrong end of the train and hear the engine away in the distance somewhere! We also converted the existing train (the locomotive of which at that time had a thatched roof!) to a similar operation and installed an intermediate passing loop for two-train operation. This proved to be the zenith of passenger operations at Cricket St Thomas and the whole system has hardly been used as intended since.

Of more mundane interest was a derailment at Cotswold Wildlife Park that caused the locomotive chimney to fall off! In fact I had used an old and damaged Avonside chimney which I happened to have and for which there were only about two bolts holding it on, the rest was filler! The Park did know about this, but it did precipitate an overhaul of the loco – and a new chimney. Some twelve years later Graham Morris was desperate for that old chimney to fit to his newly-acquired Avonside locomotive *Elidir* that had a non-original one. Too late, I'm afraid. At the Woodhead Tunnel we installed a passing loop for Murphy's at a point where the tunnel was marginally wider and this could only be used with narrow rolling stock. Also on the overhaul front we rebuilt a 14in. gauge locomotive from Frontierland at Morecambe with a new hydraulic drive system. This was manufactured in America by Alan Herschell of North Tonawanda, New York, whose ideas were taken over by Chance, and had not just two, but four, wheels floating in the middle. In addition it had a Wisconsin petrol engine and like most of its sort was very fine scale. It was returned looking very smart in new paint and worked until the railway closed.

We rebuilt a Simplex with new Perkins engine and a basic steam-outline body for long-term hire to Pembrey Park. This was very successful and even more surprisingly went on hire for its first winter, complete with its steam-outline body, to a peat moss belonging to Sinclair Horticulture. They loved it too and were very loathe to let us have it back come the spring. I think they were not used to such a modern locomotive. The railway at Pembrey declined, in part due to typical local authority inertia, and this locomotive, *Ivor*, went on hire elsewhere and was eventually sold to the Devon Railway Centre some six or seven years later.

Despite some substantial spares orders we now hit what turned out to be the nadir of Alan Keef Ltd. Fundamentally we were not making any appreciable amount of money out

of the work we were doing and Barclays Bank had had enough. Whilst not actually threatening to call in the overdraft they made it pretty plain that that was on the cards unless we sorted ourselves out. By a few weeks we had foreseen this coming, but to make matters worse it came at just the point where Susan and I were booked to go off to the Britain in Kenya exhibition in Nairobi. We debated about cancelling but in the end decided to go as everything had already been paid for and, one never knew, something useful might come out of it. We had also made some family arrangements for extra finance if needed, which it was, and poor Patrick had something of a baptism of fire whilst we were away. Upon our return the immediate move was to sell as much surplus, or not so surplus, stock as we could and to this end we sent out a flyer to all our customers with a list of material for sale. Had we sold all of it our problems would have been solved but at least we showed willing and did indeed sell enough to make an impression. A casualty of this was the little O&K MD1 locomotive that had been works shunter at Cote and again at Lea, although it was by now becoming too small for the job. The other major cash effort was for me to borrow enough from my father to pay off the outstanding purchase money to Simplex, which, although I had to pay him interest, reduced our overheads by many thousands per year. Inevitably there was a rationalization of staff that we had made our usual mistake of trying to keep on 'until times improved'. The whole exercise was exacerbated by a contract I had obtained in Tanzania to re-engine two Simplex locomotives for Lugongo Sisal Estate. This was exactly the type of job I had long hoped for from Tanzania, hoping to prove what could still be done with rail haulage. The job was to provide two replacement engine kits that we would oversee fitted to two chassis that they would refurbish in their workshops. The intention was that the work would be paid by monthly payments over six months. We started and then the money dried up, or not exactly dried up but became very erratic in payment. In the circumstances

This 15in. gauge locomotive (AK51 of 1995) for Cricket St Thomas Wildlife Park in Somerset is equipped for push/pull operation with a driving compartment at the rear of the train thus saving on turnaround times and track maintenance.

we had no spare cash to cope with this and it reached the point of the Perkins agents, quite amicably, reclaiming the engines they had supplied. Eventually it did all resolve itself and Patrick went to Africa to see the engines fitted. Although I do not think he liked Africa as much as I do (it is definitely an acquired taste) the locos did prove a point. However they were very shortly followed by a change of management to a man who would not accept the light rail/small engine policy I advocated and the whole experiment died in its tracks. No doubt much to the delight of the tractor and trailer suppliers.

In the circumstances any work was worth having and we did two jobs quite outside of our normal line of business. One was to make a complete staging for Ross Choral Society to fit into Ross church around the pillars and pulpit for the choir to stand on to perform. It is pleasing to know that this is still in use. Slightly similar was the manufacture of canopy framework for John Hall Craggs which was used at least annually for his railway fête.

Earlier in the year we had uplifted some track at ICI Nobels at Stevenston which had gone mostly to Dalmunzie Hotel near Blair Atholl, also in Scotland, where it was proposed to reinstate at least part of their very spectacular 2ft 6in. gauge railway. This had been pulled up and sold in some sort of family feud but its *raison d'être* was to carry shooting parties some two and a half miles to a lodge on a grouse moor. It was quite spectacular having a zig-zag with 1 in 20 gradients and a substantial viaduct over a mountain stream. The owners had retrieved the Simplex locomotive and two passenger vehicles and made a move towards restoring them. A good many years later this railway has yet to materialize.

The locomotive *Robin Hood* was mentioned earlier in this chapter and it must now be recorded that, after various unsuccessful attempts, the whole railway from Kilverstone was ultimately sold to Woburn Safari Park. Here it was installed by a 'friend of a friend' who made a thoroughly bad job of it. We should not really complain as it has created endless work for us for many years, but I do not like to see people taken in in this way. However, at Woburn two locomotives were needed either to provide two trains in service or to stand in as spare. It rapidly became apparent that the rebuilding of *Flying Scotsman* at Kilverstone – by a local firm of engineers and, judging by the number of second-hand components used, on a tight budget as well – had not been successful. The revamping of the hydraulic system was fairly straightforward but the net result was disappointing because the loco would hardly pull its train except with the engine running flat out the whole time. The engine fitted was a Renault tractor engine and it transpired that this particular engine was almost the last of its type to be made and was thus probably very cheap. The power curve for the engine showed that it did exactly as we had found – it did not develop its full power, which was barely enough in any case, until running at maximum r.p.m. Goodness knows what sort of tractor it was intended for. Ultimately we replaced this as well with a Samé 100.3AT engine that produced lots of power low down in its speed range, and all was well. Even so, on a daily basis *Flying Scotsman* was always second choice to *Robin Hood* for the staff who had to drive them.

The recovery from the low point was further assisted by securing a contract of which we were to obtain several over the next ten years, each with increasing levels of sophistication. Indeed this was a whole new market even if it did turn the clock back to my great-grandfather's railway at Mortimer Lodge – the garden or estate

railway. This first one, which has always been a very private affair, was the Wotton Light Railway in 15in. gauge. The details were decided and overseen by Jeff Price of The Miniature Railway Supply Co. Ltd. It comprised something like one and a half miles of track, which we did not lay, an 0-6-0 steam locomotive supplied by Exmoor Steam Railway, an 0-4-0 diesel, two carriages and three open bogie goods wagons, one of which had a guard's compartment. All were fitted with fail-safe air brakes and automatic couplers of the type designed by Sir Arthur Heywood back in the 1880s. From a business point of view it was ideal as we were able to invoice on a monthly work-completed basis which greatly helped in those somewhat parlous times. The whole railway lived up to expectations and completion of the above equipment was immediately followed by an order for an additional carriage, but this time extended slightly to be used as a dining car and to include tables and a cool box. There is a tendency to laugh at this type of railway and what they very obviously cost, but the world accepts hundreds of thousands of pounds, even millions, being spent on a motor yacht, so why not a railway?

At a more down-to-earth level, some track and locomotive work was done for Blackpool Pleasure Beach and a big heavy Simplex was supplied to Legoland at Windsor so that they had a means of pulling the Severn Lamb train off a viaduct in the event of failure;

When a new road was designed past Cherry Orchard Brickworks at Southend, provision was made for a bridge and rail track so that the claybeds could continue to be reached. The works closed whilst the road was being built but nevertheless the bridge was built and we laid the connecting track. The only train it ever saw was our ballast skip *Skippy*!

The Wotton Light Railway is a 15in. gauge garden line and was the first of several railways of this type. Here we see the first batch of equipment all together in one train comprising an 0-4-0 diesel locomotive, *Pam* (AK52 of 1996), two passenger carriages and various bogie wagons.

who later became part of Jos Achelis & Sohne Gmbh. They later became our official agents for Tanzania with a roving commission elsewhere. Their first foray produced two spare-parts orders worth some £37,000 between them with the sale in such a manner that Achelis took care of the payment side and we got paid within thirty days of despatch. Again very good for cash flow.

In the middle of the year we ran into bureaucracy and red tape at its most stupid, a state of affairs which has only got worse since. Cotswold Wildlife Park decided, quite rightly, that their existing carriages were no longer up to passenger's expectations and in some respects were downright dangerous and, as a consequence, ordered three new carriages. While these were in build they had a chance inspection from HM Railway Inspectorate and this was quite naturally mentioned. To this they had the response, 'Had they been type approved?' Blank looks all round. Now this is something that we, as manufacturers, cannot do, it has to be done by the operator. So drawings and all details were supplied to HMRI and an inspection of the finished units made and ultimately the new vehicles put into service. However it delayed delivery by at least six weeks. I have often wondered where HMRI, in particular, would have stood if there had been an accident in that period which could have been attributed directly to the perceived dangers of the existing vehicles and about which the operators were taking significant steps to remedy. The carriages were in fact bodies only, to run on existing bogies, and we built a further carriage body only (already type approved!) for the 15in. gauge Perrygrove Railway at

there was deemed to be insufficient space to de-train the passengers at that location. It will be recalled that we had supplied new Simplex locomotives to Cherry Orchard Brickworks. The track to the clay fields crossed a lane upon leaving the works and this road was to be rebuilt as a major northern access to Southend-on-Sea. Part of the contract for that included a bridge under the new road together with access cutting and associated new trackwork, and we had quoted for the provision of this track to the contractors, J. Breheny Ltd. In the period between quotation and completion of the new road the brickworks closed but the contract required that the track be installed down to and through the new bridge and this is just what we did – the fact that the only 'train' to ever run on it was our ballast skip *Skippy* is immaterial! Also among the oddities was a hand-propelled platform wagon for Birse Construction Ltd for use in new REME workshops for the Ministry of Defence. This was intended for taking engines into a wash bay and had to move a distance all of six metres, which was arranged by turning a large wheel on one side with chain drive to one axle and disc brakes to prevent a runaway. Interestingly, although originally designed to carry only two tons, it had to be redesigned and strengthened to carry five tons, not because the engines were likely to be any heavier, but because there was a 5-ton overhead crane in the workshop and somebody might therefore put five tons on it.

TPC in Tanzania came to the fore again at a convenient moment due to the good offices of Derek Porteus, formerly of RMP. He was now the English end of a firm of agents in Bremen, Germany,

3ft gauge all-enclosed carriage for the Cavan & Leitrim Railway in Ireland. This was built on an existing but much modified underframe but was internally very traditional with longitudinal bench seating. Just nosing into the picture on the right is the Kerr Stuart Brazil-class 0-4-2 No. 1 which originated from the Lochaber Railway in Scotland.

Coleford. Interestingly, when the Cotswold carriages came in for refurbishment some years later we found that the bearings in the bogie axleboxes were all just about worn out having run and run for something like twenty years. The roughest of rough calculations showed this to tally with the manufacturer's recommended bearing life of x million revolutions.

Our first track-laying job repeated itself when we re-laid the Santa Fe track for Butlin's at Minehead. We also re-laid the triangle of track out of the station for Llechwedd Slate Caverns in Blaenau Ffestiniog. This was in a very constricted space and allowed the whole train to reverse at the end of its trip and therefore the turnouts had to be very precisely made to fit. This is an interesting line that takes visitors into the old slate workings in an attempt to demonstrate how a slate mine worked in the supposedly good old days. Most of the excavation and much of the re-lay work was done by their own staff with us only providing technical assistance and supervision. Surprisingly, the most useful and interested member of their staff was deaf and dumb and it was very difficult not to try and verbally explain things to him. In addition to the Miners Tramway they also have a deep mine that is reached by an incline-car cable-hauled up a very steep gradient. We also had to re-profile the wheels of the car on this. Later in the year we also provided all new wheels for the Miners Tramway carriages.

After a great deal of cogitation, the Cavan & Leitrim Railway from Ireland ordered a fine bogie carriage which was to be built upon an ex-Bowater's wagon underframe that we had previously lengthened for the North Gloucestershire Railway Society for their line at Toddington. That project had been overtaken by the purchase of a much more interesting vehicle from Poland. As it came back to us it had had balcony ends and side steps made but by re-gauging to 3ft gauge it was possible to lengthen it further to something like thirty-six feet. Upon this we built an all-steel body with longitudinal cushioned seating, drop-light windows and some fancy ironwork on the balcony ends. This was an altogether most impressive vehicle and has found itself included in a good deal of our publicity material.

There was a spasm of selling Simplex spares in quantity to Richardson's Moss Litter. I think in part this was because their long-time fitter, Eddy Bouch, was approaching retirement and he wanted to leave the railway system shipshape when he did. In the event, his retirement coincided with a change of management at Solway Moss, closely followed by the retirement of Iain Richardson himself, and the railway closed completely almost immediately thereafter. This was followed by the closure of some of the other Richardson's railways. Opinion in the industry was that doing this would ultimately close the company altogether, which in due course it did. Late in 1997 the K.40, No. 47, which had been out on hire almost continuously since built, was sold to William Sinclair Horticulture for their new moss at Strathavon, not far from Glasgow. Sinclair are totally wedded to their railways which makes for a steady trickle of spare-parts sales. Despite our best efforts, and most of their people also seeing the logic of so doing, they have yet to buy a new locomotive. I wonder how much other equipment they have in daily use which is fifty years old and more!

After much haggling and long pauses in the negotiations, we finally bought back the two Simplex T series locomotives used on the Channel Tunnel. Both were re-gauged to 2ft and one went to the Butterley Narrow Gauge Railway at the Midland Railway Centre and the other stayed in the yard for a number of years until rebuilt for Leighton Buzzard. With passenger numbers steadily increasing at the Cotswold Wildlife Park we started a five-year program to re-lay the whole railway in new 30lbs/yd rail and at the same time added some weight to the locomotive to give it a bit more adhesion to pull heavier trains.

On the principle used throughout this book of grouping long-running events together, now is the time to deal with the accident at Peatlands Park in Northern Ireland. It will be remembered that in 1986 we had supplied new carriages for the new railway at this park and subsequently a new locomotive to go with them. In 1996 there was an accident caused by a broken axle. My understanding is that the axle had typically broken just behind the wheel seat and the long end had come up through the wooden carriage floor and two children were hurt. I gather there was a lot of blood but no serious injury. The Department of Environment (N.I.) who were the owners – although it later transpired not the operators at that time (they had franchised it out) – immediately, God bless them, had an in-depth investigation done into the equipment and in particular the broken axle. This came up with the conclusion that there was no fault in the design, materials or manufacture of the axle and to this I was going to cling during what was to follow. The point here is that it was not until a year later that we were allowed to replace the broken axle and repair the damaged bogie.

Immediately the accident happened I notified my insurance company of what had happened and, after a very long pause, a year or three, it became apparent that there was the probability of a compensation claim being made against the park. This was followed, again after a long pause, with notification that Alan Keef Ltd was to be included in the action on the basis that if the claim against the Department of Environment failed, then they could have a go at us without having to start all over again from scratch. The matter dragged on interminably with sudden bursts of action and then nothing. To me it was obvious that the claimants were deliberately stalling at each stage to the last moment to allow for the litigious attitude to become more embedded in society in order to give them a better chance of success. The insurance company was prepared to fight it largely because there were a string of further claims waiting in the wings for children who had suffered trauma and so on. The approach was quite clever in that none of the claims was for very much but in total they added to a considerable sum. Eventually the case was to be heard in the High Court in Belfast a week before Christmas in 2003 (yes, 2003!) and I had to go over yet again for the actual hearing and further discussions with solicitors and QCs. Ultimately the matter was all settled, technically out of court, at the 11½th hour with everyone including the judge in court and waiting to proceed with the case.

The punch-line with this is that the two children received £4,500 between them. Apparently it is the custom in this situation that Alan Keef Ltd, as a VAT-registered defendant, should pay the VAT on the legal fees. This bill came to just over £6,500 and there must have been at least a similar amount payable by the Department of Environment. It is fairly simple arithmetic to calculate what the legal fees must have been!

It was a year of small jobs, perhaps the largest of which was a 2ft gauge four-wheel gang trolley for Severn Lamb for a theme park railway in Egypt. This had a very small Kubota engine with an Eaton hydraulic gearbox as fitted in lawnmowers and drove on

Best described as a rail lorry, or perhaps rail pick-up, AK53 of 1997 was a maintenance vehicle supplied to Severn Lamb Ltd for a railway they were supplying to Dream World, Egypt.

one axle only. With two seats and rear platform it was more than adequate for two men going out to do a bit of track maintenance. For a similar purpose a quantity of Simplex spares and a 3ft 6in. gauge wagon which originally came with *Woto* were sold to Isle of Man Railways. The MoD started a program of closing their 2ft 6in. gauge munitions railways and a goodly amount of equipment started to get into the enthusiast world. However, most of these people wanted it at 2ft gauge so there started a process of re-gauging wheelsets to suit. This became, and continues to be, a steady business and we must have dealt with several hundred to date.

Mike Want of the Wells Harbour Railway approached us with a need to make some new carriages for his half-mile 10¼in. gauge railway that connects a caravan site and the beach with the town of Wells-next-the-Sea in Norfolk. In fact this was to be bodies only to run on existing perfectly satisfactory bogies. We made four of these and they proved very satisfactory. The following year he decided that a new diesel locomotive was required to go with them and thus was 'standardized' a version of the *Swee'Pea* design originally built for Hastings. This locomotive was named *Denzil* as being a corruption of diesel. This gave him a powerful and reliable unit so that steam operation became very much a rarity. Both he and his successor have always been very obliging in allowing our potential customers to look at this equipment.

The tail end of the year saw our track gang laying a new 15in. gauge railway at Gulliver's Land in Milton Keynes. This was an entirely new park to compliment the other Gulliver sites at Matlock and

Warrington. Unfortunately they decided to go their own way, with locomotive and rolling stock of similar style to that at Warrington. This has not been without its problems, but then the Phillips family can always be relied on to do it their way. This was followed by a major job for Tunnel Steels Ltd, ultimately for Severn Lamb, to lay approximately 1,200 metres of track for Ravensburger Spieleland which was situated about twelve kilometres south of Ravensburg in southern Germany, almost on the Swiss border. All materials were supplied by Tunnel Steels; we provided labour, expertise and equipment for the job which meant that our ballast skip *Skippy* went on a continental holiday. As usual it involved regular visits to supervise the job and this was a somewhat annoying trip as it could not be done in the day. It involved checking in at Birmingham at 5.30 a.m. for a flight to Stuttgart, then train to Ravensburg including a change at Ulm, with Chris Gorman to meet me at the other end. I could do all I had to that day, but I had to kill time the next as there was only a return flight in the evening. In railway terms it was an interesting area, as there were trams in both Ulm and Stuttgart and it being Christmas-time everywhere was lit up and jolly. We took this on with some trepidation as regards labour laws and health and safety requirements in Germany and consequently provided our men with hard hats, safety boots, high visibility vests and anything else we could think of. We need not have worried, there was not a hard hat in sight and the beer lorry came in twice a week to deliver to all the site huts dotted about the place. All was well but I had to return once on a consultancy basis to advise them on the subject of track wear and other problems. On one of these trips I took the train on to Fredrichshaven and spent the time in the Zeppelin Museum, which was fascinating.

Mike Want admires his brand new locomotive *Denzil* (AK54 of 1998) at the inland terminus of the 10¼in. gauge Wells Harbour Railway. Not to be confused with the Wells & Walsingham Railway, this hard-worked line connects Wells-next-the-Sea with a large caravan site and the beach about half a mile away.

Materials handling or a narrow gauge railway? The 3ft 6in. gauge train provided to take covers off sand filtration beds for North Surrey Water Co. at Walton on Thames included a hydraulic drive K.12 locomotive (AK55 of 1998) and about 100 yards of track. Whilst what we provided did its job admirably, the overall concept was a failure.

proposed to use were in a lattice form with each plastic slat about two inches wide and hinged to its neighbour so that a whole cover could be rolled off onto a drum. As the theory was that these covers would only have to come off each tank about once per year the cost of a fixed installation on each tank became prohibitive. We were asked if we could make a train which could remove the covers from a tank, move out of the way whilst the sand in it was being changed and then move back to replace them. Thus one set of equipment would serve all six tanks. We thought this was a marvellous idea and all concerned thought, and hoped, that every good water works should have this system.

The upshot was that we designed and built a small (10h.p.) locomotive with hydraulic drive so that we could use the hydraulics to drive the drums to wind the covers on and off. There being four covers on each tank there were four wagons, two on each side of the locomotive. The rail gauge was 3ft 6in. to give stability as the complete wagon with cover weighed about five tonnes and there was of course the side load of pulling the cover off the water. There was also a certain amount of technique in using the train because there was virtually no overrun of track at either end. Thus on the end tanks the covers had to be juggled quite carefully to make the system work. Also the ability to unwind a drum of sheet material is quite technical where control is concerned in order to avoid it all landing in a heap.

Again so far, so good. What we built did in fact work and do what was asked of it very well. The problems came with Aquatech themselves, their suppliers and the weather. Correctly, the slats forming the covers were glued together but Aquatech, perhaps to save cost, appeared to have used an inferior glue for the purpose. This meant that the covers had a habit of pulling apart if for any reason they did not pull cleanly, and for the same reason they never really overcame the problem of the initial attachment of the cover to the drum. Their suppliers, French I think, just walked away from the job which was silly of them, because this could have had great business potential. However the real problem, which was never overcome, was the wind. To, I am sure, everyone's astonishment, even quite a moderate wind seemed to manage to get underneath the covers and, with the assistance of wave action, move one over on top of its neighbour or alternatively break up the inadequately glued slats. A further wind problem was that it blew sand and dust onto the covers which in turn became home to quite large plants which had the merit of holding the covers together and stopping them moving about but it also prevented their easy removal. To be fair, Aquatech did spend a huge amount of time and effort trying to make their side of the system work but the initial weakness of the glue could never be overcome.

In the end they went out of business creating one of the very few bad debts I have ever had and left us to try and sort it out. Because the equipment had never been officially handed over John Palmer and I spent many frustrating days hauling covers for the water company, but in the end the problems were not ours – everyone

Over the years it has always happened that one tends to do business and go to certain areas for a while and then not go there again for ages whilst one then goes somewhere else. This seems to work on an international basis as well because we had hardly finished at Ravensburg when I was asked to commission a new Chance locomotive in a small park near to Konstanz on Lake Constance. I flew to Zürich where I was met by the German Chance agent and taken out to the park where we stayed in a typical German/Swiss chalet-type house and did our business the next day. The locomotive had apparently been delivered some considerable time previously and stored while the man built his own carriages and laid his railway. Despite my lack of in-depth knowledge all went well and the loco performed as it should and everyone was satisfied. However the track was laid to very coarse industrial standards and I have often wondered since how it all fared when in constant use. Having allowed myself two days on site I had a day to kill before returning so I took a deliberately roundabout return rail journey back to the airport and, to my regret, flew home without seeing any trams in Zürich.

The next large job was one that should have had a good potential, but was ultimately disastrous and therefore requires some prior explanation. In a traditional waterworks, water is filtered downwards through a layer of fine sand to remove minute impurities from it. This is done in large settlement tanks perhaps 200 feet long and sixty feet wide. The sand has to be changed at quite frequent intervals, not so much because it has become foul from the water but from debris that has blown into the tank, some of which is then able to grow in the sand. In recent times blue-green algae can also be a problem. For similar and also different reasons, swimming pools are covered to keep them fresh and clean. A firm called Aquatech Ltd from Newbury had the idea that if the water treatment tanks were covered as they did with swimming pools, then the frequency of sand changing could be dramatically reduced with a substantial saving in cost to the water authority. So far, so good. It was true, and it worked.

Where we came in was on a site beside the river at Walton on Thames where there were six of these tanks alongside each other and all of approximately the same size. The covers that Aquatech

Schoma locomotive and slave unit completely rebuilt for Levington Horticulture for their peat moss near Doncaster. This involved the fitting of a larger engine and, amongst other things, a better arranged cab air-conditioning system.

accepted that – and the whole concept was abandoned. Pity, because the idea was good.

John had another trip to TPC to fit a conversion unit in what they called the Kahe locomotive. This was a metre gauge version of Simplex's standard gauge shunter, which in turn was a version of the 60S. Basically it was a standard locomotive but with slightly longer wheelbase around which was hung a framework to carry standard gauge buffers and couplings. The Kahe loco was further confused by being fitted with a Simtram gearbox. This was a sort of automatic gearbox and was intended to compete with the Ruston hydraulic box, but was never as good. About a year after this we sold our No. 48, *Sally*, to TPC. In my usual manner, whilst work had been slack I had built a prototype 100h.p. locomotive over a period of time with the hope of having something to market when times got better. This one was based around an old Hunslet metre gauge frame and wheels, used a Perkins engine and JCB 720 series transmission and was a smart machine with soundproofed cab, comfortable seats and so on. It went on trial to Leighton Buzzard and in retrospect they wished they had found the money to buy it. It was fitted with disc brakes which are good for stopping but can create problems with greasy rails as Patrick found to his cost. He was approaching the Leedon road crossing, applied the brakes, the wheels locked up and he glissaded across the road at more or less full speed! Fortunately there was nothing in the way. However, and much more to the point, the sale of this locomotive at a fair price did more than anything else to turn the financial problems of the company round and thanks to Patrick it has not faltered since. I went out to Tanzania to commission it and

it was a sight to behold handling seventy-two 3-ton wagons of sugar-cane.

Butterley Brick Co.'s Star Lane works near Southend had a railway which ran quite a distance to the clay fields. In connection with a new housing development, this was temporarily closed and dumpers used instead. At the same time the ownership changed to the Hanson Group. When the time came to reinstate the railway Hanson would have none of it; 'They weren't having anything as old fashioned as that in one of their works.' And this despite proven pleas from the local management that the railway was a more cost-effective way of moving their clay. The upshot was that we bought all the locomotives and rolling stock. The sting in the tail was that they were sold to us at a knockdown price provided we would in turn pay for something else that the works wanted but which head office would not authorize! We refurbished and sold three of the locomotives (two of which we had built) to Richardson's Moss Litter. The fourth, which was the 40SD we were building for Simplex at the time of takeover, we sold to Volks Railway in Brighton for whom we re-gauged it to 2ft 8½in. gauge. It was also raised slightly to clear the electric pick-up rail. Despite being the world's oldest electric railway, this was needed to move cars around when the power was off in the winter. As part of the Richardson's deal, two K.12s were taken back in part exchange and one of the these was converted to 1ft 9in. gauge for Blackpool Pleasure Beach for much the same type of usage as at Volks. The other was converted to 15in. gauge for John Tennent for a private railway.

Fisons at Hatfield Moss near Doncaster had become Levington Horticulture, and enquired for a new locomotive for their 3ft gauge line. The axle loading was fairly low which suggested a double bogie locomotive, although it would have to be very 'flexible' to operate satisfactorily on a peat bog railway despite their track being fairly good. We developed a design of bogie locomotive of about 125h.p.

Iguazu Falls locomotive (AK56 of 2000) and train standing in our gateway prior to despatch. These locomotives were designed to burn natural gas fuel and the similarity between them and the Telford Tram in Chapter 7 is striking. 'Conductor' is Spanish for driver! Locomotive AK57 is identical.

Photography of the trains in action at the Iguazu Falls was difficult for a number of reasons and this is one of the very few showing the rear driving trailer and the general jungle terrain through which the railway passes.

down below the footplate so that sand did not get in and around all the hydraulics, not to mention that it should work properly; a decent seat for the driver from which he could see in both directions, not just a perch facing forward, and, luxury of luxuries, they wanted the cab air-conditioning replacing with a more robust system. And we did all this and more besides for them. We did two locomotives but unfortunately the money ran out to do the third one – you cannot win them all!

Years previously I had built the steam tram for Telford Town Park and it was a well-known photograph of this that brought an enquiry for a similar train for use in the National Park surrounding the Iguazu Falls in Argentina. The object of the railway was to allow cars to be parked away from the main centre of attraction, the falls themselves, and for visitors to be brought in by train. The original design promulgated by the park authorities was for a double bogie version of the Telford tram powered by a natural gas engine. We managed to restrain them to a four wheeled locomotive but it, and the carriages, had to have curved or waisted sides. Four of these trainsets were called for, together with a works or maintenance train and this was to be a rebuilt Simplex with some flat and tipping wagons. Visitors were to be channelled through a series of gift shops and information offices that would be in one large complex around the train station. This was one of the many cases we have come across where the track is laid out by architects who have little or no concept of how a railway works or of what its potential is. The aforementioned station was, as a consequence, far too lavish and could accommodate all four trains together regardless of the fact that when in operation only one at best would actually be there. In addition the railway was laid out as basically two separate railways, one about one and a half kilometres long and the other three kilometres with a long stretch of double track where the two lines followed the same route. The whole concept of running trains to different destinations or even in opposite directions on a single track

that would have done them well. As is always the way, cost forbade it but we did completely rebuild their two 'loco & slave' Schoma units.

These were an 8-tonne locomotive with a slave unit permanently coupled to it which weighed much the same and, being hydraulic drive, both units drove together from the same engine. John Palmer and I had looked at this idea for a number of customers but it requires quite considerable hydraulics to make the locomotive travel at the same speed either as a single unit or when coupled together. Schoma had not bothered about this and the loco simply travelled at half speed when operating with the slave unit. However this was not really the problem. Levington had a considerable shopping list of modifications. They wanted the five-cylinder engine replaced with the six-cylinder to give a bit more power; the sanding gear moved

seemed to be completely beyond their comprehension! I know the basics of time-tabling trains but try as I might it was just not possible to run a regular interval service to both destinations – there was always a train left behind somewhere!

Thus the whole contract was set up with a value well over £500,000 and, from my point of view, the customer's request to pay in stage payments was ideal. It was to be a twenty-month contract with twenty-two monthly payments. What could be better? The snag came when we got to payment five and the money stopped coming. By that stage we were well into the job with one trainset very largely built even if a long way from being finished and a good many components had been bought and delivered for all four. As always we carried on longer than we should

The contract for Iguazu Falls also included a service train of flat and tipping wagons together with a diesel locomotive to be used for track maintenance purposes. For the latter we rebuilt a 3½-ton Simplex (MR9411 of 1948) in the same style as the passenger locomotives.

before calling a halt, but the real problem was that we had put off or postponed other work because of this contract and it took time to recall that work to keep the establishment going. Fortunately we had overcome our financial difficulties or it would certainly have put us out of business. About a year later money became available again for two train sets only and the works train. The trains were arranged for push pull operation in order to speed up the turnround times as, especially in the main station, no provision had been made for running a locomotive round its train! For the first time we used radio control for this and the equipment was supplied by Cattron-Theimig who specialize in radio remote control for cranes and for locomotives cut into the middle of immense American freight trains. The system worked well and allowed for full gear change, throttle and so on. Whilst it is not a cheap system the cost is saved in the initial saving in track and point work.

In due course the first train was shipped out and I went to commission it. Along with the elaborate station there had been built an equally elaborate workshop building in which all four trains could be stored under cover and with a full-length pit under one track. Just shortly before delivery it was discovered that there was no natural gas within 500 miles of the park and nor was there likely to be within the foreseeable future! In something of a panic the engines were converted to LPG and at the time of my visit we had to bodge-up an upturned propane bottle with which to run the official opening as the LPG installation was incomplete. There was a further panic after I returned about tank certification. I supplied the standard certificate used in the UK but this was unacceptable and I rapidly came to the conclusion that someone was looking for a bribe. I discovered that the tanks were manufactured in Holland and quite by chance Christian Fuller had a friend who worked for the makers. I subsequently faxed no less than sixty-five pages of documentation to Argentina and unsurprisingly heard no more!

The track for the railway was done by Glastra, an Argentinian company who do main line work, and I had problems getting them to treat what they regarded as a toy train seriously, but they got there in the end. Incidentally they were Simplex agents for that part of the world many years ago and we have a few cast brass plates carrying their name. A further spin-off was a very neat lever arrangement for point working which included spring-loaded operation and a direction indicator. We have subsequently made our own version of this for various customers.

Moving nearer to home, in Ireland there commenced a run of work for 3ft gauge railways built on old trackbeds, most of them originally 3ft gauge but some on standard gauge (Irish) lines. These had a habit of acquiring some track and laying it in a straight line into the wild blue yonder with precious little thought of what was to be run on it. Whilst not in strict chronological order, one of these was built along the old Suir Valley line into Waterford and came under the patronage of Waterford Crystal, possibly one of Ireland's best known companies. This came at an appropriate moment and we were able to use a couple of the carriage bodies at that time left over from Iguazu together with re-gauged bogies from the same source. The carriages were unusual in that they were modified to half saloons, that is, one balcony end had doors to a saloon compartment with side bench seats and the other half of the vehicle was left in its toast rack form. Why they did not have one coach of each type, I do not know; but then the customer is always right. For a locomotive we had a 3ft gauge Simplex which was re-engined with a new Perkins engine and set to work. At least it was despatched to Ireland but was on display in the Waterford Crystal car park for a year or more whilst the railway was completed.

Again completion is a misnomer because when first opened it was just a continuous track starting in a container for a shed and running through Kilmeadon station and then some four miles alongside the River Suir. In due course it acquired a passing loop in the station but remained with push/pull operation and this is when our troubles started. It would appear that the four-cylinder Perkins engine and the 60S frame do not go together, there seem to be created great vibrational stresses which just destroy the engine mountings. Not least because Simplex offered the Perkins engine as an alternative to the Deutz we fitted it in good faith. However when we reviewed the whole picture we realized that they had only supplied one locomotive so fitted (just before the take-over) and that I had seen this derelict in Tanzania not many years later when it should really have been an operational modern machine. We had also supplied a retrofit engine kit to Guyana and had then supplied

A total rebuild of a Simplex T series locomotive for Leighton Buzzard produced this substantial and attractive locomotive (AK59R of 1999). Who would have thought that the preservation movement would ever reach the stage of buying an effectively new locomotive?

a replacement engine not long afterwards; there may have been no connection, but in retrospect it was ominous. The situation in Ireland was exacerbated by the train being run flat out on track that had been created by simply narrowing the main line bullhead track. Added to this, no great care had been taken over rail joints either, with the end result that some five years later we had to fit a new transmission unit which could be soft mounted in place of the Simplex gearbox. At the same time the opportunity was taken to give it radio control from a hand-held console so that the driver could always be at the front of the train. In this guise the whole arrangement has proved satisfactory even if it is never fast enough for their drivers!

We then supplied one of the ex-Channel Tunnel locomotives built by RFS at Doncaster Works to the West Clare Railway and this was followed the following year with two ex-Bowater's underframes, re-gauged and lengthened, upon which they have built their own bodies. This is another Irish reincarnation, this time on an original narrow gauge trackbed and starting from the triangular junction at Moyasta. If it can be reinstated in both directions to Kilkee and Kilrush it could be a successful proposition. Moving to Northern Ireland, at about the same time we had the power unit from one of the County Donegal Railways railcars at the Foyle Valley Railway in Londonderry in for re-tyring of the wheels. This came about from a visit of mine about a year previously when I had watched this machine in action. When starting there was some violent wheel spinning and I noticed (they had not!) that one wheel was not going round, or at least the wheel centre was but the tyre fitted to it was not! In practice the tyre could not escape and it ran like that for about a year before being repaired.

The success of the 10¼in./12¼in. gauge locomotives brought another for the Ferry Meadows Railway at Peterborough. This was much the same as the rest but, from our point of view, was a financial nightmare. The purchase was in part hire-purchased and there were troubles there with payment. We did not get paid as agreed and this reached the point of calling in bailiffs to take possession of the locomotive (this was a first). Some money was forthcoming very rapidly and we sent it back again but despite all that we were still out of pocket at the end of the day. Default in payment has been a real rarity in this business but it does occasionally happen.

The Leighton Buzzard Railway regretted not buying *Sally* to the point that they decided that another diesel locomotive of similar size was required. To this end we rebuilt the remaining ex-Channel Tunnel Simplex T series completely in order to provide a machine of slightly greater weight and power. In fact we turned the whole loco round and widened the buffer beams to provide a large and commodious cab, again soft mounted and soundproofed. This was such a major rebuild that it acquired its own R number in our built list. The only pity was that it retained the Simplex chain drive instead of having our otherwise standard shaft drive, but finances did not allow that luxury.

We completed the rebuilding of *Stanhope* (KS2395 of 1917) for Dr John Rowlands and to a very high standard as well. This machine had the doubtful distinction of having been cut in half at one stage before restoration!

Track-laying and maintenance for small railways has always been a major part of the business. It tends to take place during the winter when the weather can be dire but here it is obviously later in the year, installing the 15in. gauge line at Gulliver's Land, Milton Keynes.

The Kerr Stuart 0-4-2 locomotive *Stanhope* had spent most of its working life at the Penrhyn Slate Quarries in North Wales but when the remains of the chassis were acquired for preservation the then purchaser cut the locomotive in half for ease of transport! This did not improve his chances of successfully restoring it to working order and in the end the bits were bought by John Rowlands for whom Brian Gent started the long haul of a full restoration. For various reasons this petered out but not before Brian had successfully found many original parts to provide the correct feel for the locomotive. It then fell to us to complete the job and make the loco work. This we did very successfully so that it became something of a prestige job and set the scene for a number of other similar and larger jobs.

In similar style work started in earnest on the 0-6-0 Avonside *Nancy* for the Cavan & Leitrim Railway and, more spectacularly, on the 0-6-2 Dübs locomotive 5C, *Slieve Callan*, for the West Clare Railway. The latter's survival into the preservation era is not part of this story, but this is a proper main line narrow gauge locomotive and weighs in at some thirty-one tons. However it had stood on a plinth at Ennis in the Irish rain for some forty-five years and was completely rusted solid. The boiler was so well rusted into the frame that it took two 50-ton jacks to get it out and when inspected we found it had a hole in it. Some of the motion-work had to be cut apart with a gas cutter in order to make dismantling possible. Although this work was being done for the West Clare Railway, the locomotive remains the property of Irish Rail and they took a very serious interest in the work being carried out. Indeed, had it been found not possible for the restoration to proceed they would have required it cosmetically restored and returned to Ennis.

Cricket St Thomas Park changed hands having been sold to Warner's for conversion into a holiday hotel. This precipitated a deal of work on the railway to bring it up to scratch, not the least of which was training a whole new raft of people in how to use and maintain it. We fitted new tyres on the 0-6-2 locomotive and refurbished the woodwork in the old set of carriages. None of this was before time but money seemed to be even less available under the new regime than the old. As the decade and century came to a close we had a sizeable order for spares from RMP for a drainage board on the River Danube. On the materials handling front there was the supply and installation of a track in a factory for moving fibreglass components for Hatcher Components, who make such things as the spoilers on lorry cab roofs. Finally came the laying of 250 metres of track for use by Leighton Buzzard Railway at the Bedford Millennium Festival.

Above: Laying track on the private Beeches Light Railway. Chris Gorman, in the foreground of both this and the previous picture, has been doing this work for us for over twenty years. Note the quality of this track, with hardwood sleepers, Pandrol plates and clips, the quantity of ballast and the depth of excavation.

Left: Much rebuilt, our first diesel locomotive (AK2 of 1976) converted to a self-propelled ballast skip is now an integral part of track-laying operations. It is sobering to think of how many thousands of tons of ballast *Skippy* has moved. It should really carry 'GB' plates having been used in both Ireland and Germany!

Another Watery Interlude

Interests in boats and trains quite often go together but if you have no interest in marine matters feel free to skip this chapter. Susan is probably to blame for this further effort to acquire webbed feet and it is not really an interlude as it is very much ongoing. In about 1989 she saw a notice in *The Forester*, a free newspaper that we do not often see, for an open day at Lydney Yacht Club and suggested that I should go along. I have been on the waters of the River Severn and the Bristol Channel continuously ever since. The Bristol Channel is a silly place to sail. It has a reputation for being the most dangerous river estuary in the country and, with the world's second highest tidal range at fourteen metres off Avonmouth and 8 knot (9m.p.h.) currents under the Second Severn Crossing, even a layman may understand why. But having said that, one can have the entire Bristol Channel to oneself which is unheard of in most sailing waters. Sailing has been described as 90 per cent boredom and 10 per cent sheer terror, an overstatement in both directions, but it is true to say that the stories with which yachtsmen regale each other are of the times when life got difficult rather than of a soozle down-channel on a glorious sunny afternoon in midsummer. This narrative is no exception.

On that initial occasion I was taken for a short sail up-river from the yacht club's base next to Lydney Dock. I was hooked, and my previous small experience of sailing as a child at Lymington resurfaced with a vengeance. Alice, who was also into matters watery (canoeing and rowing), came with me and together we learnt to sail in the club's dinghy. For this we have to thank Colin Lee and Alan Freeman. Again Susan is to blame, having noticed an advert for a boat jumble at Portishead at which I bought a rather nice clinker-built wooden dinghy complete with a full set of sails and associated bits and pieces. Although I did not appreciate it at the time, this turned out to be something of a museum piece, being a National 12 of about 1938 vintage; I just thought of it as my sort of boat. I spent a lot of time stripping off old varnish and finally launched it into our inflatable swimming pool. It leaked badly, very badly! Some serious work was required around the centre-board casing to make it even reasonably watertight. So began a tradition, that I get as much pleasure out of working on, and even carrying out major alterations to, my boats in the winter as I do sailing them in the summer. I think Alice and I sailed it a couple of times at Lydney and once at Llandegfedd Reservoir, where everything that could go wrong did go wrong, before I followed the normal route of those who start off dinghy sailing by moving up to a small cruiser. This dinghy never did have a name by the way.

One of the problems of starting boating or sailing blind, as I was, is that boats are advertised by either make, marque or type, and reading the adverts of boats for sale can be like trying to read a foreign language. Therefore the chance discovery of a small attractive plywood sailing cruiser in a yard in Cardiff was a bonus. It was very much love at first sight as being, again, 'my sort of boat'. *Fortune* by name, she was mine for £1,100 and turned out to be of the Caprice type, designed by Robert Tucker and built in Cowes. She was 18ft 6in. long, 6ft 3in. beam and 2ft 3in. draught, had been slightly modified by the addition of a short bowsprit and cutter rig, came complete with a Seagull outboard, echo sounder, gas hob, berths for two and a variety of other useful oddments. In short, a very reliable seaworthy little boat of which at least one has been sailed round the world – twice.

Up to this point the limit of my sailing had been a variety of up-river sails from Lydney and an all-day cruise down-river in company with several other dinghies to Woodspring Bay near Clevedon. As a consequence of the conditions not being very good, Alice and I took Jim Orr with us for the trip back from Cardiff to Lydney, from whence she was brought home for the winter on a trailer. With some repainting and the renewal of the perspex windows she was ready for the next season and some very pleasant sailing out of Lydney. This boat was of a size that could be kept on what are called 'trot' moorings at Lydney. Here the boat is moored fore and aft to chains laid on the seabed allowing the vessel to rise with the tide and return to sitting on the mud when the tide ebbs away. It works well but there can be problems, such as ropes getting tangled and not

Fortune was a nice little boat and knew a good deal more about sailing than I did at the time. Here she lies on trot moorings in the River Severn outside Lydney Harbour.

allowing the boat to rise properly, which usually result in something breaking. Alternatively, one can miss the mooring in some way when returning to it and wind up high and dry in the wrong place. This requires going back when the tide returns – usually at about 2 a.m!

With a couple of equally enjoyable trips down towards Cleveden and beyond, Alice and I were getting quite confident by now, but pride comes before a fall. It turned out that our retiring Rector, the Rev'd Ronnie Hambleton, was a sailing man and I offered him a trip down-river with *Fortune*. We arranged for Alice to have a day off school and thus began a series of mistakes. One should go sailing dependent only on the weather and sea conditions, not in accordance with any land-based pre-arrangements. The weather conditions and forecast for a north-easterly wind that day were not good and we should really have cancelled; but one has made all these arrangements and does not want to disappoint, etc, etc. We had a horrendous time, the mainsail ripped, the forestay rigging screw came apart and the rest of the gory details do not concern us here. At the very least we should have stopped at Portishead or I should have asserted my authority as skipper and let us run before the wind to Penarth/Cardiff. As it was, we wound up limping into the Avon River and a berth with Portishead Yacht Club from where Susan came and rescued us by car. The sad part is that it virtually put Alice off sailing for life, and left me a bit nervous which may have been no bad thing.

The following year the club organized a week away down-channel with the intention of getting to Lundy Island if possible. This was a very useful trip where experience was concerned, as I found out where one could lay over for the night, how one arranged to use the showers at yacht clubs we visited and generally 'learnt the road' to use railway parlance. According to my log I had two nasty sails during the week, firstly down to the Severn Bridge which is something that has repeated itself on other occasions, and then from Minehead to Porlock Weir. The problem with the latter was that the rest of the boats had gone off like rockets and left me as tail-

end Charlie not having any real idea of where I was going. However some kind soul came out again to pilot me in. I had to leave the group early so never got anywhere near Lundy although I believe two boats did make it there. There were two outcomes of this trip for me; the first of which was that I got the necessary certificates, installed VHF radio and had the somewhat unnerving experience of someone trying to call me the first time I switched it on. The second, and more far reaching, was that I decided that for sensible use in the Bristol Channel I needed what is known as a motor sailer. This is just what it sounds like, a boat which will sail but also has a useful-sized engine under the floor for those occasions when life gets tricky. With a foot in both camps one has to get used to being looked down on by both the sailing and motor boat fraternities! The problem with making that decision is that there is only one motor sailer on the market for every forty or so of any other kind of boat and, as a consequence, they tend to be expensive. This was where the personal profit from extricating myself from Parry People Movers came into its own and bought me my next boat.

This was deliberately an experimental exercise to ascertain whether I was right in what I thought I wanted. I watched the boats for sale adverts in *Practical Boat Owner* and eventually alighted upon a Fairey Fisherman called *Seashell* for sale at Conway, North Wales. Alice and I went to have a look at it and, I think slightly to the owner's surprise, bought it on the spot for £8,500. The Fairey Fisherman is a boat which ought to be more sought after, as it has some huge points in its favour, the principal one being that it almost indestructible. The down side is that most were built in the 1960s just before the advent of glass fibre and they are now decidedly old – mine was built in 1966. Fairey Marine were looking for peacetime uses for their wartime aircraft manufacture processes and built a number of different types of boat basically of plywood but moulded to the hull shape and cooked in a vacuum bag in an oven. By repute the Fisherman was the largest size that the oven would take. This class looks very much like a traditional ship's lifeboat and I guess that was the hoped-for market, but unfortunately fibreglass got

Left: I had left my car overnight at Lydney Yacht Club and it was a time of spring tides when John Nash took this photograph. There is a mark on the wall halfway up the door on the left that marks a particularly high tide!   *John Nash*

Right: The first *Heather Bell* was a Fairey Fisherman (that is Fairey as of aircraft fame) and she is here waiting for the tide to allow entry to Minehead Harbour.

there first. A Perkins 4.108 diesel engine (a type I had fitted into locomotives), a roomy cabin with four berths, sea toilet, shallow draft, an open-backed wheelhouse and an ability to sit on the mud were all ideal from my standpoint. The sailing pundits would consider them under-canvassed but there is adequate to drive them along at close to hull speed.

I did all the usual chores with a new boat to get it into a state when one considers it to be one's own, launched at Sharpness dock in June of 1994 and then moved her across river to my mooring at Lydney. At twenty-eight feet this was just about as big a boat as could be kept on the trot moorings there and I was always a bit anxious for her at times of bad weather or high tides. After a few experimental trips I decided that this was indeed the type of boat I wanted. Having never liked the rather prissy name of *Seashell* I changed it to *Heather Bell* in memory, if that is the right word, of the erstwhile Wyvern Shipping boat of that name which had spent a good deal of its life on the same waters. For the record, the National 12 was sold to Peter Lockwood in the village, who has continued to race it at Lydney and other venues around the country ever since. *Fortune* was sold to a young man to use as a home for the summer whilst he worked in a boatyard; I subsequently heard that he had sailed her to the Isles of Scilly, but after that no more.

Never being content with a boat as bought, I set about her that first winter and completely renewed the cabin top including fitting a new trawler-style wheelhouse. Beauty is in the eye of the beholder and I much prefer this style with the forward sloping windows. Aside from looks, this makes visibility much better in the dark as lights

do not reflect. It also made her look very akin to the much sought-after Fisher range of motor sailers and she was often confused with them. I also kept her for considerable periods at Penarth Marina, which was a good place to sail from and, being well down channel, it gave one a head start to go anywhere. Like all marinas it was, and is, expensive – but like everything else in life one gets what one pays for; superb facilities and courteous and helpful staff. It was an interesting place to get in and out of whilst the Cardiff Bay barrage was being built, but I have to say that I have rather gone off it since that was completed. It has also become completely surrounded by housing. One of the problems with many marinas is that whilst they offer completely secure moorings it can be quite difficult to judge the weather until one has left and it takes quite a bit of courage to then swallow one's pride and go back in again. *Heather Bell* gave me some very good sailing and really got me to sailing entirely on my own, single-handed as the expression is. I travelled as far down-channel as Swansea, which may not seem far but can be quite exciting. I included a night in Porthcawl, a place avoided by most sailors and with good reason.

We had our adventures as well, the most entertaining of which, although it could have been serious, was a trip across from Penarth to Weston super Mare. I like to claim that was the first occasion that I sailed out of sight of land as it was patchily foggy and there were times when I could not see any land in any direction. My plan was to stay overnight in Knightstone harbour which is a small, rather exposed, drying harbour at the northern end of Weston sea front. Because of the renowned gentle slope of Weston beach it was necessary to creep in as the tide rose, anchor, and then creep in a bit further. This worked quite satisfactorily until I felt I just needed one more move to get me safely in behind the resident anchored boats. It was dark by now and Weston Bay was turning into its usual uncomfortable self, a state that I have subsequently come to know only too well. I was becoming a bit queasy and thought I would be better lying down. I must have gone to sleep as the next thing I knew was an almighty crash of water against the side of the boat rapidly followed by a second. I jumped up into the cockpit wondering where all these street lights had come from! It very rapidly became apparent that my anchor had dragged and I was about twenty yards off the promenade sea wall but as the tide had turned and I was aground there was no immediate danger. Had I actually been driven against the seawall the situation might well not have had a happy ending.

Despite it being 2 o'clock in the morning a crowd had congregated on the seafront and I did gather from the shouting that they had called the Coastguard and soon a flashing blue light was proof of this. It then occurred to me that perhaps I should call the coastguard and tell them what was going on. The conversation went something like this:

'Swansea Coastguard, Swansea Coastguard, yacht *Heather Bell*, *Heather Bell*. Over.'

'Yacht *Heather Bell*, this is Swansea Coastguard, we are incident working at the moment, could you please call back in about twenty minutes. Over.'

'Yes, certainly. *Heather Bell*, out.'

I thought about this for a while and then called them back and after the preliminaries said:

'I think I may be your incident,' and explained what had happened and that I was in no immediate danger.

'Ah, yes,' they replied, 'the lifeboat will be with you in about twenty minutes.'

'I'm sorry,' I answered, 'but I'm afraid they will be too late.' And they were.

When the water had dropped sufficiently for the land-based coastguard to wade out to me his first comment was, 'Well, you're here until Tuesday week!' And I was. That, in yachting parlance, is being neaped, running aground when the height of tides is in the falling cycle and one is stuck until spring tides come round again. To add insult to injury the next tide did not even reach the boat. The cause of the problem was not so much an anchor dragging as an anchor breaking. Moral – do not buy a second-hand anchor, it had been welded.

I obviously could not be on the boat continuously and I have to pay tribute to the beach staff at Weston super Mare for doing everything in their power within their normal duties to look after the boat for me. I made two items in the local paper and eventually got off and took myself round to moorings at Uphill Boat Centre where I have kept my boats almost continuously ever since. Lydney Yacht Club has an annual prize, the Awkward Cow Trophy, for those who get it most spectacularly wrong, and this episode earned me that. The interesting fact is the number of past club commodores who have won this particular trophy!

As has been said, this vessel was really to prove a point as to the type of boat I wanted and I was gently scanning the 'Boats for Sale' columns again. I came across an all-steel boat, *Steelia*, again in Conway (I keep clear of the place now!) at what seemed a reasonable price. Business took me in that general direction and I made the detour to have a look at her. Initial impressions were not good, with her having the feel of being more motor boat than sailing boat and I went no further. However the brokers continued to badger me and I went to have another more detailed look, by which time she was out of the water for winter storage. The upshot was that I made what I considered a silly offer and she was mine within a week at £7,500 less than the original asking price of £29,500! My father having died in 1996 this could be construed as my inheritance.

So *Steelia* was brought back to the yard at The Lea in midsummer of 1997 whilst I continued to sail and, at the same time, tried to sell *Heather Bell*. This I eventually did for not very much more than I paid for her despite having spent a good deal along the way. There is a saying about boats that they are a hole in the water surrounded by wood, steel or fibreglass into which you shovel money, and there is a good deal of truth in that. It is better to think of the enjoyment gained. Without wishing to confuse too much I then transferred the name to the new boat, which is *Heather Bell* hereafter.

In between boats, as it were, a word on this name of 'Heather Bell'. The name intrigues me. I have come across it in the following circumstances:

- There was an emigrant ship out of Tralee in 1849, just after the worst of the Irish potato famine, with the name *Heather Bell*, who carried 123 passengers to New York. She had been built in Nova Scotia and was registered in Limerick.
- There was a 53-ton sailing coaster out of Barnstaple built in 1869 of this name. She finally broke loose in a gale at Coverack in 1922 and broke up.
- Overlapping with this was another 45-ton vessel of the same name built at Cardigan but operated out of Barnstaple. This one was lost off the Irish coast in 1916.

- Then there is of course the canal boat *Heather Bell* used by Wyvern Shipping Co. and from which I derive the name. This is still extant and, at the time of writing, in the course of major restoration.
- There is, or rather was, a house on the quayside at Minehead with the name Heather Bell on the wall. The owner seemed mightily offended when I enquired about the name and promptly removed it!
- And finally, I came across a modern pub of this eponymous name near St Ives, Cornwall. The landlord knew nothing of boats but thought the name came from a plant as the site had once been a nursery.

So there you have it, if any reader has any positive ideas on the subject I should love to hear from them.

My *Heather Bell* was built in 1984 by Steelcraft of Aberystwyth and sold as a bare hull to someone in North Wales who spent the next three years fitting her out. A very good job he made of it too, although there were idiosyncrasies such as that all the berths were different lengths to suit the family, some of whom obviously grew and holes had to be cut into the cupboard sides to accommodate them. Her overall length is 30ft 0in. × 10ft 0in. beam × 4ft 3in. draught. One feature to which I took an instant dislike was the galley (kitchen) in the wheelhouse and my first move was to lose one short berth and re-install this as part of the main saloon. A later move was to additionally install a solid-fuel stove in the saloon, which is lovely on a cold night. Although this boat is remarkably well insulated and dry, all boats tend to be damp and a solid fuel stove not only warms but draws in fresh air at the same time.

At something over eight tons she weighed considerably more than I thought and the first moves to get her to the water were a story in themselves. A very clever firm of boat movers thought they could move her on an ordinary lorry, which I told them they could not. When I was proved correct they were more than a little surprised when I managed to whistle up a low loader in a couple of hours, and even more surprised when I refused to pay them for their abortive efforts. The upshot of that was that I bought a step-frame or semi-low trailer on which to move the boat and only have to hire a tractor unit from one of our regular hauliers. It gives a whole new meaning to trailer sailing, but for all that I am not alone as I have seen boats advertised complete with 40-foot trailer.

The big disappointment with this boat was that she did not steer well. Because she was on dry land when I went back to look at her a second time I did not have the chance of a sea trial, which I otherwise would have done and might not have bought her as a consequence. If I cannot do anything else, I do reckon to be able to steer a boat, but this one was almost uncontrollable and on my first visit to Lydney Dock I managed to put a dent in her on the lock gate. In due course I dropped her on the slipway at Lydney and had Tony Tucker of marine architect fame have a look at her. He made various recommendations as to the size of the rudder and the shape of the bilge keels which I carried out and these have vastly improved the problem; transformed would be too strong a word. In suitable conditions and especially under power the autopilot will steer her very adequately, but in bad conditions one cannot let up concentration for a moment.

Having said that, she has proved her worth in all types and sorts of conditions, some of them very bad – wind over tide in a Force 7 can be nasty. She draws a little more than I would wish and the keel configuration is such that I am a little careful as to what sort of seabed I let her settle on, deep mud or hard sand being the best. The Bristol Channel suffers from short sharp seas and her predecessor used to ride over one wave and land with a resounding bang on the next one, which could be unnerving and possibly not good for the hull. This one cuts through the waves nicely and is what is known as a good dry boat, that is, a minimum of seawater comes on board. She has suffered three major transformations at my hands that have changed her out of all recognition from the boat that I bought.

Apart from not steering very well, she did not sail all that well either, and for some reason the mainsail had been cut down in size. By now virtually all my sailing was single-handed and, with a conventional rig, to reef a sail (that is, to reduce its area to the wind) by oneself in deteriorating conditions is not easy or entirely safe. Some articles in *Practical Boat Owner* extolled the virtues of the Chinese junk rig, particularly for single-handed sailors, as all the control lines can be routed to one spot and, in theory at least, there is no need to go out on deck to alter sails.

I took this concept one step further again. When I was in Kuching I came across a Dutch boat that had the masts made in lattice form just like any other motorway lamp-standard or radio mast. The owner claimed three major advantages for this; first, he could make them himself; second, if something goes wrong at the top of the mast they are easily climbed to put it right, and third, for long distance or 'blue water' sailing as he was, exercise can be a problem and he got some by climbing up and down his mast! The latter would never be my problem but the first two appealed no end. As if to confirm that I was doing the right thing I came across a damaged copy of *Practical Junk Rig*, the 'bible' on this subject, at a bargain price at Stanfords' book shop in London. With this I set to work to design the whole thing and one interesting fact

came to light. When Tony Tucker had been looking at my steering problems he had commented that the mast appeared to have been set about half a metre too far forward on the hull. When designing the junk rig percentage comparisons were suggested for the position of the centre of effort of the sails (that is, where the driving force of the wind is concentrated) as compared with the original rig. My calculations were sort of nearly right but I was not entirely happy. I then theoretically moved the old rig to where Tony reckoned it should have been and, bingo, everything fell into place.

One of the peculiarities of junk rig is that the mast has no supporting stay wires, what is known as standing rigging; the mast just sticks up there like a flag pole. I was therefore a bit concerned as to the stiffness of my lattice mast but was completely unable to find anyone able to satisfactorily stress it. Even Alice's university professors did not want to know. In the end I worked out a figure for wind force on the sails at Force 5, on the basis that in anything above that I should have reduced sail anyway and thus the loading, and then mounted the mast horizontally and applied that force at the correct point along its length. The deflection was considered to be reasonable although the base had to be strengthened. I also made a mistake on the actual mounting in the boat by not allowing enough for deflection due to the motion of the boat and this led to some interesting *in situ* modifications. I then spent a considerable amount of time rigging the rig and used about 600 feet of rope in the process – there is an awful lot of string in a junk rig although none of it is heavily loaded. The mainsail has an electric vehicle winch to haul the whole assembly up and down. This is good going up, but a bit slow coming down.

The whole set-up has been very successful and suits my sailing very well. I can, as intended, control the whole thing from inside the wheelhouse. If I had a pound for every time somebody has commented on my masts I should be a rich man by now! It has also stood up to some fairly bad sailing conditions although I have to say that if the going gets bad I tend to lower the sails and start the engine. That, after all, is one of the objects of a motor sailer.

However I have to admit to having been caught out. The possibility of a dismasting is every sailor's nightmare and this did indeed happen in 2007, but fortunately in conditions that were little short of benign. I had left Uphill bound for Minehead with a residual swell in the sea and very little wind. Whilst still in Weston Bay there was an almighty bang and I thought something had fallen down in the cabin or that the main halyard holding up the sail had broken. But no, the mast had broken off about four feet from the deck and was gently falling over the side. Only one of the three tubes had broken so the process was somewhat in slow motion. The even more remarkable part was that the Burnham lifeboat was on exercise about quarter of a mile away and with their assistance I was able to get back onto my berth at Uphill before the water dropped too far. The broken tube was just as though it had been cut through with a saw and must have been a fatigue crack, possibly from new. However, I shortened the mast slightly, added some stiffening to it, replaced it much as before and offered up a prayer of thanks for what could have been very serious.

The second major work to the vessel was to fit a new engine. The original was the BMC 1.5, as, I believe, was fitted in many taxis. This was noisy, smoky and appeared to be under-powered. It also looked as though it had been second-hand when fitted although it was supposed to be the correct engine for the boat. My choice was

The second *Heather Bell*, now with all my pet modifications to date – junk rig, trawler style wheelhouse, and so on – approaches Lydney harbour in 2005. The tide across the pier-head is so strong that the boat is almost facing directly down stream as she fights her way across the current.
Martin Grainger

a marinized Kubota, a make that one knew to have a good pedigree anyway, type BV1903 of 43h.p. from Betamarine in Stroud. Whilst I was at it, I renewed the whole stern gear and propeller as this all appeared to be somewhat undersize, especially the prop. In practice I think I could have got away with an engine a size smaller when everything else had been corrected. This has transformed the boat and I am always getting comments about how quiet she is when under power.

The final phase of altering *Heather Bell* to my liking was to rebuild the wheelhouse. I had thought about this for a considerable time beforehand because taking the angle grinder to it to slice the old one off is a bit final. One can then only go ahead! The object of the exercise was to increase the internal height so that I could stand up straight – previously I was always slightly hunched which could be tiring – and also to produce the trawler-style forward-facing wheelhouse which I favour. At considerable expense I fitted all new windows and door which made for a very smart job. In service this has all proved as good as expected and the internal roof lined with mahogany matchboarding has been admired by many.

So, having done all this what do I do with *Heather Bell* when I am actually on the water? Well, despite its other problems the Bristol Channel has the merit of having a large number of small ports mostly some ten to twenty miles apart to which one can go: places such as Minehead, Ilfracombe, Tenby, Swansea and so on. The snag is that there are only four, Milford Haven, Ilfracombe, Swansea and Barry, that one can get into at all states of the tide and thus one's navigation and timing have to be pretty well spot-on if one is going to be in the right place at the right time. Put another way, one's every move is tide dependent and sailing single-handed places a further restriction on what one can achieve. The consequence is that I tend to follow a fairly regular pattern, not least because I do not like to be away from home and business for more than a few nights at a time. I tend to take day-trips across to Barry or a night or two away down to Minehead and Watchet. Alternatively up-river to Portishead, Lydney and Sharpness usually for some particular reason such as an annual rally. I have been into some unusual places like Porthcawl and St Pierre Pill between the Severn Bridges. Longer trips have taken me to Ilfracombe, round the corner to Westward Ho! and Bideford, and as far as Milford Haven.

I enjoy the planning of a trip and then the achieving of the intended passage in the right amount of time, and I find there is something extremely satisfying about arriving in a harbour somewhere in the evening, sometimes well after dark, and being able to settle down to a meal, a drink and a pipe (it's the only time I smoke!) and watch the world go by. The sailing can be exciting due to the weather, or it can be very relaxed. As I have said before,

---

<u>10.9.01</u> Left Watchet 10.10 about one hour before high water headed for Swansea via the Nash Passage. Wind F3 and forecast F3–4 for the day. 12.30 reduced sail and started engine as wind creeping up. Nash Point 14.20 and wind now F5. Struggled hard to clear the Tusker buoy [off Porthcawl] in rough conditions. Wind now definitely continuous F5 SW getting rougher. Kenfig buoy 16.45 and sails down but main yard got snagged in topping lifts but managed to release it. Then a steady motor across Swansea Bay. I hoped the conditions might ease but top of some waves at eye level when in the trough! Tawe Lock 18.45. Marina berth 19.40.

1) This is the first longish trip in this (second) *Heather Bell* in bad conditions especially with the lattice masts. She lived up to her appearance of being a 'go anywhere' boat. I am quite surprised, because she always seems a bit tender. She seems to heel so far – quite a long way – but nothing much makes her go further. The masts also seem to have stood the test of it with no apparent problem.

2) Once moored in the marina there was a layer of salt glistening in the sun on the wheelhouse roof. I have never seen anything like that before.

<u>18.8.01</u>

Left Swansea Marina	09.30	Nash Point	14.45
Tawe Lock	10.30	Bream Head	18.15
Kenfig	12.45	Uphill	18.45

Sounds easy does it not. Except that it was motor all the way except for about a mile in Swansea Bay. Wind F4-5-6 and even 7 at one point. Huge seas off Nash Point, even *Heather Bell* was digging her nose into them. But Weston Bay was flat calm and people were wondering how to sail their boats. Incredible. Engine a bit reluctant to start but otherwise kept pegging away, no problem [this was the old one].

<u>31.7.02</u> Left Ilfracombe 16.25. Possibly a bit early but fed up with waiting for the tide. Wind well into F4 for a start but by 18.15 had dropped away to nearly nothing. Engine on and motor sail a bit and then down sails.

Watched a rainstorm go into Lynmouth but cleared the Foreland at 19.15. However another rainstorm followed and crossed Porlock Bay without being able to see Porlock! Thank heavens for GPS. Just cleared in time to see Hurlestone point and clear visibility by Minehead. Called [on radio] Watchet to enquire gate times and told gate not open until 22.30 which did not seem right. However took it slowly for a while. Subsequently told that time not right and gate now open so made all speed on lovely clear night with a flat calm sea for Watchet. Gorgeous. Arrived 22.30 as planned.

<u>25.10.03</u> Left Portishead 05.30. Avonmouth radio advised of one ship going to Sharpness and others around Avonmouth but it was clear across King Road. Tide running very hard and fast. Under the new Severn Bridge log reading 5 knots and GPS 13 knots!! [that is, 8 knots of current, about 9m.p.h.] Overtaken by the *Arklow Mill* under the Severn Bridge 07.00 and overheard them commenting on the strength of the tide to Sharpness. Dawn broke about the Counts Buoy and arrived Lydney 08.00. Got in beside *Sadina* on *YoYo's* old berth very tidily despite going past the pier-head backwards! Motored all the way. The object of this trip was to attend the Lydney Yacht Club A.G.M. which raised a few eyebrows and some kind comments from the Commodore. I do not think anyone had come by sea before.

<u>13.8.04</u> Left Saundersfoot 07.30 in flat calm. But with F4-6 forecast. Motored about 4 miles and then tried to sail, only to find that the halyard winch had let go of the rope tail and was just revolving. Managed to move dinghy and repair, by which time no wind again but an increasing swell. Motored to past Worms Head which passed at 11.40 at fairly slow speed to ease motion. Then able to sail with wind F4. Wind steadily increased to top end of F5 and the swell with it. Possibly the most exhilarating sail I have ever had. At times boat sailing a steady 5 knots + tide so averaged a bit over 5 knots for the 12 nautical miles to the Mumbles. This trip has finally convinced me that I do not have to worry about the boat heeling over – just go with it. Rounded the Mumbles and lowered sail but could have sailed on. Swansea Bay was more sheltered than I expected. Called Tawe Lock who initially asked me to go to the assistance of a broken-down boat but a fishing boat was nearer. Came in at 15.30 and onto berth by 16.10. (33 nautical miles.) [This was part of a trip which totalled 210 N.M.]

<u>23.6.05</u> Had planned on spending the day in Ilfracombe but very hot and on the spur of the moment decided to go for a sail perhaps to Lundy. Left at 09.15 with no wind at all and mostly drifted to Bull Point. Put the engine on to get through the overfalls and drifted again until just enough wind to fill sails. Then sailed very slowly towards Lundy but always drifting gently south westwards.

About 9 miles from Lundy turned back with the tide at 14.00 and with a little more wind from 14.25 to 15.10 had an idyllic sail without having to touch wheel, tiller or sails. This has only happened to me once before! Even then it needed very little to get me a bit north to clear Bull Point. It seems one has to be within 2 miles of the coast before the incoming tide picks one up. Engine on 16.50 for the overfalls and no wind so motored on to Ilfracombe and moored by 17.40. (24 N.M.)

Boisterous makes her way through the Straits of Dover, probably headed for Rotterdam to pick up a cargo. She carries about 1,000 tons of cargo. Masts can be dropped to give her a low height, or air draught, allowing access into continental rivers.

in sailing terms these waters are extremely empty, there is a good camaraderie between sailors and one often meets boats and people one has only met somewhere else several years before. One of the more remarkable of such occasions was when I came into the outer basin at Ilfracombe the first time I went there and gently pulled up behind another boat to enquire of the local form, only to find two good friends from Lydney on board! We carried on together to Bideford. A few extracts from my log might be of interest (see left); I apologise for the nautical language.

And now for something completely different, as the saying goes. On one of my occasions at Sharpness I walked into the office of D & B Shipping Ltd beside the lock and said, 'Now here's a silly question. Does anybody buy a share in a ship these days?'

They looked at the ceiling, they looked at the floor then out of the window and replied, 'Yes. Occasionally, and it just so happens …!'

Thus it was that I came to know Edmund Dorman and became a 25 per cent owner of the *Boisterous*, a little coaster of about 1,000 tons capacity which we originally intended for moving logs from the Western Isles of Scotland to the pulp mills. In fact it was not until 2006 that she became seriously involved in this trade and in the meantime she was largely employed on general coasting work around the United Kingdom and the near continent. Before I committed cash to the project I had said that I wanted to actually see the ship: I wanted to be sure that it actually existed. So it was with a certain amount of trepidation that I went to Lowestoft and found her in the docks in the hands of the engineers awaiting hand-over. I went up the gang-plank and asked for the master, who was not on board at that moment. So I explained my business and who I was and was passed on to somebody else who was completely unconcerned about a shareholder appearing on board wanting

to look her over. It appeared to be quite the norm and I was taken on a detailed guided tour.

I had been on a ship before but it was fascinating to see one in detail. She has a box hold, which is just as it sounds and is straight down inside and does not extend under the side walkways. This makes for easier loading and unloading, as cargo can positioned exactly by dockside crane. Engine and all accommodation is aft. The main engine is a five-cylinder Calleson of around 500h.p. at 375r.p.m. max. The crew is accommodated in four, later five, cabins, with one of greater size and including office space for the master. A mess room, well-equipped galley, shower, toilets and utility room complete the facilities. The engine room also contains a four-cylinder Cummins to provide hydraulic power for winches and electric power when the main engine is not running. Finally, the forepeak contains a small Lister generating set for use when in port only, along with a glorious storage space for all things that might one day be useful. On top of all this is, of course, the bridge which is the nerve centre of any ship. The most immediate thing to strike a visitor is that there is no wheel! The ship is steered entirely by electro-hydraulic control and can be operated from out on deck with a trailing cable. Otherwise she has all necessary and required equipment in the form of radar, radio, magnetic and gyro compass, charts, tea-making equipment and so on. The crew is currently all Polish including the captain, and the mate has been with her for no less than eight years. He seems to love her dearly. It would be easy to be sentimental about 'one's own ship' but this is a totally commercial operation with everything geared to keeping her at sea in the most profitable manner possible. It never

Inside *Boisterous*' wheelhouse, talking to her master at the time. Spot the deliberate mistake? There is no wheel. She is steered by the knob extreme bottom left or from an extension lead which can be taken onto the deck outside.

fails to amaze me where the agents find the cargoes from and, like all haulage, it is the odd ones which are the most profitable and the regular bulk loads are only used, where possible, to return the ship to a port with a more profitable cargo. Avoidance of empty mileage is the name of the game. Even so, having taken a load to steel to the Shetlands, to find a return grain cargo out of Wick has to be remarkable.

However, problems arose in 2004 when she arrived in Sharpness with apparently fifty tons more cargo on board than she had when she left St Malo. The problem was a split in the double bottom and emergency repairs were carried out in the dry dock there. This raised a few eyebrows when I turned up to go underneath and have a look-see. In the eyes of the yard I was a yachtie with nothing to do with commercial shipping. My status went up several notches in the eyes of a grumpy crane driver! This could only be a temporary repair while decisions were made about her future, as the surveyor's

Steam boat *Hawk* is just a bit of nonsense. I bought her in very dismantled condition and spent some time getting her back to working order. This is her first trial after this. Clinker-built boats always leak after they have been ashore for a while as evidenced by the stream of water from the bilge pump!

reports suggested that a large amount of work was required. There was a modest amount of profit in the kitty but the shareholders were obviously going to have to cough up a lot more if the ship was not going to be laid up, which in my view was tantamount to scrapping her. In the end I had to double my investment, and at the same time reduce my shareholding, to cover the cost of her going to Poland for very extensive surgery. The plus side of this was that she did at the same time achieve her five-year survey (something like an MOT) and a cargo was found in both directions to pay for getting her there and back. Subsequently she went back to her usual haunts but that included an extended time-charter to Corus carrying general steel sections from North Wales to Belfast. Whilst on this work we were approached by Boyd Brothers of Fort William, a firm of road haulage contractors, with a view to their purchasing her for use around the Western Isles. In the event they did not go

through with that but at the time of writing she is on time-charter to them at a very satisfactory daily rate primarily hauling logs to the pulp mills, which is ironic as it is what we originally had in mind. In between times she carries general cargo, such as building material and anything else required, out to the islands – very much along the lines of the old Clyde Puffers. This has included the reinforced concrete components of a new harbour facility which were unloaded by a floating crane from Liverpool that completely dwarfed the ship!

In similar vein, somewhere along the way I became interested in steam boats and thus acquired *Hawk*. This is basically a 14-foot clinker-built dinghy into which a steam plant has been fitted. Remember that I had a National 12 sailing dinghy? Well, this may have once been a National 14; the construction is very similar. The whole came as a collection of bits with the boiler having no documentation at all and, in my view, the hull being the least good bit. However, more on the basis of who you know rather than what you know I managed to trace the boiler certification to the National Vulcan inspector with whom I dealt at Cote and all was resolved. The engine is a Stuart Turner 5A, and it does all work although maintaining adequate steam pressure is a problem not yet wholly resolved. However some fun has been had with it and Susan in particular seems to have taken to steam boating whereas sailing is not her scene.

The first ones to get away, Bagnalls 2087/8 of 1919, *Lady Luxborough* and *Leonard* at the Birmingham, Tame & Rea Drainage Board's Minworth Depot. I was offered these two at £30 each in about 1961 but could not afford the cost of transport home! One of them still had a current boiler certificate.

13

The Ones that Got Away

It strikes me as appropriate that this chapter should happen to fall as number 13! Inevitably in any business there are possibilities and potential orders which do not happen. Either one loses them to a competitor or, more frequently in our case, the job is not done at all. Over the years there have been a good number of these, but some of them have been interesting in their own right and are worthy of record for that reason if none other. By the same token, there have been more in recent years simply because we are doing a greater volume of business. An encouraging feature of many has been that small railways have been at least considered by someone for a particular use.

I have to start back in the days of being at The Red House and the inauguration of the Iron Horse Railway Society at Leighton Buzzard. They planned an American-style 2ft gauge line and it just happened that I had read the 'bible' on the subject, *The Maine Two Footers*, and it was possibly Alf Fisher who put the promoters in touch with me. In turn I drew up a modified design of carriage which might just run at Leighton Buzzard – the originals were far too big – and spoke to my church repairing friend, Peter MacKinnon, with the idea of building an all-wooden vehicle. He had a contact at Wolverton carriage works and we had a fascinating afternoon there with a crash course in carriage design and building. Needless to say the whole idea came to naught, no doubt as much due to lack of money as anything else.

When what became Cotswold Light Railways was being thought through, I did offer the project to the Cotswold Wildlife Park at Burford, a place which has cropped up a good many times in this narrative. I was turned down flat and no doubt the course of my history would have been very different if that idea had been successful, indeed this book would never have been written. Although a railway was built there not long afterwards, as with Arnolds at Leighton Buzzard they were just not interested when I asked the question.

Not very long after the railway manufacturing business became a business I was approached by Thomas Hill Ltd of Rotherham with the idea of producing small steam locomotives specifically designed to burn bagasse, which is a waste product from crushing sugar-cane. The enquiry came from the Far East, probably Indonesia, where the skills were available to maintain steam locomotives, but for diesels the availability of spares and the skills to fit them were serious problems. Although burning bagasse in the mill boilers is commonplace, using it in a mobile situation is rare. The problem is that bagasse is light, bulky and has a very low calorific value requiring huge quantities of it to keep steam. There are indeed huge quantities of the stuff available and in the Philippines, where it was used in locomotives, huge tenders are required to carry sufficient. I spent a good deal of time trawling through the Patent Office for ideas on how to burn the material but never really came to a conclusion. In reality I think it required a large amount of research and development which neither of us could afford or wanted. The project simply died.

Whilst at Cote I thought I was going to be building an entirely new, but quite short, industrial railway in Witney when a concrete works decided that a light railway would have advantages for moving materials in their works. They got as far as buying some track and bogies, ordering a second-hand Simplex loco and then went bust. Much later I had an almost exactly similar scenario with a concrete beam works in Wells, Somerset, although in this case nothing was actually bought. Similar was a proposal to build a large standard gauge locomotive for Plasmor at Knottingley, Yorkshire. This was to be used to move raw concrete blocks in and out of autoclaves for curing. Whilst it was to be some 120h.p. and fifteen tons weight, it only had to move at walking pace or less. It was to be a bogie machine and I even got as far as acquiring a couple of ex-Glasgow Underground bogies as a basis from which to work.

At the time that I did the deal buying locomotives from London Brick Co. and selling them on to Blue Circle Cement, I came across a great hunk of a Simplex locomotive at Fletton of a type which I did not recognise. I could probably have bought it but did not bother. With hindsight and the take-over of Simplex I realise that this was a Simplex 9-ton loco and possibly the only one in this country. Of academic interest only, but it was no doubt scrapped. In the same vein I probably should have taken the Fowler single-cylinder locomotive from Blue Circle but I could, quite rightly, see no commercial use for it. This at least was preserved. At much the same point in time I had talks with Booker Agriculture about building a fleet of bogie wagons for a sugar estate in Madagascar. These were to be of substantial construction on diamond frame bogies with roller bearing axleboxes. This reached the point of my going to their offices in London to discuss details and despite the obvious small size of my operation they appeared to be taking me seriously – but all to no avail. Although it never progressed to the stage of any action being taken, there was a proposal to rebuild the ex-Portugal Orenstein & Koppel *Pedemoura* for the Welsh Highland Railway.

On several occasions I have been asked to provide a long length of track (as much as a mile) and large numbers (sometimes hundreds) of four-wheel bogies upon which a pipeline could be welded up and then launched into the sea, with further lengths being welded onto the end, *ad infinitum*, until the required length was attained. The construction industry has improved, but the number of contractors who seemed to think I might have all that lying around ready to pick up in a couple of weeks' time was quite remarkable.

A major job which came to naught, but inevitably cost a lot of time and money on the way, was rebuilding of the railway on the country's longest pier at Southend-on-Sea. This was to be done in conjunction with Severn Lamb, they to build the trains and me to do the track. The railway was to be rebuilt and operated by a private individual who ran an amusement park at the landward end of the pier. In the event he either backed out or decided he could not afford it and the local council took the project on themselves. In view of the work already put in I was to be the nominated supplier for the track, but when the tenders went out they had made a 'mistake' and failed to make me such. I tried to join forces with a firm of contractors very conversant with that type of work but the job went elsewhere, with the trackwork going to Track Supplies & Services of Wolverton. I was very annoyed but managed, after considerable effort, to get a contribution to my costs from the original proposer. My first experience of light aircraft flying was on a visit to Southend with Mike Lamb, not with him as pilot I hasten to add.

In the business expansion plan produced at Cote the proposal for K.12 locomotives for Teneriffe was interesting. Apparently the mountain in the middle in Teneriffe acts like a sponge and collects rainwater. At that time the 'in' way of making a fortune on the island was to tunnel into the mountain and sell the water running out. One of the requirements was that the locomotive could be dismantled into small enough pieces that it could be carried up the mountain on a donkey! RMP, who were the agents involved, sold huge quantities of very light rail for these 'water mines' but I suspect their commission may have killed my selling large numbers of K.12s.

Again in Cote days I spent a good deal of time on a possible railway for an estate in Texas which grew flowers on what appeared to be a scale that only the Americans could cope with. They intended to install a railway with a fleet of covered wagons that would carry flowers from the growing greenhouses to a central packing and despatch point. The idea was not entirely new to me, as in my childhood there had been a flower-growing establishment near Eaton Socon which had much the same set up, albeit very small and hand pushed. In reality, at that stage of the business it would

probably have been too big for me to cope with but in the end it just went dead and I never heard any more. The latter seems to be a recurring theme with enquiries from the USA, terrific enthusiasm and then nothing. I have since read somewhere that that is how one terminates a love affair over there, so perhaps it continues through into business life as well.

There are times when I think one should have a rule in business that one does not attempt to do one's customers any favours because they are apt to rebound on one with a vengeance. One such case was the trial of a Simplex U series loco at Fisons' peat works at Swinefleet near Goole. Fisons, later Levington, were principal users of 40S Simplex locomotives and were considering new and larger locomotives, but they were severely restricted by the light rail over which they would have to run. We suggested a locomotive and slave unit which would have consisted of a Simplex U series with a unit of equivalent weight permanently attached to it but driven from the main engine hydraulics, thus spreading the weight over four axles instead of two. As a precursor to this idea we let them have a Simplex U series on trial that we happened to have and which we re-gauged to 3ft for the purpose. This machine was cabless and in the event gave considerable trouble both with the engine and hydraulics. Despite the fact it was on free loan, I think they took the view that if that was the best we could provide then they did not want to know about us, with the result that they bought identical units from Schoma which in turn had their own problems as has been related.

A similar situation arose with the sale of No. 48, *Sally*, to TPC. This was sold to them at a very favourable price at a time when they were desperate for anything that would haul sugar-cane, despite the fact that everybody knew it was under-powered when compared to the later Simplex T series conversions. When this started to give transmission trouble due to overloading the fact that it was never intended to be comparable was quietly forgotten. It was only by the sheer chance of a misdirected email that we discovered that they

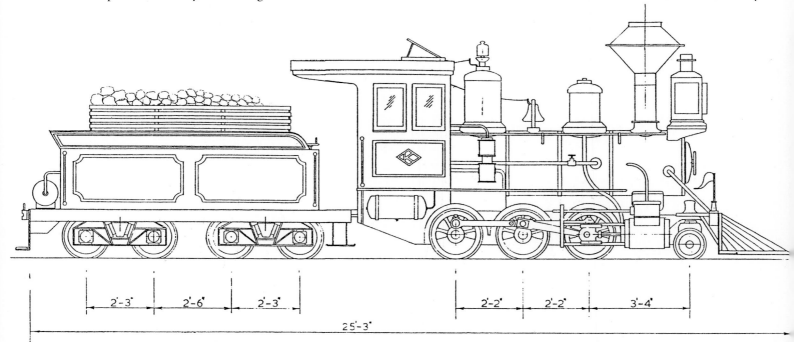

John Palmer put together this substantial design of American-style Mogul locomotive for a project in the Far East that ultimately came to naught. The tender was to have been the 'locomotive' with Perkins engine, JCB transmission and shaft drive to the wheels. Despite our best efforts we have never succeeded in selling the design to anyone else in the twelve years since.

Scale 8mm:1 foot

were seriously looking for prices for a new locomotive. With no sensible specification to work to we over-specified in some areas and again lost out on price to a bruiser of a locomotive from Schoma. Slightly more complicated were the problems with the Waterford & Suir Valley Railway in Ireland which have already been related, but again it was an attempt to provide suitable equipment on the cheap yet the customer not viewing it in that light.

In 1989 we had an enquiry from the Crown Agents for four locomotives for shunting main line wagons in cotton gins in Zimbabwe. This was before the development of the K series locomotives and we offered beefed-up Simplex 60Ss of eight tonnes weight for the job and actually got the order. Then disaster struck in that the bank would not give us any assistance in the way of increased overdraft facilities to finance the job. Bert Raven, our dour bookkeeper/accountant at the time, was particularly unhelpful into the bargain. The Crown Agents were not interested in a suitable form of stage payments and so we could not proceed. I am sure it created a wealth of ill-will towards the company that spread around the industry and which I said at the time would take us ten years to overcome. I think I was about right, it certainly cannot have helped our problems of the mid-nineties. On a personal note I was desperately disappointed by this occurrence and had I been working for any other organization I would have resigned on the spot. I very nearly did, and would have done so had my personal finances not been at a particularly low ebb at that moment in time. It is certainly true to say that I lost my overriding enthusiasm for the business with that *débâcle* and it is just as well that Patrick was there with his determination to carry it forward.

I have always been disappointed, although not as seriously so, that my efforts through the 1990s with the Tanzanian sisal industry never really bore fruit. I was very new to Africa and doubtless naive as to the ways of the continent, in particular the necessity for somebody to be paid off for anything at all to happen. Initially at least I was largely dealing with Europeans with whom this certainly

did not seem to be required. Two other things might have helped. The first would have been to set up my own business in Tanzania to deal in second-hand equipment, very much as the business had started in this country. I obviously could not do it myself and finding someone with the enthusiasm and honesty to do it for one would have been all but impossible. The second was to find a source of grant-aid finance to pay for what needed to be done. I did find someone who claimed he could do this but he wanted between 10 and 15 per cent on all subsequent transactions and I turned him down, which may have been a mistake.

The proposed railway in the bird park to which I went on my abortive trip to Turkey was a good idea in principle but was far too elaborate in conception. The idea was to take people from their cars, coaches and even a new railway station, through the park to the newly opened visitor centre and then on to the site of an old fortress on a hilltop from which there certainly were some panoramic views of the area. The distance would have been some six kilometres. However the coaches for this railway were to be a pure replica of road motor coaches complete with air conditioning, tinted windows and so on. As a consequence it needed to be at least 3ft gauge and the costs just escalated out of all proportion. To make matters worse, Ismir is the commercial capital of Turkey and not really a tourist area at all. I subsequently went there a second time for an equally abortive exercise. This time the proposal was for a series of diesel powered tramways, complete with street running in places, to connect inland villages to the sea, this time in an effort to promote tourism. One of these was at least reasonably sensible and could have been viable. I believe part of this scheme had been an electric tramway at one time, but again nothing came of it.

Not once, but twice, I attempted to sell new locomotives to British Steel at Shotton Steel Works. John Palmer and I went there the first time to view what was needed, and that was massive. The locos were used to transfer incoming steel coils either direct from mainline wagons or from the stockyard into the works for

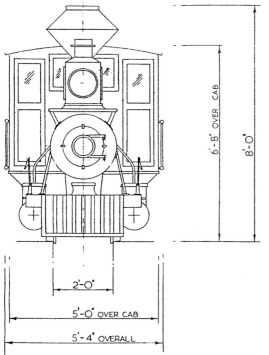

Taken from a Motor Rail sales leaflet, this is a 9-ton Simplex locomotive. The picture is certainly at a London Brick Co. works and it might have been the only one in use in this country. It could have come my way if I had realized its rarity at the time. There are still a few at work in Fiji.

Whilst we had the consolation prize of rebuilding their existing Schoma locomotives, to have built this Bo-Bo locomotive for Levington for use on their peat workings would have been impressive indeed. For environmental reasons the long-term future of the site precluded the capital cost involved.   *Scale 8mm:1 foot*

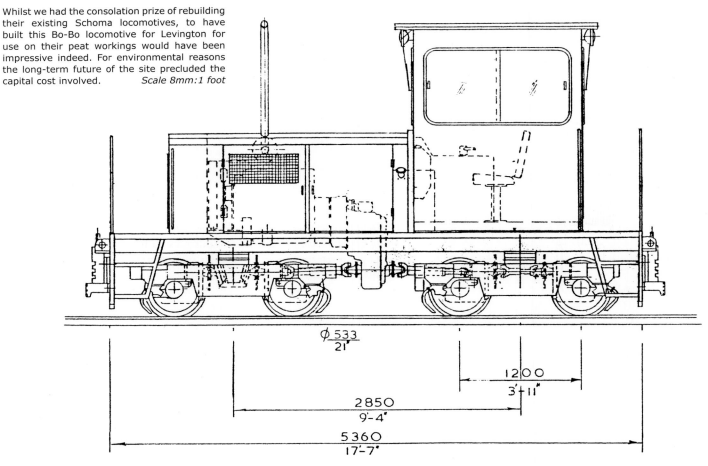

$\phi \frac{533}{21"}$

$\frac{1200}{3'-11"}$

$\frac{2850}{9'-4"}$

$\frac{5360}{17'-7"}$

processing. Sufficient to say that the wagons had signs on them stating that the load was not to exceed sixty tons! The existing locomotives comprised three Hudswell Badger (formerly Hudswell Clarke) 0-6-0s based on their mining locomotives on the outside tracks and a Hunslet Plantation class plus some Greenwood & Batley electric locomotives used inside. I think they liked what we had to offer in the official tender and on both occasions assured us that in due course it would genuinely happen – but it never did, and now the whole plant has closed.

Patrick went to St Kitts in 1997 with a view to a tourist train over part of the 'round the island' sugar-cane railway. This was eventually done by a consortium from Alaska, of all places, but we had no part in it. A couple of lesser projects were a replica brake van for the Cavan & Leitrim Railway for which they had found, or scrounged, a number of original parts, and a short 12¼in. gauge line in a bird park in Lanzarote. The latter was actually owned by a man who came from the next village to Lea.

At Jeradong Park in Brunei there is a 15in. gauge railway supplied by Severn Lamb and managed by Kieth Watson of Perth, Australia. We always hoped to supply a proper diesel locomotive for it, but this has never happened. A third locomotive has been offered twice to Chhatak Cement Co., and on the first occasion would have been ordered except that the government had given the company six months in which to make the works profitable or they would withdraw subsidies. Therefore, despite the fairly desperate need, no money was being spent. The second time round it just went dead. Similarly several offers have been made to Pakistan Ordnance Factories, but to no avail; this was a Simplex customer and the

locomotives were unusual in requiring aluminium/bronze wheels to avoid the possibility of sparks.

Mention has been made of potential railways in Brunei and Sarawak. The former was to have been from a base on the river, which could easily be reached by boat, up into the hinterland to a guest lodge, yet to be built, at a fork in the river beyond which it was only possible to walk. As the river was fast-flowing and therefore rising quite rapidly, the gradients were going to be quite steep. Added to this was a deep valley for a small tributary that had to be crossed. This involved a considerable detour that did at least allow more distance in which to gain height, something that I simply could not get those involved to understand. The line also started off with what would have been a sizeable bridge, perhaps 200 feet long, across the river, it apparently not being possible to disembark from the ferry on the other bank. Not only would the railway have carried guests to the forest lodge, but also all supplies to and rubbish away. They were fairly pragmatic about what was wanted – a diesel locomotive that perhaps paid lip-service to steam outline, carriages with wide overhanging 'eaves' in order to keep off the worst of the frequent tropical downpours, together with suitable vehicles for stores, staff and rubbish. It would have been a fascinating railway both to build and operate but, because they would not keep it simple, for instance avoid the river bridge, the cost escalated to the point of being ridiculous. On my second visit, when the Chinese were involved, the situation just got worse. Because they understood even less about railways they covered for it by producing all sorts of side issues that they did understand, such as fancy gardens and street lighting, which merely drove the costs even higher.

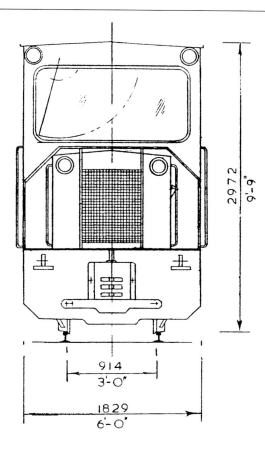

there mostly via RMP and a local agent, North Borneo Trading. In Brunei, and again in Kuching, I came across one of their offices and in both cases called to see if there was still any business to be done. In Kuching they were at least aware of the existence of Simplex locomotives but explained that to the best of their knowledge there were effectively none in operation, indeed the logging railway itself was a thing of the past. At least it was nice to know.

I spent a considerable amount of time and travelling for a firm called KK Balers Ltd who made a roller crusher to compact material into waste containers as used in local authority waste disposal sites and industrial situations. This consisted of a roller on the end of a hydraulically operated arm that rolled and crushed the waste material in order that it took up less space in the container with consequent savings in ultimate haulage costs. Our part in the exercise was to mount the crushing unit as a self-propelled unit on rails that could thus serve several waste containers on the same site. This had been attempted by others but far from successfully. The whole concept was good but ultimately of no avail.

During Patrick's trip to Kashmir he had time to visit the railway museum in Delhi and there dutifully left his card. In due course this filtered through to the fact that the Darjeeling Himalaya Railway was looking for new steam locomotives. By some other means we acquired an agent in New Delhi who at least had some idea of railways, although he had some difficulty in getting away from huge diesel locomotives. He arranged a trip for Patrick to Darjeeling to see the existing locomotives and their maintenance facilities at first hand. If nothing else it was worth it to have had this sort of opportunity; it is what makes it all worth while.

At the time, SLM of Switzerland were endeavouring to market a twenty-first-century brand of steam locomotive upon which the Indians had become hooked. To be fair, the design was revolutionary in that it had such sophisticated boiler insulation that

Mulu Caves, which as the crow flies are only about fifty miles from the up-river railway site in Brunei, was an even more grandiose version of the same idea, to take tourists to see the jungle and in this case the caves themselves. The idea was sound and the finance appeared to be no problem, and I genuinely think it would have happened if the Far Eastern economies had not all suffered a major collapse at the critical moment.

The large Mulu Hotel was already there and attracting visitors. It could have been halfway along a line about twelve miles long that was to join the caves to the hotel, to the airport and on to further caves. It was to have been of 2ft 6in. gauge to allow for large rolling stock to carry a (small) plane-load of people all at once and several miles of it would have been on stilts above the ground. This was partly to allow the jungle floodwater to pass underneath and partly for environmental reasons of not disturbing the forest floor. The hotel itself is also on stilts for the same reasons. Its operation would have had to be quite sophisticated as it was intended to operate a considerable service including through trains to the caves and short workings to the airport only. It was all being taken sufficiently seriously that if it had happened it was proposed to close most of the roads in the area. The scheme reached a situation where orders were close to being placed, but then there were international problems with the national economies of the area and it was put on hold. Alas, despite it having raised its head once since then, I fear it has to remain a might-have-been and the only railway in the area was a hand-worked one from the river bank to bring in materials for the extension of the hotel.

Brunei, Sarawak and Sabah had collectively been North Borneo and part of the British Empire. As such, Simplex had sold huge numbers of locomotives, several hundreds, to the logging industry

One major scheme that has as yet come to nothing is a railway to the Mulu Caves, the world's largest, in Sarawak. This line to bring materials from river boats to the hotel extension is as near as it has so far been managed.

it hardly became cold and was fitted with electric heating elements programmed so that steam could be raised within minutes of opening the shed doors. Needless to say it was oil fired. They had sold two of these in rack-locomotive form to the Brienz Rothorn Bahn where they appeared to be very satisfactory. However the down side was the cost, which was at least twice that of a conventional locomotive, and in our view it was highly unlikely that the facilities at Tindharia workshops would have been capable of maintaining such a machine. Accordingly, we decided to offer an upgraded version of the original B Class Sharp Stewart locomotives, which after all had served the railway well for a hundred years, with the only major concession being to oil firing.

The tender forms were based on the SLM model and, with Indian bureaucracy being what it is, it became almost impossible to explain to anybody just what we were trying to achieve. In particular, because they had never heard of the Laidlaw Drew system of oil firing, they just did not seem able to accept that if at that time all of the United Kingdom's larger narrow gauge railways used it, it probably worked satisfactorily! In the end they did not buy a steam locomotive from either us or SLM, presumably because of cost. However they did subsequently manufacture one to their preferred design in India but by all accounts it has been singularly unsuccessful. In the meantime they bought some Schoma diesels built under licence in India which have, understandably, transformed operations on the DHR and the possibility of any new steam locomotives must be considered dead. For the record, ours were going to cost about £500,000 each.

Shortly after this a development officer rang up from the Falkland Islands enquiring about a railway system to move calcified seaweed from the seashore to a point inland on the island's road system. Apparently on the windward, or western, side of the islands there are great banks of seaweed which have calcified into a very weak limestone. The intention was to grind this down to form a fertiliser

with which to reduce the acidity of the cultivatable land and also for export sale. The reason for a railway was that a good deal of the intervening land was more or less peat bog and, as in commercial peat operations, the railway would spread the load. In addition, a railway would leave a very small 'footprint' on the landscape when the operations were complete.

I was sent detailed plans of the area and on these I laid out a suitable line some three to four miles long with the best gradients obtainable and at the same time allowing for connection to a second site at a later date. The theory was that the train(s) would consist of flat wagons carrying box skips of material that could then be unloaded by forklift either into a crusher or into lorries for onward transit. Again in theory, one trainset was just adequate for the proposed level of production although I felt that they should allow for two and a spare locomotive as well. Track was to have been basically light Jubilee track on steel sleepers. I did look into the possibility of reclaiming track from sisal estates in Tanzania and this proved possible, although whether the only marginally reduced costs would have been worth while is arguable. One thing in the Falkland Islands Company's favour was that they had their own ships, so transport from almost anywhere in the world was not a problem. Indeed one of the objects of the exercise was to provide return cargoes for their ships.

Once again this was all set up to go and then fell at the penultimate fence for a somewhat unexpected reason. Wisely they carried out quite a large experiment to see that what was proposed was indeed possible. It turned out that the calcified seaweed was in fact only a crust, albeit a fairly thick one, over not very much underneath. Consequently there was simply not enough material available to make the project viable. This was sad as I was looking forward to a trip to the Falklands; not least because I hoped I might be able to do a deal for one or both of the remains of two Kerr Stewart

Abigail was designed specifically to suit the Bure Valley Railway and reached the fully-detailed specification stage complete with this artist's impression. With 7in. × 11in. cylinders, superheated boiler and roller bearings throughout, fourteen coaches at 25m.p.h. would have been no problem.

'Wren' steam locomotives which exist out there and had originally been part of a peat operation. Subsequently they came back to the attack, with possibilities for restoring one of these locomotive which have been lying in the harbour for over fifty years! But again, nothing.

Early in the new century we had one of our rare head-to-head competitions with Severn Lamb, over a railway in Dubai. This was a theme-park railway of the type which they typically provide and included a couple of train sets and about a mile of track. We offered very competitively and were very well placed to obtain the order to the point where I went to London to meet the consulting engineers. I subsequently went to Dubai to see them again and also to look at another project for which we were, hopefully, the only supplier involved. Although it was admitted that we were the most competitive on price and that they would have preferred to deal with us, I was told that they 'couldn't have our equipment even if we gave it to them'! So who was paying off whom I wonder? The other job was looking fine but then the project was abandoned completely. So much for Dubai, until next time.

Back in the UK we were approached by British Nuclear Fuels Ltd for a complete railway system for the removal of contaminated waste during the decommissioning and dismantling of Trawsfynedd nuclear power station. This was to consist of a remote-controlled battery-electric bogie vehicle that would take a 35-tonne container through suitable air locks into the contaminated area in which it would be filled and sealed. It would then come out into a new building for external washing and decontamination before being moved to a storage area or loaded direct to transport away from site. The vehicle would have made about one movement a week at most! We went through a terrific rigmarole of tendering for this and liked to think we were well placed. Eventually the project was cancelled in its entirety for reasons that were never entirely clear although it seems that they downgraded the category of the waste so that all this decontamination was not necessary. However the most extraordinary thing was that BNFL never let us know. Having bombarded us with paperwork it was only when we rang to enquire what, if anything, was happening that they told us it was effectively nothing. Pity, it would have been an interesting and prestigious job.

Following the success of *Mark Timothy* at the Bure Valley Railway, Alan Richardson asked for proposals to provide another locomotive for this line. Ian Gaylor designed *Abigail* specifically to suit the railway but to use, where possible, components that were common to their existing locomotives. The specification called for the capability to handle a 14-coach train at a continuous 25m.p.h. with power to spare. The upshot was a 2-8-0 tank engine with 7in. × 11in. cylinders, superheated boiler, Lempor exhaust, roller bearings throughout and a commodious cab. This may appear an odd design but it should be borne in mind that locomotives on this railway only work in the forward direction. A tank engine has maximum adhesion with most of its weight on the driving wheels and the absence of a tender allows another carriage in the train. This project reached the full specification stage, including an artist's

The cabs on the locomotives on the Darjeeling Himalayan Railway locomotives are intended for the local population and Patrick had something of a squeeze to get into the driver's position. His visit was to obtain further information prior to quoting for two new locomotives.

impression from Jonathon Clay, and the cost (close to £250,000) was only one of a variety of reasons why it fell by the wayside. By any standards *Abigail* would have been an impressive machine with a truly stunning performance. Perhaps the world was just not ready for her!

The other fairly long-running saga over the years has been the possibility of building rope-worked passenger funicular railways for various uses and in various places. We became deeply involved in making new bodies for the water-balanced incline at the Centre for Alternative Technology at Machynlleth in Wales, but so far no business has resulted although it did give me a useful insight as to how these things work, particularly the safety-brake system.

A slightly similar fate befell a project near Cork in Ireland for two funiculars on a golf course. We were approached by the supplier of the winch to do the trackwork and build a suitable car to carry the golfers and their golf caddies. The owners had bought, or been given, a some lengths of very second-hand ex Irish main line 5ft 3in. gauge track and were insistent that this should be used. Anything less suitable is hard to imagine and I effectively refused to use it. The owners seemed unable to appreciate the safety risks and went off in a huff with nothing being done. This was more than a pity as there were reputed to be several other golf courses in Ireland waiting to see how this idea worked out.

2006 turned out to be one the most difficult years I remember and Patrick had a very hard time of it despite all the hard work he put in. The memory is rather of what did not happen rather than what did. For instance, we retained a locomotive number, 75, for a new locomotive for Wicksteed Park to be delivered for the 75th year of operation of their railway. It has yet to happen. The year was supposed to kick off with major work for Fintown Railway and whilst this has happened, it was mid-2007 before it

Pibroch, almost the last Clyde Puffer to be built, does not look as bad in this photograph as she actually is. Had she not been almost as far away as one can get in the far west of Ireland I might have been persuaded to attempt to save her!

was completed. Major track alterations at the Cotswold Wildlife Park were postponed until the autumn, after we already had the materials on site. We actually received a substantial order from the UK Atomic Energy Authority and four days later it was cancelled!

Some ten or twelve years ago we quoted for a railcar for the Air Traffic Control authorities for use on the Snaefell Mountain Railway on the Isle of Man. This was for service and emergency use to a tracking station on the summit and normally would only be used in the winter when the icicles at the top are reputed to be horizontal! In summer the normal electric car service suffices. John Palmer put together a design for this but the final contract went to Hugh Phillips Engineering. In 2007 we were approached to refurbish and modify this vehicle; again the contract went elsewhere, reputedly on cost but, because no proper specification was provided, like may well not have been compared with like.

Relating to the last chapter rather than the railway industry, by a series of coincidences I became interested in the Clyde Puffer *Pibroch*, more as bit of nonsense than anything else. This was the last genuine Puffer to be built, albeit always diesel powered, and a very handsome little ship she was/is too. Quite by chance I came across a copy of *Sea Breezes*, a magazine for those who had been to sea but of which I had never seen a copy, and, lo and behold, there was a report about *Pibroch* and where she was lying in the far west of Ireland near to Clifden in County Galway. I persuaded (he did not need much persuasion) Michael Kennedy of the Cavan & Leitrim to go and have a look and send me some pictures. This he did, including details of the owner and that she could be bought for £9,000. At face and photographic value it seemed like a good idea. The snag was getting her back and then what would I do with her? A friend of a friend in the Isle of Man who had a tug as part hobby, part business quoted me £18,000 to tow her back, It still looked feasible – just.

This was at the time when I was going to Ireland regularly in connection with the Lartigue project and I persuaded Edmund Dorman that he should find some business in Ireland, which he did with alacrity, and together we went to have look at her. Oh,

dear; what a sorry sight she made. She was largely all there and, although I think she had been at least temporarily sunk, she was just afloat. The hatches were up and the hold full of water and the owner told us that there was a minor (how minor?) leak in the bows. The accommodation was complete and not in bad order; the engine room was absolutely filthy from the engine having been run with a broken exhaust pipe but again everything was more or less there. The topsides were as rusty as hell, there is no other adequate description, and there remained the burning question of what was I going to do with her?

There is no doubt that I could have bought her very cheaply, almost literally given away, and got her towed home for usefully less than quoted. Alternatively, a week or so's work on site could probably have had the main engine running and she could come back under her own power. Maybe; it is very much the real Atlantic off the west of Ireland and not to be trifled with. If I had had the time, which then I did not, and had had total dedication, which I did not really want to have, she could have been transformed back into her real self and possibly found some work servicing fish farms or some such. Alternatively, she could have made a personal yacht, houseboat or whatever. No. Very reluctantly I turned it all down and kept the money in the bank. Subsequently I have heard of attempts to preserve her but they appear not to have been successful. I saw her again some five years later and to say she is a depressing sight is an understatement. Let's leave it at that.

On an equally different note, and before I got involved in ships, my beloved Mkonge Hotel in Tanga came up for sale. A 50-bedroom hotel, even in Tanga and even in a run-down state, had to be worth £60,000. After all, it is in the most gorgeous position on a cliff top overlooking the bay which forms the natural harbour of Tanga and has extensive gardens with it. Whether it could have been made to tick at long range is probably another matter altogether but I was very annoyed at being 'used' to push a local Indian consortium into buying it. In the event they largely abandoned the place and it was left to the minority shareholder and his Dutch wife to actually try and do something with it. It is interesting that they have done, or are doing, most of the things that I had in mind, although not necessarily in the same order. Good luck to them.

14

New Millennium

Our computer, along with everyone elses, entered the new millennium without a hitch and Alan Keef Ltd entered upon a period of great, ongoing and profitable activity. However the work was slightly unusual in that it consisted of a number of very large jobs which all went on for a very long time and for which we were paid in stages along the way, which is what really turned our cash flow round. Indeed it started a period when the usual ongoing mass of small jobs which could be wrapped round the big ones became decidedly thin on the ground; or maybe it is just that the numbers have stayed the same but the big jobs have got bigger.

The new millennium kicked off to a good start with a short railway for Pavilion Gardens in Buxton. This was the replacement by the local authority of a very run-down line that had been operated by a concessionaire. The locomotive and rolling stock were very similar to those which we had supplied to the Wells Harbour Railway, but this time was in 12¼in. gauge to give a little more stability. However we had to design new bogies to suit and these in turn were a further permutation of our standard design. The line was short, about 300 yards, but the day-to-day operation was complicated by the use of a short but very substantial tunnel for storage of rolling stock and the train had to be split in two at night and reassembled in the morning. However it has been a resounding success and helps to keep the rates down in Buxton.

Bicton Gardens in Devon changed hands at about this time, from Clinton Devon Estates to an individual operator. The whole place was fairly run-down, and the railway particularly so. Simon and Valerie Lister, the new owners, were out to make money with which to refurbish the place and viewed the steam railway as something of an anachronism, even though they accepted that it was an integral part of the park. All the equipment having come originally from Woolwich Arsenal, by this time it was just about worn out. They made, what was to us, a very sensible decision. They would buy a complete new trainset that would require minimal staffing and maintenance and sell the old equipment to whoever would buy it. Thus we built an 18in. gauge version of our standard 2ft gauge steam-outline diesel locomotive. Because of the narrow gauge it had outside frames and was thus some 5ft wide and wider than the 2ft gauge equivalent. Initially this was run with the existing carriages until such time as we could manufacture new ones. In due course these were supplied and the whole train looked a fine sight painted in royal blue. The train at Bicton had been one of those that crawled round its track at a pace that would have been slow for a snail and initially it was very difficult to get their drivers to drive at a reasonable speed. They used to run a train every forty-five minutes and the idea that actually one every twenty minutes was perfectly practical took a long time to penetrate. After various false starts for an overseas sale, the old equipment was ultimately sold to the Royal Gunpowder Mills restoration project at Waltham Abbey. This site was, if anything, a forerunner to Woolwich Arsenal, so a better home could hardly have been found.

Right: *Charles* (AK58 of 1999) after delivery to the Ferry Meadows Railway at Peterborough. So far as anything that we build is standard, this was a standard 0-6-0 in 10¼in. gauge.

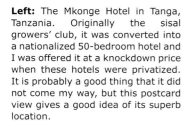

Left: The Mkonge Hotel in Tanga, Tanzania. Originally the sisal growers' club, it was converted into a nationalized 50-bedroom hotel and I was offered it at a knockdown price when these hotels were privatized. It is probably a good thing that it did not come my way, but this postcard view gives a good idea of its superb location.

Left: To make the point, this is the same locomotive as AK58, but in 12¼in. gauge! (AK60 of 2000). Alice drives a trial train through what was still a building site at Pavilion Gardens, Buxton. This is an attractive little line that is a great draw to the public in a restored public park.

Below: Bicton Park Gardens, Devon. Ex-Woolwich Arsenal locomotive, *Woolwich*, in steam for the last time for the benefit of a potential purchaser. This and the associated rolling stock ultimately went to the Royal Gunpowder Mills Museum at Waltham Abbey.

On the trackwork front there was considerable activity with some of our ongoing customers, notably Cotswold Wildlife Park, Blenheim Palace, Marwell Zoo, Cricket St Thomas Park and the National Grid in Woodhead Tunnel. An odd one was a 10¼in. gauge railway for the Melton Mowbray Town Trust. At Llechwedd Slate Caverns we re-laid a section of track on raised steel sleepers so that the water could run out underneath. These were bolted to a concrete base and left the rails some four inches above it. Even so the track still floods occasionally when the Welsh rain is at its worst! That was done at the beginning of the season and the turning triangle at the inner end of the line was done at the end of it. At Blenheim we not only re-laid track but re-engined the locomotive as well. We also secured a hire contract which went on for about two years, to supply track and hand-pushed wagons to a firm clearing contaminated waste at the Harwell nuclear research establishment. Before the job started they wanted purchase costs for the material hired in case it got so badly

Left: Replica Heywood 0-4-0 locomotive *Katie* and a train of original and replica stock on the railway at Eaton Hall, near Chester. Except for being in colour, this picture could have been taken 100 years ago.

Right: The original was unusual and this was no less so – the replica trainset for the reincarnated Listowel & Ballybunnion Railway in Ireland. This is a diesel version of the original, and the track is only some 500 yards long, but sufficient to demonstrate the operation of the system. AK62 of 2001 on an early trial run.

contaminated that it could not safely be returned to us! Of particular note was the first call from Eaton Hall, home of the Duke of Westminster. There had been a 15in. gauge railway here from about 1895 to 1947, that had been provided by the redoubtable Sir Arthur Heywood, the purpose of which was to haul coal and materials from the local station to the house and estate. A circular line a mile or so in length had been laid, together with a spur back into the original carriage sheds, in order to provide a taste of what had been. A replica Heywood steam loco, *Katie*, had been obtained, along with some of the original rolling stock from the Romney Hythe & Dymchurch Railway. The problem was that this had all been handed over to the Duke's helicopter pilot who, presumably having mechanical knowledge, was supposed to know how to make it all work! There ensued some fairly frantic teaching and learning, allied to minor repairs, to produce a working railway. This was followed over a number of years with some extensive track alterations as the original had not been well laid, together with more substantive repairs to the locomotive. Efforts to sell them a diesel for maintenance and immediate use if required regrettably fell on deaf ears.

There then followed the job to build a replica of what was possibly the most unusual railway ever to be built and operated. This was the Listowel & Ballybunnion Railway in Ireland which was built on the Lartigue Monorail principle. The whole idea was the brainchild of a M. Lartigue, a Belgian, with the idea of producing a transport system that could be easily laid and operated for use primarily in what we would now call developing countries. The monorail principle seems to have a singular fascination to some engineers, most of whom should know better. The general public are just as bad, they deem it futuristic and therefore it must be good. After innumerable attempts, most of them failures, the fascination continues to this day. The Listowel & Ballybunnion was different insofar that, firstly, it was actually built as a commercial operation and, secondly, it operated for forty years, from 1886 to 1926. By that time its equipment was life expired and the motor vehicle was beginning to make its presence felt against all railways, even in the

One of my most frequently asked questions is 'How do you transport them around?' The answer is, of course, 'On the back of a lorry', and this is No. 61 passing Taunton Deane services on the M5 on its way to Bicton Gardens.

far west of Ireland. One is tempted to say that 'Only in Ireland …' could such a thing have been built (in fact there was a short-lived one in France as well) and, also, that only in Ireland could a replica have been built. The idea of building such a reincarnation had long been a dream in and around Listowel, but it was not until the local MP, Jimmy Deenihan, got hold of the idea, found some money and was prepared to push and search for more, that the dream became a reality.

This particular monorail had the main weight of the stock carried on a single rail on top of an A frame with horizontal wheels working on guide rails slightly below the level of the crossbar of the A. From our point of view the problem was that we only had the published drawings and photographs to work from, although James Boyd kindly provided some large copies of the best known pictures taken from the original negatives. The biggest problem with any monorail is how you transfer from one track to another, as with a set of points on a normal railway. Lartigue's answer was to use a turntable but it was a turntable with a difference. On the conventional turntable it is only possible to connect any two opposite tracks together. In the Lartigue system the turntable is curved, and its centre is not on the centre of the track, and by this means there are a combination of five positions where the tracks join up 'straight through' as it were. Ingenious to say the least. These turntables were never used for turning locomotives and stock, they were not strong enough, and there were separate straight turntables for that purpose.

The object of the scheme was to provide a short run of some 500 yards, with a run-round loop at each end, together with shed and sidings to demonstrate just what

Left: On arrival in Listowel the locomotive was greeted by a pipe and marching band from the USA, blessed by the local priest, together with speeches from all concerned. All in the pouring rain as only it can rain in Ireland!

Right: The 'turntables' which deputise for sets of points in the Lartigue system are ingenious in their own right. The track is curved and is not centred over the centre of the circle, but for all that will give up to five different permutations of track connections.

the Lartigue was. This was done on the old mainline track bed at Listowel, just over the fence from where the original ran. It was always to be a diesel replica. The original steam locomotives had twin boilers, one either side of the track, and an 0-3-0 locomotive in between. For our purposes we made the tender the 'locomotive' and the front part a simple 'push-along' that looked the part. For the record, the originals were made by Hunslet Engine Co. Ltd. One of the originals had had a most enormous light fitted to it, quite out of all proportion to the machine itself, and by chance it was this locomotive which was most frequently photographed – perhaps because of that light. I have seen pictures of exactly the same style of light fitted to old-time locomotives in the Wild West and I guess somebody brought one back. Whatever, it was our job to replicate this feature and replicate it we did. All the original rolling stock straddled the tracks like panniers on a bicycle. Carriages had first and second class compartments and were fully enclosed. Each train included a set of steps so that passengers could cross to the other side as it was patently impossible to walk across the track. The two carriages we built were more of a compromise than the locomotives, as all these features of the railway had to be included in them. They also had to be suitable for passing holiday trade. As a consequence they were all welded out of box section and steel sheet, included a dummy guards compartment and on one of them was built a set of steps. They were also fully open with only one door each side. The old myth was that a fat lady one side had to balanced by two pigs on the other, but sadly for legend it is not true. The guide wheels are heavily spring applied and all is perfectly stable.

Having made all the track and been well on the way with the rolling stock, this job also came to a grinding, if temporary, halt because of the foot and mouth epidemic in England. The Irish government were very wisely not allowing any imports that were not essential. The Lartigue was hardly that, and when the track was finally sent it all had to be disinfected before despatch. The arrival of the locomotive was cause for great rejoicing in Listowel. We stopped in a lay-by about five miles away to give it a thorough polish and then timed its arrival to fit in with some majorettes and a

marching band from the USA who happened to be touring Ireland. There was much speech making, a final blessing from the local priest and then a tour twice round the town before unloading; the whole operation taking place in the pouring rain as only it can rain in Ireland. Everybody was well satisfied. In the speech I was called upon to make I remarked that large numbers of people had said to me that it looked just like the old ones but, I replied, 'They would have been very disappointed if it hadn't!'

Whilst all this was going on there was the usual array of smaller jobs, albeit they would have been significant not that many years previously. We sold-on most of the railway at Alton Towers to the newly-opened East Links Family Park at Dunbar, near Edinburgh. We carried out some major repairs to a Lister locomotive from Leighton Buzzard and there was a large spares order to Guyana. On an altogether larger front, we were asked by Beamish Museum in County Durham if we would be willing to undertake work on a new replica steam locomotive they were building. Beamish were building a replica of a six-wheeled locomotive of about 1815 vintage, which they had designed from a single oil painting of the original and some other basic information. It was known as the *Steam Elephant* because of its immensely long tapering chimney. To have designed it at all from so little information was in itself no mean achievement. They were well on the way with the project but had run into problems with finding someone with the knowledge and in-house skills to complete the work. Thus it came our way and was to occupy a chunk of our workshop for the next year or so. For largely financial reasons it was being built piecemeal by Beamish with almost each part ordered and paid for separately and this also applied to the procurement of forgings, castings and so on. Fundamentally we had to take the parts we were given, machine as necessary, assemble and ultimately make the whole thing work. It sounds easy, but that is just what was achieved. Not only that, but the *Steam Elephant* has worked consistently at the museum since then.

The next major saga starts with a question, 'Why would railway engineers need life jackets and tide tables?' The answer is, 'When

To put us on our mettle, 24 hours before the tests were due to take place they asked if we could arrange to produce actual figures for the loads required to pull, push or stop the loaded trolley. Fortunately we knew where to obtain a load cell and were able to provide the figures they wanted. I'm sure it was a try-on to see how good we were. On the strength of this we then designed and built a proper trolley which was fully galvanized, as the production units would be, and this went to their headquarters at Poole for further in-house testing. This was obviously successful as manufacture followed on from there.

The first two units were installed at Southend-on-Sea (which place seems to have major implications in this saga!) and these were 'sideways mounted' and the track was further complicated by having to be cut into a relatively thin concrete deck. In fact, having standardized the trolley it is the track which has become the variable and very varied it can be. For a brand-new lifeboat station at Salcombe we arranged the track to go down into the sea so that the lifeboat could be launched direct without it having to be craned as well. To date we have supplied these ART and SART

the Royal National Lifeboat Institution becomes a major customer.' This all started with the usual cryptic phone call from a firm of consulting engineers asking if we could supply a few short rails for a lifeboat station at Salcombe, and in the time since that call the RNLI has become our largest ongoing customer. By the nature of what they do, the RNLI are a very professional organization, very particular about what they need and have some difficulty in finding firms willing to do just what they want. However, doing that is exactly what we are always having to do and indeed probably what we do best. The whole lifeboat saga, which is ongoing, has become almost Alice's private fiefdom. She has done most of the design work and followed this up with organizing and supervising the on-site installation of whatever it is we are doing.

The initial project was to provide a rail-mounted trolley to carry an Atlantic 75 inshore lifeboat out of a building so that it could then be lifted into the sea on a davit or small crane. It sounds very simple, but the issue was complicated because they wanted to try and standardise on rail gauge, make the trolley suitable for all three sizes of inshore lifeboat, make it possible to move the boat either fore and aft or sideways, and for the loaded trolley to be pushed and, more particularly, stopped by two average-sized men or women. They were quite prepared to pay for a prototype and the setting up of a short piece of test track to experiment with all these things.

The upshot was that we made a somewhat crude trolley and loaded it with old Simplex cast iron ballast weights to represent the boat and were able to perform the trials they wanted. By jacking and packing the track we were also able to test differing gradients.

The *Steam Elephant* is remarkable in having been designed from a single original painting by Beamish Museum in Northumberland. Whilst we did not build it in total, we finished off the mechanical side and were responsible for final steaming and commissioning. Here it is in steam on rollers outside our workshop doors.

installations to lifeboat stations at Crosshaven (Ireland), Gorleston, Hartlepool, Harwich, Kilkeel (Ireland), Salcombe, Southend on Sea (2), Sunderland, together with track only at Newhaven.

The RNLI also have a system of trailer-launching these lifeboats. They are taken down to the sea on a trailer with the outboard engines running from an onboard supply of cooling water so that as soon as they float, even if only on the top of a wave, they can be on their way. This system also has the ability to 'catch' an incoming boat riding in on a wave in F6 or F7 wind and sea conditions. They then wanted this set up as a rail mounted system for the lifeboat station at St Abbs in Scotland. In this instance, the trolley is shaped like a giant tuning fork and is extremely massive and heavy to prevent it being lifted off the rails in heavy seas. In case that is not enough, it also has retaining cleats which catch under the head of the rail. At St Abbs the slipway rail was also very heavy, 50lbs/yd, and also had a considerable vertical curve where it came off the slipway into the level boathouse. Again we were successful in developing what was required and have supplied similar systems at Port Erin and Kirkcudbright.

Returning to more conventional railway matters, a new steam-outline diesel locomotive was supplied to the Alford Valley Railway. This had been a long-term dream of James Gordon whose brainchild that railway is. He had spoken about it for years and finally achieved his objective. The railway has a supporters' association and they asked if we could supply and fit the loco with name-plates *James Gordon*, but not to let James know we were doing this. We were delighted to fall in with the idea. Poor James, he is a diffident man and was so embarrassed to find an official naming ceremony on his hands and then that it was named after him!

A Simplex locomotive was taken in part exchange for this and, about a year later, was sold to a Ken Zadnichek in Alabama, USA, for a line he was building around his developing trailer park. This line was to be based upon Welsh narrow gauge practice and to be marketed as such. He also had plans for other railways in the miniature gauges with the idea that visitors would come with little locos, stay in his park and use them on his railway. He had us build a number of four-wheel underframes on which he has since built

carriages and he also had a new steam locomotive from Exmoor Steam Railway. This was all followed by a number of smaller orders for point levers and couplings. With typical American generosity he sent us a subscription to *Trains* magazine which gives an insight into how American railroading works and how different it is from what we are used to here.

The track-laying side of the business then took a major spurt, with the short but often complicated bits for lifeboats, a ghost train track at Great Yarmouth and the laying of a complete track at the National Forest Park to take a Severn Lamb train. This work was done in association with Tunnel Steels who supplied most of the materials. As so often, this suffered from being landscape architect designed and had more curves in it than were really necessary. This was followed by the relaying of an existing track at Pleasure Island, Cleethorpes, which was again a Severn Lamb railway. At Cricket St Thomas two of the cattle grids were completely rebuilt; the standard of the originals got worse the further one got along the railway – perhaps money was getting shorter when it was being built!

The Woodhead Tunnel continued to provide useful work with a lengthy hire of locomotive and wagons to Wormald Fire Systems Ltd who were installing a fire-fighting system in the tunnel. In addition some new wagons were supplied to National Grid to create a fire-fighting train. The locomotive at Blenheim was repainted red instead of the rather drab estate green of previous years. The overhaul of *Nancy* reached the point at which it became a complete rolling chassis with tanks and cab. Although we had been regularly attending Leisure Industry Week exhibition for the leisure trade we felt that we had not given ourselves much exposure to the industrial market and lacking a suitable exhibition we tried SED

Above: Quite remarkably, the Royal National Lifeboat Institution has become our largest ongoing customer. This all started from building a trolley for hand moving inshore lifeboats out of a building for launching. Here the prototype is being tested at Poole.

Right: The DART is a large and substantial affair able to take the Atlantic 85 lifeboat, which is capable of 36 knots! In this picture at St Abbs, Scotland, the boat is being experimentally retrieved but in due course it will be turned round so that it can leave the boathouse with engines running and be off as soon as it hits the water. The trolley has grippers fitted to prevent it being washed away when conditions are rough.

(Site Equipment Demonstration) held outdoors at Milton Keynes. To our surprise a small stand within a large tent produced two lots of business. The first was the use of a 2ft gauge railway for moving the shredded branches of trees from thinning operations. With burning being frowned upon, apparently there are literally mountains of this material that nobody knows quite what to do with. The second one was somewhat similar but involved the monorail being almost literally floated on a Norfolk fen for the removal of brushwood in conservation operations. In fact the two companies involved knew each other quite well.

We have often argued as to which is the oddest job we have ever done and the consensus is that that for Bath University takes second place. For them we built

Above: The Alford Valley Railway near Aberdeen is a very local affair and is the justified pride of those who have initiated and built it. Of those, James Gordon is the most prominent and this locomotive (AK63 of 2001) is named in his honour. A year or so later we also built this rather splendid carriage for the line.

Left: A number of projects vie for the accolade of being our most unusual railway. A strong contender has to be the bobsleigh track for Bath University, upon which the Olympic team is trained.

Below: *Pompey* (AK64 of 2001), named after the owner's cat, is a double bogie diesel locomotive in 15in. gauge fitted with cab heating, de-mist and sound proofing and has proved very successful in service.

a bobsleigh track, or at least the first bit of one! This was a straight but vertically curved rail track with a fall of about thirty feet and then a lift up to help slow the cars down. The object was the training of the British Bobsleigh Team and apparently to save a hundredth second on the push-off helps towards gaining a tenth of a second at the end of the run. The mind boggles!

The owner of the Wotton Light Railway asked for a new diesel locomotive for this private railway. This was to be a much more powerful and sophisticated machine than anything else he had, or, for that matter, that we had built before in 15in. gauge. It was to be called *Pompey* after his cat and was to have such luxuries as a heated cab so that owner and said cat could travel in comfort. The reality was a double-bogie locomotive of about 65h.p., with a cab at one end only, that proved both fast and comfortable to ride in. About two years later we then built a fully enclosed carriage with full sound insulation, sliding doors, carpeted floor and cushioned seats which was apparently a Christmas present to his wife.

For quite a long time there had been rumblings about a new railway to be installed at Margam Park at Port Talbot in South Wales. As so often happens, consultants had been called in by the local council, who were the site owners, and an extremely ambitious project had developed. Due to financial restraints this had to be modified into something more reasonable. The resulting railway was about 700 metres long with a balloon loop at each end, connected the castle itself to a wooden fort for children to play on at the other and ran alongside the lake and over the dam at its end. For this we supplied a locomotive and two carriages. This produced a successful railway although it was marred by the fact that no covered accommodation was, or has yet been, provided so the train has to stand outside in all weathers winter and summer which does not help its appearance. The original intention was for the railway to bring visitors from the car park at the bottom of the hill up to the castle, and ultimately this did happen.

For me personally, our most prestigious job has to have been the building of two new open carriages for the new Welsh Highland Railway. Not least because this takes the wheel full circle back to my volunteering days on the Festiniog Railway, part of which involved uplifting the last remnants of the erstwhile Welsh Highland. These new vehicles were to be improved versions of a previous batch built by Winson Engineering Ltd. The WHR provided the bogies, ex South Africa, together with a set of the original drawings, and the rest was up to us. Due to space requirements we took on a rented unit in Ross on Wye in which to build these as they were going to take some time and needed to be kept clean in the process. The fabrication work was too large for us and we put this out to A.J. Lowther Ltd and then set about the conversion of the steel shell into a finished carriage. It pulled in all sorts of trades and skills that we had not troubled with before, such as obtaining melamine faced plywood, some very complicated electrical fittings, particular flooring, and the whole having to be of a high standard of finish. Considering where this business began I am inordinately proud of the doorsteps with my name and the year, 2002, cast into them! I went to see the first one put into service and it certainly seemed to

do all that was asked of it and we live in hope that one day there will be some more to build.

Apart from the WHR carriages which carried on somewhat independently of everything else, it turned into an extremely busy year with some sizeable spares orders to Fiji, Guyana (which included a new Simplex gearbox), TPC and some biggish ones within the UK as well. We built an additional carriage for Bicton Gardens and fitted bodywork, if that is the right word, on the four-wheel carriages used in Llechwedd Slate Caverns. We re-laid the track at Legoland, Windsor, in conjunction with Tunnel Steels Ltd and, at the end of the year, built a new railway at Flamingoland in North Yorkshire to take a Chance locomotive and train which we had bought from Chessington Zoo and sold on to them. Because of a shortage of British 20lbs/yd rail we used some Spanish S10 section for this and subsequently had serious problems with rail wear. Corus claim to make the best rail in the world and our experience is that it is true. There was some minor re-lay work at Cricket St Thomas and some rail was supplied to Hythe Pier for restoration work after a dredger had knocked a piece out of the pier. A small industrial job was the fitting of a cab to one of the Lister locomotives used by Painter Bros in Hereford. During the summer the RNLI added to the pace with a trolley and track for a new lifeboat station at Salcombe in Devon.

Private railways again came to the fore with the spectacular 15in. gauge Difflin Lake Railway at Raphoe in County Donegal, Ireland, for Sir Jerry Robinson. This really was a model railway in the grand manner and was installed in completely new gardens being added to an existing Georgian house. These included a new lake and a castle as a folly. For our part we supplied an 0-4-0 diesel locomotive, two fully-enclosed bogie carriages, two open four-wheel carriages together with four-wheel and bogie wagons. We also made ten sets of points for the job. The whole was laid and installed by local labour and a good job they made of it. The bogie carriages were something else again, as the saying goes. Whilst the whole railway was given a flavour of the County Donegal Railways, the carriages were of all-timber construction with full height doors and traditional drop-light windows with leather straps. One was a three compartment all third and the other had a guard's compartment for wheel chairs together with side duckets for the guard to see along the train. This vehicle also had a first class compartment with cushioned seats, mirrors and carpets on the floor. Both were stained and grained in the traditional manner throughout on the inside.

When it came to despatch, the whole lot went on one 40-foot trailer except for the first class carriage. When the driver came for this he commented, 'I thought you said this had a first class compartment.'

'It has,' I replied.

'Where is it?' he said.

'I'm in it,' I answered.

'But it says "Third" on the outside.'

And it did too.

One of two open carriages built for the Welsh Highland Railway, here seen following delivery to Dinas. On a personal note I have always been inordinately proud of these vehicles and hope that one day we may build some more.

Despite our best explanations, the signwriter had written 'Third' on all the doors. We totted up that at least eight people had seen the carriage, all of whom were aware of the first class compartment, and not one had noticed it! There was no choice but to send it as it was and rustle up a signwriter in County Donegal to re-write it on arrival. He, and most other people, thought it was the best laugh in ages.

A new departure altogether was the manufacture of a battery electric locomotive for Llechwedd Slate Caverns. Historically, and for various good reasons, I had always tended to keep away from battery locos; not least because there are other manufacturers of this type of locomotive, and so far as second-hand ones are concerned the batteries tend to deteriorate rapidly unless used. However we

Lea Line. This track layout was very largely determined before we moved in, although the paint shop spur and the multi-gauge track were added later. The temporary railway used when building the house ran down the driveway. *Scale 1:500*

had a good working relationship with Llechwedd and this seemed as good an opportunity as any to, firstly, build a locomotive specifically suited to their operation and, secondly, give us a start into that market. In this we were initially only partly successful. From Cote days I had known CBL Electric Vehicles in Bampton and had always called on them for anything resembling electric traction. With our connivance I think they tried to be a bit too clever with the electric control and they in turn were badly let down by their suppliers. The result has been a series of silly failures, when the locomotive will run completely trouble free for months and then stop dead. This has now been resolved and they do need a second loco that we hope we shall build one day.

Mark Timothy arrived at about this time and work started in earnest in mid-2002 and was to carry on for something over a year. This machine had been built for Alan Richardson as a 2-6-4 steam locomotive with the general appearance of those on the County Donegal Railway. It was intended for use on the Bure Valley Railway in Norfolk but in fact had never turned a wheel in anger and was to remain so for some time yet. This was sad as the locomotive was a memorial to the owner's son who had died in a white water rafting accident.

Aside from the RNLI, this was Alice's first prestige project and her responsibility all the way through but ably assisted in the more technical aspects by Ian Gaylor. At an early stage it was decided that the locomotive would be revamped to the maximum size that the Bure Valley Railway loading gauge could accept, and eventually the Leek & Manifold Railway locomotives were thought to be a good prototype for it to be based upon. Once stripped down we realized just how badly it had been built and what a journey there was to go. Just about everything had to be remade or renewed and at the end of the day only the boiler, wheels and frame were original, and even the latter was lengthened and strengthened. In order to balance the weight more evenly a new smoke box was rolled from plate 40mm thick! A Lempor blast nozzle was fitted and whilst new piston valve cylinders were perhaps not essential they transformed the performance. One snag with all this was that it was deemed that the connecting and coupling rods were no longer strong enough, so these had to be replaced as well. In order to get the appearance and position of windows and seats right I made a mock-up wooden cab which, when it was no longer needed, somebody took off for his grandchildren to play in! The end result was a very splendid and elegant locomotive that was both powerful and fast. On test it was capable of hauling a 13-coach train at speeds up to 25m.p.h. Not bad by any standards. And incidentally we supplied a further set of the same cylinders for one of the other BVR locomotives.

This was a time when the effect of the litigious society was beginning to bite in the UK and insurance premiums had begun to rise rapidly as a consequence. It was also the aftermath of the Hatfield rail crash. We had just got our teeth into a major track-laying job worth some £130,000 for the National Grid in the Woodhead Tunnel when our insurance company decided that it could no longer insure us for track-laying work. In true insurance company style we were notified of this just four days before the previous policy expired! There was no small panic whilst our brokers

AK65 of 2001 *Margam* starts up the three-quarter mile 1 in 45 gradient at Margam Park in South Wales. The initial railway here was quite short but was subsequently extended down the hill to the car park. Testing the air brakes in a simulated runaway for HM Railway Inspectorate was an entertaining exercise.

ran around and managed to rustle up some cover at Lloyds. Even so we worked for about three days without any cover. The cost of this was about equal to the rest of our insurances put together and added about £4.50 a metre on our track-laying costs for the rest of the work we had in hand that winter. The surprising thing was that those customers affected by this took the extra costs without quibble, all of them having suffered similarly with their problems. It should be recorded that at that time invoices for National Grid were sent to the delightful address of Cat & Kittens Lane, Wolverhampton.

Again the wheel turned full circle with a requirement for a larger and more powerful locomotive at the Cotswold Wildlife Park. It will be remembered that I built my first steam-outline diesel locomotive for this establishment shortly before we left Cote, and it had run virtually all the trains for the intervening sixteen years. Having been built round the ubiquitous Simplex 20/28, this railway suffers from being constrained in width and the new loco had to follow suit. The result was a chunky and attractive machine with outside wheels that really did look like a big sister to my original concept. One result of a more powerful locomotive was an order for an additional carriage for the train a few years later.

Which tidily brings us to what I think is the best of the garden railways with which we have been involved so far. It started in mid-2003 and so far as we were concerned went on in a big way for over a year with odds and bits continuing to the present day. This was the Beeches Light Railway for Adrian Shooter at his home near Banbury. It should be said at the outset that he is chairman of Chiltern Railways, one of the most successful train operating companies hived off from British

Rail, and as such is extremely knowledgeable about railways. Added to this he knew from the beginning exactly what he wanted to achieve and in overall terms this made our life easy. The concept was to build a short 2ft gauge railway around his house and garden upon which he could run one of the Sharp Stewart 0-4-0 steam locomotive from the Darjeeling Himalayan Railway in India. In fact this engine had 'escaped' from India some years previously and he bought it in the USA.

The first move was to completely rebuild a 20/28 Simplex with new Perkins engine and complete with air brakes that were vital in view of the gradients, up to 1 in 22, on the new railway. This was followed by the regauging and air-braking of some ex-MoD flat wagons and vans. The latter were fitted with curved corrugated iron roofs as in correct Darjeeling practice complete with signwriting in Hindi and English.

In the meantime his contractors had started serious work on the trackbed which involved the excavation of cuttings into a shale-type rock up to six feet deep and embankments at least as high. With this started we in turn were able to start on the track-laying proper. This was in 35lbs/yd rail, Pandrol clipped to hardwood sleepers, the first time we had done this. There are no less than thirteen sets of points in this fairly short line but the *pièce de résistance* has to be a diamond crossover with two of the tracks going out on a curve. This was fitted with air operation so that the four turnouts within

Nancy (AE1547 of 1908) originally worked on the Eastwell iron ore quarrying system and was saved when the line closed. It has been rebuilt for the Cavan & Leitrim Railway in Ireland and is seen completed but awaiting a new boiler that is currently under construction.

it all operate together. We developed a point lever similar to one that I had seen in Argentina which, whilst locking the blades in position, allowed them to be trailed.

His locomotive was overhauled by Tyseley Museum and he had two replica Darjeeling carriages built by the Festiniog Railway that were dual air and vacuum braked so that they could be run there as well. Being something of a railway of the superlatives he also had the Festiniog Railway build him a Parlour Car based on the one at the Sandy River & Rangely Lakes Railway of Maine, USA. This brought back memories of all those years ago when I was considering something similar for the newly-preserved Leighton Buzzard

Above: Except that it was built to the unusual gauge of 1ft 8in., AK66 of 2002 for Woburn Safari Park was identical to its sister at Margam. This is the official naming ceremony by Lady Alexandra of *Lady Alexandra*, assisted by her mother, the Duchess of Bedford. The elephants having come along as well to see that the job is done properly.

Above: AK66 of 2002, *The Earl of Oakfield*, stands outside the new locomotive and carriage shed on the 15in. gauge Difflin Lake Railway in County Donegal, Ireland. These carriages, of all timber construction with drop-light windows in the doors, are after the style of those on the erstwhile County Donegal Railway.

Left: The same locomotive with a rake of goods rolling stock and also showing the 'model railway' style of this line. It is all very new with the grass and trees yet to grow.

Patrick and Helen leave on *Woto* after their wedding on 12 October 2002. How many weddings have been arranged round the date of expiry of a locomotive boiler certificate, I wonder?

turnouts for this line as being a good starting point to go at this seriously. In the event we decided, rightly I think, that this was all going to be a bit complicated at this stage of our abilities and had settled on Hofa Engineering of Port Talbot to make them for us. With the big double crossover just about finished they went into liquidation. Perhaps having seen the writing on the wall, their design engineer and works foreman had already handed in their notice and were going to work for K.G.J. Price Ltd of Cardiff who specialized in main line track repair work but did not have their own manufacturing facility. As a temporary measure we brought four of their people to The Lea and used our equipment to complete these turnouts and they then went on make another twelve or fifteen turnouts for other customers until K.G.J. Price had their own

Light Railway, except that this one is premium class in all directions. It has a balcony at each end, sitting area with loose chairs, dining area and full kitchen with hob, oven, wine glass racks and so on. Again this is built to Festiniog loading gauge so that it can be used there and on the rebuilt Welsh Highland Railway when that is complete but it is, shall we say, on the large side for a garden railway.

There was a hiatus in the middle of all this. We had for some time been working towards being able to design and make our own turnouts and to this end had installed a modest sized planer and other equipment to do so. We had considered making all the

workshop set up to receive them. This suited both parties very well and Price's have gone on to make all our turnouts ever since. This is perhaps just as well as the planer has been in almost continuous use on steam loco overhaul work.

Whilst all this was going on, Hunslet Barclay of Kilmarnock had for sale some of the 100h.p. 12-ton locomotives that they built for the Jubilee line extension. We bought four, or rather three and a half, as one had a missing wheelset. The one and a half we sold to the Welsh Highland at Portmadoc and they were delivered there direct. One of the others was earmarked for Adrian Shooter and

Opposite: Lea Line, 2004. The house and garden are in the foreground with the works behind, the roofs of offices – permanent and temporary – beyond that, with the A40 road at the top. The white area to top left is the site of the old Gloucester–Ross railway which was in deep cutting at this point. There is not a huge amount of railway interest in this shot but the crane is poised over the frame of West Clare Railway *Slieve Callan* with *Carnegie* from Bicton Gardens to its right. In front of those is *Princess Anne* from Southport. Beside the gate are stacks of monorail track together with the power units.

Right: For a variety of good reasons we have tended to keep clear of battery electric traction but this is a K20E (AK66 of 2002) coming out into the daylight (and snow) on the Miners Tramway at Llechwedd Slate Caverns, Blaenau Ffestiniog, North Wales.

his Beeches Light Railway. This was modified with new cab and suitable air connections such that it can be driven from inside his parlour car and thus meals can be taken on the move. The other one went to Leighton Buzzard on trial as a spare diesel that could deputise for steam and was accepted for that purpose.

At Woburn Safari Park we installed a balloon loop at the station end of the line so that they no longer had to run round trains, including turning locomotives, and could thus improve their service. This was to be in conjunction with buying a new train, locomotive and carriages, which they duly did the following year. The ageing Hudswell Clarke equipment had served them well but was expensive to maintain and, not having enclosed cabs

At an open day on the Beeches Light Railway, *Taffy* shunts a couple of vans onto the back of the passenger train. These are ex-Ministry of Defence vehicles modified to give them a Darjeeling 'feel' and are in fact lettered in Hindi on the side away from the camera. The station building is a replica of those typical to the DHR.

together with poor adhesion, could not be used when the weather was wet. The whole operation has thus been transformed and irritable queues of passengers are a thing of the past. The original two locomotives and four carriages were sold for preservation and went to Cleethorpes for temporary storage. They have since moved on for use on the North Bay Railway in Scarborough.

Patrick went to Jersey to look at a potential railway in the grounds of the Gold Centre there, but in the event this came to nothing. However he also made a contact with the Jersey New Waterworks Co. who have a number of pumping installations perilously mounted on cliff edges around the island. One of these had a rope-operated incline for access, and over the next year or two we supplied a couple

of special bogies, rope rollers and various track spares which more than covered the costs of his abortive visit. The supply of spares to TPC continued unabated through 2003, there was also a large order from Chhatak Cement and a few Simplex spares were sent to enthusiasts in Sweden. There was also a lengthy hire to AMCO who were working in the Woodhead Tunnel but, unusually on this occasion, the National Grid allowed them to use their locomotive and wagons as part of the job. I think they must have regretted it. We had some problems with a K.40 on hire, which took a long time to resolve, but they virtually destroyed the Grid's equipment and there was a bill for several tens of thousands of pounds to repair it all after the job was over.

Left: *Mark Timothy* (AK69R of 2003). A 15in. gauge locomotive that we rebuilt in the style of the Leek & Manifold Railway locomotives. Fitted with piston valve cylinders and Lempor exhaust it here pulls out of Aylsham station with a 13-coach train on the Bure Valley Railway in Norfolk.

Right: Ex-Darjeeling Himalayan Railway B class thunders up the 1 in 22 gradient on the private Beeches Light Railway. The vehicle behind the tender is a very splendid parlour car based on those used on the 2ft gauge railways of Maine, USA. This is followed by two replica DHR carriages.

The old adage says that one man's meat is another man's poison and this certainly proved to be the case with Wicksteed Park at Kettering. We had always done a small amount of business with them as they had the only locomotive that Simplex ever built (in 1977) specifically for the leisure market, an Americanized 40S, which is modestly attractive. Otherwise they had two Baguley locomotives dating from 1930 when the line was built. In September 2003 they had a derailment in which a few passengers were hurt, two of them sufficiently to be taken to hospital. This was correctly reported to the Railway Inspectorate. I happened to be in the area a few days later and, at Wicksteed's request, was asked to go to have a look myself. Over the years the railway here has had, I think, rather more than its fair share of problems and reportable incidents. However there may be a moral in that most of the HMRI recommendations had been studiously ignored and primarily on the basis of this the Health & Safety Executive took them to court where they were heavily fined. This was unfortunate as it did not really help the situation. Most unusually, HMRI reported with a long diatribe on best practice but did not actually offer any reason for the derailment; indeed I think I may be the only person who does know what happened. I would very happily have taken the powers that be to task on this but Wicksteed chose to admit guilt and quote all the work they were now going to do as mitigating circumstances and I think they lost out accordingly.

However that may be, Alan Keef Ltd set about relaying the railway with heavier rail, as had been recommended earlier, and re-routing it slightly so as not to be quite so near the edge of the lake. As often happens, the railway had been left very much to its own devices in the care of someone who had picked up his knowledge from his predecessor. As a consequence there were anomalies in how it operated and was maintained. These we were able to sort out for them and a set of four new carriages went a long way to solving their problems by allowing them to maintain the throughput of visitors with only one train instead of the complications of running two. The railway remains their second most popular ride and this is one of the most heavily used railways of its type in the country, carrying towards 250,000 passengers in a season. This is surprising as it is a park that many people have never heard of.

Slieve Callan, or 5C, has been mentioned, and finally work started on this in earnest. After dismantling, the frame went away

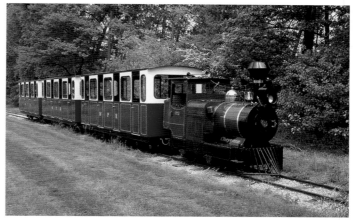

Carrying in the order of 250,000 passengers each season, the railway at Wicksteed Park, Kettering, is one of the most heavily used of its type in the country. We supplied four new carriages in 2004 and here three of them are seen in service with the Simplex locomotive *Cheyenne* (MR22224 of 1966). This was Simplex's only essay into the leisure railway market.

to be built up where it was badly rusted and was shot blasted and painted. We could then fit new horn guides, rebuild the axleboxes and fit them to the re-machined wheels and axles. The cylinders were repaired where they were cracked and work was in hand on a brand new boiler when the usual sort of problems arose – but with a twist in the tail this time. We knew payments for this work had been largely grant aided and they were paid to us through the owner's accountants. Curiously, there always seemed to be some problem; either they were delayed, which is not unusual for Ireland anyway, or they were made out in the wrong name, or something else was not right. This came to a head and it transpired that a member of his accountant's staff had absconded with no less than £300,000 of his money and goodness knows how much of other people's. Fortunately the man was caught, but needless to say the job came to an abrupt stop and took the best part of a year before it could restart.

This actually played to our advantage as we had an ex-First World War Baldwin 4-6-0 steam locomotive in from Leighton Buzzard for complete overhaul and there was some pressure to get on with it. This one had spent most of its life hauling sugar-cane in India and, whilst complete, was in atrocious condition. We had to strip down to every last nut, bolt and pin and start from there. All holes had to be bushed, the frames were built up and planed off true, the motion was straightened out and fitted with new brasses throughout, the axle boxes given new whitemetal and re-machined, the loose slipper horns were replaced, the bogie was fitted with new axles and, although not our direct concern, a new boiler was made. New tanks, cab and bunker were made by a 'Friend of the Leighton Buzzard Railway' and, as has become normal, it was our job to pipe it all up and make it work. This it did very satisfactorily and it has since put in stalwart service at Leighton Buzzard since its arrival there in the spring of 2007.

Also dating from the First World War was the rebuilding of a 40h.p. Simplex that

Simplex built many of these armoured locomotives for the First World War. After spending many years hauling sugar-cane in Antigua, this one (MR435 of 1917) was repatriated and we completely rebuilt it for use on the Festiniog Railway. Bryan Lawson tries it out on the multi-gauge track.

worse there was no continuity of operator, with a new driver every season not to mention a change of supervisory management almost as frequently. We came very close to the point of refusing to keep it going as we did not want our name to be attached to what we foresaw as an inevitable disaster. Since then, decisions have been made that they cannot function satisfactorily without the railway and funds have been made available to upgrade the track. What a difference from Cotswold Wildlife Park who had not only bought a new locomotive but now had their carriages refurbished and upgraded to match! Thorpe Park reappeared on the scene after many years with some last-minute track repairs to their Severn Lamb railway just before the season opened.

The closure of the ammunition storage depot at RNAD Dean Hill near Salisbury and the subsequent sale by tender of the railway equipment brought the unexpected purchase of a Baguley diesel locomotive and, more deliberately, a large number of stillages of spare parts. The latter are always useful and can be sold on to enthusiasts and others over a long period of time. We deliberately avoided the large number of wagons and vans being sold but picked up a good deal of useful work refurbishing and re-gauging for those who did buy them.

The Groudle Glen Railway had us rebuild a BEV battery electric locomotive with a centre cab as a replica of *Polar Bear*, one of the BEV locomotives that had worked there at one time. This apparently simple exercise was in fact quite complicated in order to make it look right. In June of that year, York Railway Museum was to hold a major exhibition and steam event celebrating 200 years of railways and we were invited to attend. We were a bit dubious as to whether this would be worth while, especially as it lasted about ten days, but we took *Polar Bear* and certainly gained some useful publicity from it.

was one of the many hundreds supplied to that conflict and which put Motor Rail Ltd on their feet. This had been converted to 2ft 6in. gauge and also used for sugar-cane haulage, but this time in Antigua. It was very badly rusted in places and replacement of both headstocks and some other frame members was required, including the heavy curved body sections. This was one of what was described as the protected type that could withstand rifle fire as opposed to armoured version that would, hopefully, withstand something heavier. It was regauged and fitted with couplers for use on the Festiniog Railway, wheels, axleboxes and gearbox sorted out and then fitted with a four-cylinder Gardner engine which had been taken out of a Jaguar car! Apparently this latter was at one time a surprisingly common conversion. To my mind the more remarkable part of the exercise was that somebody was willing to pay what it cost to carry out this restoration on a 'mere' diesel locomotive, and not a very uncommon one at that.

Whilst on the subject of restoration we also carried out major work to the wheels, axleboxes and motion on the Barclay locomotive *Doll* from Leighton Buzzard, and also for *Caledonia* – also a Barclay – from the Hollycombe Steam Collection at Liphook. It is perhaps significant with the latter that whilst the locomotive had generally been adequately maintained, they had not the facilities to lift the loco off its wheels and so no major work had been done to this part of the machine since it left Dinorwic Quarry in the 1960s.

The whole railway at Blenhiem Palace had been causing us some anxiety at this time. Because of the nature of its use it tended to be grossly overworked, with trains being turned round at each end as fast as was possible. Both equipment and track were suffering. The engine in the locomotive suffered a major calamity and had to be replaced but they were very reluctant to spend anything over the minimum on the track or train. To make matters

Polar Bear (AK72R of 2004) is a rebuild of a more modern BEV battery locomotive to look like an original that worked on the Groudle Glen Railway on the Isle of Man. It is here seen at the Railfest exhibition in York complete with polar bear on the front!

Bryan Lawson

15

Church and State

It will be recalled that whilst at school I considered becoming a priest, but decided against it feeling that I could do more good from outside than inside the Church of England. As a consequence, a fair proportion of my spare time over the years has been involved in matters ecclesiastical. Do not be alarmed. I have no intention of trying to convert the reader to the Christian or any other faith, indeed the person who announces himself as a 'Christian' is apt to set all my alarm bells ringing; I have known several such whose ethics leave a lot to be desired. However, for those who wonder how the Anglican Church, and the Church of England in particular, works, this chapter may be instructive.

As with so much of mine and probably most peoples lives, one has to go back to the beginning or possibly before. My grandfather was sufficiently well thought of by the parish of Framfield that they erected a plaque in his memory on the outside of the church after he died. My parents were both staunch 'church people', especially in later life, although I think they did blow a bit hot and cold about it at times. As a consequence, church going was something I was brought up with and was expected to do. I was sent to Sunday school at Eaton Socon and remember being thoroughly bored. In those days children did not attend main services although I do remember going to evensong fairly regularly and that that was much preferable to Sunday school. Whilst I was in Cumberland we did go to church officially on Sunday mornings, but apart from the fact that the church was dedicated to St Mungo (lovely name – should have been a dog!) I do not remember much about it.

It was the move to Leighton Buzzard that brought my church life to the fore. My parents, quite rightly, wanted to see me confirmed, but equally rightly felt that to be 'done' *en masse* at school was not a good idea as it would inevitably mean very little to me. The consequence was that I received instruction on an individual basis from the Rev'd Wyndham Edgar who was the parish priest of St Barnabas, Linslade, and I was in due course confirmed by the Bishop of Oxford. I think my parents did not bargain for what was to follow. Wyndham Edgar was something of an odd character but a good priest and very 'high' Church, indeed some said he was only just not a Roman Catholic. As a consequence morning communion services, especially on festival Sundays, could be a riot of choir, servers, cross, banner and candle bearers, incense and so on. It was this that I was now invited to join. Although they doubtless knew the services backwards I do not think my parents had much idea of the how and why of all that was done. I, however, took to it as a duck to water and it has stood me good stead ever since.

It was this enthusiasm which prompted thoughts of the priesthood, but Bedford School, wisely, treated it for what it was, a teenage infatuation. In those days one could, and many did, go straight from school to theological college. Nowadays it is preferred that you should have worked elsewhere for a few years at least before you will be accepted for training and the ranks of the clergy are definitely the better for it. The move to Woburn brought all this to a stop although it need not have done. Whilst a regular attender at church I did not get involved in the same way, not least because the Rev'd Robin Osborne, who was the new vicar there, was building his own team of servers from the 'young lads' of the village and there was no place for an 'old hand' like me! My parents were on the Parochial Church Council (PCC) and Susan's father, when I came to know him, had been churchwarden for more years than he liked to remember. By a somewhat similar route, Susan had been inculcated into the life of the church and this is one of the many strands in life which we have in common. Our wedding was perhaps the culmination of all this and included choir, crucifer and servers; the local boys in their 'winkle picker' shoes and Teddy Boy haircuts!

Aston Clinton was a complete change of scene. St Michael & All Saints church was very 'low' church and had a vicar completely stuck in his ways. I actually felt very sorry for him because he was a very sincere man but he should have moved on to pastures new a good many years previously. By that time he would have been in his late fifties and the thought of uprooting himself and starting anew in a new parish no doubt frightened him and so he was stuck until he could decently retire. Although traditional, it does not do for clergy to get stuck in one place and here is as good a place as any to explain how it happens.

Although paid by the diocese, and until recently that meant by the Church Commissioners, the clergy are not employed by the diocese in the normal sense of the word. They have what is known as the freehold of the parish in which they find themselves. This means that technically they own the house and grounds in which they live although they cannot actually sell it. They own this freehold for as long as they like or until they retire. The effect of this is that as long as they take a minimum requirement of services and do not actually infringe the rules of the Anglican Church they cannot be kicked out. This has led to the traditional image of the vicar as being old, doddery and completely of another world. However times have changed and many priests nowadays are on seven- or ten-year contracts in their parishes, often team ministries, and if they do own the freehold they are encouraged to move on in about the same timescale. This encourages new blood, new life, new thinking and prevents them getting stale as was the problem at Aston Clinton. There are currently proposals for a system of 'Common Tenure' that would allow the clergy to come within the country's employment laws, which they are not at present.

Being new to the place and with ideas as to how things were done elsewhere, we got involved and were young and enthusiastic. We were on the Parochial Church Council and not long before we moved away I was voted to be churchwarden, something I knew very little about at that time. My co-churchwarden was extremely elderly and perhaps they thought I would balance it a bit. Patrick was christened at Aston Clinton, but whether we left any motivation for the future, or whether they just dropped back into their traditional ways, I know not.

The early years at Cote, which was in the parish of Aston, were not overly taken up with Church matters. There were two reasons for this; first, that the children were small and being at a service could be a bit of a trial for all concerned and, second, that when South Cerney was operating we had to be there, although we never opened on Good Friday, much to the chagrin of site owners. However, once again we found ourselves involved. First Susan was on the PCC and later I was; we have never been keen on both of us being on a PCC together as we feel that it creates too much of one opinion.

From this I was appointed to be a manager (now governor) representing the church on the local village school managing body. This position I held for ten or twelve years until we left. I was high-jacked into being secretary somewhere along the way when my predecessor suddenly ceased to be secretary for reasons which were never explained. This was an interesting assignment and at times a little daunting when one had to appoint teachers to teach one's

Although strictly speaking outside the time-frame of this book, a hand operated railway has been installed into the church of St John the Baptist, Cirencester, to assist with the complete renewal of the floor. It is raised on a timber 'viaduct' to maintain a level with the ground outside.
Bryan Lawson

own children. At that time there were six managers and the head teacher was in attendance, although not officially a manager, and, in conjunction with the Local Education Authority, I think we did a fair job. There were two of us with children at the school and the remainder were local farmers and the like. We coped with a major building exercise for a new hall and all the usual functions of a school. I was there when the concept and actuality of parent governors was introduced and I have always held the view that this was a mistaken move – it is better to have governors who just happen to have children at the school. My reasons for this unorthodox opinion are that parent governors have a very intense but very short-term interest in a school, five years at most, and that is very little, even in the life of a village primary school. The consequence is that pet ideas can be brought in which have to be unravelled when the parent with the enthusiasm ceases to be a governor. I also saw the beginnings of the inundation of head teachers with reporting paperwork which now almost prevents them from having time to teach. Not long after we left Cote we were invited back for a leaving party for the lady who had been head throughout my period as school manager/governor. I did ask her if the reason for her early retirement was because of the paperwork and her answer was an unequivocal 'Yes'.

We had come to Cote in the retiring years of the Rev'd Selwyn Taborn, who was again something of the old school of priest, whose one claim to fame in my eyes was that he could get through a service at truly remarkable speed whilst still doing it sincerely, without omitting anything and without gabbling. He was replaced by the Rev'd Derek Frost, a young man in his first parish, but who at the time was unable to drive which seemed a remarkable achievement when he had five churches to contend with! However he was much of our age and we had considerable empathy with him.

The spire of Aston church was just under 100 feet tall and my knowledge of building and surveying came into its own when the top twenty feet had to be rebuilt. I have two very vivid memories of this job. The first was when I was discussing some detail with the foreman mason and he said, 'Well, come and have a look at it then', and then set off up the ladders like a rabbit out of a hat. I have always had a reasonable head for heights, but straight off the cuff like that was a bit disconcerting but I followed regardless. I think he was testing me out. For the second, we made a new weathercock to go on the top as somebody had put a .303 bullet through the old one and Martin held the steps on the top of the scaffold while I put himself in place; in fog so thick we could not see the ground! Later the floor in Aston church started to collapse in the area where we normally sat which caused considerable mirth in all directions. In due course the whole of the wooden floor on either side of the aisle had to be renewed.

It is a stock interviewer's question as to what is the worst thing that has ever happened to one. Whilst I would not describe it as the worst, possibly the most alarming thing to happen to me was on one occasion when I was at a Good Friday service. Whoever was supposed to take the service did not turn up and the then churchwarden approached me and asked me what *I* was going to do about it. Considering that he was a retired headmaster I have always thought he should have been better qualified to cope than me. Anyway, after a bit of thought I lasted about twenty minutes which I have always thought pretty good. I have had to take quite a number of services since, but I have always had a bit longer in which to think about it!

In due course, and with a certain inevitability, I became churchwarden. This is a very ancient office of the Church of England and one is officially the bishop's representative in the parish. One is elected separately and independently by the parish as a whole at the annual meeting and not by the congregation, although in practice these are often one and the same. The job is no sinecure. In times past the wardens were responsible for such things as road maintenance and relief of the poor; nowadays it is very much maintaining an active church presence in parishes that no longer have resident clergy. One is responsible for the church buildings and all that goes on in them and for the good conduct of the vicar for the time being. Bishops will sit up and take notice of comments or complaints from churchwardens. Thus it was that for the first time I became in part responsible for the appointment of a new vicar and also for the running of a group of parishes during an interregnum, which is the gap between one vicar leaving and the next taking office. Also, this was when what had a been a loose group of parishes became amalgamated into one benefice (the area looked after by one priest), something which was to occupy my time considerably from here on. The Anglican Church in this country was just entering a period, that we might now just be moving away from, when clergy numbers were falling and they therefore had to be spread more thinly on the ground. The days of one vicar to one parish have long gone. This is in part due to lack of suitable persons coming forward for ordination and in part due to the inability of parish churches to find the money to pay them. More of all that later.

The Rev'd Andrew Scott was our new vicar. He was a retired naval chaplain and, as he described it, on his way south from County Durham to ultimately retiring in Plymouth. He was a bachelor with a dry sense of humour and very precise and sincere in all he did. He had a passion for Scottish dancing but was not everybody's choice in the villages. He had to contend with the reorganization of the parish in what was to be one of the many experiments with using clergy more effectively. In this case each church retained its churchwardens

and church council but they in turn sent representatives to a benefice parochial church council who conducted the affairs of the group as a whole. At some stage I wound up as secretary to this body. Whether this arrangement has continued I do not know, but it was good experience and I think is a slightly better way of doing things than that which I came to be very involved with in Herefordshire.

Also at this time came the new services of the *Alternative Service Book* which were intended to make church-going easier and more intelligible to those who were unaccustomed to it. This caused a lot of heartache for a lot of people but, by and large, I found it acceptable and certainly better than that which has come since. It is true that the language of the *Book of Common Prayer* written in 1662 is archaic, but the Anglican Church has always been capable of skewing the rules and adjusting its services to suit time and place.

Above: The secret of the K.40 is the drive box mounted on the axle and these we manufacture ourselves. This one is having the gearwheel tolerances set up.

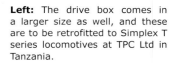

Left: The drive box comes in a larger size as well, and these are to be retrofitted to Simplex T series locomotives at TPC Ltd in Tanzania.

The bodywork can be quite complicated, as with this picture of the Lartigue replica in course of manufacture.

Whether tinkering with the language has brought any more people to their Church and their God has, I think, to be questionable. It was also the beginnings of serious moves for the ordination of women and opinions were requested from PCCs and others. At the time I was against the concept, and still have some reservations, but always vowed that if it came to pass they would have my wholehearted support. At the time people would say, 'Well, look at Margaret Thatcher.' To which my comment was, 'Precisely!' Twenty years later people are getting heated about the possibility of women bishops, but if one is going to ordain women to the priesthood then a woman as a bishop is as inevitable as night follows day.

Thus we moved to The Lea and out of the diocese of Oxford and into the diocese of Hereford. We have kept in touch with Andrew Scott over the years (he has retired to Plymouth) and he has spent a number of Christmases with us. As if to emphasise the move to a truly rural area we had an almost immediate problem. Alice moved into the local village school but it was not as good as that at Aston, and after a couple of terms we moved her to a well-reputed convent school in Cinderford. We then found ourselves with a deputation of the local rector, the Rev'd Ronnie Hambleton, and one of the churchwardens complaining not so much that we had moved her from the school but that we had moved her to a Roman Catholic school. I could not believe my ears; Northern Ireland, here we come! Despite this I was a school governor at The Lea for a few years at a later stage.

Susan and I had said that we were going to have respite and not get involved in local church matters for at least a couple of years after we moved. It nearly worked. I think I was suborned onto the PCC about eighteen months after the move, and not very long after that one of the churchwardens (not the one above!) suffered a major illness. When he recovered he asked me to act as his deputy if either it happened again or he was temporarily unable to perform his duties. Very unexpectedly, about a year later he died and so I found myself in at the deep end. My co-churchwarden Bill Edwards, although rather pernickety and beginning to get elderly, had a good grasp of things and I did not have to think too hard. However another hand

seemed to have control of the tiller and I was about to get involved in Church affairs at a much higher level and away from purely local issues. My first brush with this came with the retirement of Ronnie Hambleton and being involved in the appointment of the Rev'd Tim Alban-Jones and the inclusion of The Lea into what was to become the Ross Team Ministry. Tim was a very likeable and personable young man for whom this was his first parish. He later made a national name for himself as vicar of Soham in Cambridgeshire where two young children were murdered. It was a very high-profile affair and it is typical of him that he accepted an MBE on behalf of all the other clergy who have to cope with the same problems but without the media attention.

To make sense of what happens next it is necessary to give some further explanation of how the Church of England works. It has a series of tiers of governance of which the parochial church council is the lowest and most local, the real 'grass roots'. If a parish is part of a team or group, this may have its own council to decide mutual issues. The next official body is the deanery synod which covers a large area of perhaps thirty to forty churches and one of the clergy within that deanery will be appointed rural dean and will automatically be chairman of that synod. All churches within the deanery send representatives to deanery synod and this body in turn sends representatives to diocesan synod. This, as its name implies, is, if you like, the parliament of the diocese and is chaired by the bishop. Diocesan synod sends representatives to general synod which meets twice a year in London or York (the two archbishoprics) and this is chaired by the Archbishop of Canterbury as head of the world-wide Anglican Communion. Over and above all this is the Lambeth Conference, when all the Anglican bishops from all over the world meet once every ten years to discuss policy and more serious issues. Thus in theory a matter can be raised at a local PCC and be passed right up the tree to general synod for discussion or, conversely, matters raised at general synod are passed down to the parishes. It is cumbersome but it does work; it takes time, as none of these bodies meet more than three or four times a year, but then time is not a serious issue. The Christian Church has survived 2,000 years and despite the prophets of doom continues to prosper so whether something happens next week or next month is neither here nor there. If that is a surprising statement, bear in mind that the average member of the Anglican Church is female, black and aged twenty-two! Finally, for administrative purposes most dioceses are divided into archdeaconries comprising several deaneries in the care of an archdeacon who is fundamentally the personnel officer looking after the posting of clergy, their housing and other problems. There is also bishop's council, a fairly august body that is the 'cabinet' of the diocese. And finally, finally there are numerous committees taking care of individual aspects of the Church's work.

Returning then to my personal position in all this, I was at some stage voted by the PCC to be The Lea's representative on Ross & Archenfield Deanery Synod (Archenfield is a corruption of Ariconium, the Roman Sheffield of Great Britain which remains unexcavated between The Lea and Ross). Deanery synod has a fully justified reputation for being a pretty deadly exercise without much purpose, something I remembered from keeping the minutes when I was at Aston. However its presence is required by statute and it is the first step up the communications ladder. I possibly made a name or a nuisance of myself early on by suggesting that the clergy should be listed in the telephone book under a general heading of Church of England rather than under their individual names so that one could contact a church elsewhere if one wished. Apparently this did get passed to Bishop's Council for consideration and was turned down, but I note that it has since happened. It was the first of a number of things like this that have occurred. I also got on to a sub-committee set up to discuss the anticipated reduction in the number of clergy, the involvement of lay people in worship and other issues. This got nowhere and I have always thought of it as one of the bishop's red herrings to make people think. That, if anything, was its only merit – it meant that people were thinking about the problems that were to come and that the Hereford Diocese did not get caught out in the way that some did. Much more interestingly, I was voted on to the Archdeaconry Pastoral Committee which concerned itself with the appointment of clergy, the amalgamation of parishes, clergy housing, parish land and other such problems. I have been on this committee for at least fifteen years, at one stage as a co-opted member.

Not long before my first trip to Tanzania there was a local Deanery event at which I met the Bishop of Ruvumu from southern Tanzania who was in England for the Lambeth Conference. From this I discovered that there was a link between Hereford Diocese and the Anglican Province of Tanzania, that is, the whole country. Having heard a number of dire traveller's tales prior to that first trip I stashed the man's name away in my head as a last resort if everything went wrong and I needed someone to vouch for me, hoping that he would remember! The second time I went to Tanzania I asked the Archdeacon if there was anything I could take with me that was needed out there. Big mistake! I took a piece of computer equipment that was needed urgently at the hospital at Muheza near Tanga. Apart from raising a few eyebrows with customs officials this in itself was no problem. When I got back, one Sunday evening I found I had the Bishop of Hereford, the Rt Rev'd John Oliver, on the phone with the question, 'Would I be chairman of the Diocesan Overseas Committee?' I did not even know that the diocese had an overseas committee, never mind that I should be chairman of it! It was to be quite a stormy ride.

The problem was that the Overseas Committee had bumbled along for many years without any sure direction and very little idea of what it was supposed to be doing. The committee was large, twenty-five people, of whom nearly two-thirds were representatives of various missionary societies, each of whom were ploughing their own furrow with little regard for any overall pattern. They included both my favourite and least favourite charities and if they had all put their heads together

(unlikely!) they could have dictated policy to the diocese in the field of missionary activity. Maybe the diocese was finding similar problems with some of its other committees but my principle undertaking was to produce a new constitution for the committee and that involved my presenting draft ideas to Bishop's Council and Diocesan Synod. All a bit daunting. In the end the deed was done and the committee was cut down to size with the charities being jointly represented by one of their number. Greater emphasis was to be placed on the Tanzanian link which was reduced to the dioceses of Dar es Salaam, and Tanga with Zanzibar in the north with Masasi in the south. That one of this country's least populous dioceses should cover the whole country was just ridiculous. There was, and is, also a link with the Lutheran Church in Germany but this was always a personal project of the Bishop and never came under the Overseas Committee despite my best endeavours. I believe it has now with a change of bishop.

On a more practical level, a certain amount of good began to be done and in the process I came across some truly remarkable people. Dominic Mchopa was a young priest from Mtwara in the far south of the country who was training at a college in Bristol. Susan and I offered him some hospitality one Christmas. It was an eye-opener to hear of him having to cope with twenty-five churches in an area some seventy-five miles by thirty miles with only a bicycle for transport, not to mention having to spend the odd night in a tree with lions wandering about at the bottom! Whatever were we worrying about in England? Despite a considerable effort to do so, it is my regret that I never met Canon Robin Lambourn who founded the Kindwitwi Leprosy Mission. He had retired from life as a priest in Africa when he discovered that leprosy victims were sent to an area near the mouth of the Rufuji river south of Dar es Salaam, there to live or die as best they could. He founded a settlement to care for them and I used to take parcels out for

There are always large lumps to manhandle about as in the fitting of the boiler to this Baldwin 4-6-0 locomotive, and for this our mobile crane has to be brought into the workshop. Phil Kent on left.

him which were left at the International School in Dar. He used to write me the most delightful letters complaining of hippopotamus damage to their crops – perhaps I could come out and say 'Shoo' or shoot them or something! I had afternoon tea with Archbishop Ramadhani, Archbishop of the Anglican Province of Tanzania, on the veranda of his house at Korogwe, again not too far from Tanga. He was an enormous man, taller than I am, and I met him again in Hereford, when he was attending the Lambeth Conference. I visited St Marks Theological College in Dar es Salaam and then sent Joyce Banbury out there to teach English and Church history for three months. She thoroughly enjoyed the challenge but found it difficult teaching Church history to a group of people who had never heard of the Romans!

As might be imagined, all this took up a good deal of my time, not least because I suddenly found myself an *ex officio* member of various other diocesan committees such as Diocesan Synod, a steering committee (fairly useless) and, when required, attending Bishop's Council. I also attended a couple of day-conferences in London with USPG, again not frightfully useful. In the event it was taking up too much time and with the problems the business was facing in the mid-nineties I had to give it up. At the time I felt nothing much had been achieved but when I see how the Tanzania link in particular has blossomed since, maybe I did not do too badly.

I remain on both Deanery Synod and the Pastoral Committee so when I volunteered to represent the Pastoral Committee on the Redundant Churches Uses Committee I received a round of applause! There is a myth that due to increasing costs, lack of clergy and so on, churches are going to be closed all over the place. Hereford Diocese has a firm policy that if there are some few people, be they ever so few, who will maintain and love a church it will not be closed. And this in a diocese which has the distinction of being the least populated of any English diocese; a fact which is emphasized by there being over 200 parishes with less than 200 population. Having said that, there are inevitably a few which have little or no future. There are many and varied reasons for this, some were duplicated in the Victorian era of church building when travel was not as easy as now; in some the population has moved away over the centuries (we have one which is one and a half miles from a made road with the final 300 yards on foot only across a field, but with a Norman castle at the church gate); others where the desire and ability to maintain a church has faded away and still others which are literally in the garden of the local mansion – which I should imagine makes church-going somewhat daunting. Some are taken over by organizations such as the Friends of Friendless Churches, some are sold for houses or, just occasionally, they rise to the occasion and find the means to carry on. It is remarkable and humbling to see what can be achieved. All have their problems as far as alternative uses are concerned with vehicular and sometimes even pedestrian access usually being top of the list.

As an ancillary to this I have also become responsible for redundant church furnishings for which the diocese has a small church, itself redundant, that is half-full of church furniture. This has been taken out of other churches in various reorganizations but is too good to scrap or to sell for secular use. This includes several pulpits, stone fonts, sets of choir stalls, altar rails and so on. I am just getting to grips with this one.

So, back to local matters. When Tim Alban-Jones departed for Soham, The Lea, as part of the Ross Team, came under the able care of the Rev'd Tirsh Grigor, a rumbustuous Scot with a great sense of fun. The Ross Team Ministry was itself in a bit of a hiatus just then, undergoing change and expansion as a number of other parishes came under its wing and the number of clergy was reduced yet again. At the time the buzz-words were 'team ministry' where a number of team vicars worked under a team rector and could thus, by working together, provide a better service over a larger area. Some teams work very well indeed; but they are like schools, only as good as the headmaster or mistress at the time. I think it is now admitted that the Ross Team has never really worked – but whether in this instance it is because of the clergy, the people or the place is anyone's guess. The problems inherent with all this ultimately caused Tirsh to leave for a group of parishes in Gloucester Diocese where she can be her own master and she is undoubtedly the better and happier for it.

Before she left, Susan took over from me as churchwarden. I think she makes a better job of it but the role has become expanded to the point where churchwardens are virtually running their parishes and, in the long term, I am not sure that that is a good thing. The present buzz-words are 'collaborative ministry', but again I remain to be convinced. More to the point, she has had a hard time with the appointment of a successor to Tirsh and after three attempts we shall have our own incumbent, albeit for six parishes, by the time this appears in print. This, inevitably, is a chapter without an end. As the hymn says, 'Christ is working his purpose out as year succeeds on year', and despite its problems, to which I have had my small input, the Christian Church in general, and the Anglican Church in particular, will carry on, even if the African churches have to start sending missionaries to England!

I headed this chapter 'Church and State' because it had a nice ring about it but in truth there has been very little 'State'. Possibly my involvement in schools could come under that heading, but local councils I find so petty that I just feel I could not cope. Patrick at least manages to be on the local Parish Council. Part of the problem may be that I have never been a political animal but I have come to have very strong views on the subject of the European Union. I fully subscribe to the view that as a nation we were conned into it in the referendum of 1973 and I will admit that I voted in favour at that time. Like many people I thought we were only embarking on a free trade area not the wholesale take-over of our country by what is effectively a foreign power. I have made modest contributions to organizations that are opposed to the EU and have equally modestly helped local parliamentary candidates in this area. The real problem, and I think it will cause the ultimate death of the European dream, is the lack of democracy within that organization. It appears to be run by bureaucrats for the benefit of the political elite and seems prepared to stamp on any dissent from its one-party-state type policies. Historically, countries run that way do not last but whether it will fall within my lifetime or not remains to be seen.

I will end this chapter with something surreal and slightly scary as it seems about the only place to put it. It has long been my habit to walk round the premises on Christmas morning just to see that everything is OK and get a breath of fresh air before Christmas lunch. When doing this about a year after my father died I found lying in the yard one of his business cards – I did not know that he even had a business card and had certainly never seen one. Make of that what you will!

16

Retirement

Too often have I seen businesses where the founder cannot let go, and is doggedly running the show into his seventies and more – to the great frustration of those around him, particularly if they are family. Alternatively, he insists on coming in just to do a bit of filing or something, and is nothing more than a damned nuisance. I was determined that I was not going to fall into this trap and so, from a few years before reaching the watershed of sixty-five, I started to take at least one day a week off; after all, it allowed a bit more time to go sailing! The reality has been that this has worked quite well and that now I simply get called in when required and the day-to-day running of the firm is down to others. One of the curiosities of this period has been the reappearance of customers with whom we have not done business since the very earliest days, perhaps twenty-five to thirty years ago. One has to hope that we do not always have to wait that long for repeat orders. Of these, the most notable are Whipsnade Zoo, Longleat House and the Chemin de Fer Touristique du Tarn.

A replica locomotive on a large scale was the commencement of work on *Puffing Billy* for Beamish Museum. This had been under discussion for some time and depended on their obtaining adequate funding for it, which in the event proved easier than expected. This time, unlike the *Steam Elephant*, we were involved from the beginning and had at least some input into how the job was done. My abiding memory of this one is the number of times the boiler came from and went back to the boiler-makers. This came about because various items had to be fitted to the boiler before the next stage of manufacture could proceed. One is only left to marvel at the original builders who had to overcome the problems as they went along, without really knowing whether what they were making would even work. All in all, for us the job went very smoothly and is another feather in the cap of everybody involved. I was struck forcibly by the fact that despite the intricacies of its construction it worked faultlessly from the first moment it was steamed, and all credit must go to Dave Potter, who also designed *Steam Elephant*, for this remarkable achievement. As a family we all went to Durham for the opening ceremony which was performed by Sir William McAlpine, another name from the past.

The railway at Margam Park, for which we had built stage one, had always been intended to connect the car park at the bottom of the hill with the castle that was at the top. There had been an idea

to connect the new line into the visitor farm and I came up with a layout that included a spiral, but still had fairly stiff gradients. In the end they opted for the straightforward route which was effectively the shortest possible with a ruling gradient of not more than 1 in 40. Even so there were to be some 1,200 metres of this from more-or-less a standing start at the bottom. With this possibility in mind, the locomotive had at least been given enough power and weight to cope with it. The earthworks were substantial, with a cutting about fifteen feet deep and embankments some ten feet high.

The exciting part came when HMRI came to inspect. Whilst the train was fitted with fail-safe air brakes they, not unreasonably, wanted to test whether in fact the brakes would do all that was intended of them, especially as a third carriage was to be added to the train. The upshot was that the train was fully 'loaded' with bags of animal feed, and various tests carried out with the train in 'free fall' down the gradient. I have to say that we were surprised how well it stopped from a speed of around 15m.p.h. More interesting still was a need to check where and how the air brake pipes would part company in the event of a coupling failure; they were anxious that the train would not 'hang' on the air pipes as had happened on one well-known railway. Therefore I took the various components to Gloucester Rope & Tackle and tested them on the chain test rig. The answer was that the souxie pipe would pull out of its union first but, more surprisingly, a common-or-garden brass pipe fitting took four tons to break!

Among the many railways being rebuilt was that into the old Laxey mines on the Isle of Man which originally had some absolutely

Technically this replica *Puffing Billy* was built by Beamish Museum but for our own convenience we gave it works number 71 of 2004, even if the works plate is buried under the floor. This is its first official journey at Beamish following the official launch by Sir William McAlpine.

For The Great Laxey Mine Railway on the Isle of Man we built two carriages, or manriders, as they are known in this context. This is the first one with locomotive *Bee* and gives an idea of just how small these locomotives are. We carried out major work to its *confrère*, *Ant*. *Andrew Scarffe*

minute steam locomotives built by the redoubtable Stephen Lewin of Poole. We had hoped that we might build the replica locomotives but unfortunately these went elsewhere. The consolation prize was to build a manrider to carry only eight people through the tunnel. However three years later by way of poetic justice we not only built a second manrider but had one of the locomotives, *Ant*, in for major modification.

Almost from its inception, the Alford Valley Railway had had a large wooden-bodied carriage which ran on a couple of old skip frames for bogies. In my opinion it was really too big for a small 2ft gauge line but it worked and suited them. In his efforts to see the railway complete and set up for the future, James Gordon had us build a new carriage of very similar proportions but in steel and very smart it turned out to be. In order to finance it they decided to sell their rare 0-6-2 Fowler steam locomotive, *Sacharine*, which in reality had become more trouble than it was ever worth as an attraction. This we sold to an enthusiast who will cherish it dearly.

Then came a very remarkable garden railway for Graham Lee who had a large farm near Tamworth. This started off as a fairly modest 2ft gauge line around his garden crossing a couple of ornamental ponds in the process. For this he had acquired a steam-outline Simplex and an underframe (on our bogies) on which to build a carriage. It was supposedly for his grandchildren. He bought the last Hunslet steam locomotive built, a 2ft 6in. gauge Brazil class 0-4-2ST, that was on a sugar plantation in Java. Not only that, but he also brought back from the same country a small Orenstein & Koppel and an 0-4-4-0 Mallet by the same maker. Just to add

to the complications, his family then bought him as a retirement present the 18-ton 0-6-0 Peckett originally ex Harrogate Gas Works upon which I had worked in my volunteering days at the Festiniog Railway. Ultimately it had been restored by David and Bill Best in Kent.

Thus what had been intended to be a spur off the garden railway to the farmyard for access purposes became the main line and was to be mixed 24in./30in. gauge in 50lbs/yd rail with pointwork to suit. The provision of the turnouts and laying of this heavy track was done in conjunction with K.G.J. Price Ltd. To all this he added a very spacious three-road engine shed complete with overhead crane and separate turntable. The railway was then extended to about three-quarters of a mile with stage four yet to come, which eventually made it up to around one and a half miles. The sad part about all this, and it was the root cause of later complications, was the inordinate haste with which it all had to be done. Insufficient thought was given in the early stages with the result that earthworks and, indeed, track layouts had to be changed at a later date.

Soon after the project started he bought some of the locomotive business of Hunslet/Barclay to become part of his principal company in contractors' plant and railway component overhaul. As part of the exercise he set up Hunslet Steam to build several 'Quarry Hunslet' steam locomotives, hoping to sell them to enthusiasts and preserved railways. Along with his private railway this all operated from his farm premises which by now included substantial workshops and

12¼in. gauge 0-6-0 diesel locomotive (AK73 of 2005) for a private line in North Devon. Although thought-out by different people and built nearly thirty years apart, the similarity between this and No. 16 in Chapter 8 is remarkable.

several full-time employees. I think he may have been somewhat surprised to discover us tendering against him in some international tenders which in turn may have had something to do with a major row that started over the ballast used on his railway. This in turn led on to arguments about turnout design and the installation of the track. After carrying out remedial work with which he refused to be satisfied he ultimately presented a claim for a very substantial sum in compensation. Regrettably we simply could not afford the potential costs that might have been incurred to defend this claim. Eventually it was settled for rather more than half the sum claimed, an amount even then considered by some to be extortionate. It wasted a huge amount of time, money and effort, particularly on Patrick's part, that it will take the company some years to overcome.

One of the shocks of 2004 was Severn Lamb Ltd going into liquidation. Only time will tell whether this will be generally a good or bad thing as far as Alan Keef Ltd is concerned, but it is always sad to see a well-known name go down even if they were a competitor. It is worth recording that in 2004 Alan Keef Ltd achieved a one million pound turnover for the first time.

Perhaps the most ghostly of reincarnations from the early days was an 0-6-0 diesel locomotive in 12¼in. gauge for William Heller for a private railway in North Devon. Except that it had curved bonnets and roof and featured coupling rods, this was visually almost an exact repeat of the locomotive built for Commander Francis of the Wells and Walsingham Railway all those years ago. Unlike most of the private railways dealt with to date, this one is being built slowly with the owner enjoying the doing of it rather than it all being constructed at once. To this end we have supplied several sets of points, rail and fastenings on a piecemeal basis.

One of my first commercial customers was the railway at Whipsnade Zoo, and we suddenly found ourselves carrying out major bogie refurbishment. This railway used equipment almost exclusively from the Bowater's paper mill railway and passenger carrying bodies were built on the old wagons. Alterations to the springing arrangements transformed these carriages as twenty to thirty passengers do not weigh anything like the ten tons of paper for which they were designed. We also supplied two batches of new FR-type couplers to replace those currently in use. As these have the ability to keep the train tight, passenger comfort is again improved. They also purchased an ex-MoD Baguley diesel locomotive from us, which was of course the right gauge for them.

Some emergency trackwork at Thorpe Park has been mentioned, but a year later they came in for some more substantial work with the straightening of the track layout through the Canyon of their railway. There was a further section of trackwork at Wicksteed Park which was complicated by including three level crossings, two bridges and lowering the track in the tunnel. With some minor realignment the result

was a considerable improvement on what had gone before. A major re-lay and re-grading was carried out in the camel enclosure at Woburn Safari Park. The survey work for this was entertaining and, to Patrick's and my eternal regret, we neither of us had a camera with us that day. When entering the animal enclosures it is necessary to have a member of staff and a Land Rover in attendance in case of problems. The camels are quite mild but trying to look through a surveyor's level with two or three of them bundling round and generally getting in the way was something that should have been recorded for posterity. At Eaton Hall we laid in a crossover to create a passing loop and also realigned the triangular junction so that it worked with all their rolling stock rather than just some of it. This was yet another case of us having to put right work done by others. A.J. Lowther Ltd have been mentioned as steel fabricators that we use, but they have a short length of track in their factory for moving steel for shot blasting or painting. To improve the efficiency of this we supplied a crossover made up in square steel bar for this 'railway'. Another oddball piece of trackwork was a three-metre length of standard gauge track in S7 rail for W. Bance & Co. Ltd made up so that it could all be dismantled and put in the back of a car and taken to exhibitions. This was for demonstrating their maintenance trolleys and it was later extended for test purposes in their works.

TPC and Fiji Sugar Corporation continued to buy spares, and an increasing amount of business was done in Ruston spare parts which business had come our way with the closure of Esca Engineering. Being a Ruston locomotive enthusiast, Bryan Lawson has taken this one very much in hand. North Sea Camp is a prison on the coast near Boston and has the dubious claim to fame of being where Sir Jeffrey Archer was imprisoned recently. This establishment has had from its inception a 2ft gauge railway originally for sea defence work, latterly for use in conjunction with the prison farm and most recently not used at all. It was home to many Lister locomotives and I did call there once to try and drum up some business but in mid-2005 it was all put up for sale by tender. Most of the equipment was

Howard and *Denzil* (AK74 of 2005 and AK54 of 1998), 10¼in. gauge 0-6-0 locomotives, mechanically very similar but of different appearance on the Wells Harbour Railway, Wells-next-the-Sea, Norfolk. The owner's daughter is trying the new locomotive for size!

well life-expired, but we did acquire a couple of good Jim Crows for bending rails.

In parallel with building the locomotive for William Heller we built another 0-6-0 for the Wells Harbour Railway. Mechanically this was basically the same as the previous one that had given yeoman service over the years. In order to make it look different it was given an overall saddle tank after the style of *Prince* on the Festiniog Railway and was painted blue. Nearly as expensive in cost terms was a major overhaul of the Simplex, *Cheyenne*, for Wicksteed Park. It is worth recording that the Kerr Stuart *Diana* was finally completed as far as we were concerned and left after all those years.

Selling our sort of 'trainset' on the Internet may sound unlikely, but this is just what happened with a locomotive and two carriages sold to Lithuania. It was with some reluctance that the purchasers even took the trouble to come and see us, and even then we did not know precisely for what they were intended. All we could get out of them was that it was for a 'kids' park'. The equipment was perfectly standard but a good order nevertheless and left in time to be a static exhibit in the city square at Vilnius over the Christmas season. It was not until late spring 2006 that I went to Lithuania to commission them and discovered what it was all about. The so-called park was something that we do not have in this country, a summer camp for the children of the employees of Lithuanian Railways, who were in fact the end users. The consequence of this is that our little locomotive and two carriages are numbered into Lithuanian Railways' stocklist! The railway itself is a circular track about 800 metres long although it has pretensions to extend to the local main-line station and possibly become something of a tourist attraction in its own right. It is at least in a tourist area.

2006 turned out to be a most difficult year and Patrick had a very hard time of it despite all the work he put in. The memory is rather of what did not happen rather than what did. For instance we retained a locomotive number, 75, for a new locomotive for Wicksteed Park to be delivered for the 75th year of operation of their railway; it has yet to happen although it is still being spoken of. The year was supposed to kick off with major work for Fintown Railway and whilst this has happened, it was mid-2007 before it was completed. Major track alterations at the Cotswold Wildlife Park

were postponed until the autumn after we already had the materials on site. We actually received a substantial order from the UK Atomic Energy Authority and four days later it was cancelled! Due primarily to the pressures all this put on our cash flow I personally spent most of the year completing our new offices and thus did all the internal carpentry work including flooring and second fixing.

Despite the postponement at Cotswold there was a good batch of ongoing trackwork with a major re-lay of the loop at Woburn Safari Park, a further section at Wicksteed Park and some repairs at Thorpe Park. Under the same heading could also come slipway tracks for the RNLI at Kikcudbright, Scotland, Port Erin, Isle of Man and at Kilkeel in Northern Ireland. In due course the trolleys were also supplied to go with these, two of them being of the big DART variety to take the latest Atlantic 85 inshore lifeboats which have a speed of no less than 36 knots. The provision of a new turning loop and siding to new locomotive and stock sheds was undertaken on the 10¼in. gauge miniature railway of Michael Whitehouse. Later in the year this also included the refurbishment of a petrol locomotive as well. Possibly under the track-laying heading also comes what we consider to be the most unusual railway we have ever supplied. This was for a railway on a ship.

The ship in question, the *Wave Sentinel*, had been a roll-on roll-off ferry and was later converted to a cable-laying ship. Apparently cable laying was in the doldrums at the time and the owners were going to use the vessel for some salvage operations. The requirement was for a means of moving the salvaged material, which was apparently very heavy, from cranes and winches at the stern to the various holds further forward. The situation was confused by having to negotiate a metre-wide gangway between two enormous winches that were part of the cable laying operation. The track was to be purchased and the rolling stock to go on it hired in six-week sessions. For the latter we supplied two heavy wagons with locations to take two stillages each and a Schoma locomotive that had the merit of being very narrow. The track was partially prefabricated and a welder and myself went to Portland and welded it to the deck. The total length was about 100 metres

This trainset, AK76 of 2005 plus two carriages, was effectively bought from our website with our having very little knowledge of what it was for. It turned out to be for a summer camp for the children of the employees of Lithuanian Railways. Both locomotive and carriages are numbered into the state railways' stock!

Left: Another odd job is this railway installed on a ship. The vessel was a RoRo ferry subsequently converted to a cable ship now to be used for salvage, and the railway was required to move the salvaged material along the deck to be unloaded into the various holds.

Mark Armstrong

Right: Galvanizing and steel fabrication are major industries in Hereford with three companies in the business. All of them use internal narrow gauge railways for moving steel sections about but only that at Painter Bros Ltd is locomotive worked. This second-hand Clayton battery locomotive was rebuilt for use on their line.

and as the salvage operation could only be undertaken in seas of three metres height or less we reckoned the train would not have to contend with more than about 1 in 30 gradients! It all happened for one six week period and nothing more has been heard, so perhaps the operation was uneconomic, who knows?

There was the usual array of smaller jobs to be done which helped to keep the works turning but it was not enough to prevent us from having to lay off two of our workshop staff and having a rearrangement of duties amongst the management. Amongst these smaller jobs were re-profiling locomotive wheels for the Devon Railway Centre, repairs to a steam locomotive from the Wotton Light Railway, some new wheelsets for Blackpool Pleasure Beach, an ongoing supply of spare parts and the supply of some air brake equipment to the County Donegal Railways. We also stored the remains of a wagon from the Kington Tramway for Herefordshire Museum Services. Although it is no more than a very rusty iron frame, people who know suggest that it is probably amongst the top

Cutting edge technology in 1816. A replica plateway wagon made to stand beside the canal at Brecon, Wales, near the terminus of the tramway from there to Hay on Wye and Kington. At thirty-six miles, this claimed to be the longest railroad in the world at the time. The two ladies are reading an inbuilt board explaining its significance.

ten of the oldest railway vehicles in the country. Chronologically slightly further ahead, in late 2007 we made a plateway wagon and a few sections of track for display beside the canal at Brecon as a reminder of the Hay Tramway which started there. This in turn connected to the Kington Tramway and at the time, 1816, was claimed to be the longest railway in the world at thirty-six miles! Most surprisingly, a pattern for a wheel for one of these wagons was found that had been made in the 1970s for a similar exercise. All cutting-edge technology from 200 years previously!

Curiously, Hereford, of all places, seems to be becoming a centre of industrial railways. We supplied a service exchange engine for one of the Lister locomotives used for moving steel girders at Painter Bros and subsequently supplied a second-hand battery locomotive for use on one of their other internal railways with a second one being supplied a year later. Galvanizing is a major industry in Hereford; Hereford Galvanisers have several short hand-worked lines for which we have on occasion supplied bogies, and Joseph Ash & Co. have also approached us for a battery locomotive in their works but this has to be an unusual gauge, something like 4ft 3in.

As always, it is an ill wind that precipitated an order that had been part of the original project but never done. A major breakdown in midsummer at Bicton Park Gardens left them without a train service and the total rebuilding of their existing steam-outline Ruston locomotive resulted. This job was done almost in its entirety by our apprentice, Matthew Knight, and was in effect his 'apprenticeship piece'. It earned him, and it, a picture in our 2008 calendar. However the order of the year has to go to a new steam 2-6-2 tank locomotive, *Lydia*, for Alan Richardson, although to be used at the Perrygrove Railway at Coleford in the Forest of Dean. Like *Abigail*, the concept of this locomotive came from Ian Gaylor, but because he was unable to follow through with the detail design Phil Kent has picked up this baton and will have the locomotive to his credit. It is not due for delivery until 2008 but, after a lengthy gestation, it is beginning to look like a locomotive and will be a chunky

AK80 of 2007 is a standard 12¼in. gauge 0-6-0 supplied with three carriages to a reincarnation of the railway in Hotham Park, Bognor Regis. Being painted in British Railways steam livery with the carriages in malachite green is unusual but appropriate to the location.

materialized once their grant aid was in place and they were able to purchase a large carriage from the closed Shanes Castle Railway that was about the one item of rolling stock that did not go to the Giant's Causeway. We subsequently fitted it with air brakes and extended it slightly to give proper wheelchair access. Along with this we rebuilt their Simplex T series locomotive, again ex Shanes Castle, in the general style of the one we did for Leighton Buzzard. Once again this conversion has produced a very satisfactory 'large' locomotive, both physically and in terms of power, for a preserved railway. This now often works on a push/pull basis with the ex-County Donegal Railways railcar No. 18, which is, of course, back on its old stamping ground.

After much discussion we set about building what was something of a new departure in diesel locomotives for us, but of a type I had always had in mind.

and powerful beast when completed. Right at the end of the year an order was also received for a new 12¼in. gauge locomotive and three carriages to our standard design for the rebuilding of the miniature railway in Hotham Park at Bognor Regis. This was followed by a request for a carriage to carry disabled passengers a year later.

Similarly, the work on 5C, *Slieve Callen*, has been ongoing but in fits and starts as and when finance has been forthcoming. At last money has been raised for a new boiler for *Nancy*, the Avonside from the Cavan & Leitrim Railway, and this is likely to be finished off within the foreseeable future. The work for the Fintown Railway

This is a 15in. gauge 0-6-0 with jackshaft drive using the K.40 drive box mounted in the front of the frame giving the appearance of some of the locomotives built by Fowler and Hudswell Clarke. Although exact figures are not available, it seems that the railway at Longleat may be the most heavily used railway of its type in the country with annual passenger numbers over the 400,000 mark. Sufficient to say that this locomotive had a warranty problem after having been there for slightly over a fortnight, and the speedometer registered over 400 miles travelled and that on a railway only one and a quarter miles long!

Right: *Flynn* (AK79 of 2007) is something very different amongst our passenger locomotives. Loosely based on early Hudswell Clarke or Fowler designs it has mechanical transmission and jackshaft drive through a K.40 drive box under the front bonnet. Built for the railway at Longleat House the speedometer recorded over 400 miles travelled in its first ten days on site!

Left: Alice about to drive off on *Taffy* with a train-load of guests on her wedding day, 29 September 2007. Richard, an airline pilot, appears to be running his usual checks of the instruments to see that all is in order.   *Philip Price*

In the steam locomotive line came a new style of work altogether; this was renovation of axleboxes, connecting rods and other mechanical parts for RMS Locotec of Dewsbury. Their principle business is the hire of diesel shunters but they also overhaul small standard gauge steam locomotives for enthusiasts and liked our ability to understand and carry out this type of work.

It was also a time of supplying sets of points, albeit that they are now made by K.G.J. Price Ltd as recounted previously. In two batches, six went to the Rhyl Miniature Railway, three to Laxey Mines, and one in 60lbs/yd rail to Whipsnade Zoo. As well as turnouts there was track-work all over the place, with the delayed track-work at Cotswold Wildlife Park eventually being done. This railway was always curious in that whilst it was roughly circular the two ends did not meet by about 100 yards. This work was to complete that link and involved three level crossings, filling in the ha-ha and moving the emu pen, which may account for it not being done originally. It has certainly improved and simplified the operating capacity of the railway. We also supplied and installed new turnout components on Southend Pier and also a turnout and storage siding at Flamingoland. Also winding the clock back to Day One of the business was some work on the Santa Fe or Peter Pan track at Butlin's Minehead. It will be recalled that the re-lay of the original track here was not only the first job directly for Butlin's but also our first track-laying job ever. The railway at Thorpe Park was cut back to a circle of about 400 yards from something like one and a half miles following the closure of the visitor farm. In due course we bought the remaining track and redistributed it around the country. The triangle

Above: AK78R is a rebuild of Simplex T series 102T007 of 1974 for the Fintown Railway in County Donegal, Ireland. It is seen working push/pull with ex-County Donegal Railways railcar No. 18 on its first day in service. This is on the old CDR branch to Glenties with Loch Finn to the right and typical Donegal scenery.

Above: AK75R of 2006, *Bicton*, for Bicton Gardens in Devon is a complete rebuild of their existing Ruston locomotive (RH213839 of 1942) including new engine, hydraulic transmission and bodywork. This is the official ex-works photograph taken on site early in 2007.

at Bicton Gardens was re-laid with new turnouts made to fit the site, which has greatly improved the operation. In the disastrous flooding in the summer of 2007 the railway at Chesterfield had large amounts of ballast washed away which in turn raised issues of the general safety of the track, but all was resolved in the end. One of the other disasters of the year was that Corus, in the process of transferring rail manufacture from Workington to Scunthorpe, stopped rolling light rail sections and although this was half expected, the most disappointing part was that they failed to tell anybody and scrapped the rolls without giving someone else the chance to use them. Light rail now has to be imported and the best quality is coming from South Africa but is most readily available from China.

Along with the track-work there was also a spasm of wheel work, with bogie repairs at Blenheim, Margam Park and Marwell Zoo together with new bogie wheelsets for Wells Harbour Railway. Again going back to the earliest days of the business, we found ourselves making six heavy-duty carriage bogies in 500mm gauge for the Chemin de Fer Touristique du Tarn in France, to whom it may be recalled I sold two ex-Butlin's carriages perhaps thirty years previously. The replica carriage which is normally used with *Rocket* at York Museum was to go to a railway event in Holland with *Puffing Billy* from Beamish Museum. It fell to us to modify the air brake system so that the two were compatible. We acted as agents to sell *Emily* and train from Drusilla's Zoo to a private customer in Denmark. Talks are in progress for a tourist railway into some caverns in Denmark in which cheeses are also matured, so the railway could have mixed industrial and tourist use and that would certainly be a first. Patrick carried out a feasibility study for a possible railway beside the Kielder Reservoir (of Swales mine and wagon fame) but whether this will go ahead or not remains to be seen.

The Monorail found itself another unusual job. Silbury Hill, near Marlborough in Wiltshire, is the largest prehistoric earth mound in Europe. It is 130 feet high and dates from about 2400BC and, despite various excavations over the years, no-one knows just what its purpose was. For stabilizing and other conservation work the Monorail was hired to have two wagons rope-hauled up the side of the hill. From our point of view this required some vertically curved track sections at the top to bring it onto level ground and the whole thing painting dark green to make it inconspicuous whilst it was there. This work carried on for the better part of a year.

After several years in the planning and gestation stage we obtained an order for a funicular for private use some forty metres in length to serve two houses beside the River Thames. These things sound very simple until one starts to get deeply into them. The principal problem is the safety requirements of a man-riding winch and the fact that the haulage speed has to be significantly high. Forty metres may not seem far, but one does not want to be on it for more than a couple of minutes at most before it becomes tedious, especially if it is raining. As a consequence, the winch is liable to cost as much as the rest of the project put together. It was this cost that almost killed this one, which would have been unfortunate because there is the potential for another in a neighbouring property. The issue here is also muddied by there being an existing one in the next-door garden which has been there for many years. This was built using second-hand crane components and is very satisfactory even if a bit slow and, I gather, requires a fair amount of tender loving care to keep it working. It is always difficult to explain to people that the owner could build his own funicular and at worst hurt himself but that I simply cannot take that risk and that therefore the cost is going to be accordingly high. This has indeed come to business in the end, but is very slow in progress due primarily to arguments as to whether it could be construed that it is for public use and therefore just what regulations it comes under. At the time of writing the site has been cleared, the winch is in production and foundations are being designed, but it is very much anyone's guess when it will be operational. Matters are further complicated by very restricted space at the top not to mention that access to the bottom for materials and building work has to be by boat!

Some years previously we bought back from Singapore two Hunslet/Jenbach locomotives in the anticipation that one would go to the Eaton Hall Railway but in the event that never happened. They languished in the yard, seeing some use with the occasional shunting exercise, until quite unexpectedly both were sold together. One went to a new line in 12¼in. gauge being built locally and this we re-gauged and refurbished to suit. The other went to the Fairbourne Railway with them to reduce it to the same gauge.

The whole concept of the Parry People Mover moved on a stage when their vehicles were approved for use on the three-quarter mile Stourbridge branch. After much discussion they gave us the order to manufacture underframes for the two cars required together with assembling the flywheel drive units and associated hydraulics. In other words, to provide a complete operating chassis upon which the body could be directly placed. When it came to it, Phil Kent found himself having to design the final drive gearboxes on the powered axles. Whilst not strictly a

Simplex down under. The ubiquitous 20/28 Simplex really travelled the world and this one (MR7369 of 1939) is at the Cobdogla Museum in South Australia. It was one of a batch of fifteen built in ten weeks for a housing contract in Glasgow and subsequently exported to the Queensland sugar fields. With our advice it has been much rebuilt with a Perkins engine and enlarged cab.   *Dean Adamson*

locomotive, they are self-propelled units and consequently will carry our works numbers 81 and 82.

Works No. 83 will probably be earning its living by the time these words appear in print and is to be an 0-6-0 diesel locomotive in 10¼in. gauge for the Newlyn Branch Line of the Lappa Valley Railway in Cornwall, again one of my very earliest customers. And so it goes on. Somebody has to do all this work!

Having reached the end of the history part of this book it has been suggested that I should reflect a little on the changes that I have seen and have taken place since I started.

The first, and most obvious, is the almost complete demise of the industrial narrow gauge railway. This trend was well on the way when I started and has accelerated over the years. Fashion, in that railways have been out of fashion for the last forty and more years, has had a lot to do with this, see the saga at Star Lane Brickworks. Added to this, the chips have been stacked against them. Back in my days at Merry's, railway lines attracted rates whereas a roadway did not; how it stands today I do not know. Crossing a road or public right of way is now almost impossible with a railway but not with a dump truck. Small railways would continue to function after a fashion in the most incredibly derelict condition and the salesman who could offer anything, almost anything, that would apparently do a better job was on to a winner. They also tend to be labour intensive both in operation and maintenance and efforts in this direction, such as the Simplex remote control and my Hydrotip wagons, came too little and too late. There has never been any attempt to influence the market as, for instance, the Japanese did with the mini-digger. This was ridiculed when it first appeared but is now ubiquitous.

Added to this there has never been a concerted effort to sell light railways as a means of materials handling. Worse still, the user tended to have to buy the components from a selection of different suppliers, locomotives from one, wagons from another and track materials from a third – whereas Caterpillar, say, could supply it all from one very well organized basket. In fairness, Robert Hudson went a long way in this direction but the buyer still had to know what he wanted. Even then they only sold the materials, they did not market the concept. With everything getting larger all the time a similar situation has arisen in light rail strongholds like mining and tunnelling. The very high capital cost has also precluded light railways in new installations for traditional uses like sugar-cane harvesting, despite it being generally acknowledged as the best tool for the job. So the industrial railway has only survived where there are very specific reasons for it, such as on a peat bog or in the Woodhead Tunnel.

The passenger railway has been a growth industry for entirely opposite reasons. Some park railways, such as Wicksteed, have been around for a long time and many of them had become run-down over the years – perhaps not as badly as their industrial counterparts, but to the point where the owners had to decide whether to keep or remove. Most have decided to keep and upgrade as these are usually significant profit centres within their organizations, again unlike the industrial version which is always a cost centre. As far as Alan Keef Ltd has been concerned, this has been aided by the continuing bite of safety issues and the litigious society in which we now live. The passenger railway too has grown bigger with heavier rail, larger locomotives and increased train lengths to accommodate the very

Most of the locomotives we have built are still at work with their original customers. Inevitably, however, a few have gone into preservation and one such is this K.12 (AK6 of 1981), originally built for Richardson's Moss Litter Co., here seen converted to 15in. gauge on the private railway of John Tennent in South Wales in 2006.   *John Tennent*

large numbers of passengers now being carried. By any standards several hundred thousand passengers in a season is significant business.

Then there are the oddball jobs such as bobsleigh tracks, funiculars and railways on ships, not to mention the RNLI, that are difficult to categorise. These may have always been there, but seem to come our way with increasing frequency.

The market that is almost entirely new since I started is what is now termed the Heritage Railway. This is basically the preserved railway from the large standard gauge affair such as the Severn Valley Railway down to static exhibits in museums. For us, and particularly Patrick, the overhaul of steam locomotives in all sizes for use on this type of operation has become a major part of the business. Similarly, the supply of rolling stock and diesel locomotives, even effectively new ones, has a great significance for us. Added to this are repairs and renewals together with the supply of Simplex and Ruston spares which all help to keep the wheels turning. Possibly because of the demise of the country's industrial base, some of the preserved railway organizations are surprisingly short of skilled personnel to carry out repairs and restoration and that is where we can step in.

Despite the number of small railways there are, one of today's major problems is the lack of people who actually understand them. HM Railway Inspectorate are very professional and fully understand what they are all about but beyond that there are a whole raft of safety inspectors who really ought to know better. We have had two cases recently where great issues have been raised without said inspector even having seen the operation in question! Lateral thinking and the ability to evaluate the risks, or lack of them, rather than just 'tick-the-boxes' seems to be beyond their ability. Safety is something that is very difficult to argue against, but a whole industry has arisen which has to be self-perpetuating in order to survive and for whom 'using common sense' are dirty words. In similar, but not quite such aggravating, vein is the role of consultants in any project. Again they are often lacking in specific knowledge and do not understand the issues involved. They seem merely to be there to cover somebody's back and thus add to the cost of the enterprise.

One other thing that I find curious (perhaps its my age!), and it does not apply only to railways, is that nothing seems to be done without immediate recourse to grant aid of some sort from some public body or another. The sources seem to be endless; the lottery fund, the local authority, central government, the European Union, trust funds and charitable organizations. I really do wonder where all this money comes from. Wearing my Alan Keef Ltd hard-nosed businessman's hat, who am I to care about all these things? But I do. We do. I have been to places where the whole economy appears to live on handouts and the only new vehicles on the road belong to aid organizations. The prospect is not edifying.

I started this book with mention of the railway in the garden at Mortimer Lodge belonging to my great grandfather. It must be stated that the garden railway is still very much alive and well, ranging from large and substantial affairs such as that of Adrian Shooter to the smaller miniature line of Michael Whitehouse. Long may they all last!

Above: Open days have been a feature of the business and at Cote we borrowed *Pixie*, the late-lamented Rev'd Teddy Boston's Bagnall, to help raise money to rebuild the church spire. In 2006 this locomotive visited us again at The Lea.

Above: The event at The Lea was started for the same purpose but has become a major event of the railway calendar. In 2005 *Taffy* comes forward to take over from *Pixie*, Leighton Buzzard's Kerr Stuart, with *P.C. Allen* lurking in the background. Alice is on the extreme left.

Left: Almost exactly twenty years after the move to The Lea we moved into our new offices. Compare this with the photograph in Chapter 9 that was taken from about the same position.

17

Epilogue

It is difficult to know quite where to stop with this book because under Patrick's management Alan Keef Ltd is going from strength to strength and I always have the feeling that I should wait for such-and-such a contract to materialise or another one to be completed before I write 'Finis'. However, by the time this appears in print I shall have retired from the active management of the company although I remain company chairman for a variety of reasons, mostly financial. We will also have spent a year or more in our splendid new office building, which to have managed at all is no small achievement when I look back to the crises of the past. I am now a year or so past the magic age of 65 and am claiming my pension, so all these things make it a suitable point at which to draw the proverbial line. However there remain a number of items which do not fit tidily into the text and this is as good a place as any to record them.

Perhaps chief among these are the open days that we have held over the years. Originally they were by invitation only, usually to celebrate the completion of a major contract of some sort. The first was for the trains for the Iranian Navy and another was held to demonstrate the new steam locomotive for de Efteling. However back in Cote days we did borrow *Pixie* from the Rev'd Teddy Boston and held a public open day in aid of the rebuilding of Aston church spire. As I remember it was not as successful as we had hoped.

As so often seems to have been the case, history repeated itself at The Lea when the rebuilding of the church spire coincided with Patrick having *Woto* completed and thus was born an annual steam up and open day which now might be difficult to stop. It is now in its fifteenth year and over those years we have had a variety of steam locomotives available for the event. *Woto* and *Taffy* have obviously been regular performers, but there have been others that we have had in for overhaul, such as *Stanhope*, and still others that have just come visiting for the weekend, such as *Peter Pan*. On a couple of occasions we have added in a 'bunker sale', the railway equivalent of a car boot sale, which has been a good means for our disposing of material which might be useful to somebody but which would otherwise be scrapped. The event now brings around 500 visitors from, quite literally, all over the country and beyond, and raises some £2,500 that is divided between the local church and school. We have always had a policy of welcoming visiting railway enthusiasts and this has the merit of tending to concentrate them into one occasion.

Whilst obviously not a public event, Patrick and Helen's wedding in October 2002 was very much railway orientated. This was not least because the date was in large part determined by the expiry of *Woto*'s boiler certificate! I wonder how many weddings have been arranged thus. I had often been derided for thinking that the workshop building would make a good venue for a family wedding, but we came close to it when a marquee was fitted into the yard with the works being the base for the caterers. A good time was

had by all and engraved off-cuts of rail used as place markers grace a remarkable number of mantle-pieces. Perhaps the difficult bit came with Alice's wedding in September 2007 and how to make it different. This we achieved by carrying out quite major earthworks in the garden so that the marquee could be there. Entrance was gained via the field rather than the main gate and *Taffy* came to the fore as a means of entertaining guests. Richard is an airline pilot and I think his colleagues were quite bemused by the whole event. On a personal note, a surprise was that one of his friends turned out to be of the same family as my Aunt Kathleen's husband in South Africa, and one of Alice's to be related to my cousin Oliver's mother! Almost exactly in the middle between these two events fell our ruby wedding anniversary in 2004. This created a good family gathering with quite a number of original guests being available to be there. In particular the Rev'd (now Canon) Robin Osborne, who had married us, came to celebrate the Sunday morning service to which all were invited and many came.

John Palmer retired from his position of chief engineer in 2003, leaving a vacancy in the country's knowledge in the design of small locomotives. Although he started his working life and worked for twelve years with Brush, he spent eighteen years with Simplex and a further sixteen with us, so there can have been few with his experience. Alice took over from him with some considerable trepidation but is coping admirably. The business has always had an Achilles heel in the form of its workshop manager. Because the work is so far flung I, and nowadays Patrick, have always tended to be on the road almost as much as we have been in the office. The consequence is that there has always had to be someone else to run the workshop in our absence. Workshop managers have been many and various over the years. Despite our best endeavours we always seem to see the best ones in other people's workshops but not in our own! In 1999, Bryan Lawson, the son of one of my earliest customers, came to work for us in a sales and administrative capacity and he has become well known as the telephone voice of Alan Keef Ltd. Quite rightly we are often complemented on how helpful and courteous he is.

It was in 2002 that we achieved something that I had long dreamt about. That was to produce our own calendar; not just to buy one the same as other peoples, but one with pictures of our own activities on it. We had in fact done something like it back in the late 1970s, but that was a fairly crude 'large number' calendar organized by Ken Whittaker through some printers local to him. It was quite well received for all that, but this time we wanted to produce something that could become a collector's item. This I hope we have achieved and it is sobering to see them hanging in pride of place on office walls. It would be nice to have twelve pictures and a month to a page but it is quite hard enough sorting out six suitable pictures each year from the many we have. It has become a bit of a sales gimmick to promise potential customers a picture of their new locomotive in our calendar!

My elder daughter Florence deserves mention even if she has nothing to do with Alan Keef Ltd. School and Florence did not go well together and she left at the age of sixteen. She had become interested in woodworking and took a trade apprenticeship with a firm of furniture restorers in the village of Aston, of which Cote is a part. When we and the business moved to The Lea she effectively got left behind; this always worried Susan and myself but in reality was no different than, say, her going off to university. From there, and with the aid of a local technical college, she obtained her City & Guilds and we have a very beautiful oval table mirror with curved drawers underneath which was her trade piece for that. From there she moved on to West Dean College at Chichester and was the first teenager they had accepted onto the furniture restoration course. As a measure of the calibre of what she was being taught, there was said to be over a million pounds-worth of furniture on display at her graduation ceremony.

Whilst at West Dean the restorers in Aston closed down due to one of the partners going blind suddenly and they sold her the entire contents of their workshop from the coffee mugs to the machinery at almost a free-gift price. No prizes for guessing where this was to be stored in the interim! After working for a variety of people she went off to see the world for two or three years. This included Australia, where she had chicken pox in Darwin; New Zealand and the countries of Central America where she was nearly imprisoned in Honduras and was loaned restaurant premises in Guatemala. When in Australia she did some furniture work and after her return her employer there tried hard to persuade her to emigrate permanently. Meanwhile, whilst she was 'down under' her employer in Bath kept ringing us up to find out when she was coming back! She was obviously good at her job.

Not too long after she returned she moved to London and eventually in 2001 set up on her own as a furniture restorer in Battersea. Her customers are primarily the top end of the antique trade with a few private customers from as far afield as New York thrown in. Furniture she has restored goes to the likes of the Grosvenor House Antique Fair and the major auction houses. It is hard to visualise the quality of the work that she does – I like messing with a piece of wood but she can fit two pieces of wood together with greater precision than Alan Keef Ltd can do in steel with all their facilities. While it may not be strictly true, my comment is that she does not touch a piece of furniture worth less than about £10,000 and I know that recently she restored a modest-sized mirror that had a price tag of £280,000!

Looking back I think it is highly unlikely that any of the masters who taught me at Bedford School would have laid bets on my ever doing anything to make an autobiography possible or worth writing. Their consolation must be that they gave me an education that could cope with the vicissitudes of life and thus make it all possible. Possibly the most frequently asked question is, 'How did I get into this oddball business?' After all, it is not exactly a business that one would set out to be in. My answer is always that it is a hobby that got out of hand and that is as near the truth as anything can be. More to the point, what has been achieved? It has had its hairy moments (and still does!) but it has taken me to many parts of the world that most people do not reach, I have met and done business with all manner and types of people, it has paid for the education of my children and hopefully, if indirectly, will take care of my retirement. It has produced a business which my children want to carry on and that will leave Patrick to write volume two of this history covering the next twenty years or so! In short I have had a very interesting and varied life and that is possibly all that I ever set out to achieve.

The family outside the office door early in 2008. From the left, Helen and Patrick, Susan and Alan, Alice and Richard, Florence with Angus hogging the show in the foreground.

Appendix 1: Locomotive Drawings

The K12 was intended to be – and was – about as simple as one could get with a small locomotive. The engine and gearbox were mounted across the locomotive on a pivoted sub-frame so that jacking it up adjusted the chain tension. The gearbox forward/reverse lever poked through into the cab for easy operation. All were built with cabs but could easily have not been.

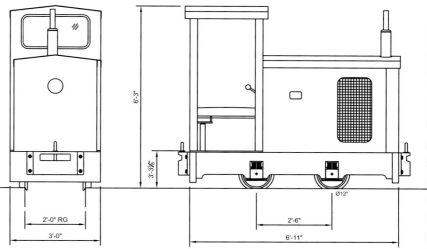

A good example of our standard bogie design even if it is not wholly typical. Made in 500mm gauge for the Chemin de Fer Touristique du Tarn in France these are a particularly heavyweight example. Also, unusually, the bolster support points for the body will be outside the bogie frames. This is an unbraked version.

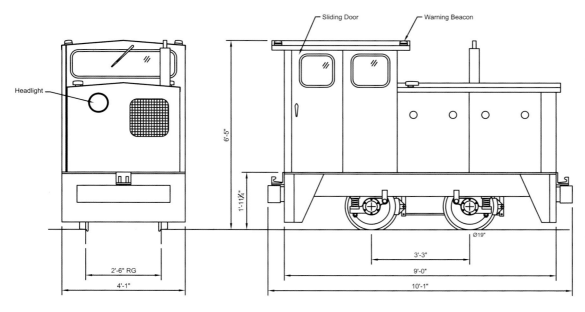

The four K.30s built for ICI Nobels Explosives were not entirely typical, being slightly longer and with more commodious cabs than normal. Added to this they had a broad sprung buffer to cope with long four-wheeled, double buffered wagons. The engine is off-set to one side, hence the off-centre radiator grill, with the large hydraulic motor above the frame on the opposite side. The cabs were internally soundproofed, had a sliding door and were on the low side to allow access to buildings.

Scale: All drawings are at a scale of 8mm:1 foot

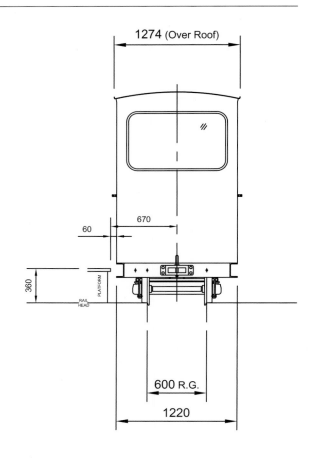

Drilling the headstocks and ballast weights for 3ft 6in. gauge locomotive No. 36.

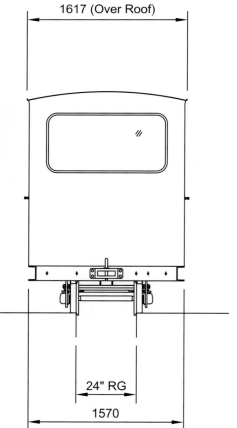

New 2-6-2 15in. gauge steam locomotive, *Lydia* (AK77 of 2007), stands on rails for the first time. Built for the substantial gradients of the Perrygrove Railway in the Forest of Dean it should be completed at about the same moment as this book goes on sale.

Semi-open carriage, suitable for use with the locomotive on p. 172, that would run on our standard bogies, one of which would be air braked. Note the lift-up seat and hinged end panel to allow disabled access. The roof keeps off the worst of the rain and the glazed ends prevent unruly passengers from trying to climb to the next carriage. It has happened!

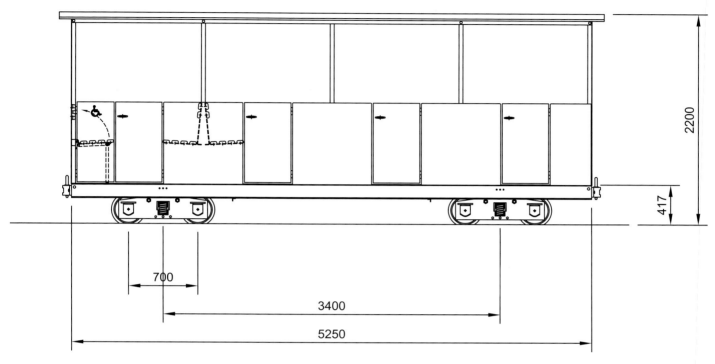

Scale: All drawings are at a scale of 8mm:1 foot

Semi-enclosed and larger carriage running on heavy-duty bogies. Disabled access is provided in much the same way as on the open version. Doors are a generously slack fit to avoid trapping small fingers and seats are varnished mahogany slats, floors aluminium treadplate.

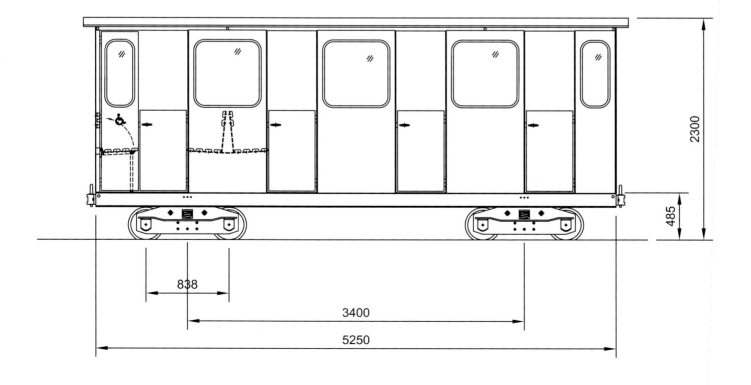

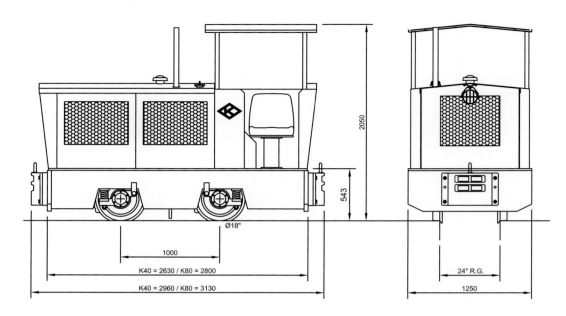

2050

543

Ø18"

1000

K40 = 2630 / K80 = 2800

K40 = 2960 / K80 = 3130

24" R.G.

1250

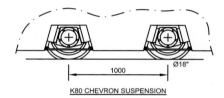

1000

Ø18"

K80 CHEVRON SUSPENSION

The K.40/K.80 designs are very similar, with the latter being simply more powerful, heavier and having the distinguishing feature of using a rubber chevron suspension. Both use the same JCB transmission and final drive arrangement. Most were built without cabs but the photographs show what is possible. The two-slot buffer belongs to the K.30/K.40 and the K.80 had the Simplex three-slot buffer/coupler.

Scale: All drawings are at a scale of 8mm:1 foot

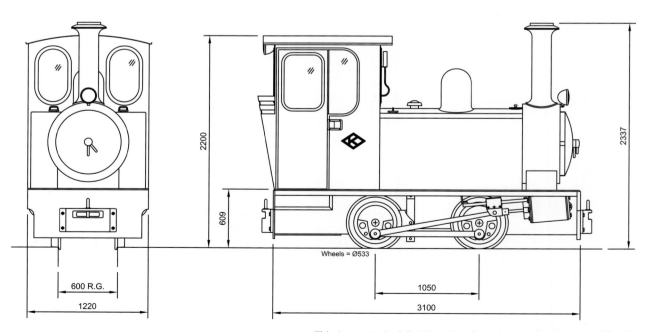

2200

609

600 R.G.

1220

Wheels = Ø533

1050

3100

2337

This is our typical 0-4-0 park railway locomotive as exemplified by No. 76 supplied to Lithuania. Narrower gauges or larger versions have outside frames with fly cranks to carry the rods. The doorway is one side only, specific to the operator, and is often without an actual door. There is a sliding window the other side. The 'door' is stepped off the smokebox to allow a free flow of engine-cooling air.

Appendix 2: Alan Keef Ltd – New Locomotives

This list has been compiled by Ken Scanes primarily from information supplied by Alan Keef Ltd. Locomotives up to and including No. 20 were built at Cote with Nos 21, 22 and 60SD757 being started there and completed at Lea Line.

Works No.	Plated year	Number/ Name	Type	Gauge	Class	To	Comment	Page Ref
1	1974	Trixie	0-4-0ST OC 4.75t 6in. × 9in. cyls	2ft	Trixie	First steamed at Cote 5/9/74. Demo at Bala Lake Rly. Demo at Centre of Alternative Technology, Machynlleth 30/10/74. Sold to Merion Mill Rly, Dinas Mawddwy (after 12/74, before 2/75). Returned to AK in 1976, and resold to Rail Rebecq Rognon, Belgium, where renamed Paula. 2005 with CF Chanteraines, Paris	Alan Keef Ltd did not actually build Trixie, though they were heavily involved in the conception, design and sale. The actual builder was Trevor Barber, former manager of the Whipsnade and Umfolozi Rly (see text for details)	42 43
2	1976		4wDM, 1.5t Lister LD2 engine mechanical transmission	2ft	K12	Richardson's Moss Litter Co. Ltd, Nutberry Works, Eastriggs 24/9/76	Prototype K12. No bodywork. Loco returned to Cote in 1977. Mechanical parts used in Works No.3. Frame of No.2 used to build a motorized end tipping skip (Skippy), used by Alan Keef Ltd on track-laying contracts.	44 118
3	1977	Redgauntlet	4wPM, 0.75t Morris 1000cc engine mechanical transmission	15in.		Romney Hythe and Dymchurch Rly, Kent 7/4/77	Rebuild, involving new frame, of loco built by M. Jacot in 1964. Not allocated an Alan Keef Ltd wks number	46
	1978		4wDM, 1.5t Lister LD2 engine mechanical transmission	2ft 6in.	K12	Richardson's Moss Litter Co. Ltd, Solway Moss, Gretna 25/9/78	As built had no bodywork, though RML later added an engine cover. Included mechanical parts from No.2. Sold for scrap c.2001	50
	1979	Thomas	4wVB VCG 1cyl Tram	2ft		Telford Development Corporation, Town Park, Telford	Frame was built by Kierstead Systems & Controls, Telford; engine & boiler by Peter Bridges, Oundle; the rest by Alan Keef Ltd. To Telford Horsehay Steam Trust c.1987	51
4	1979		4wDM, 1.5t Lister ST2 engine mechanical transmission	2ft	K12	Country Kitchen Foods Ltd, Wilmslow 6/11/79	First K12 to have body & cab; electric starting	51
5	1979		4wDM, 1.5t Lister ST2 engine mechanical transmission	2ft	K12	Croxden Compost Ltd, Chat Moss 2/1/80	Hand start	51
6	1981		4wDM, 1.5t Lister ST2 engine mechanical transmission	2ft 6in.	K12	Richardson's Moss Litter Co Ltd, Solway Moss, Gretna 24/4/81	Regauged by RML c.1994 to 2ft for use at Creca Moss. Purchased by AK 16/9/98 & sold to John Tennant, Brecon	56 163
7	1982		4wDM, 1.5t Lister ST2 engine mechanical transmission	2ft	K12	Richardson's Moss Litter Co Ltd, Nutberry Works, Eastriggs 6/8/82	Purchased by AK 16/9/98 & sold to Blackpool Pleasure Beach Rly	55
8	1982		4wDH, 2.5t Lister ST2 engine hydrostatic transmission	2ft	K30	Norit-Klasmann Ltd, Penicuik, Scotland 12/82	Prototype K30	58
9	1983		4wDH, 3.5t Lister ST2 engine hydrostatic transmission	2ft	K30	O'Connell Peat Ltd, County Donegal 16/6/83	Stand up cab. Later resold per AK to Midland Irish Peat 7/88	60
10	1983		4wDH, 3.5t Lister ST2 engine hydrostatic transmission	2ft	K30	Milton Hall Brick Co. Ltd, Cherry Orchard Works, Southend-on-Sea 26/8/83	Wlw A Gartell, Templecombe	61
11	1984		4wDH, 4t Perkins 4.108 engine hydrostatic transmission	2ft	K30	Thorpe Park, Chertsey, Surrey 2/84	Steam outline bodywork fitted by customer	62

Works No.	Plated year	Number/Name	Type	Gauge	Class	To	Comment	Page Ref
12	1984		4wDH, 4t Perkins 4.108 engine hydrostatic transmission	2ft	K30	Thorpe Park, Chertsey, Surrey 3/84	Steam outline bodywork fitted by customer. Wlw Lynton & Barnstable Rly Association	62
13R	1984		4wDH, 3t Perkins 4.203 engine hydrostatic transmission	2ft		Hire loco. Hired to Shellabear Price Ltd, Solva Sewage Works, Dyfed 7/1/85	Rebuild of RH 452280 of 1960. Later regauged to 15in. and sold to Littlecote House, near Hungerford, Wiltshire, for use on a pleasure railway. Wlw Markeaton Park Light Rly, Derbyshire	65
14	1984		4wDH, 3.5t Lister TS3 engine hydrostatic transmission	2ft	K30	Redland Bricks Ltd, Nutbourne Brickworks, Surrey 31/7/84	Wlw Billing Aquadrome, Northamptonshire	64
15	1984		4wDH, 2t Petter P600/2 engine hydrostatic transmission	2ft	K20	Hire loco. Hired to Shellabear Price Ltd, Solva Sewage Works, Dyfed 20/12/84	Hired to Woburn Abbey c.7/85, rtn Cote by 1/86. Hired to Trevor Guy, Filey (old Butlin's camp) 25/5/86–13/7/86. To new works at Lea Line 3/11/86. Hired to Boothby Peat 2/5/87 to 18/5/87. Hired to Billing Aquadrome c.6/87. Exported to Pakistan c.11/87	64
16	1985		6wPM, 1.5t Ford 1600cc engine mechanical transmission	10¼in.		Wells and Walsingham Light Railway 6/6/85		68
17	1985		0-4-0DH steam outline 2.5t Perkins 4.108 engine hydrostatic transmission	2ft	Tyrone	Cotswold Wildlife Park, Burford 10/3/86		70
18	1985		4wDH, 4t Perkins 3.152 engine hydrostatic transmission	2ft 6in.	K30	Nobels Exposive Co. Ltd, Ardeer Works, Strathclyde 27/8/85	Wlw William Sinclair Horticulture Ltd, Ryflat Moss, Strathclyde	69
19	1985		4wDH, 4t Perkins 3.152 engine hydrostatic transmission	2ft 6in.	K30	Nobels Exposive Co. Ltd, Ardeer Works, Strathclyde 27/8/85	Wlw William Sinclair Horticulture Ltd, Ryflat Moss, Strathclyde	69
20R	1986		4wDH, 3.5t Deutz F3L912 engine hydrostatic transmission	2ft	K30	Butterley Building Materials Ltd, Cherry Orchard Lane Works, Southend-on-Sea 6/6/86	Rebuild of RH 283513 of 1949. Wlw A Gartell, Templecoombe. Wlw William Sinclair Horticulture Ltd, Bolton Fell, Cumbria	70
21	1987		4wDH, 4t Perkins 3.152 engine hydrostatic transmission	2ft 6in.	K30	Nobels Exposive Co. Ltd, Ardeer Works, Strathclyde 30/1/87		73
22	1987		4wDH, 4t Perkins 3.152 engine hydrostatic transmission	2ft 6in.	K30	Nobels Exposive Co. Ltd, Ardeer Works, Strathclyde 30/1/87		
60SD 757	1987		4wDM, 6t Deutz F4L912 engine mechanical transmission	3ft 6in.	60S	Ghana Bauxite 1/87	Subcontract from Simplex Mechanical Handling Ltd	72
40SD 530	1987		4wDM, 3.5t Deutz F3L912 engine mechanical transmission	2ft	40S	Butterley Building Materials Ltd, Star Lane Works, Southend-on-Sea 6/8/87	Subcontract from Simplex Mechanical Handling Ltd. Re-purchased by AK 5/98. Regauged to 2ft 8½in. and sold to Volks Electric Railway, Brighton 23/6/98	74
23	1988		0-4-0DH steam outline 2.5t Ford SD425 engine hydrostatic transmission	2ft	Tyrone	East Hayling Light Rly, Warner Bros Holiday Camp, Hayling Island, Hants. 29/7/88		76
24	1988		4wDH, 10t Deutz F6L912 engine hydrostatic transmission	2ft	U-series	Kyung Dong Coal Mine, South Korea 31/5/97		76

Works No.	Plated year	Number/ Name	Type	Gauge	Class	To	Comment	Page Ref
25	1988		4wDH, 10t Deutz F6L912 engine hydrostatic transmission	2ft	U-series	Kyung Dong Coal Mine, South Korea 31/5/97		76
26	1988		4wDM, 3.5t Deutz F3L912 engine mechanical transmission	2ft	40S	Butterley Building Materials Ltd, Star Lane Works, Southend-on-Sea 22/9/88	Re-purchased by AK 5/98. Sold to L. & P. Peat, Nutberry Moss, Dumfries 16/9/98	5
27	1988		4w-4wDH, 1.25t Lister LD2 engine hydrostatic transmission	9.½in.		John Hall-Craggs, The Lawns, Brightwalton, near Newbury, Berks. 15/4/89	Used bogies from one of the Severn Beach Miniature Rly locos	80
28	1989		4wDM, 3.5t Deutz F3L912 engine mechanical transmission	2ft	40S	Butterley Building Materials Ltd, Cherry Orchard Lane Works, Southend-on-Sea 19/6/89	Re-purchased by AK 5/98. Sold to L. & P. Peat, Creca Moss, Dumfries 26/6/98	5
29R	1989		4wDM, 8t Perkins 4236 engine mechanical transmission	3ft 6in.	60S	Chemicals and Fertilizers (Nigeria) Ltd, Kaduna, Nigeria 19/12/89	Rebuild of MR 11004 of 1955	82
30	1990	Taffy	0-4-0VBT VC	2ft		Built for Alan Keef	De Winton replica. Works number was originally allocated to an order for a miniature steam loco, which was subsequently cancelled. Works number retrospectively given to Taffy, which was built over several years (frame complete by 7/9/88, first publicly steamed 1994)	82 160
31	1990	Swee' Pea	0-6-0DH steam outline Perkins engine hydrostatic transmission	10¼in.	Swee' pea	Hastings Miniature Rly 29/3/90		84
32	1990		4wDH, 4t Perkins 3152 engine hydrostatic transmission	2ft	K30M	Nigerian Coal, Enulu Colliery, Nigeria 11/90	Fitted with Pyroban flameproofing equipment	85
33	1990		4wDH, 4t Perkins 3152 engine hydrostatic transmission	2ft	K30M	Nigerian Coal, Enulu Colliery, Nigeria 12/90	Fitted with Pyroban flameproofing equipment	85
34	1991		0-4-0PH steam outline 2.5t Ford 1300cc engine hydrostatic transmission	2ft	Tyrone	Singapore Zoo 20/8/91		98
35	1991		4-4-0PH steam outline 2.5t Ford 1300cc engine hydrostatic transmission	2ft	Fiji	Singapore Zoo 22/8/91		98
36	1990		4wDM, 8t Perkins 4236 engine mechanical transmission	3ft 6in.	60S	Morris (Nigeria) Ltd, Minna, Nigeria 21/8/90		83
37	1990		4wDM, 10t Perkins 4236 engine mechanical transmission	3ft 6in.	85S	Chemicals and Fertilizers (Nigeria) Ltd, Port Harcourt Docks, Nigeria 1/91		83
38	1991	Tryntje	0-4-0T OC, 7t 7in. × 10in. cyls	60cm		De Efterling B.V., Kaartsheuval, near Tilborg, Holland 15/1/92		98 100
39	1992	Sir Winston Churchill	0-6-2DH steam outline Perkins 109/19 engine hydrostatic transmission	15in.	Blenheim	Blenheim Palace 20/3/92		101

Works No.	Plated year	Number/Name	Type	Gauge	Class	To	Comment	Page Ref
40	1992		4wDH, 3.5t Perkins 3.152 engine hydrokinetic transmission shaft drive	2ft	K40	Prototype K.40. Built for demonstration and hire. First trial was at Woodhead Tunnel 10/7/92	Demonstrated at Scot. Ag. Ind., Bolton Fell, and L. & P. Peat, Eastriggs, during 10/92. Hired to Donelon Contractors, Portway, Bristol mid-93. Hired to Donelon Contractors, Bradford 11/93. Hired to Kier Construction, Mansfield Outfall Sewer, from 1/12/93 to late 1994. Sold to De Efterling, Holland 20/4/95	103
41	1992	Gilbert Swift	0-6-2DH steam outline Perkins 109/19 engine hydrostatic transmission	15in.	Blenheim	Haigh Hall, Wigan 14/5/92	Name subsequently removed	102
42	1992		0-6-2DH steam outline Perkins 3.152 engine hydrostatic transmission	15in.	Blenheim	Build for exhibition. First exhibited at Leisure Industry Week, NEC, Birmingham, 9/92	Sold to Whitworth Hall, near Spennymoor, Co. Durham 10/3/95. Exported 3/96 to Bear Creek Park, Surrey, Vancouver, Canada	104
43	1992		4wDM, 5t Perkins 4236 engine mechanical transmission	metre	60S	Guyana Sugar Corporation 8/11/92		102
44	1993		4wDH, 3.5t Perkins 3.152 engine hydrokinetic transmission shaft drive	3ft	K40	Peatlands Country Park, Derryhubbert, Co. Armagh 27/4/93		104
45	1993		4wDH, 8t Deutz F4L912 engine hydrokinetic transmission shaft drive	610mm	K80	Chhatak Cement Co., Bangladesh 22/12/93		106
46	1993		4wDH, 3.5t Deutz F3L912W engine hydrokinetic transmission shaft drive	2ft	K40	National Grid, Woodhead Tunnel 22/11/93.		105
47	1994	Mary	4wDH, 4t Perkins 3.152 engine hydrokinetic transmission shaft drive	2ft	K40	Built as hire loco	Hired to Kier Construction Ltd, Mansfield Outfall Sewer c.17/1/94. By 1995 on hire at Woodhead Cable Tunnel. Rtn Lea by 26/2/95. Hired to Balfour Beatty / AMEC joint venture, Jubilee Line Extension contract 11/95. Rtn Lea 3/4/97. Sold to William Sinclair Horticulture Ltd, Springfield Works, Lothian 9/97	103
48	(1994?)	Sally	4wDH, 10t Perkins 1004.4 engine hydrokinetic transmission shaft drive	2ft	K100	Built as demo loco. To Leighton Buzzard Narrow Gauge Railway for trials 1/97. Remained at Leighton Buzzard until mid-1998. Sold and exported to TPC, Moshi, Tanzania (a sugar plantation) 22/7/98		107
49	1994	Sandy	4wDH, 4t Perkins 3.152 engine hydrokinetic transmission shaft drive	2ft	K40	Taylor Woodrow, Southall 4/7/94	On closure of the works at Southall, the loco went to Morgan Est, Rugby, for storage. Later bought by Tunnel Steel, Swansea and moved to Alan Keef Ltd	107
50	1994		4wDH, 8t Deutz F4L912 engine hydrokinetic transmission shaft drive	610mm	K80	Chhatak Cement Co, Bangladesh 19/10/94		106
51	1995		0-6-2DH steam outline Perkins 109/19 engine hydrostatic transmission	15in.	Blenheim	Cricket St Thomas Wildlife Park 11/4/94		63 108

Works No.	Plated year	Number/Name	Type	Gauge	Class	To	Comment	Page Ref
52	1996	*Pam*	0-4-0DH Kubota D722-E engine hydrostatic transmission	15in.		Jeremy Sullivan, private railway near Oxford 22/8/96		110
53	1997		2w-2DHR Kubota engine hydrostatic transmission	2ft		Dreamworld, Egypt 8/97	Rail lorry; subcontract for Severn Lamb Ltd	112
54	1998	*Denzil*	0-6-0DH steam outline Perkins engine hydrostatic transmission	10¼in.	Swee' Pea	Wells Harbour Railway, Norfolk 14/7/98		112 159
55	1998		4wDH 12hp Lister Type LPA2 hydrostatic transmission	3ft 6in.	K12H	North Surrey Water Company, Walton Treatment Works, Desborough Island, Walton-on-Thames by 22/12/98		113
56	2000		4wGasH 7t Ford CSG-649 Engine hydrokinetic transmission shaft drive	600mm	K80	National Park, Iquazu Falls, Argentina 18/11/2000	Frame built by 7/4/99, loco then 'on hold'. Work re-started mid-2000. Tram style bodywork	114
57	2001?		4wGasH 7t Ford Engine hydrokinetic transmission shaft drive	600mm	K80	National Park, Iquazu Falls, Argentina 8/6/2001	Frame built by 7/4/99, loco then 'on hold'. Work restarted 12/00. Tram style bodywork	
58	1999	*Charles*	0-6-0DH steam outline Hydrostatic Transmission	10¼in.	Swee' pea	Ferry Meadows Rly, Peterborough 8/99		135
59R	1999	*Beaudesert No 80*	4wDH Hydrokinetic transmission	2ft	K120	To LBNGRS 26/6/99 for special event. Returned to Lea 28/6/99 for completion. To LBNGRS 3/8/99	Used frame, engine & transmission of SMH T-series 101T018/9	116
60	2000		0-6-0DH Perkins engine Hydrostatic transmission	12¼in.	(Swee' Pea ?)	To Pavilion Gardens, Buxton 17/5/00		136
61	2000	*Sir Walter Raleigh*	0-4-0DH Perkins engine	18in.		Bicton Woodlands Rly 25/5/00		2 137
62	2001		0-2-0+2aDH steam outline. Perkins 23½kw engine	Lartigue Monorail		Listowel and Ballybunion Rly, Ireland 19/3/2002		137 138
63	2001	*James Gordon*	0-4-0DH steam outline. Perkins 37kw engine	2ft		Alford Valley Railway 25/7/01		141
64	2001	*Pompey*	4w-4wDH Perkins 52hp engine	15in.		Jeremy Sullivan, private railway, Oxford 3/11/2001		141
65	2001	*Margam Castle*	0-4-0DH steam outline. Perkins 46.9kw engine	2ft	(Similar to no.63)	Margam Country Park 21/12/2001		144
66	2002	*The Earl of Oakfield*	0-4-0DH, Perkins 103.10 engine, Linde pump, SAI motor	15in.	(Similar to no.52)	Difflin Lake Rly, Co. Donegal, Ireland end 3/2003.		145
67	2002		4wBE, 3 tonne, 12kw	2ft	K20E	Quarry Tours, Llechwedd 31/1/2003		147
68	2003	*Bella*	0-4-0DH steam outline, 80hp	2ft		Burford Wildlife Park, Oxon. 20/6/2003		70
69R	2003	*Mark Timothy*	2-6-4T OC	15in.		Bure Valley Railway, Norfolk 28/7/2003	Rebuild of Winson 20 of 1999	148
70	2004	*Lady Alexandra*	0-4-0DH steam outline. Perkins 46.5hp engine	20in.		Woburn Safari Park 2/4/04		145
71	2004	*Puffing Billy*	0-4-0 VC	4ft 8½in.		To Beamish Museum 24/4/2006		157

Works No.	Plated year	Number/Name	Type	Gauge	Class	To	Comment	Page Ref
72R	2004	*Polar Bear*	2-4w-2BE	2ft		Groudle Glen Rly, Isle of Man 2/7/04	Rebuild of WR 556801. Replica of *Polar Bear* BEV 313	150
73	2005		0-6-0DH, Perkins 22hp engine.	12¼in.		Wm Heller, Devon 17/10/2005.		158
74	2005	*Howard*	0-6-0DH steam outline, Perkins 22hp engine.	10¼in.		Wells Harbour Rly 29/7/2005.	Mechanically similar to *Denzil* but bodywork different.	159
75R	2007	*Bicton*	4wDH steam outline. Perkins engine.	1ft 6in.		Bicton Woodlands Rly, Devon 4/4/2007	Rebuild of RH 213839/42	163
76	2005		0-4-0DH steam outline Perkins 5H3XL2 50hp engine	600mm		To Lithuania 14/12/2005. (Mokmasis Gelezinkelis 'Ingnalina' – a summer camp for the children of employees of Lithuanian Railways)	Numbered into Lithuanian Railways fleet – 15001	160
77	2007	*Lydia*	2-6-2T OC 5½in. × 8in. cyls, 7 tonnes, 200psi.	15in.		For Perrygrove Rly		170
78R	2007		4wDH	3ft	K120	Fintown Railway, Ireland, 19/7/2007	Used frame, engine & transmission of MR 101T007	163
79	2007	*Flynn*	0-6-0DM, Perkins 47hp Hydrokinetic transmission	15in.		Longleat Light Rly 27/9/2007		163
80	2007	*Boris*	0-6-0DH s/o Hydrostatic transmisssion.	12¼in.	Swee' pea	Hotham Park, Bognor Regis 24/5/2007		162

Industrial Monorails

Works No.	Plated year	Type	To	Comment
M001	1987	2a-2DH, 0.75t Lister LV1 engine hydrostatic transmission	Built for demonstration, exhibition and hire. First exhibited at the International Construction Equipment Exhibition, NEC, Birmingham 6/11/87	Eventually sold to Mrs White's Gardens Ltd, contract at Strand-on-the-Green, London, 12/88 (subsequently disappeared)
M002	1989	2a-2DH, 0.75t Kubota EB300 engine hydrostatic transmission	Built for hire use. First hire to Mowlems, Paddington Station 1/89	
M003	1989	2a-2DH, 0.75t Kubota EB300 engine hydrostatic transmission	Built for exhibition / hire use. First exhibited at NEC Birmingham 18/9/89	

'Beware of the Train', AKL and Lithuanian style!

Appendix 3: Alan Keef/Alan Keef Ltd – Second-hand Locomotives

This list has been compiled by Ken Scanes from information supplied by Alan Keef Ltd, Bob Darvill, The Narrow Gauge Railway Society and The Industrial Railway Society. In its original form it included every locomotive to pass through my premises even if only in transit on a lorry or for one of our open days together with those that came and went on a fairly regular basis for repair or overhaul. This became repetitive and was probably only of interest to the diehard enthusiast, so, with Ken Scanes' permission, I have edited it to cover only those locomotives where there has been a change of ownership or destination through the good offices of Alan Keef Ltd. This has produced its own anomalies in that some that have been on the premises for a considerable time for major overhaul, such as the Levington Schoma's or Baldwin 778, are not included. However most of these are covered in the main text.

For the uninitiated there follows a list of abbreviations customarily used for locomotive manufacturers sufficient to cover this list:

AK — Alan Keef Ltd, Ross on Wye, Herefordshire
Barnes — A. Barnes & Co, Rhyl, N. Wales
BD — Baguley Drewry Ltd, Burton on Trent, Staffordshire
Bg — E.E. Baguley Ltd, Burton on Trent, Staffordshire
CE — Clayton Equipment Ltd, Hatton, Derbyshire
Chance — Chance Manufacturing Co. Inc., Wichita, Kansas, U.S.A.
Corpet — Corpet Louvet & Cie, Seine St. Denis, France
De W — de Winton & Co, Caernarvon, N. Wales
Diema — Diepholzer Maschinenfabrik, Diepholz, Germany
FH — F.C. Hibberd & Co. Ltd, Park Royal, London
GB — Greenwood & Batley Ltd, Leeds
Guest — Guest Engineering Ltd, Stourbridge, Worcestershire
HC — Hudswell Clarke & Co. Ltd, Leeds
HE — Hunslet Engine Co. Ltd, Leeds
HLH — Hunslet Locomotive Hire Ltd, Killamarsh, Derbyshire
JF — John Fowler & Co. Ltd, Leeds

KS — Kerr, Stuart & Co. Ltd, Stoke on Trent, Staffordshire
L — R.A. Lister & Co. Ltd, Dursley, Gloucestershire
Minirail — Minirail Ltd, Frampton Cotterell, Bristol
Morse — R.H. Morse, Potter Heigham, Norfolk
Moss — A.J. Moss, Scarisbrick, Lancashire
MR — Motor Rail Ltd, Bedford
OK — Orenstein & Koppel AG, Berlin (later Dortmund), Germany.
RFS — RFS Engineering Ltd, Doncaster
RH — Ruston & Hornsby Ltd, Lincoln
RSH — Robert Stephenson & Hawthorns Ltd, Darlington
Schoma — Christoph Schöttler Maschinenfabrik, Diepholz, Germany
SMH — Simplex Mechanical Handling Ltd, Bedford
WB — W.G. Bagnall Ltd, Stafford
Wkm — D. Wickham & Co. Ltd, Ware, Hertfordshire
WR — Wingrove & Rogers Ltd, Kirkby, Liverpool

Gauge	Number/Name	Type	Make	Wks No.	Year	Date	Ex	To
2ft 0in.		0-4-0PM	Bg		1918	1962	Associated Portland Cement Manufacturers, Bidwell Clay Pit, Houghton Regis, Beds.	R.P. Morris, Longfield, Kent c./65
1ft 10¾in.	Kathleen	0-4-0VBT VC	DeW	760	1877	c.6/65	R.P. Morris, Longfield, Kent (wfw Penrhyn Slate Quarries)	Walcroft Brothers, Pershore, Worcs. b.5/68
3ft 0in.	Llanfair	0-4-0VBT VC	DeW		1895	c.1966	Mr Hughes, Llanrwst (wfw Penmaenmawr Granite Quarries)	Walcroft Brothers, Pershore, Worcs. b.5/68
2ft 0in.		4wDM	L	25919	1944	c.5/68	Southern Gas Board, Poole Gas Works	M E Engineering, Cricklewood Depot by 12/68 (wlw Richardson's Moss Litter Co. Ltd Eastriggs)
2ft 0in.		4wDM	RH	243388	1946	c.5/68	Dealer, Swindon (wfw Devon County Council, Beacon Down Quarry, Parracombe)	M E Engineering, Cricklewood Depot by 12/68
2ft 0in.		4wDM	L	18557	1942	c.12/68	Southern Gas Board, Poole Gas Works	Cotswold Light Rly, Cotswold Water Park, South Cerney, for construction 4/71. Rtn Cote b.10/71. To P.C. Vallins, 15 Smith Road, Reigate c.1/73. ? then to Brockham Museum b.1/76
2ft 0in.		4wDM	OK	4013	1930	c.12/68	M.E. Engineering, Cricklewood (wfw Diamond Tread Co. (Chart) Ltd, Kent)	Hampshire NGRS, Durley, Sussex 9/71
2ft 0in.		4wDM	OK	5125	1935	c.12/68	Maidenhead Brick & Tile Co., Sussex (per M.E. Engineering)	Hampshire NGRS, Durley, Sussex 9/71
2ft 0in.		4wDM	MR	8969	1945	1969	Edward Redden Ltd, Little Irchester Scrapyard, Northants; prev Bedford Corporation Water Board, Manton Lane Waterworks, Bedford.	Mixconcrete Aggregates, Earls Barton Sand & Gravel Quarry, Northants. by 1971

Gauge	Number/Name	Type	Make	Wks No.	Year	Date	Ex	To
2ft 0in.		4wDM	L	4228	1931	17/6/69	R.P. Morris, 193 Main Road, Longfield, Kent	resold to R.P. Morris, Longfield, 31/10/71
2ft 0in.		4wDM	RH	277273	1949	1969	L.W. Vass Ltd, Scrap Merchants, Ampthill, Beds. (wfw Woodside Brick Co., Croydon)	Hired to A. Waddington & Sons Ltd, Farningham Sewer Contract c.4/72. To J. Marshfield-Hutchings, Quinton Road Rly Society, Bucks. 17/4/73. To Boothby Peat 11/74 per AK
2ft 0in.		4wDM	HE	2207	1941	c./70	B.W. Goodchild, Wychwood, Leamington Spa, Warwicks. (wfw Trevor Quarry)	To Cotswold Light Rly, Cotswold Water Park, South Cerney c.7/71. To M. Haynes, Sheppards Boat Station, Saltford, Bristol c.4/72
2ft 0in.		4wDM	MR	8575	1940	c.11/70	B.W. Goodchild, Wychwood, Leamington Spa, Warwicks.	Moved direct to Mixconcrete, Northampton area, c.11/70
2ft 0in.		4wDM	MR	8681	1941	c.1/71	J. & J. Jackson Ltd, Heaton Mersey Plant Depot, Lancs.	Haunchwood Lewis, Rosemary Tileries, Cheslyn Hay, Staffs. 1972
2ft 0in.		4wDM	MR	7304	1938	c.1/71	J. & J. Jackson Ltd, Heaton Mersey Plant Depot, Lancs.	To new works at Lea Line 3/11/86. To Midland Irish Peat 11/89
2ft 0in.		4wDM	MR	8588	1940	c.2/71	Flettons Ltd, King's Dike Brickworks, Whittlesey	Exported to Bian Haut Hardware Pty Ltd, Singapore, 6/71
2ft 0in.		4wDM	MR	8592	1940	c.2/71	Flettons Ltd, King's Dike Brickworks, Whittlesey	Haunchwood Lewis Brick & Tile Ltd, Rosemary Tileries, Cheslyn Hay, Staffs. c.10/71
2ft 0in.		4wDM	MR	8611	1941	c.2/71	Flettons Ltd, King's Dike Brickworks, Whittlesey	Exported to Bian Haut Hardware Pty Ltd, Singapore 6/71
2ft 0in.		4wDM	MR	8620	1941	c.2/71	Flettons Ltd, King's Dike Brickworks, Whittlesey	Exported to Bian Haut Hardware Pty Ltd, Singapore 6/71
2ft 0in.		4wDM	MR	8862	1944	c.2/71	Flettons Ltd, King's Dike Brickworks, Whittlesey	Exported to Bian Haut Hardware Pty Ltd, Singapore 6/71
2ft 0in.		4wDM	MR	8882	1944	c.2/71	Flettons Ltd, King's Dike Brickworks, Whittlesey	A. Waddington & Sons Ltd, Farningham Sewer Contract c.10/71. Loco to Motor Rail Ltd, Bedford b.4/72. To Cote for repair. Rtn Farningham b.6/72. To Haunchwood Lewis Brick & Tile Ltd, Sold to Rosemary Tileries, Essington Works, Staffs. 11/73. See also later
2ft 11in.		4wDM	MR	5606	1931	3/71	Scrapyard in Bedford originally from London Brick Co. Ltd, King's Dike Wks	Whipsnade Zoo (2ft 6in. gauge) 1971
2ft 0in.	7	4wDM	FH	?	?	c.6/71	Flettons Ltd, King's Dike Brickworks, Whittlesey	E.N. Jones, Leeds c.5/73
2ft 11in.		4wDM	MR	11206	1962	15/7/71	London Brick Co. Ltd, Hicks No1 Works, Peterborough	APCM Sundon, Beds. (3ft) 1971
2ft 11in.		4wDM	MR	10159	1950	15/7/71	London Brick Co. Ltd, Hicks No1 Works, Peterborough	APCM Sundon, Beds. (3ft) 1971
2ft 0in.		4wDM	MR	22031	1959	c.10/71	Anglo-Scottish Plant Ltd, Peterborough	A. Waddington & Sons Ltd, Farningham Sewer Contract c.12/71
2ft 0in.		4wDM	MR	22032	1959	c.10/71	Anglo-Scottish Plant Ltd, Peterborough	A. Waddington & Sons Ltd, Farningham Sewer Contract c.12/71
2ft 0in.		4wDM	RH	222094	1946	c.10/71	Cremer Whiting & Co. Ltd, Ospringe Brickworks, Oare, Kent	Exported to Singapore c.3/72
2ft 0in.		4wDM	HE	4187	1948	c.10/71	W. Donald, dealer, Kings Langley, Herts. (wfw Marples Ridgeway, contract in Sudan)	Earls Barton Silica Co Ltd, Northants., for tracklifting 1/72. Flettons Ltd, King's Dike Brickworks, for tracklifting 3/72. Exported to Singapore c.3/72.
2ft 0in.		4wDM	FH	3502	1954	c.10/71	W. Donald, dealer, Kings Langley, Herts (wfw Marples Ridgeway, contract in Sudan)	To Cotswold Light Rly, Cotswold Water Park, South Cerney c.8/72. Rtn Cote c.7/74. To Dowty Rly Preservation Society, Ashchurch, Glos. c.9/74
2ft 0in.		4wDM	OK	7595	1937	c.12/71	Mixconcrete Aggregates Ltd, Earls Barton Sand & Gravel Quarry, Northants.	To new works at Lea Line 3/11/86. To Brian Clarke, Midford, 8/95
2ft 0in.		4wDM	MR	9416	1949	12/71	Bell Rock Gypsum Industries Ltd, Staunton in the Vale, Notts.	Exported to Bian Haut Hardware Pty Ltd, Singapore, c.3/72

Gauge	Number/Name	Type	Make	Wks No.	Year	Date	Ex	To
2ft 0in.		4wDM	MR	9417	1949	12/71	Bell Rock Gypsum Industries Ltd, Staunton in the Vale, Notts.	Exported to Bian Haut Hardware Pty Ltd, Singapore c.3/72
1ft 10in.		4wDM	MR	9263	1947	1971	J. & J. Jackson Ltd, Lancs.	Regauged to 2ft. Hired to A. Waddington & Sons Ltd, Farningham Sewer Contract c.12/71. Exported to Singapore c.5/73
2ft 0in.		4wDM	RH	187045	1937	1/72	Bell Rock Gypsum Industries Ltd, Staunton in the Vale, Notts.	Exported to Singapore c.3/72
2ft 0in.		4wDM	RH	339209	1952	1/72	Bell Rock Gypsum Industries Ltd, Staunton in the Vale, Notts.	Great Bush Rly, Tinkers Park, Hadlow Down, East Sussex 16/9/78
3ft 0in.		4wDM	RH	256169	1948	c.2/72	Wm Bush & Sons Ltd, Alfreton, Derbys. (wfw British Gypsum Ltd, Fauld Mines, Staffs)	Stripped for spares. Frame scrapped c.5/73
2ft 0in.		4wDM	FH	2544	1942	c.3/72	W. Bush & Sons, Alfreton	To Cotswold Light Rly, Cotswold Water Park, South Cerney c.10/72. To John Crosskey, Mitcham 22/12/73. Rtn Cote b.21/6/75. To Long Eaton Light Rly, West Park, Long Eaton, Derbys. 22/10/75
2ft 0in.		4wDM	MR	8627	1941	c.3/72	West Lancs. Light Rly, Hesketh Bank, near Preston	Cumberland Moss Litter, Kirkbride c.5/72
2ft 0in.		4wDM	MR	8711	1941	c.3/72	West Lancs. Light Rly, Hesketh Bank, near Preston	Sheppey Light Rly, Leysdown on Sea, Isle of Sheppey, Kent 5/72. See also later.
1ft 10in.		4wDM	MR	5851	1933	c.3/72	West Lancs. Light Rly, Hesketh Bank, near Preston	Regauged to 2ft. Exported to Singapore c.2/73
2ft 0in.		4wDM	MR	9235	1946	c.5/72	London Brick Company, Kempton Hardwick, Beds.	Stripped for spares, scrapped c.4/78
2ft 0in.		4wDM	FH	2051	1937	c.5/72	London Brick Company, Kempton Hardwick, Beds.	To ? (Possibly Eddie Jones?)
2ft 0in.		4wDM	MR	8789	1943	c.5/72	B.C. Hawkins, dealer, Green Street Green, Kent (wfw Aylesford Sand, Kent)	Cotswold Light Rly, Cotswold Water Park c.5/72. Returned to Cote 1973, Exported to Bian Haut Hardware Pty Ltd, Singapore c.5/73
2ft 0in.		4wDM	RH	175413	1936	8/72	ECC Ball Clays Ltd, Norden Clay Mines, Dorset	Exported to Bian Haut Hardware Pty Ltd, Singapore c.10/72
2ft 0in.		4wDM	RH	179889	1936	8/72	ECC Ball Clays Ltd, Norden Clay Mines, Dorset	Sheppey Light Rly 16/5/73
2ft 0in.		4wDM	MR	22070	1960	c.8/72	London Brick Company, Kempton Hardwick, Beds.	Hired to Butlin's, Clacton 7/74 for three weeks. To H. Frampton-Jones, South Eastern Steam Centre, Ashford, Kent 15/10/75
3ft 0in.	Dinmor	4wDM	JF	3900011	1947	20/9/72	Dinmor Quarries Ltd, Anglesey	Regauged to metre. To Cotswold Light Rly, Cotswold Water Park, South Cerney 3/7/73. Rtn Cote 30/7/79. Regauged to 3ft. To new works at Lea Line 3/11/86. To Cahir Rly Museum, Ireland, end 1989. Wlw Cavan & Leitrim Rly, Dromod
1ft 10½in.		4wDM	RH	226302	1944	8/10/72	G.J. Mullis, Wychbold, Droitwich	J. Crosskey, 46 Homefield Gardens, Mitcham, London 25/2/73. See also later
2ft 2in.		4wDM	RH	200766	1941	10/72	British Gypsum Ltd, Glebe Gypsum Mines, Gotham, Notts.	Regauged 2ft & exported to Singapore c.2/73
2ft 0in.		4wDM	RH	224308	1944	10/72	British Gypsum Ltd, Kingston-on-Soar Gypsum Mines, Notts.	Exported to Singapore c.2/73
2ft 0in.		4wDM	MR	11311	1966	10/72	London Brick Company, Kempton Hardwick, Beds.	Moved direct to Reed & Mallik, Plant depot at Romsey, Hants. Used on Fechlin Aqueduct Contract
2ft 0in.		4wDM	MR	8960	1945	3/1/73	W.R. Nichols & Sons, Plant Dealers, Burney St, Greenwich, London	Exported to Singapore c.5/73
2ft 0in.		4wDM	RH	189945	1937	1/73	British Industrial Sand, Dullatur Quarry, near Cumbernauld	?? Scrapped by 4/73
2ft 0in.		4wDM	MR	5943	1936	1/73	British Industrial Sand, Dullatur Quarry, near Cumbernauld	Hired to White Moss Peat Co., Kirkby c./74. Rtn Cote c.6/76. Stripped for spares, remains scrapped 15/8/78

Gauge	Number/Name	Type	Make	Wks No.	Year	Date	Ex	To
2ft 0in.		4wDM	MR	21282	1959	2/73	London Brick Co., Kempston Hardwick, Beds.	Hired to Elmet Industrial (Tractors) Ltd, South Milford, N. Yorks. 2/74 (used on contract for Yorkshire Water Authority at Booth Ferry Bridge, Asselby). Hired to Haunchwood Lewis, Cheslyn Hay Wks c.6/74. Rtn Cote b.4/75. Hired to Butlin's Ayr c.5/75–31/5/75. Sold to Meirion Mill Rly, Dinas Mawddwy, Gwynedd 6/75
2ft 0in.		4wDM	HE	4476	1953	2/73	N.H. Greaves & Co., Plant Dealers, Bypass Road, Mexborough, W. Yorks.	Exported to Singapore c.5/73
2ft 0in.		4wDM	OK	3685	(1929?)	13/3/73	P.C. Vallins, 15 Smith Road, South Park, Reigate, Surrey	Island Narrow Gauge Rly, Newport, Isle of Wight, 15/8/74
2ft 0in.		4wDM	MR	8696	1941	c.4/73	Motor Rail Ltd, Bedford, property A. Waddington & Sons Ltd, ex Farningham Sewer Contract	Hired to CJB Pipelines, Chat Moss in 1976. To White Moss Peat Co., Simonswood Moss, Merseyside c.8/76
2ft 0in.	Sue	4wDM	RH	476106	1964	c.5/73	Wm Bush & Sons Ltd, Birchwood Sidings, Somercotes, Alfreston, Derbys.	Steam Outlined. Butlin's, Heads of Ayr Holiday Camp 5/74. Per J.H.Rundle Ltd, New Bolingbroke, Lincs.
2ft 0in.		4wDM	HE	2477	1946	c.5/73	Track Supplies & Services Ltd, Old Wolverton, Bucks.	Exported to Singapore c.5/73
2ft 0in.		4wDM	MR	5821	1934	14/8/73	Redland Bricks Ltd, Nutbourne Brickworks, Hambledon, near Godalming, Surrey	Long Eaton Light Rly, West Park, Long Eaton, Derbys. 4/8/75
2ft 0in.		4wDM	MR	5243	1930	14/8/73	Redland Bricks Ltd, Nutbourne Brickworks, Hambledon, near Godalming, Surrey	Stripped of useable parts. Frame used as a welding bench. To new works at Lea Line 3/11/86. Scrapped 1991
metre	The Rock	0-4-0DM	HE	2419	1941	c.8/73	W.R. Nicholls & Sons, Plant Dealers, Greenwich; prev. Admiralty Dockyard, Gibraltar	Cotswold Light Rly, Cotswold Water Park, South Cerney c.7/74
3ft 0in.	No1	0-4-0ST OC	KS	3024	1916	c.9/73	Whipsnade & Umfolozi Rly, Whipsnade Zoo, Bucks. Originally with Lochaber Rly, Scotland per Hampshire Narrow Gauge Rly.	To new works at Lea Line 3/11/86. To Cavan & Leitrim Rly, Dromod 10/7/94 (Dromod)
2ft 0in.		4wDM	RH	221603	1943	16/10/73	Sheppey Light Rly	Scrapped c.7/77
2ft 0in.		4wDM	RH	175116	1935	28/11/73	West Kent Main Sewerage Board, Long Reach Works, Littlebrook, near Dartford, Kent	exported to Singapore c.3/78
2ft 0in.		4wDM	MR	8592	1940	11/73	Haunchwood Lewis Brick & Tile Ltd, Cheslyn Hay Wks., Staffs.	Sam Henry & Partners, Killingholme, Humberside c.7/74.
2ft 0in.		4wDM	RH	432664	1959	11/73	Haunchwood Lewis Brick & Tile Ltd, Cheslyn Hay Wks., Staffs.	P. Nicholson, c/o Pen-yr-Orsedd Slate Quarry 20/7/76
2ft 0in.		4wDM	RH	187056 (plated 264242)	1937	11/73	Haunchwood Lewis Brick & Tile Ltd, Cheslyn Hay Wks, Staffs.	Exported to Singapore c.7/74
2ft 0in.		4wDM	RH	264242	1949	11/73	Haunchwood Lewis Brick & Tile Ltd, Cheslyn Hay Wks, Staffs.	? by 1/79
2ft 0in.		4wDM	MR	8979	1946	1973	M. Jacob c/o J.M. Baldock, Hollycombe	Elmet Industrial (Tractors) Ltd, South Milford, S. Yorks. 2/74. (Contract for Yorkshire Water Authority at Booth Ferry Bridge, Asselby.)
2ft 0in.		4wDM	HE	2607	1942	19/5/74	Caledonian Peat Products Co. Ltd, Gardrum Moss	Festiniog Rly c.9/75. Rtn Cote c./76. To R.P. Morris, c/o Pen-yr-Orsedd Slate Quarry 20/7/76
2ft 0in.		4wBE	WR	5537	1956	c.6/74	Wheal Jane Mine, Cornwall	Dowty RPS, Ashchurch 20/6/74. Rtn Cote 9/74. To Festiniog Rly 27/9/75
3ft 2¼in.		4wDM	RH	266561	1948	c.6/74	Burlington Slate Mines, Kirkby in Furness, Lancs.	Scrapped 23/9/83 (Couplers used on AK30 Taffy)
3ft 0in.		4wDM	RH	398088	1956	c.12/74	G. Dew & Sons, Contractors, Esgreen, Oldham, Lancs.	Cross Channel Tunnel Contractors, Dover, Kent 12/74. Rtn Cote 20/1/75. To Caledonian Peat Products Ltd, Gardrum Moss, Shieldhill, near Falkirk 13/2/75

Gauge	Number/Name	Type	Make	Wks No.	Year	Date	Ex	To
1ft 6in.		4wBE	WR	G7177	1967	1974	Parnell Plant, Rugby	Mineral Industries Ltd, Scraithe Hole Mine, West Allendale, Northumbria 10/74
2ft 0in.	Cilgwyn	4wDM	RH	175414	1936	c.3/75	Welsh Highland Light Rly (1964) Ltd, Portmadoc	Vale of Teifi Rly 3/85
2ft 0in.		4wDM	MR	11004	1955	4/75	Reed & Mallik Ltd, Fechlin Aqueduct Contract, Inverness-shire	Hired to Balfour Beatty, Second Dartford Tunnel Contract c.12/75. Rtn Cote 4/77. Regauged to 4ft. To Taylor Woodrow, Glasgow Underground Rly 1978
2ft 0in.		4wDM	MR	11311	1966	4/75	Reed & Mallik Ltd, Fechlin Aqueduct Contract, Inverness-shire	Hired to Balfour Beatty, Second Dartford Tunnel Contract c.9/75. Rtn Cote 4/77. Scrapped c.11/82
2ft 0in.		4wDM	MR	11177	1961	4/75	Reed & Mallik Ltd, Fallin Plant Depot, Central Scotland, ex Fechlin Aqueduct Contract	Llanberis Lake Rly 8/10/75
2ft 0in.		4wDM	MR	5342	1931	5/75	Cattybrook Brickworks, Almondsbury, Avon	Scottish Agricultural Industries Ltd, Bolton Fell Mill, Cumbria 16/8/75
2ft 0in.		4wDM	MR	9215	1946	5/75	Cattybrook Brickworks, Almondsbury, Avon	Scottish Agricultural Industries Ltd, Bolton Fell Mill, Cumbria 16/8/75
3ft 0in.	1	4wDM	MR	11206	1962	5/75	APCM Sundon, Beds.	Regauged to 4ft, to Taylor Woodrow, Glasgow Underground Rly 1978
3ft 0in.	2	4wDM	MR	10159	1949	5/75	APCM Sundon, Beds.	Fisons, Swinefleet 5/75
3ft 0in.	3	4wDM	MR	10118	1949	5/75	APCM Sundon, Beds.	Scrapped c.10/86
2ft 0in.	10	4wPM	MR	9104	1942	1975	M.E. Engineering (wfw C Shear, Winkleigh Airfield)	Hired to Beecroft Peat, Alsager 6/75; hire ceased and sold to Moseley Industrial Tramway Museum c.8/76 but loco remained on site at Alsager until 8/85
2ft 0in.		4wDM	MR	8729	1941	c.9/75	C.F. Rawlinson Brickyard Ltd, Skegness Brick & Tile Works	Used on contract work at Butlin's, Minehead 12/75-2/76. Used on contract work at Butlin's, Filey 3/76-c.5/76. Hired to Scottish Agricultural Industries Ltd, Bolton Fell Mill c.8/76. Rtn Cote 1977. Used on contract work at Butlin's, Pwllheli c.11/77-c.1/78. Sold to L.J. Smith, Battlesbridge, Essex 1978
1ft 11½in.		4wDM	RH	277265	1949	9/10/75	Llanberis Lake Rly	H. Frampton-Jones, Dorking 20/1/77
2ft 0in.		4wDM	RH	264252	1952	c.12/75	Foraky Ltd, Colwick, Nottingham	H. Frampton-Jones, Dorking 20/1/77
2ft 0in.		4wDM	RH	174139	1935	c.12/75	Foraky Ltd, Colwick, Nottingham	Track Supplies & Services, Wolverton 2/76
metre	Cambrai	0-6-0T OC	Corpet	493	1888	21/2/76	NG Rly Museum, Tallyllyn Rly	Northants Loco Group, Irchester 4/6/83
4ft 8½in.		4wDM	RH	235511	1945	b.3/76	H. Frampton-Jones	To ? b.1/79. (to Northampton Ironstone Railway Trust, Hunsbury Hill b.1/82)
2ft 0in.		0-4-0DM s/o	Bg	3235	1947	26/5/76	Butlin's, Filey	D. Preece, Pengally Farm, Cornwall 2/11/79
2ft 0in.	Digger	4wDM	MR	8882	1944	6/76	Haunchwood Lewis Brick & Tile Co. Ltd, Rosemary Tileries, Essington Wks, Staffs.	Hired to White Moss Peat Co., Simonswood Moss, Liverpool c.11/76, rtn Cote b.15/11/77. Hired to A. Streeter & Co., contract at Bordon, Hants. 7/78. Hired to Christiani & Nielsen Ltd, Bournemouth Pier contract 28/8/79-c.4/80. To new works at Lea Line 3/11/86. Hired to Boothby Peat 2/5/87-22/6/87. Hired to Stoke on Trent Festival Garden 29/2/88. Used by AK on track renewal contract at Woodhead Cable Tunnel 22/1/92-24/3/92. Hired to Pirelli Ltd, Woodhead Cable Tunnel, 7/6/92-8/92. (List of hires is not exhaustive!)
2ft 0in.		4wDM	MR	7170	1937	6/76	Haunchwood Lewis Brick & Tile Co. Ltd, Rosemary Tileries, Essington Wks, Staffs.	Used on contract work at Butlin's, Minehead c.1/77-c.5/77. Exported to Singapore 4/79
2ft 0in.		4wDM	MR	8681	1941	6/76	Haunchwood Lewis Brick & Tile Co. Ltd, Rosemary Tileries, Cheslyn Hay Wks, Staffs.	Scrapped c.11/82
2ft 0in.		4wDM	HE	1974	1939	18/6/76	P. Briddon, Wey Valley Light Rly, Farnham, Surrey	P. Briddon, Bala Lake Rly 13/10/77

Gauge	Number/Name	Type	Make	Wks No.	Year	Date	Ex	To
2ft 0in.	Trixie	0-4-0ST OC	AK	1	1974	b.7/76	Meirion Mill Rly, Dinas Mawddwy, Gwynedd	Exported to Rail Rebecq Rognon, Belgium 4/77
2ft 0in.		4wDM	MR	5713	1936	20/1/77	John Crosskey, Surrey	Wey Valley Light Rly, Farnham, Surrey 15/12/80
2ft 0in.		4wDM	RH	304439	1950	4/77	Sheppey Light Rly	Hired to Doddington Light Rly, Chipping Sodbury, Avon c.4/7/78–5/5/79. Sold to ICI Ltd, Nobels Roburite Works, Shevington, Manchester c.6/79
2ft 0in.		4wDM	MR	8711	1941	4/77	Sheppey Light Rly	Hired to T.H.Contractors Ltd, Swale District Council Contract, Faversham, Kent ?/77–10/78. Rtn Cote. Exported to Singapore 4/79
2ft 0in.		4wDM	RH	179889	1936	4/77	Sheppey Light Rly	Exported to Singapore 3/78
2ft 0in.	Sue	4wDM s/o	RH	476106	1964	20/4/77	Butlin's, Heads of Ayr Holiday Camp, Strathclyde	To new works at Lea Line 3/11/86. To Vale of Teifi Rly a.20/6/87 b.31/8/87
2ft 0in.		0-4-0DM s/o	Bg	3232	1946	c.5/77	Butlin's, Clacton Holiday Camp	Butlin's, Minehead c.6/78.
2ft 0in.		4wDM	MR	40SD505	1977	4/7/77	New, ex Motor Rail, Bedford	Imperial Iranian Navy, Bandar Abbas jetty, Iran 8/77
2ft 0in.		4wDM	MR	40SD506	1977	4/7/77	New, ex Motor Rail, Bedford	Imperial Iranian Navy, Bandar Abbas jetty, Iran 8/77
2ft 0in.		4wDM	MR	7057	1938	11/10/77	Caledonian Peat Products Co. Ltd, Gardrum Moss	Stripped of useable spares. Frame used to carry a hydraulic press. To new works at Lea Line 3/11/86. Scrapped c.10/92
1ft 9in.	Old Sparky	4wDM s/o	RH	487963	1963	c.3/78	Butlin's, Pwllheli	To new works at Lea Line 3/11/86. Regauged to 2ft. To H. Frampton-Jones, Horsham end/88.
2ft 0in.		4wDM	HE	2536	1941	3/78	Richardson's Moss Litter Co Ltd Letham Moss	Chalkpits Museum, Sussex 4/8/80
1ft 3in.	Michael	4-4-2 OC	Barnes	105	(1928?)	c.4/78	Entam Leisure Ltd (orig. Rhyl Miniature Rly)	Rhyl Miniature Rly 24/6/78
1ft 3in.	Clara	0-4-2DM	Guest		1961	c.4/78	Dudley Zoo	Rhyl Miniature Rly 24/6/78
2ft 0in.		4wDM	MR	40s371	1970	24/6/78	Mixconcrete Aggregates Ltd, Charlecote, Warks.	Regauged to 2ft 6in. To Richardson's Moss Litter Co. Ltd, Solway Moss 25/9/78
2ft 0in.		4wDM	MR	21505	1955	24/6/78	Mixconcrete Aggregates Ltd, Charlecote, Warks.	Richardson's Moss Litter Co. Ltd, Letham Moss 25/9/78
2ft 0in.		4wBE	CE	5667	1969	9/8/78	Taylor Woodrow Plant Ltd, Greenford Depot, London	L.J. Smith, Battlesbridge, Essex b.2/79. Loco later to Ayle Colliery, Alston c.8/85, per AK.
2ft 0in.		4wBE	CE	5667	1969	9/8/78	Taylor Woodrow Plant Ltd, Greenford Depot, London	Ayle Colliery, Alston c.4/85
2ft 0in.		4wBE	CE	5667	1969	9/8/78	Taylor Woodrow Plant Ltd, Greenford Depot, London	Ayle Colliery, Alston c.4/85
2ft 0in.		4wDM	HE	3109	1944	16/9/78	Great Bush Rly	Scrapped c.10/78
2ft 0in.		0-4-0DM s/o	Bg	3232	1946	10/78	Butlin's, Minehead Holiday Camp	To L.J. Smith, Battlesbridge, Essex 6/10/78
4ft 8½in.		4wDM	MR	9909	1958	1978	H. Frampton Jones, South Eastern Steam Centre, Ashford MPD, Kent	Regauged to 4ft. To Taylor Woodrow, Glasgow Underground Railway 9/78
2ft 0in.		4wDM	MR	60s362	1968	c.12/78	W Ainscough, Mossy Lea Road, Writhington, near Wigan (orig. Pilkingtons)	Regauged to 3ft. To Caledonian Peat Products, Ryflat Moss, Carstairs c.2/79
2ft 0in.		4wDM	MR	60s382	1969	c.2/79	W. Ainscough, Mossy Lea Road, Writhington, near Wigan (orig. Pilkingtons)	Regauged to 3ft. To Caledonian Peat Products, Gardrum Moss c.6/79
2ft 0in.		4wDM	MR	11141	1960	21/3/79	W. Ainscough, Mossy Lea Road, Writhington, near Wigan (orig. Pilkingtons)	To new works at Lea Line 3/11/86. Exported to Singapore 1987 a.20/6/87, b.24/10/87
4ft 8½in.		4wDM	FH	2893	1944	3/79	James Friswell & Son Ltd, Banbury. wfw Grain Silo (Oxford) Ltd, Banbury Rd, Oxford	Gloucester-Warwickshire Rly Society, Toddington Goods Yard, Glos. 23/7/82
2ft 0in.	Layer	4wDM	JF	21294	1936	7/5/79	Great Bush Rly, E. Sussex	Leeds Industrial Museum 8/86
2ft 0in.		4wDM	MR	21513	1955	6/7/79	Llanberis Lake Rly	Redlands, Nutbourne Brickworks, Surrey 31/7/79
2ft 0in.		4wDM	MR	5862	1934	31/7/79	Redland Bricks Ltd, Nutbourne Brickworks, Surrey	Hired to Croxden Gravels Ltd, Chat Moss 8/79–10/1/80. Exported to Singapore 5/80.

Gauge	Number/Name	Type	Make	Wks No.	Year	Date	Ex	To
4ft 0in.		4wDM	MR	9909	1958	7/9/79	Taylor Woodrow, Glasgow Underground Rly Contract	To new works at Lea Line 3/11/86. Scrapped 10/88
1ft 8in.		4wDM	L	33937	1949	18/9/79	W.H. Collier, Marks Tey Brickworks, Essex	Chalkpits Museum 1/8/80
2ft 0in.		4wDM	OK	3444	1929	18/9/79	Rugby Portland Cement Co., Barrington, Cambs.	P. Briddon, Sheffield 1/10/79
2ft 0in.	Owl	4wDM	RH	283513	1949	23/9/79	Great Bush Rly, E. Sussex	Hired to A. Streeter & Co., contract at Bagshot 11/79–c.4/80. Rebuilt as 4wDH AK20R of 1986. To Butterley Building Materials, Cherry Orchard Works, Essex 6/86
2ft 0in.	Bear	4wDM	RH	339209	1952	23/9/79	Great Bush Rly, E. Sussex	Wynne Slate Quarry, Glyn Ceriog, Clwyd 4/80
2ft 0in.		4wDM	MR	22220	1964	18/10/79	Severn Trent Water Authority, Minworth	Regauged to 75cm. To Bullrush Peat, Co. Antrim 21/1/80
2ft 0in.		4wDM	MR	22237	1965	18/10/79	Severn Trent Water Authority, Minworth	Hired to Cristiani & Nielsen Ltd, Bournemouth Pier Contract 19/11/79. Rtn Cote c.4/80. Sold to Jones & Bailey, contract at Harton Coal Staithes c.4/81
2ft 0in.		4wDM	MR	40s309	1968	18/10/79	Severn Trent Water Authority, Minworth	Regauged to 75cm. To Bullrush Peat, Co. Antrim 21/1/80
2ft 0in.		4wDM	MR	40s307	1968	19/10/79	Severn Trent Water Authority, Minworth	Regauged to 75cm. To Bullrush Peat, Co. Antrim 21/1/80
2ft 0in.		4wDM	MR	22239	1965	19/10/79	Severn Trent Water Authority, Minworth	Hired to Cristiani & Nielsen Ltd, Bournemouth Pier Contract b.4/80. Rtn b.10/81. Sold abroad (Denmark) b.2/83
2ft 0in.		4wDM	MR	40s343	1969	19/10/79	Severn Trent Water Authority, Minworth	Hired to Woburn Abbey Narrow Gauge Rly 8/80–c.11/80. Hired to Surrey and Hampshire Canal Society 12/80–c.6/81. Sold to Norit-Klasman Ltd, Penicuik 26/6/81. See also later
1ft 3in.		4w-4wPM	Guest		1953	c.6/80	Dudley Zoo Miniature Rly	Rebuilt as 4w-4wDH with Perkins engine, and sold to Cricket St Thomas Wildlife Park, Chard c.4/85
1ft 3in.		6w-4PM	Guest		1960	c.6/80	Dudley Zoo Miniature Rly	Blenheim Palace Rly 1981
1ft 3in.	Dmr359	4-4wPM	Morse		1939	by 6/80	Dreamland Miniature Railway, Margate	Rhyl Miniature Rly 6/80
2ft 0in.		2-4wBE	WR	887	1935	7/7/80	Wm Bush, Alfreton, Derbys.	John Crosskey, Surrey 28/6/82
1ft 3in.		2w-2DMR	Minirail		c1976	8/80	Dudley Zoo Miniature Rly	Converted to a 2ft gauge coach by 2/83. Scrapped c./84
2ft 0in.		4wDM	MR	22253	1965	4/81	Anglian Water Authority, Haddiscoe via a London Dealer who bought it at Chelmsford Cattle Market	Hired to Surrey & Hants Canal Society 1981, rtn Cote c.10/81. Sold to Norit-Klasman, Penicuik c.7/82
2ft 0in.		0-4-0DM	HE	5222	1958	c.5/81	Hibernian Rly Society, Ireland	R.J. Washington, Cheltenham 11/81
1ft 8in.		4-6-4DM s/o	HC	D570	1934	1981	Morecambe Miniature Rly	Kilverstone Wildlife Park, Thetford c4/82
2ft 0in.		2w-2PMR	Wkm	1309	1923	c.5/82	Wey Valley Rly, Surrey	Scrapped c.10/86
2ft 0in.	Robin Hood	4wDM	MR	11297	1965	3/6/82	Leighton Buzzard Narrow Gauge Railway Society	South Tynedale Rly, Cumbria 10/7/82
2ft 0in.		4wDM	MR	60s318	1966	3/6/82	Leighton Buzzard Narrow Gauge Railway Society	T. & G. Mining, Chilmark Quarry c.4/85
2ft 6in.		4wDH	MR	115U093	1970	7/82	Mogul of Ireland Ltd, Shalee Silver Mines, Co. Tipperary	To new works at Lea Line 3/11/86. Regauged to 3ft. Loaned to Fisons, Swinefleet c.9/88, rtn Lea c.10/88. Sold to Cavan & Leitrim Rly, Dromod 9/2/95
2ft 6in.		4wDH	MR	115U094	1970	7/82	Mogul of Ireland Ltd, Shalee Silver Mines, Co. Tipperary	To new works at Lea Line 3/11/86. To William Sinclair Horticulture Ltd, Springfield Works, Lothian 17/9/96
2ft 0in.		4wDM	MR	40s343	1969	c.9/82	Norit-Klasman, Penicuik	Hired to Milton Hall Brick Co. Ltd, Essex, Cherry Orchard Works 6/83–9/83, and Star Lane Works 9/83–c.14/11/83. Used at Thorpe Park, Staines early 1984. Sold to Richardson's Moss Litter Co. Ltd Letham Moss 12/4/84

Gauge	Number/Name	Type	Make	Wks No.	Year	Date	Ex	To
1ft 8in.	*Flying Scotsman*	4-6-2DM s/o	HC	D582	1933	b.11/82	Morecambe Miniature Rly	Kilverstone Wildlife Park, Thetford 17/11/82
2ft 0in.		4wDM	MR	40s383	1971	c.1/83	Severn Trent Water Authority, Minworth	Hired to Streeters & Co., Bagshot, contract, Surrey 2/83, rtn Cote by 6/83. Hired to Pyleford Marina Contract 6/83, rtn Cote 8/83. To Richardson's Moss Litter Co. Ltd Eastriggs 12/4/84
2ft 0in.		4wPM	L	962	c.1930	5/83	E. Evans, Scrap Dealer, Birmingham	A. Neale, c/o T. Hall, North Ings Farm, Lincs. 22/10/83
2ft 6in.		4wDM	MR	5606	1931	6/83	Whipsnade & Umfolozi Rly, Whipsnade Zoo, Beds.	To new works at Lea Line 3/11/86. Regauged to 2ft. Exported to Angola per RMP 1987 a.20/6/87, b.24/10/87
2ft 6in.		4wBE	WR	1393	1939	6/83	Whipsnade & Umfolozi Rly, Whipsnade Zoo, Beds.	Richardson's Moss Litter Co. Ltd Fannyside 12/4/84
2ft 6in.		4wBE	WR	1616	1940	6/83	Whipsnade & Umfolozi Rly, Whipsnade Zoo, Beds.	Scrapped 7/83
2ft 6in.		4wBE	WR	1801	1940	6/83	Whipsnade & Umfolozi Rly, Whipsnade Zoo, Beds.	Scrapped 7/83
2ft 0in.		4wDM	MR	8738	1942	6/83	Pleasurerail Ltd, Knebworth Park, Herts.	Norit-Klasman, Penicuik 20/6/84
15in.		4wDM	L	54183	1964	10/83	ex H. Gamble, Whitstable, Kent. wfw M.E. Engineering, wfw W.H. Collier, Marks Tey Brickworks.	Regauged to 60cm. To Midland Irish Peat, Co., Westmeath 11/83
2ft 0in.	S 1380	4wDM s/o	RH	?	?	b.4/84	Billing Aquadrome, Northampton	Exported to New Zealand b.9/84 (loco wks number probably one of: 182137/36, 226278/44, 229631/44 – all missing 'Leisuretrack' locos)
2ft 0in.		4wDM	RH	213834	1942	b.4/84	R.J. Washington, Cheltenham	Brian Clarke, Midford Station, Avon c.3/86
2ft 0in.		0-4-0DM	HE	5222	1958	b.4/84	R.J. Washington, Cheltenham	Ayle Colliery, Cumbria b.4/84 (possibly moved direct)
2ft 0in.		4wDM	RH	213853 or 217973	1942 or 1941	12/4/84	Richardson's Moss Litter Co. Ltd Solway Moss	To new works at Lea Line 3/11/86. To Glendale Forge, Monk Street, Thaxted, Essex 14/12/90
2ft 0in.		4wDM	MR	21513	1955	8/84	Redlands, Nutbourne Brickworks, Surrey	Hired back to Redlands, Nutbourne Brickworks, 11/10/84–23/2/85. Steam outline bodywork transferred from MR 8993. To Knebworth Park c.6/85
2ft 0in.		4wDM	RH	452280	1960	6/84	Richardson's Moss Litter Co. Ltd Eastriggs	Rebuilt as 4wDH AK13R of 1984. Hired to Solva Sewage Wks. Rtn Cote 6/85. Rebuilt to 15in. gauge. To Littlecote House, Hungerford 3/86
2ft 0in.	No1	4wDM	RH	222089	1943	6/84	Richardson's Moss Litter Co. Ltd Eastriggs	Exported to Singapore 12/85
2ft 0in.	No2	4wDM	RH	235641	1945	6/84	Richardson's Moss Litter Co. Ltd Eastriggs	Scrapped c.11/85
1ft 5in.		4w-4wRER	? (Holland)		1976	b.11/84	Southsea Miniature Rly, Hants.	Mr L. Wastie, Barnard Gate, near Witney, Oxon. c.10/86
2ft 0in.		4wDM	MR	8993	1946	b.2/85	Pleasurerail Ltd, Knebworth Park, Herts.	Steam outline body transferred to MR 21513. Exported to Singapore 12/85
2ft 0in.	Adam	4wDM s/o	MR	9978	1954	3/86	Cotswold Wildlife Park, Burford	Hired to Drusilla's Zoo, East Sussex. Rtn Cote 14/7/86. To new works at Lea Line 3/11/86. To Brian Clark, Avon by 7/4/87
1ft 3in.	Silver Jubilee	4-6-4PE s/o	?		1935	b.4/87	Coney Beach Miniature Rly, Porthcawl, Mid Glamorgan	John Tennent, Hampton Lode b.6/4/87
2ft 0in.		4wDH	AK	14	1984	7/87	Redlands, Nutbourne Brickworks	Billing Aquadrome 8/87
2ft 0in.		4wDM	MR	9546	1950	c.1987	G. Evans, Cornwall	Exported to Singapore c.1987
2ft 0in.		4wDM	SMH	104063G	1976	26/2/88	Old Kiln Rly, Surrey	ERS Mining, Whittle Colliery c.7/88
4ft 0in.		4wDM	MR	11004	1955	31/3/88	Taylor Woodrow, London	Rebuilt as AK29R. Exported to Nigeria 19/12/89.
4ft 0in.		4wDM	MR	11206	1962	31/3/88	Taylor Woodrow, London	Chalk Pits Museum a.28/5/88, b.7/9/88
4ft 8½in.		4wDM	MR	9932	1972	31/3/88	Dunlop, Birmingham	Regauged to 2ft. Hired to Balfour Beatty, Woodhead Cable Tunnel 10/10/88–c.4/89. Sold to Chilmark Quarry c.27/6/89

Gauge	Number/Name	Type	Make	Wks No.	Year	Date	Ex	To
2ft 0in.		4wDM	RH	393327	1956	17/4/88	Gloddfa Ganol	Dare Valley Rly, Aberdare 12/7/91
2ft 0in.		4wDM	RH	432664	1959	17/4/88	Gloddfa Ganol	Scrapped by 6/91
3ft 6in.	Woto	0-4-0ST OC	WB	2133	1924	6/5/88	P. Elms, Romford	(Property Patrick Keef)
2ft 0in.	Ivor	4wDM	MR	8678	1941	29/7/88	East Hayling Light Rly	Hired to Balfour Beatty, Woodhead Cable Tunnel 9/1/89–end 2/89. Sold to Wm Blythe, Far Ings Tileries, Humberside, via J.W. Stamp 6/89
4ft 8½in.	Army 9113	4wPMR	Bg	3539	1959	b.9/88	J. Hirst & Sons, St Mary Bourne, Hants.	Rebuilt as 2ft gauge carriage, to Leighton Buzzard Narrow Gauge Railway 26/8/89
2ft 0in.		4wDM	L	10498	1938	11/88	Alan Gartell, Templecombe	Regauged to 15in. To Jackman's Garden Centre, Woking
2ft 0in.		4wDM	RH	195846	1939	1/89	M.E. Engineering, London	Mosely School 2/9/89
2ft 0in.		4wDM	RH	223700	1943	1/89	M.E. Engineering, London	Leicester Museum b.28/2/89
2ft 0in.		4wDM	MR	11111	1959	1/89	M.E. Engineering, London	Vale of Teifi Rly 28/3/89
2ft 0in.		4wDM	MR	9543	1950	1/89	M.E. Engineering, London	Midland Irish Peat 2/10/89
2ft 0in.		4wDM	FH	3583	1954	1/89	M.E. Engineering, London	Leighton Buzzard Narrow Gauge Railway 16/6/89
2ft 6in.		2-2wPM	Wkm	3414		1/89	M.E. Engineering, London	Moseley School b.28/2/89
2ft 6in.		2-2wPM	Wkm	3564		1/89	M.E. Engineering, London	Moseley School b.28/2/89
2ft 6in.		2-2wPM	Wkm	?		1/89	M.E. Engineering, London	Moseley School b.28/2/89
metre		4wDM	HE	6648	1967	1/89	North Gloucester Rly Co., Toddington Goods Yard	Regauged 2ft and frame and wheels used for AK48 Sally
2ft 0in.	Mavis	4wDM	RH	7002/0967/6	1967	b.28/2/89	R.D. Geeson Ltd, Ripley, Derbys	Hired to Butlin's, Minehead 17/3/89–3/11/89. Sold to Knebworth Park 12/89
2ft 0in.		4wDM	MR	8683	1941	28/3/89	Vale of Teifi Rly	Scrapped c.10/92
2ft 6in.	18	4wDH	SMH	101T018	1979	8/4/89	NCB Allerton Bywater (orig. Ledston Luck)	Regauged to 900mm. To Transmanche-Link, Channel Tunnel Contract c.6/89
2ft 6in.	19	4wDH	SMH	101T019	1979	8/4/89	NCB Allerton Bywater (orig. Ledston Luck)	Scrapped 12/9/2002
2ft 6in.	20	4wDH	SMH	101T020	1979	8/4/89	NCB Allerton Bywater (orig. Ledston Luck)	Regauged to 900mm. To Transmanche-Link, Channel Tunnel Contract 7/7/89
2ft 0in.	Liza	4wDM	MR	21282	1957	26/7/89	Fisons, Kirkbride	Hired to Taylor Woodrow, Woodhead Cable Tunnel 23/7/90. Rtn Lea 20/8/91. Used on track lifting at Hewlitts Farm 9/91. Hired to Taylor Woodrow, Isle of Grain b.12/91. By 1/6/92 on hire at Rochdale Canal. Rtn Lea by 28/9/92. Sold to Lea Bailey Mine, Newtown, Glos. 9/93
								J.M. Parry Associates, Overend Road, Cradley Heath, Birmingham c.2/90
2ft 0in.		2w-2BE	J Peat			11/89	J. Peat, Shaftsbury, Dorset	Hired to Taylor Woodrow, Woodhead Cable Tunnel c.7/90. Rtn Lea c.8/91. Exported to Angola per RMP 9/91.
2ft 0in.		4wDM	MR	21513	1955	12/89	Knebworth Park	Brian Gent, Oakhanger 11/1/94
2ft 0in.		4wDM	MR	7066	1938	12/89	Fisons, Kirkbride	Rebuilt as steam outline. Hired to Pembury Country Park during 1995. Rtn Lea 10/95. Hired to William Sinclair Horticulture Ltd, Auchencorth Moss, Lothian 10/95–14/3/96. Hired to Pembury Country Park by end/3/96. Rtn Lea 20/5/99. Hired & then sold to Devon Rly Centre, Bickleigh Park 8/6/99
2ft 0in.		4wDM	MR	8875	1944	12/89	Fisons, Kirkbride	
2ft 0in.	Ivor	4wDM	MR	8877	1944	12/89	Fisons, Kirkbride	
2ft 0in.		4-2-4DH s/o	Chance	64-5031-24	1964	6/3/90	Butlin's, Minehead	Sandyholm Garden Centre, near Larkhill, Strathclyde 19/11/90
2ft 0in.	(No21)	4-2-4PH s/o	Chance	76-50145-24	1976	5/90	Butlin's, Head of Ayr	Glendale Forge, Monk Street, Thaxted, Essex 5/90
2ft 0in.	(15)	4wPM	MR	5861	c.1920	18/9/90	Ian Jolly, Clwyd	Brian Gent, Oakhanger 12/11/93
2ft 0in.		4wDM	MR		1934	18/9/90	Llanberis Lake Rly	FMB Engineering 29/3/93
2ft 0in.		4wDM	SMH	104063G	1976	b.4/91	ERS Mining, Whittle Colliery	Tim Shelton, Corfe Mullen, Dorset 5/7/91
2ft 0in.	3	4wBE	CE	5554/3	1968	c.6/91	Wheal Jane Mine, Cornwall	Identity unsure. Regauged to 4ft 8½in. To Tilbury Construction, Waterloo & City Line contract, Waterloo Station, London 25/6/91

Gauge	Number/Name	Type	Make	Wks No.	Year	Date	Ex	To
2ft 0in.	23	4wBE	CE	B2289A	1980	c.6/91	Wheal Jane Mine, Cornwall	Identity unsure. Regauged to 4ft 8½in. To Tilbury Construction, Waterloo & City Line contract, Waterloo Station, London 20/6/91
2ft 0in.	7	4wBE	CE			17/6/91	Wheal Jane Mine, Cornwall	Walker & Partners Ltd, Inkersall Road Estate, Staveley, Derbys. 10/3/92
2ft 0in.	8	4wBE	CE			17/6/91	Wheal Jane Mine, Cornwall	Walker & Partners Ltd, Inkersall Road Estate, Staveley, Derbys. c.3/92
2ft 0in.	15	4wBE	CE			17/6/91	Wheal Jane Mine, Cornwall	Walker & Partners Ltd, Inkersall Road Estate, Staveley, Derbys. 10/3/92
2ft 0in.	16	4wBE	CE			17/6/91	Wheal Jane Mine, Cornwall	Walker & Partners Ltd, Inkersall Road Estate, Staveley, Derbys. c3/92
2ft 0in.	20	0-4-0BE	WR	L1021	1983	17/6/91	Wheal Jane Mine, Cornwall	Colin Saxton, Moseley Museum by 26/4/92
2ft 0in.	Kate	4wDM	MR	7215	1938	19/6/91	Vale of Teifi Rly	Hired to Taylor Woodrow at Isle of Grain b12/91, rtn Lea 2/92. Hired to Pirelli Ltd at Woodhead Cable Tunnel 24/3/92. By 1/6/92 on hire at Rochdale Canal, rtn Lea by 28/9/92. On hire to Taylor Woodrow, Southall, early/94-early/95. Sold to Joseph Metcalf Ltd, Chat Moss 11/95
2ft 0in.		4wDM	L	52579	1961	6/9/91	John Quentin, Herts.	Regauged to 15in. To John Tennent, Hampton Loade 17/10/91
2ft 9in.		4wDM	HE	8819	1979	b.14/12/91	D Hichman, dealer, Neath. (Loco was stored at Nutley's Garage, Crick, Gwent.) (Loco was originally at NCB Nantgarw Colliery.)	Regauged to 2ft 6in. To Hatton Craft Village, Hatton, Warks. c.9/93
2ft 0in.	Brecon	4wDM	MR	7902	1939	b.14/12/91	Brecon Mountain Rly	Hired to Murphy, contractors, Woodhead Cable Tunnel c.12/94-b.7/3/95. Hired to Chilmark Quarry c.6/95-c./late/95. Sold to Legoland, Windsor 3/3/96.
11¼in.		4wBE	K Peacock		1960s	12/91	Ken Peacock, Buscot	Chris Sibley, Reading 10/92
4ft 8½in.		0-4-0DH	TH	132c	1963	8/2/93	Royal Ordnance Factory, Glascoed	Rutland Rly Museum, Cottesmore 19/4/93
4ft 8½in.		0-4-0DH	RSHD/WB	8366	1962	8/2/93	Royal Ordnance factory, Glascoed	Tarmac, Caldicot depot, Gwent 1/96
2ft 0in.		4wDM	Schoma	1676	1955	b.5/93	Midland Irish Peat	FMB Engineering 2/6/93
2ft 0in.		4wDM	MR	9239	1947	b.5/93	Midland Irish Peat	Scrapped c.9/93
2ft 0in.		4wDM	RH	193974	1938	b.5/93	Midland Irish Peat	P. Westmacott, Studley, Warks. 10/93
2ft 0in.		4wDM	FH	2306	1940	b.5/93	Midland Irish Peat	Jim Hay, Liphook, Hants. 12/8/94 per FMB.
2ft 0in.		4wDM	MR	22212	1964	c.9/93	John Appleton, Leiston, Suffolk (in dsm condition)	Frame used as an engine/transmission test bed. Scrapped by 19/4/94
2ft 0in.		4wDM	MR	8969	1945	c.9/93	Leighton Buzzard Narrow Gauge Railway (frame only)	Scrapped 9/6/2005
2ft 0in.		4wBE	CE	5074	1965	30/4/94	Chatterley-Whitfield Museum	Ayle Colliery, Alston by 17/6/94
2ft 0in.		4wDM	RH	444200	1960	c.8/94	Pembury Country Park	Bromyard & Linton Rly 2/95
2ft 0in.	Mavis	4wDM	RH	7002/0967/6	1967	13/9/94	ex hire at Pembury Country Park	Moseley School 30/3/95
3ft 0in.		4wDM	SMH	60SL750	1980	12/2/95	Cavan & Leitrim Rly, Dromod (orig. Bord na Mona).	Scrapped mid-1999
2ft 0in.		4wDM	Diema	1600	1953	4/95	De Efterling. Holland	Light Railway Association, Turvey, Beds. c.8/95
2ft 0in.		4wDM	MR	8704	1942	c.3/96	Legoland, Windsor	William Sinclair Horticulture Ltd, Springfield Works, Penicuik c.2/97
900mm		4wDH	SMH	101T018	1979	w/e 23/8/96	Transmanche-Link, Channel Tunnel Contract, Sevington, Kent	Rebuilt as AK59R of 1999. To Leighton Buzzard Narrow Gauge Railway 3/8/99.
900mm		4wDH	SMH	101T020	1979	w/e 23/8/96	Transmanche-Link, Channel Tunnel Contract, Sevington, Kent	Midland Rly Centre, Butterley 17/5/97
3ft 0in.		4wDM	RH	418770	1957	b.6/12/96	John Craven, Notts.	Matthew Giquel, Tavistock (by c.7/97?)
2ft 0in.		4wDM	FH	2163	1938	b.6/12/96	John Craven, Notts.	Simon Lomax, Leics. 16/3/99
2ft 0in.		4wDM	FH	2306	1940	1/1/97	Jim Hay, Liphook, Hants.	Simon Lomax, Leics. 25/5/99
2ft 0in.		4wDM	MR	7066	1938	c.1/97	Jim Hay, Liphook, Hants.	
2ft 0in.		4wDM	MR	9411	1948	b.17/7/97	Mr White, Home Farm, Anstey	Iquazu Falls, Argentina 5/01

Gauge	Number/Name	Type	Make	Wks No.	Year	Date	Ex	To
3ft 0in.		4wDM	MR	60S362	1968	9/97	William Sinclair Horticulture Ltd, Gardrum Moss	Scrapped mid-1999
3ft 0in.		4wDM	MR	60S382	1969	9/97	William Sinclair Horticulture Ltd, Gardrum Moss	Rebuilt. To Waterford & Suir Valley Rly, Kilmeasdon, Co. Waterford, Ireland 11/7/00
2ft 0in.		4wDH	SMH	101T022	1982	1/98	South Tynedale Rly	Regauged to 60cm. To France w/e 3/7/98
2ft 0in.		4wDM	MR	22128	1961	13/2/98	Gloddfa Ganol	Sinclair Horticulture Ltd, Bolton Fell, Cumbria late 3/98
2ft 0in.		4wDM	MR	22238	1965	13/2/98	Gloddfa Ganol	Sinclair Horticulture Ltd, Bolton Fell, Cumbria late 3/98
2ft 0in.		4wDM	MR	40S308	1967	13/2/98	Gloddfa Ganol	Regauged to 2ft 6in. To Sinclair Horticulture Ltd, Cladance Moss, East Kilbride late 3/98
2ft 0in.		4wDM	MR	40S412	1973	13/2/98	Gloddfa Ganol	Sinclair Horticulture Ltd, Bolton Fell, Cumbria late 3/98
2ft 0in.		4wDM	RH	235711	1945	10/3/98	Gloddfa Ganol	Devon Rly Centre, Bickleigh Park 8/6/99
2ft		4wDM	L	37366	1951	mid 3/98	Sinclair Horticulture Ltd, Bolton Fell, Cumbria	M. Strange and J. Poyser, Matlock 22/7/98, per FMB.
2ft		4wDM	L	55730	1968	mid 3/98	Sinclair Horticulture Ltd, Bolton Fell, Cumbria	Hired to Tilbury Douglas Ltd (contractors), Denton Waterworks, Manchester 20/4/98. Rtn Lea Line off hire by 10/7/98. To Peter Smith, Newbury 2/00
2ft		4wDM	MR	8614	1941	end 5/98	Butterley Building Materials, Cherry Orchard Lane Works, Rochford, Essex	Hired to Taylor Woodrow, Southall 10/1/00. Rtn Lea Line end 1/00. Hired to Amec, Woodhead Tunnel 11/1/01. Rtn Lea Line 2/7/01. To Alaska & Environmental Contracting, Wareham, Dorset 8/01
2ft		4wDM	MR	21520	1955	end 5/98	Butterley Building Materials, Cherry Orchard Lane Works, Rochford, Essex	L. & P. Peat Products Ltd, Letham Moss 16/9/98
2ft		4wDM	AK	40SD530	1987	end 5/98	Butterley Building Materials, Cherry Orchard Lane Works, Rochford, Essex	Regauged to 2ft 8½in. To Volks Electric Railway, Brighton 23/6/98
2ft		4wDM	AK	26	1988	end 5/98	Butterley Building Materials, Cherry Orchard Lane Works, Rochford, Essex	L. & P. Peat Products Ltd, Nutberry Moss, Eastriggs, Dumfries 16/9/98
2ft		4wDM	AK	28	1989	end 5/98	Butterley Building Materials, Cherry Orchard Lane Works, Rochford, Essex	L. & P. Peat Products Ltd, Creca Moss, near Eastriggs, Dumfries 26/6/98
3ft	Rs101	4wDH	RFS	101L	1989	21/8/98	Transmanche-Link, Channel Tunnel Contractors, Sevington Stores Depot	West Clare Rly, Moyasta, Co. Clare, Ireland 30/4/99
2ft		4wDM	AK	6	1981	16/9/98	L. & P. Peat Products Ltd, Creca Moss, Dumfries	Regauged 15in. To John Tennent & P. Smith, Brecon, Powys c.6/99.
2ft		4wDM	AK	7	1982	16/9/98	L. & P. Peat Products Ltd, Nutberry Moss, Dumfries	Regauged to 1ft 9in. To Blackpool Pleasure Beach by 22/12/98
15in.		2w-2PM	Moss		1992	c.6/99	John Tennent & P. Smith, Brecon, Powys	Cleethorpes Coast Light Rly 8/99
2ft		4wDM	MR	8717	1941	5/9/99	Moseley Rly Trust	Mid Wales Stone Supplies, Tyn Rhyd, Welshpool late 9/01, as a wagon
2ft		4wDM	MR	8995	1946	(5/9/99?)	Moseley Rly Trust	To Statfold Barn Rly, Staffs. 31/7/07
2ft 6in.		4wDM	HE	7495	1977	1999	MoD Dean Hill, Hants.	Vale of Rheidol Rly, Aberystwyth (for conversion to a flail mower) late 1999
10¼in.		4w-4wDH	A Mills	1393	1993	b.10/4/00	Ferry Meadows Rly, Peterborough	John Crosskey, North Cheam 6/00
2ft 6in.		4wBE	WR		1939	w/e 2/6/00	L. & P. Peat, Solway Moss Wks, Cumbria	Rebuilt as works shunting loco
2ft 6in.	Fanny	4wDM	MR	21619	1957	w/e 2/6/00	L. & P. Peat, Solway Moss Wks, Cumbria	To Adrian Shooter, The Beeches Light Railway, Oxon. 27/11/03
2ft 6in.		4wDM	MR	9710	1952	w/e 2/6/00	L. & P. Peat, Solway Moss Wks, Cumbria	Scrapped 16/10/03
2ft 6in.		4wDM	MR	5879	1935	w/e 2/6/00	L. & P. Peat, Solway Moss Wks, Cumbria	Regauged to 2ft. To Charles Doble, Salisbury, 4/10/2003
2ft		4wBE	WR	D6912	1964	6/00	John Crosskey, Surrey Light Rly	To Cadeby 16/8/03
18in.		0-4-4-0DM	HE	4524	1954	c.10/00	Bicton Woodlands Rly, Devon	To Royal Gunpowder Mills, Waltham Abbey 13/12/04
2ft	166	4w-2-4wPH S/O	Chance	79.50166.24	1979	2/01	Chessington Zoo, Surrey	Hopewell Colliery Museum, Forest of Dean 8/01

Gauge	Number/Name	Type	Make	Wks No.	Year	Date	Ex	To
4ft 8½in.	*Steam Elephant*	6wVCG	Dorothea Restorations		2001	1/5/01	Dorothea Restorations	To Manchester Museum of Science and Industry 8/01. Rtn. To Beamish Museum 7/11/01
2ft		4w-2-4wPH S/O	Chance	76.50141.24	1976	c.6/01	Chessington Zoo, Surrey	To Flamingoland, Kirby Misperton, Yorks. 12/01
2ft		4wBE	WR	(red)		c.6/01	Quarry Tours, Llechwedd	To c/o John Perkins, Ladybridge Farm, Cheadle Hulme 19/12/04 (for Threlkeld Museum)
2ft		4wBE	WR	(yellow)		c.6/01	Quarry Tours, Llechwedd	To c/o John Perkins, Ladybridge Farm, Cheadle Hulme 19/12/04 (for Threlkeld Museum)
2ft		4wDM	MR	5342	1931	27/7/01	Alford Valley Rly, Aberdeenshire	Scrapped immediately
2ft		4wDM	MR	22129	1962	27/7/01	Alford Valley Rly, Aberdeenshire	Wales West R V Park, nr Silverhill, Alabama, USA 1/2/02
2ft		4wDM	MR	5877	1935	7 or 8/01	Moors Valley Railway, Dorset	To Stevington & Turvey Rly 27/7/07
2ft		4wBE	WR	556801	1988	30/10/01	P. McCail, yard at Red Cow, Morpeth. (Loco orig. Norwest Holst, Liverpool)	Rebuilt as AK72R 2004, 2-4w-2BE, replica of original Groudle Glen battery electric loco. To Groudle Glen Railway 2/7/04
2ft		4wDM	HE	9337	1994	30/5/02	Exmoor Steam Rly	Regauged to 15in. To Exmoor (or Perrygrove?) 2/1/03
2ft		4wDM	MR	40SD502	1975	13/12/02	Ron Lurcroft, c/o Greyhound Plant Yard, Knockin, Oswestry	Steve Clarke, Devizes, Wilts. (by 9/03?)
2ft		4wDM	MR	8720	1941	5/3/03	Slate Museum, Wynne Quarry	Bob Bailey, house at Horsehay, Telford 8/11/03
2ft		4wDM	RH	339209	1952	5/3/03	Slate Museum, Wynne Quarry	To LBNGRS 15/7/04 (initially on trial; purchased by end of 2004)
2ft		4wDH	HE	9347	1994	12/3/03	Hunslet Andrew Barclay, Kilmarnock	To Adrian Shooter, The Beeches Light Railway, Oxon. 11/12/04
2ft		4wDH	HE	9349	1994	12/3/03	Hunslet Andrew Barclay, Kilmarnock	Hired to Woodhead Tunnel 13/6/03. Rtn AK for repairs 6/11/03. Back to Woodhead 26/11/03. Rtn AK 22/4/04. Sold to East Links Park, Dunbar 25/11/05
2ft	*Sandy*	4wDH	AK	49	1994	4/6/03	Tunnel Steel, Swansea	
2ft	*Linsay*	4wDH	Schoma	5239	1991	31/10/03	Tunnel Steel, Swansea	Hired to Woodhead Tunnel c.6/11/03. Rtn AK 27/11/03. Hired to Global Marine, Portland Port, Dorset 3/06–18/5/06 (used on the deck of *Wave Sentinel*). Sold to Amberley Museum, W. Sussex 5/10/07
2ft 6in.	*Jenny*	4wDH	Schoma	5240	1991	31/10/03	Tunnel Steel, Swansea	Festiniog Rly 18/6/04
2ft 6in.		4wDM	HE	6659	1965	3/3/04	MoD Dean Hill	Joe Nemeth, Tockington 17/8/04
2ft		4wDH	BD	3753	1980	3/3/04	MoD Dean Hill	To Adrian Shooter, The Beeches Light Railway, Oxon. 8/4/04
2ft		4wDM	RH	200512	1940	13/2/04	John Quentin	
2ft		4wDH	HLH	001	1996	22/12/04	Sam Ward, Killamarsh, Derbys.	To 'private site in Devon' 17/10/05
3ft	*Handyman*	0-4-0ST OC	HC	573	1900	7/1/05	Midland Railway Trust, Derbys.	(For Ireland)
2ft 6in.		2w-2BE	GB	3547	1948	13/4/05	Omega Pacific, Trecwn	
900mm		4wDH Rack	HE	9282	1988	15/6/05	Bob Darvill c/o Roger Harvey, Walton-on-Naze	
900mm		4wDH	RFS	L106	1989	15/6/05	Bob Darvill c/o Roger Harvey, Walton-on-Naze	
2ft		4wBE	CE	5806	1970	19/4/06	SPA Poddington, Beds.	Painter Brothers, Hereford 27/6/06
2ft		4wDH	HE	9334	1994	23/5/06	Jan Pan, Singapore	Regauged to 12¼in. To Tintern Rly, Monmouthshire 14/11/07
2ft		4wDH	HE	9654	1994	23/5/06	Jan Pan, Singapore (plated 9332)	To Fairbourne Rly 14/11/07
2ft 6in.		4wDM	RH	221625	1943	1/9/06	Whipsnade Zoo, Beds.	
2ft		4wBE	CE	B0142B	1973	28/2/07	AMEC, Staffs.	Painter Brothers, Hereford 7/6/07

Index

One the enthusiasts missed!